Japan's Reluctant Realism

Foreign Policy Challenges in an Era of Uncertain Power

Michael Jonathan Green

A Council on Foreign Relations Book

palgrave

The Council on Foreign Relations, Inc., a nonprofit, nonpartisan national organization founded in 1921, is dedicated to promoting understanding of international affairs through the free and civil exchange of ideas. The Council's members are dedicated to the belief that America's peace and prosperity are firmly linked to that of the world. From this flows the mission of the Council: to foster America's understanding of other nations--their peoples, cultures, histories, hopes, quarrels, and ambitions--and thus to serve our nation through study and debate, private and public.

From time to time, books and reports written by members of the Council's research staff or others are published as a "Council on Foreign Relations Book."

THE COUNCIL TAKES NO INSTITUTIONAL POSITION ON POLICY ISSUES AND HAS NO AFFILIATION WITH THE U.S. GOVERNMENT. ALL STATEMENTS OF FACT AND EXPRESSIONS OF OPINION CONTAINED IN ALL ITS PUBLICATIONS ARE THE SOLE RESPONSIBILITY OF THE AUTHOR OR AUTHORS.

First published 2001 by PALGRAVE™
First published as paperback by Palgrave Macmillian in June 2003
175 Fifth Avenue, New York, N.Y. 10010 and Houndmills, Basingstoke, Hampshire, England RG21 6XS. Companies and representatives throughout the world.

PALGRAVE™ is the new global publishing imprint of St. Martin's Press LLC Scholarly and Reference Division and Palgrave Publishers Ltd (formerly Macmillan Press Ltd).

ISBN 0-312-23894-0 hardback -- ISBN 1-4039-6235-9 paperback

Library of Congress Cataloging-in-Publication Data

Green, Michael J.
   Japan's reluctant realism : foreign policy challenges in an era of uncertain power / Michael J. Green.
       p. cm.
   Includes bibliographical references and index.
   ISBN 0-312-23894-0
   1. Japan—Foreign relations—1945–1989. 2. Japan—Foreign relations—1989–
I. Title.
DS889 .G64   2001
327.52—dc21

                                                                00-051472

A catalogue record for this book is available from the British Library.

Design by Letra Libre, Inc.

First edition: May 2001. First published as paperback by Palgrave Macmillian in June 2003
10 9 8 7 6 5 4 3

Printed in the United States of America.

Japan's Reluctant Realism

Contents

Acknowledgments

I have many people to thank for their assistance with this book. The proving ground for my argument was a graduate seminar in Japanese Foreign Policy I taught at the Johns Hopkins University Paul H. Nitze School of Advanced International Studies from 1994 to 1998. The students in those classes kept me honest and gave me confidence that this book was worth writing. In 1998 I secured generous support from the Smith Richardson Foundation to conduct research trips and establish a study group at the Council on Foreign Relations to review draft chapters. I also received support from the John M. Olin Foundation. At the Council I came to rely on the hard work and skillful observations of my research associates and intellectual companions, Nagashima Akihisa and Furukawa Katsuhisa. I have no doubt that both men will play a central role in their country's future foreign policy and I am grateful for their contributions to this effort. They helped me to organize a team of experts for our study group that grilled me for a solid year, making this a better book, whatever its remaining shortcomings. The members of the study group were C. S. Ahn, Michael Armacost, Thomas Berger, Daniel Bob, William Breer, Patrick Cronin, Gerald Curtis, Peter Ennis, Joseph Ferguson, Ellen Frost, Paul Giarra, Seth Hurwitz, Katō Yōichi, Kobayashi Hideki, Kōno Masaharu, Edward Lincoln, Robert Manning, Nao Matsukata, Mishima Ko, Mike Mochizuki, Ronald Montaperto, Nagashima Akihisa, Kongdan Oh, Douglas Paal, George Packard, James Przystup, Samantha Ravich, Saitō Toshio, Robin "Sak" Sakoda, Richard Samuels, Robert Scher, Benjamin Self, David Shear, Shimura Hitoshi, Neil Silver, Richard Solomon, Allan Song, Bruce Stokes, Seth Sulkin, Tada Yukio, Daniel Tarullo, Tanaka Nobuo, Tezuka Hiroyuki, Nathaniel Thayer, Nancy Tucker, and Robin White. In addition, I benefited from the email comments of several scholars not then in Washington, D.C., particularly Chris Johnstone and Shinoda Tomohito.

In researching this book I conducted dozens of interviews with Japanese and U.S. officials. While this book is critical of Japanese and U.S.

foreign policy in certain areas, I hope that it is clear that I have great admiration for the dedication of both countries' diplomats, who work long hours on difficult issues, often without full political or even budgetary support at home. I also spent many hours discussing foreign and security policy with politicians from all of the major parties in Japan—a dialogue I enjoyed immensely and one which gives me confidence that Japan is nurturing a new generation of political leadership that will serve the country well. Almost all of these politicians and officials spoke on condition of anonymity, but I appreciate their time even though I cannot acknowledge them by name. In addition I was fortunate enough to arrange meetings with most of Japan's Prime Ministers for the period covered by this study: Miyazawa Kiichi, Hosokawa Morihiro, Hata Tsutomu, Hashimoto Ryutarō, and Obuchi Keizō. I agreed not to quote them directly in order to gain insights into the foreign policy process that one might not normally encounter in the press coverage of the events analyzed in these pages. Finally, I want to thank the editors at Palgrave, and particularly Toby Wahl, for their hard work on the final stage of this book project.

All Japanese names are presented here with family name first, unless the individual's English-language work is being cited and the author has put the family name second.

List of Figures

Introduction

When I told a friend in the Japanese media that I planned to write a book about his country's foreign policy, he replied by joking, "*Japanese* foreign policy? Let me know if you find any!!" Many would agree with this skeptical view. After defeat in World War II, Japan avoided playing a prominent role in international affairs. Japan's relations with other nations were guided by the principle of "omnidi-rectional" foreign policy, a risk-free formula that suggested no national strategy at all. To the extent there was an international security strategy, it was directed from Washington, not Tokyo "when you want shade, find the largest tree," as some politicians put it in the 1950s. Japanese passivity in postwar international affairs was reinforced by a cumbersome, consensus-oriented political system in Tokyo. Prime ministers were only first among equals in the ruling Liberal Democratic Party (LDP). Bureaucracies and industrial groupings struggled to protect turf. Japan was, in the words of one Western critic, a state which "has no top," where the "buck" stops "nowhere."[1] It is no wonder that many observers have despaired that Japanese foreign policy is "mired in immobilisms"[2] and that Japan is a "reactive state,"[3] unwilling to take risk or assert its interests in the world.[4]

Others have seen more sophistication to Japanese foreign policy, however. They argue that Japan's apparent passivity in international affairs is, in fact a "low-cost, low-risk, benefit-maximizing strategy that has served national self-interest extraordinarily well."[5] If one assumes that Japanese national self-interest is determined in terms of economic power, Japan's foreign policy has indeed been impressive for many decades. In this view, Japan's model of foreign policy should be seen as incorporating "techno-economic security interests—including, but not limited to, those associated with military security—as central considerations in state policy."[6] Based on this focus on techno-economic security, Japan has come to influence its environment through foreign direct investment and overseas development assistance (ODA), as "the network organization that characterizes the Japanese state" has "gone regional."[7]

Traditional military and political instruments of state power may therefore be less important, since "Japan will have more influence over international security relations in the years to come by virtue of its economic and technological strengths alone."[8]

Still other observers find unsatisfactory the argument that Japan will continue to express its national interests exclusively through economic power. They argue that economic growth, rather than offering a new definition of national security, will eventually drive Japan to pursue independent military power, including possibly nuclear weapons. This view of an economic superpower transforming inevitably into a military superpower emerged with Japan's amazing economic growth in the 1960s and expanded with the appreciation of the yen in the 1980s.[9] More recently, it has been reinforced by the perceived emergence of multipolar rivalry in Asia and "the rise of China as a major industrial and military power," which will "slowly but inevitably produce a reappraisal of the security strategy that Japan has followed for the past 50 years."[10]

The end of the Cold War appears to have added little clarity to which view of Japan is correct. Compared with the sweeping changes that have occurred in Eastern Europe, South Africa, or Germany, the parameters of Japanese foreign policy have been remarkably consistent since the fall of the Berlin Wall. Japan has reaffirmed its alliance with the United States. The Japanese Peace Constitution remains intact. Japan continues to focus its international activities on economic trade, investment, and aid.

At the same time, however, we do know that the domestic Japanese political economy is undergoing a painful transformation in the post–Cold War period—that economic growth has been essentially flat for a decade; that rival *keiretsu* industrial groupings have been forced to merge their core banks; and that the Socialist Party has collapsed while the LDP struggles to survive through shaky coalitions. We also know that the world is changing around Japan in important ways—that Russian power is declining while Chinese power is on the rise; that information technologies and currency flows have heralded a new era of globalization; and that the United States has emerged from the Cold War as an unchallenged superpower. Is it possible that Japanese foreign policy can remain immune to these changes?

This is not the first time that Japanese policies and institutions have appeared stubbornly resistant to change. As historian Carol Gluck points out:

The problem faced by any conception of Japanese history is to explain the lastingness, the conspicuous durability, of Japan's institutional structures, often to the point that they seem to violate historical common sense. Consider what one might call the Long Bakumatsu, or the Long End of the Tokugawa shōgunate. Although the Tokugawa shoguns remained in power from 1600 to 1868, the shōgunal ending played itself out slowly over a half-century.[11]

But if one cannot see changes clearly in a new constitution, new political leadership, or a new foreign policy doctrine, how is one to make judgments about the future direction of Japanese foreign policy? The answer lies in careful inspection of what Gluck calls the "loose changes that lie around at present."

The Approach

This book goes through the "loose changes" of Japanese foreign policy in the decade since the end of the Cold War. It recognizes that the bilateral relationship with the United States is the indispensable core of Japan's position in the world. Indeed, this book's main lessons are for the U.S.-Japan alliance. However, the case studies in this volume examine not U.S.-Japan bilateral trade and security negotiations per se, but rather how the United States and Japan interact in relations with the rest of the world. The case studies include: China, the Korean peninsula, Russia and Central Asia, Southeast Asia, the international financial institutions, and multilateral forums (the United Nations, the Asia Pacific Economic Cooperation Forum (APEC), and the ASEAN Regional Forum (ARF). In each case, Japan is conducting foreign policy with one eye carefully on Washington, but it remains, nevertheless, *Japanese* foreign policy. As we will see, this foreign policy still converges with the United States on fundamental issues, but it is also increasingly independent. While it remains low risk, it is more sensitive to balance-of-power considerations. And while it is still reactive, it is far less passive. In short, it is time to recognize Japan as an independent actor in Northeast Asia and to assess Japanese foreign policy on its own terms.

In order to understand patterns that are emerging in Japanese foreign policy since the end of the Cold War, each case study considers:

- Japanese objectives
- The effectiveness of Japanese diplomacy in achieving those objectives
- The domestic and exogenous pressures on policymaking

- The degree of convergence or divergence with the United States in both strategy and implementation
- Lessons for more effective U.S.-Japan diplomatic cooperation in the future

To provide context for the case studies, the first chapter looks at the unfolding debate about strategy and identity in Japan. The second chapter then dissects the domestic institutions that conduct foreign policy in Japan and explores the implications of their current transformation. These ideas and institutions are important. While the case studies demonstrate that the broad parameters of Japanese foreign policy are shaped primarily by material factors—that is, the balance between state resources and external threats and opportunities—foreign policy choices are filtered through the powerful ideational lens of Japanese norms, aspirations, and insecurities and are implemented by divided and often dysfunctional institutions. These ideational and institutional factors are a drag on the state's response to external changes—hence the "immobilist" and "reactive state" labels for Japan—but as we will see, they are not impervious to shifts in Japan's material position in the world, nor are they necessarily perpetual determinants of Japanese preferences or behavior.[12] After the two background chapters, the book turns to the case studies.

The final chapter of the book returns to the lessons of Japanese diplomacy in the 1990s for U.S.-Japan relations. It also considers the longer-term implications of Japan's emerging diplomacy, drawing from the case studies to explore what variables might lead to more revolutionary change in Japan's world role.

The Findings

The case studies examined in these pages demonstrate strong continuity in the parameters of Japanese foreign policy since the end of the Cold War. Specifically:

1. *The centrality of the United States.* Japanese foreign policy continues to take its bearings from Washington, in spite of growing independence at the margins (particularly in Southeast Asia). On issues of fundamental interest to the United States, Japan remains deferential and cautious. In terms of security, there is a broader consensus on the need for the U.S.-Japan alliance than at any previous point in Japanese postwar history—though there is much more

disagreement on the specifics of issues like U.S bases. Japan remains dependent on American hegemony for its own security in East Asia. While Japan is pressing for greater influence and recognition in international organizations and in the region, it is not challenging U.S. primacy in these settings. Indeed, much of Japanese diplomacy is aimed at buttressing U.S. leadership in the United Nations and the international financial institutions.

2. *The primacy of economic tools.* Despite a growing focus on traditional security concerns and a recognition of declining relative economic resources, Japanese foreign policy continues to rely primarily on economic tools for power and influence. These tools include foreign aid and contributions to international organizations as well as overseas foreign direct investment. In response to regional political and security crises in the 1990s, Japan's first responses have usually been financial.

3. *Constraints on the use of force.* The normative and institutional constraints on the use of force remain strong, though more flexible. New missions and capabilities for peacekeeping, noncombatant evacuation operations, space surveillance, and logistical support for U.S. forces in regional contingencies all give Japan more tools in its security kit bag. However, the use of force—whether in peacekeeping or in support of U.S. forces—is highly contentious and strictly controlled by the rulings of the Cabinet Legal Affairs Bureau. Consequently, the Japanese government has deployed military forces only against clear violations of Japanese territory or with the unambiguous permission of countries receiving the forces (whether for United Nations–mandated peacekeeping or for humanitarian relief or emergency evacuation). This is both a matter of ideology and a policy of continuing risk aversion by the political elite in Tokyo.

4. *No alternate strategic vision.* No political leader has articulated a clear alternative to the current doctrine of Japanese foreign policy. Political leaders have heralded new initiatives toward Russia or Southeast Asia, but there has been no political mandate for bolder reformulation of Japan's world role. In part this reflects the weakness of the current senior leadership in Japanese political parties, but it also is based on the conservatism of the Japanese public about international affairs and a distrust of demagogues. In the current climate of political realignment, leaders who take clear ideological stands on foreign policy have difficulty building a broad enough coalition to govern.

Within these areas of continuity, however, the case studies reveal new ideas and new patterns of diplomacy since the end of the Cold War that do represent a pronounced departure from the past. These are changes that are occurring *not* because of the growth of Japanese economic power, as many predicted, but instead because of the demise of the Japanese economic model. They are occurring *not* because of the decline of U.S. influence, but because of anxiety about the rise of Chinese power and the unilateralism of the United States. And they are occurring *not* because of a great national debate, but instead because of a growing consensus among a new generation that Japan must assert its own identity in international society. There are six trends worth watching:

1. *A greater focus on balance of power.* Japanese foreign policy is increasingly being shaped by strategic considerations about the balance of power and influence in Northeast Asia, particularly vis-à-vis China. Where Japan's relations in East Asia were primarily determined by the conjunction of mercantile interests and U.S. strategy in the past, they now tend also to reflect a self-conscious competition with China for strategic influence in the region. Confidence that Japanese economic leadership would integrate China on Japan's terms has ebbed and a new realism has emerged regarding the limits of Japanese economic influence and the growing power aspirations of Beijing.

2. *With growing realism, frayed idealism.* With this growing realism about power relations in the region and the threat of diminishing indigenous economic resources, Japan has less room for sentimentality, idealism, or guilt in its foreign policy in Asia. Where the Japanese debate about a world role in the 1980s was framed in terms of the "international obligation" (*kokusai koken*) or "obligation" (*giri*) of the world's largest creditor nation, today foreign policies must be justified to the public in terms of "national interest" (*kokueki*). Japanese host-nation support for U.S. bases in Japan, apologies to China for historical transgressions, even dues to the United Nations—all are under increasing domestic scrutiny and pressure, as politicians call for an end to Japan's international "taxation without representation."

3. *A higher sensitivity to security.* The Japanese body politic is far more sensitive to external security threats than even during the height of the Cold War. This reflects the external shocks of the 1995 Chinese nuclear tests, the 1996 Taiwan Straits crisis, the

1998 North Korean Taepodong missile launch, as well as uncertainties about Japan's own economic future. With the collapse of the old Socialist Left and the emergence of a new generation of political leaders unburdened by war guilt, there is a more permissive political environment for advancing the national security agenda. As a result, U.S. *gaiatsu* (external pressure) on Japan has less saliency in Japan's own defense debate, while U.S. failure to respond to perceived security threats has a more deleterious impact on Japanese confidence in the U.S. security commitment. Increasingly, Japan has demonstrated a readiness to take unilateral actions in response to perceived threats when the United States has been passive.[13]

4. *A more determined push for "independent" foreign policy.* Japan is pushing harder for a more independent diplomatic identity in the world. This reflects the confidence of a new generation of politicians in international affairs as well as the search for national purpose and identity after the demise of the Japanese economic model. It also reflects the Japanese people's growing focus on the integrity of the nation-state. This ideational drive for independence collides with the practical need for a close alliance with the United States to manage the rise of China and security threats from North Korea. Thus, while reaffirming alliance ties with the United States, Japan has simultaneously attempted to expand its own influence and agenda in East Asia and in international organizations. In the 1990s Tokyo proposed a string of new initiatives toward Southeast Asia, Russia, and in the international financial institutions. Whether these initiatives are truly "independent" is debatable, since they represent more of a tactical divergence from the United States than a competitive strategy. Nevertheless, Tokyo is clearly placing a higher premium on raising Japan's international political profile.

5. *A focus on Asia.* To the extent Japanese foreign policy has developed "independent" characteristics, it has done so by highlighting differences between Washington and the nations of East Asia. Japanese divergence with the United States over Burma and Cambodia in the 1990s reflected Association of Southeast Asian Nations (ASEAN) concerns that Washington was emphasizing human rights at the expense of regional stability. Similarly, Japanese initiatives in response to the 1997 financial crisis reflected Asian alarm at the insensitivity of the International Monetary Fund to regional conditions and political stability. The expansion

of trade and investment in East Asia has naturally heightened Japanese sensitivity to the region's priorities, particularly in Southeast Asia. This is true both because of the exposure of Japanese firms to political and economic developments in the region and because of the Asian dimension of the Japanese identity. However, the "Asianization" of Japanese foreign policy should not be overstated. As we will see, the security and financial crises of the 1990s reinforced for Japanese policymakers the indispensable nature of U.S. military deterrence and U.S.-led global financial institutions for Japan's own position in the region, while the legacy of Japan's wartime history hampers the growth of a new pan-Asian identity.

6. *A more fluid foreign policy making process.* The transitional state of Japanese domestic politics has done more to complicate foreign policymaking than add clarity. The dominant institutions of government in Japan—the LDP, the factions, the bureaucracy—are still in charge, but they have all become more brittle, less cohesive, and less hierarchical. Meanwhile, the limitations of coalition government and the pressing challenges of domestic economic restructuring have prevented sustained attention to international problems by senior political leaders. Finally, media and Diet scrutiny of foreign policy has increased as the Japanese polity develops a stronger sense of civil self-determination, both nationally and at the local level. Together, these trends have created a more pluralistic and less predictable foreign policy–making process, where contentious policies are more difficult to sustain and reactions to external shocks are often more assertive and even nationalistic. Because this is a transitional period, however, the patterns of interaction between the United States and Japan are quietly shaping the worldview of a new generation of politicians and bureaucrats who will not be captive to the current sources of immobilism in the future.

In short, Japan is changing. After years of cautious international behavior and paralyzing domestic debates about security policy, a broad consensus is forming that Japan should assert its national interests more forcefully. While there is not yet a coherent strategy, there is an emerging strategic view—a reluctant realism—that is being shaped by the combination of external material changes in Japan's international environment, insecurity about national power resources, and aspirations for a national identity that moves beyond the legacies of World War II.

Japan, in spite of—indeed because of—its economic travails, is set to be a larger actor in international relations.

Implications for the United States

Why should the United States care about these changes in Japanese foreign policy? U.S. interests in Japan should be self-evident. Japan hosts 47,000 U.S. troops and is the linchpin for forward U.S. presence in that hemisphere. Japan is the second largest contributor to all major international organizations that buttress U.S. foreign policy—the International Monetary Fund (IMF), the World Bank, the United Nations, and the Asian Development Bank. Japan is the bulwark for U.S. deterrence and engagement of China and North Korea—the reason why those countries cannot assume that the United States will eventually withdraw from the region and leave them alone. Japan, by its self-constrained military policies and alliance with the United States, is the model for Asia's emphasis on economic development over military competition.

It is clear from this study that Japan will continue to face many constraints on its international role. In spite of continuing political realignment and the emergence of dynamic younger politicians, for example, Japanese leadership is still drawn from the ranks of the "old guard" of the LDP—men unable to grasp the restorative powers of deregulation and information technology for the Japanese economy. In spite of a growing focus on balance-of-power realism and the decline of old taboos on security policy, coalition politics have forced on the Japanese leadership a consensus-oriented, risk-averse approach that means new public attitudes are not matched by coherent national strategies. And in spite of a growing identification with Asia, the Japanese are losing their tolerance for Asian criticism of Japan's past, without having agreed with many neighbors on a sustainable formula for moving forward.

At the same time, however, this study also suggests that U.S. policymakers can no longer assume Japan's automatic compliance with U.S. diplomacy—and certainly cannot assume Japanese passivity. In order to sustain its own position in Asia, the United States will have to do more to demonstrate reciprocal support for Japanese diplomatic initiatives. The United States will have to frame its policy toward East Asia and multilateral organizations in terms that give Japan responsibilities at all stages of diplomacy—from conceptualization, to funding, to implementation on the ground. And at each stage, the United States will have to raise the bar of expectations on Japan—giving more responsibility, but insisting on more sharing of the risk. The United States will have to establish agreement with Japan on strategy and allow for divergence in tactics. In short, the United States will have to sustain a focus on Japan when its help is not required for U.S. diplomacy, so that Japan is more forthcoming when its help becomes essential.

If U.S.-Japan diplomatic cooperation breaks down or drifts, Japan may not go the way of Gaullism, but U.S. leadership in the world will be less effective. The United States will lose leverage in its bilateral relationships with other Asian countries and in multilateral institutions as Japan joins in ad hoc coalitions with Europe, or even Russia and China, to constrain U.S. unilateralism; or as Tokyo refuses to fund U.S. initiatives. Tokyo's confidence in the U.S. commitment to Japanese security will wane, leading to more hedging strategies, redundant indigenous military capabilities, and exacerbated tensions throughout Asia. Concern about U.S. unilateralism will lead to more legal and political constraints on the use of U.S. forces based in Japan. Frustration with the asymmetrical aspects of the alliance could mount to the point that U.S. forward presence becomes at risk. Diplomatic leadership sharing, in short, is a critical complement to the core military aspect of the U.S.-Japan security relationship.

It is striking that larger U.S. and Japanese foreign policy objectives have not diverged in the decade since the end of the Cold War. The logic of a strong U.S.-Japan security relationship is well understood in Tokyo at present, particularly given the options. Japan is a status quo power in the sense that none of the realistic alternatives look much better than the status quo. If a Pax Nipponica is not likely, then Tokyo clearly will prefer a Pax Americana to a Pax Sinica in Asia. But if strong security relations with the United States are indispensable, they are also maddeningly constraining. A sustainable U.S.-Japan diplomatic partnership must therefore not assume that all roads lead through Washington. There is no question that the partnership must begin with clear strategic principles from the United States, but U.S. policymakers must also understand and address Japanese foreign policy on its own terms.

CHAPTER ONE

The Search for Strategy and Identity

Introduction

To understand Japanese foreign policy on its own terms, one must begin with the evolution of the debate about Japan's role in the world and its relationship with the United States. It was Prime Minister Yoshida Shigeru, the bespectacled former diplomat and crafty political strategist, who established the formula for Japan's foreign policy and set the terms of the debate after World War II. What later scholars and diplomats canonized as the Yoshida Doctrine centered on close alliance with the United States, minimal military rearmament, and a focus on economic recovery. This basic formula has served as the framework for Japanese foreign policy ever since. At the time, however, the Yoshida Doctrine was really more of a political compromise than it was a strategic doctrine per se. The fractured state of Japanese politics after the war left Yoshida little time for contemplative policy planning. Former leaders from the *zaibatsu* and economic ministries wanted to focus on rebuilding Japan's economic strength. Anticommunists wanted to reconstitute Japanese military power to deal with the domestic and international threats from the Cold War. Pacifists wanted a strict interpretation of Article Nine of the Constitution. Idealists wanted the United Nations to prevent further conflict so that Japan would need neither armament nor protection. Others wanted to restore Japan's ties to Asia.

The Yoshida Doctrine was the only foreign policy paradigm that would accommodate these broad views into a platform for long-term conservative rule. As John Dower explains in his biography of Yoshida, "the reconsolidation and recentralization of conservative authority during the Yoshida era was inseparable from the strategic settlement reached between the United States and Japan."[1] Alliance with the United States provided technology transfers, economic assistance, and markets for those conservatives who were concerned primarily with economic recovery. For the hawks, the alliance provided a source of military technology, defense assistance, and external political support for some level of rearmament. For the doves, the alliance provided a cap on that rearmament, or, in the words of one foreign minister, "an honorable watch-dog" (obankensama) over Japan.[2]

However, while the strategic settlement with the United States temporarily froze in place the conflicting views of Japan's future among the mainstream conservatives, it also left a profound sense of incompleteness. Alliance with the United States created a dilemma that small states aligned with superpowers have experienced since Thucydides and the Pelopennesian Wars—the dilemma between entrapment and abandonment. Entrapment results when the smaller state allows the larger state to dictate its internal and international affairs. Abandonment results when the smaller state tries too hard to maintain distance and therefore loses utility as an ally. To escape this dilemma and empower itself within the alliance, the smaller state can: establish its own military capabilities (a difficult thing for Japan given the political cleavages that would result); broaden relations with other countries (useful until it alienates the larger ally); or strengthen its own economic capabilities (the obvious choice, though it does not resolve the fundamental military dependence on the larger ally unless the larger ally becomes economically dependent on the smaller ally).

Yoshida initially looked on Article Nine of the Constitution, "the peace clause," as the most important insurance policy against entrapment in American Cold War adventures. As Yoshida told a young Miyazawa Kiichi at the time (later Prime Minister in the early 1990s), "it is indeed our Heaven-bestowed good fortune that the Constitution bans arms. If the Americans complain, the Constitution gives us a perfect justification. The politicians who want to amend it are fools."[3] At the same time, however, Yoshida never had any intention of seeing Japan remain dependent on the United States for security indefinitely. Ozawa Ichirō, the author of Blueprint for a New Japan and an advocate of Japan taking on more risk at home and abroad, notes that Yoshida admitted that his strategic settlement with the United States was "rather sneaky" and that Japan should not "continue to remain at the level where it depends on another country for its defense."[4]

As Japan's economic power grew in the postwar period, the pressure for a revision of Yoshida's formula mounted. Subsequent Japanese political and intellectual leaders pushed for a national strategy and identity beyond economic recovery and alliance with the United States. The Foreign Ministry signaled the need to move beyond alliance with the United States in the first *Diplomatic Blue Book* (*Gaikō Seisho*) in 1957, which expressed the hope that Japan's world role would rest on three pillars: alliance with the United States, UN-centered diplomacy, and Asia.[5] Many conservatives focused on revision of the Constitution and independent defensive capabilities as the essence of Japan's future identity, successfully including constitutional revision as a platform of the newly formed LDP in 1955. The Left, meanwhile, continued to challenge the very constitutionality of alliance with the United States through the Socialist Party in the Diet. Yet with each challenge to the Yoshida Doctrine in the postwar period, the result was almost always a further institutionalization of Yoshida's views and a renewed emphasis on a combination of economic power and alliance with the United States.

In the post–Cold War era, the broad parameters of the Yoshida Doctrine are still in place. For the first time there are no national leaders in Japan who are self-consciously "anti-Yoshida." The Left has collapsed. The Socialist Party exists only as a shell, and even that entity now accepts the legitimacy of Japan's Self-Defense Forces and alliance with the United States. The Right, represented in part by Ozawa's Liberal Party, now expresses its proactive internationalism as the logical extension of Yoshida's own vision. Only the Communist Party remains squarely outside the framework established by Yoshida, and even that party indicated a willingness to compromise in order to enter into an anti-LDP coalition in the summer of 1998. The bipolar ideological clash of the Cold War has ended. It has been replaced by a plurality of values and ideas that exist for the most part within the Yoshida framework. Today the diversity of views on Japan's international identity and foreign and security policies would better be captured by a bell curve than by two opposing poles.

Within that bell curve, however, a vibrant debate is taking place about Japan's international purpose. There is relatively little disagreement that alliance with the United States is essential or that Japan's primary power remains economic. However, the intellectual debate is now characterized by "*sōron sansei, kakuron hantai*"—agreement on the principle and disagreement on the specifics. The Japanese are struggling to define an independent strategy and identity at a time when U.S. military and financial power appear unrivaled and Japanese security dependency on the United States undiminished, when China is challenging

Japan's diplomatic agenda in Asia, and when Japan's own economic model is under intense pressure from the forces of globalism. Japanese intellectual leaders are being forced to reconsider the sources of their nation's power. And they are still uncertain about the direction of Japanese purpose. Is Japan's strategy and identity defined entirely by the U.S.-Japan alliance? By Asia? Is the answer in the United Nations, multilateralism, or economic regionalism? Or is the ultimate solution constitutional revision? The difficult economic and strategic circumstances of the 1990s provided no clear answer to these questions, but the pressures to clarify Japanese power and purpose are unrelenting.

Many of these themes about Japan's international identity are the same that Yoshida grappled with five decades ago. Before turning to the present debate in more detail, therefore, we briefly return to the story line we began with Yoshida and trace the evolution of his strategic vision to the present.

The Yoshida Doctrine

No sooner was Yoshida's formula for Japanese foreign policy set in the early postwar period than certain of his successors began an effort to reshape the relationship with the United States and Japan's own identity in the international system. Yet with each tack in policy, the original formula was strengthened. The first challenge came from Hatoyama Ichirō, who as prime minister attempted in 1956 to reassert Japanese autonomy in the relationship with the United States by normalizing relations with the Soviet Union and by revising the Japanese Constitution. He failed on both counts. His successor, Kishi Nobusuke (who, like Hatoyama, had been depurged by U.S. occupation authorities only a decade earlier), tried a different tack. Instead of seeking distance from the United States, Kishi sought and won a revision of the U.S.-Japan security treaty in 1960. The revised security treaty removed clauses giving the U.S. military a role in Japanese internal security and replaced them with "mutual" obligations, under which Japan granted U.S. forces bases for the security of the Far East and the United States pledged to defend Japan against attack. This led to a more balanced alliance relationship, but the explicit alignment with the United States in the Cold War provoked the most violent protests in postwar Japanese history. Desperate to maintain their consensus and majority, the LDP scrambled back to the economic focus of the Yoshida line. Yoshida's protégé, Ikeda Hayato, assumed the leadership of the party from a battered Kishi in 1960 and promised to double Japan's national income by the end of the decade. He achieved the goal in almost half that time, locking in the LDP for several more decades of uninterrupted rule based on the success of the Japanese "economic miracle." A decade after the end of the occupation, the twin pillars of alliance and economic recovery were as firm as ever.

Japan's economic boom in the 1960s led to further institutionalization of Yoshida's original formula. Among other laws and policies relating to security, the Ikeda and Sato cabinets introduced a geographic limitation on the scope of the U.S.-Japan Security Treaty in order to avoid entrapment in the Vietnam conflict. In 1967 Sato established the Three Non-Nuclear Principles to outlaw possession, transit, or stationing of nuclear weapons in Japan. At the same time, however, rapid economic growth sparked new questions about the relevance of the Yoshida Doctrine. By the end of the 1960s, Japanese economic and technological power was approaching that of the United States on many levels. Meanwhile, Washington was sending signals—most notably the 1969 Guam Doctrine—that it wanted its Asian allies to carry more of the burden for their own defense. Many within Japan's industrial and political elite were prepared to turn Japan's newly won economic power into more explicit military power. Most notable in this movement was an ambitious young Defense Agency director-general named Nakasone Yasuhiro, who in 1970 mobilized support in the Diet and heavy industry for a new five-year defense plan that would have doubled Japan's military spending.

The push for autonomous defense created a political paralysis that was resolved only by U.S. President Richard Nixon's opening to the People's Republic of China in 1972. Suddenly the same industrialists who had favored a more independent defense policy were now far more interested in the allure of the China market. No longer constrained by U.S. anticommunism, Japan could explore the Asian dimension of its identity. Tanaka Kakuei, the rough-hewn master of LDP machine politics and no disciple of Yoshida, became the Yoshida Doctrine's greatest champion in this period, normalizing ties with Beijing in 1972 and placing a "peacetime defense" limit on military spending. Throughout the rest of the 1970s, Tanaka and his successors reinforced the consensus around the Yoshida Doctrine along three lines. First, in 1976, dovish Prime Minister Miki Takeo institutionalized constraints on Japanese defense policy in the form of strict arms export control rules, a limit of 1 percent of gross national product on defense spending, and a new National Defense Program Outline (NDPO). Miki also initiated discussions with the United States on new defense guidelines that would legitimize the role of the Japanese Self Defense Forces (JSDF) and clarify the U.S. commitment to defending Japan against larger threats. Miki's successor, Fukuda Takeo, completed these guidelines negotiations in 1978 and announced the outlines of a Fukuda Doctrine, his own corollary to the Yoshida Doctrine that emphasized political interaction with Southeast Asia based on antimilitarism and Japan's growing economic leadership in the region. Fukuda, a successor of the anti-Yoshida group in LDP factional politics, could not have been more faithful to the original Yoshida line.

The 1980s opened with the clearest articulation of how Japan might translate its economic power into an international political role. Prime Minister Ōhira Masayoshi, the direct successor of the original Yoshida faction, initiated a series of research groups in 1979 to chart Japan's agenda for the next decade. He died in 1980 before the work was complete, but under his successor, Suzuki Zenkō, the research commission on "comprehensive security" issued a report arguing that Japan could address its international obligations and security threats through non-military "comprehensive" measures ranging from diplomacy, to foreign aid, and to diversifying energy resources. Nakasone Yasuhiro succeeded Suzuki in 1982 with a commitment to incorporate many of Ōhira's ideas into his own agenda.

A champion of "autonomous defense" in 1970 and a fervent anti-Yoshida campaigner in his earlier career, Nakasone was now poised to lead Japan based on the coordinates Yoshida had originally set. Nakasone emphasized an activist political agenda for Japan in the region and in global affairs. His approach was based on strengthened security ties to the United States in the context of expanded Soviet threats to Asia and the Third World and on utilization of foreign aid and other economic tools that were the legacy of Yoshida's vision. By sticking closely to alliance with the United States, Nakasone found the political consensus necessary to increase defense spending by 6 percent a year (something he never achieved with the mantle of "autonomous defense"). Meanwhile, under Nakasone and his successor, Takeshita Noboru, the rapid appreciation of the yen had made Japan the world's largest donor of ODA and the world's largest creditor nation. The United States, meanwhile, had become the world's largest debtor nation.

As the 1980s ended, it appeared that the collisions between pro- and anti-Yoshida thinkers had led to a broader synthesis that was much closer to Yoshida's original line than not. Japan had problems, to be sure. Ballooning trade deficits with the United States threatened to put the U.S.-Japan alliance itself at risk. Japan faced intense international pressure to recycle its massive surpluses through aid, investment, and, the most difficult task of all, market opening. Questions arose about the adequacy of Japanese burden-sharing during the Cold War. The Japanese people themselves asked why there were so many lifestyle constraints if they had the highest per-capita gross domestic product in the world.

However, even as the debate about *kokusaika* (internationalization) and Japan's *kokusai kōken* (international contribution) raged, the tools to manage these challenges appeared at hand. The ebbing of Cold War confrontation promised to ease security threats in Japan's neighborhood. Economically, Japan was powerful—some economists even predicted that its GDP would surpass that of the United States in the next century.[6] East Asia appeared ready to move in the direction of European economic integration based on Japanese investment and aid. Japan led in five of the twenty-two critical technologies assessed by the U.S. Government in 1989.[7] Comprehensive techno-economic security and regional interdependence all promised to give Japan an upper hand in managing the post–Cold War international environment.[8]

Bubbles Burst

Then the rules changed. First, the outbreak of the Gulf War in 1990 called into question the purpose of Japanese power in this new era. Japanese officials failed to predict the onset of the war, failed to predict the overwhelming victory of the United States, and then failed to send personnel to the conflict, in spite of unprecedented international pressure to do so. Even a $13 billion contribution to the U.S.-led coalition forces drew derogatory charges at home and abroad that Japan was shirking its international duty by relying instead on "checkbook diplomacy." With the purpose of Japanese power now in greater doubt, the source of Japanese power itself next came into crisis. Between July 16 and October 1 in 1990, the Nikkei index plummeted by 12,951 yen, approximately 40 percent, revealing that expectations about the continuing strength of the Japanese economy had been artificially inflated by speculation in the stock and real estate markets caused by the yen's rapid appreciation in 1985.[9]

The Gulf War and the collapse of the bubble economy were not quite Commodore Perry's Black Ships or the arrival of U.S. B-29 bombers at the end of World War II, but they did wreak considerable havoc on the Japanese worldview. At first Tokyo's reaction was predictably "reactive." The government launched a fiscal stimulus package to jump-start the economy and fought to introduce UN peacekeeping operations (PKO) legislation that would allow the dispatch of the JSDF to the Gulf. The stimulus packages had little long-term effect, however, and the PKO legislation had to be reworked to put greater constraints on the JSDF before being passed in 1992—too late for the Gulf War. Public and international pressure mounted on the LDP, and when the party proved unable to deliver promised political reform in 1993, enough splinter groups broke away to help form an unwieldy eight-party coalition government under Hosokawa Morihiro. Forty-seven years of stable LDP rule came to a halt. Japanese politics appeared wide open—and with that came an opportunity to define a different vision for Japan's future world role.

A Small and Shining Japan or a Normal Japan?

Great leaders are born from national crisis. Meiji oligarchs like Yamagata Aritomo emerged from the chaos caused by the arrival of modernity and the Black Ships. Postwar democrats such as Yoshida Shigeru arose from the ashes of defeat in World War II. In the wake of the Gulf War and the collapse of the bubble economy, a new generation of politicians in Tokyo also scrambled to prove that they had the vision to chart Japan's future in uncertain times. At one point, the field of potential visionaries became so crowded that one contender—Hashimoto Ryūtarō—published a book with the plaintive title *I Too Have Vision*. Hashimoto eventually did become prime minister, of course, but in the first part of the 1990s the contrasting writings of two other politicians dominated the debate over Japan's choices for the future. Both were former members of the LDP; they were Ozawa Ichirō and Takemura Masayoshi.

Ozawa had been the archetypal LDP machine politician, rising without particular luster through the party ranks based on a secure seat in his father's old district in the northern prefecture of Iwate.[10] By the time of the Gulf War, he had earned the trust of senior Tanaka faction leaders and was frequently tapped to resolve contentious trade and security issues with the United States. That position put him right in the middle of the collision over Japan's role in the Gulf War. Like many conservative politicians, Ozawa initially concluded that the problem of Japan's failure in the Gulf lay in the Constitution. With support of party elders, he led a commission within the LDP in 1992 on Japan's Role in International Society, which he and others in the party thought would open the door to writing a new Constitution. Instead, however, the commission members found themselves increasingly focused on Japan's right to participate in UN collective security actions, based on the Constitution's preamble—a more realistic goal than the divisive old mission of constitutional revision.[11] This theme animated Ozawa's career from that point forward and figured prominently in an influential book he produced in 1993 titled *Blueprint for a New Japan*.[12] Ozawa's argument combined the experiences of the Gulf War and the collapse of the economic bubble to call for a more "normal" Japan. By "normal," Ozawa meant a Japan that was deregulated and that participated in collective security, but, more to the point, a Japan that accepted risk in foreign and economic policy in order to maintain and even enhance national power and prestige.

Takemura also was a product of the LDP, but his background was in local politics and the Left wing of the party. As Ozawa's vision gained momentum with the conservative press and intellectuals, and particularly with American observers, Takemura fought to tug the Hosokawa coalition and the country back to a more pacifist and minimalist vision of Japan's future. The title of his 1994 book, *Japan: A Small But Shining Country*, said it all.[13] Where Ozawa called for "normalcy" and greater risk and reward in international society and domestic politics, Takemura urged Japan to relax and enjoy the benefits of economic success and the end of the Cold War. He argued against participation in collective security or even permanent membership in the United Nations. While he supported devolution of power to local government, he cautioned against deregulation policies that might end the paternalistic and egalitarian dimensions of Japanese economic philosophy. In contrast to Ozawa's yearning for respect and opportunity in the world, Takemura enticed the Japanese public with images of safe national retirement and a low international profile.

Would Japan emerge in the post–Cold War era as a normal country—a Britain of the East? Or would it cash in on its long, exhausting investment in economic modernization and maturity to became a quiet and respected Switzerland of Asia? In reality, Japan would become neither Britain nor Switzerland, but these opposing visions of the nation's global role set the first themes of the national debate for the rest of the decade.[14] In the years after their books hit the best-seller lists, Ozawa and Takemura saw their own political stars begin to fade. Takemura disappeared into obscurity, while Ozawa struggled to maintain control of his dwindling forces as he moved back and forth between the LDP and opposition camps. However, their opening debate about Japan's purpose after the Cold War set the tone for the rest of the decade. And the debate became far more complex as questions about the future of Japanese purpose were superceded by more distressing questions about the future of Japanese power.

A Deeper Problem

Fifteen years passed between the arrival of the Black Ships until the Meiji restoration in 1868. Whatever conservative and reactionary thinking survived the initial shock of confrontation with a modern industrial fleet was eventually converted by the mounting evidence of how much Japan's position had deteriorated in the international system. Since the middle of the 1990s, Japan has also been faced with the reality that its international position is under increased pressure.

First and foremost has been the prolonged anemia of the Japanese economy. When the bubble collapsed, many argued that the problem was temporary and not structural, but by the end of 1997 Japan had seen five consecutive quarters of negative growth and few believed any longer that its problems were only the result of cyclical adjustments. Vowing to turn around the Japanese economy, the Obuchi administration injected mammoth spending programs in 1998 that pushed Japan's ratio of debt to GDP to more than 130 percent, the highest of any major economy in the industrialized world. For the first two quarters of 1999, Japanese GDP growth grew at 1.5 percent, but as public spending flagged in the third quarter of 1999, the economy began to contract again.

Long-term growth of 1 to 2 percent per year is still possible in Japan, but clearly not based on stimulus packages alone. Real growth will require the Japanese economy to break from the old formula of intrusive government intervention, controlled competition, and lifetime employment. Bad debts totaling at least $500 billion (according to the Japanese government), and possibly twice that amount (in the view of some outside experts), have already forced the private sector to begin restructuring along these lines. Banks from rival *keiretsu* industrial groupings have merged and major companies like Nissan have accepted partial takeover by foreign firms like Renault. Prolonged restructuring and downsizing in the first decade of the twenty-first century is unavoidable, a realization that led over 70 percent of respondents to a 1999 *Nihon Keizai Shimbun* poll to express concern that they could lose their jobs—an unthinkable number the decade before. Japan's economic problems are only compounded by the longer-term challenges of sustaining a rapidly aging society. By about 2006 the Japanese population will peak and contraction will begin. Already in the 1990s the percent of the Japanese population over sixty-five years old expanded from 11 to 18 percent. The transformation of the Japanese economy has predictably led to huge debates about economic policy, but its implications for foreign policy are no less significant.

The second corrosive trend on Japanese confidence in the current modus operandi has been the changing security environment in Northeast Asia. The biggest change has been in relations with China. For decades, the Japanese view of China was shaped by a faith in the powers of economic interdependence. Japan never fully embraced U.S. confrontation with Beijing in the first decades after World War II. Then it rushed to establish full diplomatic relations with Beijing after U.S. rapprochement in 1972. In the early 1990s, Japan enjoyed a special relationship with Beijing, serving as a bridge between China and the West in the wake of the 1989 Tienanmen incident. By the middle of the 1990s, however, a pronounced Sino-Japanese rivalry began to emerge. In 1995 Chinese nuclear tests outraged both the hawkish Right and the antinuclear Left in Japan, leading to an unprecedented, though limited, suspension of about $75 million in grant aid to China. China rattled the Japanese public again in March 1996 by bracketing Taiwan with ballistic missiles, some of which landed near Japanese shipping lanes south of Okinawa. Beijing's increasingly strident attacks on Japanese defense cooperation with the United States and Japan's "treatment of history" further reinforced impressions in Tokyo that China prefers a weak and passive Japan. In 1985 only 17.8 percent of the Japanese public polled by the Prime Minister's Office expressed unfriendly feelings toward China, but by 1996 that number had increased to 51.3 percent.[15] Whether strong and assertive or weak and unstable, China has become a huge question mark in Japan's future.

North Korea is also shaking the Japanese sense of security. As the Cold War ended, Japanese politicians attempted to maneuver deftly between the two Koreas without abandoning Japan's de facto alignment with the South. In 1990 LDP political kingpin Kanemaru Shin met with Kim Il Sung and vowed in a tearful statement to normalize relations with the North as soon as possible, dangling the possibility of billions of dollars in aid (reparations, from the North's perspective). However, the promise of improved relations with Pyongyang based on economic inducements disappeared in a hale of missile firings and threatening rhetoric from the North. In 1992 the Japanese media discovered that North Korean commandos had kidnapped innocent Japanese citizens to teach spies in the North. Japanese anxiety about the North was further exacerbated in 1993 by the first of North Korea's

Nodong missile tests and in 1994 by the confrontation over the North's suspected nuclear weapons program. Then in August 1998 the North test-fired the longer-range Taepo-dong missile right over northern Japan—a brazen act that shook the Japanese out of their remaining complacency about North Korea the way *Sputnik* shook the United States in 1957.

Economic interdependence, underpinned by a large Japanese economic lead, no longer provides a reassuring context for Japan's future role in East Asia. Longer-term relative Japanese economic power is in greater doubt. The efficacy of economic power to build a benign external environment appears limited. The debate is no longer about how to define Japan's international contribution, as Ozawa and Takemura framed it at the beginning of the 1990s. It is now also about how to retain Japan's international position and influence in an era of uncertain power.

Japan's Options

What are Japan's options in this new era? The debate has focused on the same themes that confronted Yoshida when he established the future coordinates of Japan's world role a half century ago: alliance, the Constitution, Asia, the UN, and economic power.

Alliance or Autonomy

In the end there is no better strategic option for Japan than alliance with the United States. The priority of that alliance for Japan was clearly articulated in April 1996, when President Clinton and Prime Minister Hashimoto issued a Joint Security Declaration "reaffirming" the U.S.-Japan alliance and the basing of 47,000 U.S. forces in Japan, and promising to revise the 1976 U.S.-Japan Defense Guidelines so that Japan could provide support in regional contingencies. This strengthening of the security relationship was possible—even after the rape of a young Okinawan girl by U.S. servicemen in late 1995 caused national protests—precisely because of Japanese concerns about North Korean threats and growing Chinese power. Strategically, Japan has noplace else to go.

If strengthening the alliance was necessary to reassure Japan against abandonment in a potentially more hostile world, however, it has also raised the specter of entrapment. The unipolar power of the United States and the perception of American hubris have caused a backlash among many intellectuals in Japan. As the *Mainichi Shimbun's* Kawachi Takashi noted in 1998:

> Since [1997] Japanese newspapers and magazines have carried one article after another calling for greater independence and distance from the United States. The authors are predominantly conservative thinkers, not the traditional left-wing types that dominated mainstream anti-American thinking in the past. . . . What all these critics have in common is their resentment of America's self-seeking arrogance and their concomitant disgust with Japan's obsequious adherence to the United States.[16]

Leading this backlash are commentators such as former Tokyo University professor Nishibe Susumu, who argues that "Americanism" is "swallowing" Japan's independent identity.[17] Others warn that American hegemony puts Japan's future economic security in the hands of an unstable U.S. political system. *Asahi Shimbun* writer Saeki Keishi, for example, predicts that "America could end up interested only in its own national interests, losing interest in the global economic order, thus creating an international crisis."[18] American hegemony also carries the danger that U.S. policy may become more unilateral in Asia, ignoring Japanese security interests. President Clinton's heralding of a new "strategic partnership" with China in 1998, for example, confirmed for a number of Japanese observers the trend toward "Japan passing."[19] From the Right and Left, commentators are warning that Japan has no better choice than alignment with the United States but that this carries inherent dangers.

It is this fear of entrapment and frustration with U.S. domination that has led many intellectual and political leaders in Japan to call for more Japanese control of the alliance mechanisms. *Asahi Shimbun's* Honda Masaru noted in his feature story on the fortieth anniversary of the U.S.-Japan alliance in January 2000, for example, that government officials now stress "autonomy" as a major theme in security relations with the United States.[20] Senior Ministry of Foreign Affairs (MOFA) officials, he said, argue that "Japan must paint its own self portrait" in security, while Japan Defense Agency (JDA) officials warn that "treatment of U.S. bases will no longer be handled the same."[21] At one point, the opposition Democratic Party (DPJ) went even further, flirting with proposals for an "alliance without permanent U.S. forces," but the proposal was dropped when the DPJ expanded in the spring of 1998 to include more ex–LDP members.[22] For now, polls show that 67 percent of the Japanese people favor a reduction in bases,[23] but the pressure for significant withdrawal is not immediate. Indeed, at the end of 1999, polling by *Yomiuri* and Gallup showed higher support for the alliance than at any time since 1984.[24] The political sensitivity toward U.S. bases will probably grow in the future, particularly in Okinawa, but it is clear that the external uncertainties presented by China and North Korea mitigate against these. Nevertheless, the consensus is strong in Japan that the United States must increase consultation on base issues, the deployment of U.S. forces, and other security issues.

Others have argued that Japan can seize more control of its destiny and hedge against abandonment by strengthening unilateral military capabilities. The LDP's National Security Committee argued in 1997, for example, that "it is totally natural for Japan, as an independent nation, to keep a minimum required defense force."[25] Opposition DPJ candidate Hatoyama Yukio won his party's presidency in 1999 with a platform calling for more "autonomous defense," making this a prominent theme for the two major parties in Japan for the first time ever. There is no question that the political environment for defense policy in Tokyo is becoming more permissive. In 1999 the Japanese government approved a project to develop independent surveillance satellites, for example, and some young Diet members began calling for independent "counterattack capabilities."[26] However, the corrosion of normative constraints on defense policy has not resulted in fundamental changes in missions or capabilities. The defense budget remains flat and the JSDF has not moved beyond defensive missions, with the exception of peacekeeping, humanitarian relief, and noncombatant evacuation.[27] Support for a purely autonomous defense policy remains low. A poll taken by the Prime Minister's Office in 1997 demonstrated that only 7.1 percent of respondents favored scrapping the alliance and rearming, while 68.1 percent favored maintaining the current alliance.[28] Moreover, the hedging at the margins of Japanese defense policy is not new or unique.[29] In terms of real security, Japan has no place else to go.

Yet even with this recognition, the most pro-alliance intellectuals in Japan are uneasy with dependence on a nation that is seen as increasingly unilateral. As respected Kobe University scholar Iokibe Makoto puts it: "Recently American national security policy has been conspicuous for its emphasis on domestic opinion and national interest. It is therefore problematic to assume we can relax because of the U.S.-Japan alliance or that we can leave judgment on Asian regional problems to the United States."[30]

Constitutional Revision

With the uneasy sense of returning dependence on U.S. power, many Japanese political and intellectual leaders have also focused in recent years on constitutional revision. Revision represents a goal that will lead to greater self-identity without taking the self-defeating step of weakening the alliance with the United States. As influential television journalist Tawara Sōichirō writes: "To tell the truth, I still do not really want to demonstrate autonomy. Much stronger for me is the desire to get rid of subordination to the United States. Probably, most Japanese have the same feeling." To break this "subordination" without taking on the risks of "autonomy," Tawara argues, means that the next big theme for Japan must be to rewrite the American-drafted Constitution.[31]

There is no question that support for this once-taboo issue in Japan has grown in the decade since the Cold War ended. In a 1993 *Yomiuri Shimbun* poll, more than half the respondents favored constitutional amendment for the first time ever.[32] This prompted the *Yomiuri* editorial staff to issue a proposed new Constitution, sparking an editorial war with the liberal *Asahi Shimbun* throughout the decade.[33] In 1997 an LDP poll discovered that 75 percent of respondents were either in favor (41 percent) or somewhat in favor (35 percent) of constitutional revision. Interestingly, more DPJ supporters (78 percent)—who tend to be younger—favored revision than did LDP supporters (74 percent).[34] The growing momentum for revision among the younger generation was exposed again in a *Yomiuri* poll of Diet members in 1998, in which 90 percent of those politicians under fifty years of age favored changing the Constitution.[35]

The LDP polls demonstrate that the growing support for constitutional revision does not represent a desire to scrap Article Nine and push for independent remilitarization, so much as a readiness to clarify and render Japanese this fundamental document. The *Yomiuri's* draft Constitution, for example, does not eliminate the clause in Article Nine renouncing war as a sovereign right. Instead, the draft clarifies Japan's right to participate in collective security (UN missions) and collective defense (providing reciprocal military support to the United States). Many advocates of constitutional revision are not supporters of independent rearmament either. This mainstreaming of the constitutional issue has had its effect. In 1999 the Diet established commissions in both houses to study constitutional revision. While the LDP agreed to a five-year moratorium on actual proposals, the momentum toward revision appears irreversible. Whether change in the Constitution will dramatically improve Japan's strategic position is another question, but the issue has clearly grown as a focus of national purpose in an era of uncertain power.

Asia or the West

Asia also remains a central theme in Japan's debate about strategy and identity. By 1995 Asia surpassed North America and Western Europe as Japan's major trading zone (41 percent to Asia and 40 percent to North America and Europe). Meanwhile, on the front page of the *Asahi Shimbun* coverage of Asia-related stories increased from 1,000 in 1985 to 6,000 in 1995.[36] In the early 1990s Japan played a leading role in the establishment of the Asia Pacific Economic Cooperation (APEC) forum and the ASEAN Post-Ministerial Conference (PMC). This Asianist wave in Japan was heralded by the writings of Senior Foreign Ministry official Ogura Kazuo, who claimed in 1993 that Western-style modernization and industrialization had reached a dead end and that Japan and Asia must now advance a universally applicable "Asian theory of capitalism,"[37] and by the *Asahi Shimbun*'s Funabashi Yōichi, who put the United States on notice in a 1992 *Foreign Affairs* article that the "Asianization of Asia" was under way.[38] This trend in thinking became so pronounced by 1995 that Kyoto University professor Noda Nobuo was compelled to warn that the "dangerous rise of Asianism" would leave Japan alone and exposed in the region with an unpredictable China.[39]

By about the time of Noda's warnings, however, the Japanese view of Chinese power and intentions began to change. In subsequent years, the growing security threat from North Korea and the malaise of the Japanese economy further undermined the Asianists' vision. These developments have put the Asian dimension of Japanese strategy and identity in a new and somewhat different context. Asia is important in Japanese strategy now, not because of a Sino-Japanese centered integration, but because Japan needs ties in the region to constrain China from moving in unfavorable directions, and to sustain Japanese economic growth. As a 1997 strategy paper prepared by the LDP Foreign Policy Research Commission noted with regard to China: "Not only must we make the Japan-U.S. alliance a key dimension of our China policy, but we must also strengthen the cooperative countries, South Korea and Australia— nations which also have reason to be concerned about China's future course."[40]

Yoshida biographer and international relations scholar Kōsaka Masataka predicted decades ago that Japan's torn identity between East and

West would eventually become more acute because of the rise of Chinese power. As Itō Ken'ichi noted in his own writings on Japan's identity in 1999:

Thirty years ago the renowned international political scientist Masataka Kōsaka argued in his *The Vision of the Maritime Nation of Japan* that Japan belongs to neither the West nor the East and is consequently troubled by a loss of identity and he forecast that, despite the fact that Japan's defeat in World War II, its subsequent dependence on the U.S., and its attempts to Americanize had led it to forget this concern for a time, the emergence of China as a major power would once again force Japan to confront the ambivalence of its stand between West and the East, indeed a perennial problem for Japan and the Japanese that today has once again been thrust before us.[41]

Political scientist Kitaoka Shin'ichi argues that Japan has no choice to escape from this dilemma other than to return to the Meiji leaders' concept of Japan as a bridge between East and West, "a country that sits on the outskirts of Western civilization but continues to thrive as an independent civilization not completely overwhelmed by Western culture." "This example," he argues, "is perhaps the most important message that Japan can send to other cultures."[42]

This formulation of Japan's Asian identity as allied with America but serving as Asia's breakwater against the chaos of Anglo-American capitalism and culture has become powerful in recent years. As Japan's former ambassador to Indonesia, Watanabe Taizo, argued in 1997: "It is said that we've gone from Japan-bashing to Japan-passing, but in that region [Southeast Asia] there is no such talk. Expectations for Japan are extremely high."[43] Billions of dollars in financial assistance and Tokyo's criticism of the IMF in the wake of the 1997 economic crisis won political influence and respect for Japan in the region. Tokyo has drawn on these cards to counter U.S. and European Union (EU) criticism of sluggish Japanese economic growth, participating in symbolic "ASEAN Plus Three" meetings with China and Korea that exclude the United States and Oceania. Nevertheless, this remains essentially a defensive vision of Asianism, driven by the realization, expressed by Funabashi Yōichi in *Foreign Affairs* in 1998, that "Japan, the locomotive of the regional economy, accounting for about 70 percent of Asia's GDP, has ground to a halt."[44] If anything, the trend in the 1990s was one of globalism rather than the Asianization once anticipated by many observers. Organizations such as APEC have largely fallen behind the World Trade

Organization (WTO) and IMF in defining the international economic agenda. The once-vaunted "yen bloc" has proven elusive as global capital flows and a failure to internationalize the yen keep Asian financial needs and exposure global. As economic nationalist commentator Kikkawa Mototada laments in his 1998 book *The Loss of the Money War,* "APEC has been taken over by the United States and Australia" and the financial crisis has ended in "a victory for the Treasury Department Wall Street axis."[45]

The Asian dimension of Japanese strategy and identity is also held back by the unresolved legacy of history. The Japanese government has offered official apologies for its actions in Asia in various forums and forms since the end of the war—most notably with South Korea in 1998. And to be fair, in recent years Japanese textbooks have begun addressing in explicit terms issues such as the invasion of China and the Nanjing massacre, in spite of criticisms to the contrary from Asian and Western observers.[46] However, the historical cloud will not dissipate quickly for several reasons. First, few Japanese politicians are willing to challenge the status of the emperor with a comprehensive condemnation of the war.[47] Even when centrist or Left-wing politicians attempt to do so, as Prime Minister Murayama did on the fiftieth anniversary of defeat in 1995, conservative opposition politicians or members of the cabinet invariably disagree, undermining the original gesture and raising the ire of the region. Second, many Japanese feel their nation also to be a war victim, purged of guilt by the horrific atomic bombings of Hiroshima and Nagasaki.[48] Third, anti-Japanese history education is well entrenched in most East Asian countries, ensuring that generations that did not experience the war will inherit a suspicion of Japan (though there are signs of progress in Japan-Korea relations, as we will see). Finally, younger Japanese politicians and intellectuals feel less culpability for the actions of their parents and bristle at China's use of the historical card to contain Japanese ambitions. The fact that revision of the Japanese Constitution is still viewed in China and Korea as a dangerous taboo suggests that the Asian dimension of Japanese identity may be as much of a constraint as a source of autonomy.

It is likely that Japanese investment in the region and dependence on Asia for manufacturing will continue to expand as the Japanese population ages and the domestic workforce shrinks. It is also possible that regionalism will return as the more powerful force in the twenty-first century, depending, in large measure, on how the United States manages the Bretton Woods system in the future. Moreover, there is no doubt that Japan will continue to be pulled between its Asian and Western identities, forever seeking a synthesis. However, as Kyoto University's Noda Noboru predicted in 1995, Tokyo's ability to use the Asia card against the United States will more likely be limited by Japan's own vulnerabilities in the region.[49]

Multilateralism

Beyond Asia, Japan has also sought to be a good global citizen and to establish greater influence and empowerment vis-à-vis the United States in international organizations. In 1957 the Japanese government began expressing the importance of UN-centered diplomacy, and after the Gulf War the Japanese internationalist elite invested much of their hope for a clearer international identity in the goal of permanent membership in the UN Security Council (UNSC). With time, the government has also won over a once-skeptical Japanese public. The internal debate between minimalists like Takemura and great-power internationalists like Ozawa about permanent UNSC membership is essentially over. According to polls by the Prime Minister's Office, the pro-UNSC side has won in the battle for public opinion in Japan, with 56 percent supporting Japan's bid in 1994 and 64.5 percent in 1997.[50] The problem is that in the court of international public opinion and in the Byzantine world of the United Nations itself, Japan's bid has gone nowhere since 1994. There is still relatively little debate against the United Nations in Japan (certainly compared with the United States), but as UN expert Fukushima Akiko warns, increasingly the "skewed balance between Japan's role and contribution may antagonize UN sympathizers in Japan."[51]

In international financial institutions such as the IMF and World Bank, Japan's status as number-two contributor behind the United States was accomplished a decade ago. Since that time, Tokyo has attempted to turn this position into one of intellectual leadership. The failed attempt to establish a separate Asia Monetary Fund in 1997 was a gesture in that direction. In the World Bank and IMF Japan has formed coalitions with the United States and at times with the Europeans and Asia, influencing the debate about the future of the international financial architecture. However, the state of Japan's own economy has severely undermined efforts to advance alternate approaches to development and international finance. In fact, on the fundamental issues of international economic policy and development, Japan diverges little from the United States. Nevertheless, Japan continues a struggle to shape the definition of international economic policy. As Nomura Research Institute's Fukushima Kiyohiko warns, "American control of the strategic decision making in important international economic organizations" has given rise to "a Market Fundamentalism and idealization of the Anglo-American type capitalism" that is "dangerous and counterproductive."[52]

Economic Growth or Economic Security

Ultimately, the contemporary debate over international identity and strategy is a mirror of the debate over change in Japan's domestic social and economic structure. Those who assert Japanese economic nationalism believe that economic autonomy can be maintained or even enhanced. Tokyo governor Ishihara Shintarō falls into this category with his argument that Japan can just say no to the United States and "global standards."[53] So also do the economists who wrote the 1998 book *A Japanese Economy that Can Grow at Zero,* which argues that the combination of zero growth and a low birth rate will keep per-capita GDP high and allow Japan to protect itself economically as a "stock" (as opposed to a "flow") superpower.[54]

However, the majority opinion, even among those arguing for Japanese resistance to Anglo-American market fundamentalism, is that structural change in the economy is inevitable. Fukushima, for example, acknowledges that Japanese corporate governance is rapidly moving in the direction of the United States.[55] And while Mitsui Trading Company strategist Terashima Jitsurō complains that "global standards are nothing more than Washington standards," he points out that Japan is inevitably moving toward greater deregulation, though perhaps only to the level that 20 to 25 percent of Japan's GDP would be regulated—a figure still higher than the 7 percent level of regulation he calculates for the United States.[56] For Fukushima, Terashima, and many in the corporate and government sectors, even in the midst of change and restructuring, Japan must assert a unique economic philosophy and identity.

The contrasting view is powerful, however. Longtime globalists like Ōmae Ken'ichi now feel their arguments are justified and that Japan is finally moving away from "national" concepts of the economy and focusing instead on the global dimension.[57] Rhetorically, at least, the global standards perspective has won important backers in big business and politics since the deepening of Japan's malaise in the late 1990s. In 1998 the business roundtable Keizai Dōyūkai issued a "Declaration of Market Ideology,"[58] and Keidanren's (the Federation of Economic Organizations) 21st Century Institute recommended to the government's Economic Strategy Council that "the business community must adopt a positive stance toward structural reform based on thorough implementation of free-market economic ideals and complete acceptance of the principle of self-responsibility."[59] The Keidanren institute asserted further that this new globalism must now define Japan's role as the head of the free-market flying geese in Asia, arguing that "if we in Japan are to urge others to move forward with liberalization, then we have to set an example by freeing up the sectors of our own economy in which liberalization is lagging."[60] This same free market ideology has been embraced by Left and Right political challengers to the status quo. Former DPJ leader Kan Naoto wrote in *Bungei Shunjū* in 1998 that instead of "reacting against global standards, Japan should learn from the United States."[61] On the Right, Liberal Party leader Ozawa Ichirō championed reform in his 1993 book *Blueprint for a New Japan*.[62] A more recent convert, LDP conservative Kajiyama Seiroku began arguing that Japan will have to go for restructuring, letting the uncompetitive banks fail, "even if that means a hard landing."[63] (Kajiyama died in the spring of 2000.) These politicians are not free from the old economy—Kan is backed by labor unions and Ozawa by construction companies—but they have seized on a theme that they believe defines the future.

For a nation that defined national purpose and power primarily through economic performance, reconciling restructuring with autonomy has been extremely difficult. Arguments that Japan can maintain its autonomy and international weight class as a "stock superpower" or by rejecting global standards are rapidly losing credibility in Tokyo. Writers like Fukushima and Terashima are probably correct that Japan will not completely embrace Anglo-American standards of transparency and deregulation. However, the trend economically is clearly toward some degree of convergence and some decline in relative economic power. This has forced and will continue to force rethinking about the power and purpose of Japan's world role, even as the parameters set by Yoshida remain in place.

Reluctant Realism

While the debate over Japan's identity and strategy at the dawn of the twenty-first century has not yielded a new synthesis and has not changed the fundamental coordinates set by Yoshida, it has established one new principle that will have important implications for the conduct of Japanese foreign policy in the future. That principle is simply that Japan must take more proactive steps to defend its position in international society and that these steps can no longer be defined by the U.S.-Japan alliance or by facile assumptions about economic interdependence alone, even as alliance and economics remain at the core of Japan's world role. The broad support for this more assertive and in some ways more desperate expression of Japan's world role is evident in a series of commissions and study groups formed to chart Japan's objectives for the new millennium at the end of the 1990s. An examination of three follows.

The first group formally to consider how to maintain Japan's weight in a period of economic and political restructuring was commissioned by the Comprehensive Foreign Policy Bureau of MOFA in 1997. While the diplomats and scholars in the group rejected an increase in military power to compensate for economic problems, they note in their March 1999 final report, *Challenge 21:* "Given that another leap is hard to expect if our foreign policy dependence on economic strength remains unchanged, we must reconsider where we should find the sources of our national power that would support our diplomacy."[64] Though the specific policy proposals recommended by the report are ambiguous, the theme is clear: Japan must wield all of its available power assets more assertively and more independently within the parameters set by Yoshida.

The second comprehensive effort to chart Japan's foreign policy in this new setting was *Japan's Initiatives towards U.S., China and Russia,* a report prepared by the independent Japan Forum on International Relations and endorsed by seventy-eight leading scholars, business leaders, and politicians in 1999. The authors of *Japan's Initiatives*—pro alliance all—acknowledge that the entrapment-versus-abandonment dilemma in relations with the United States has distracted Japan from forming its own strategy: "post-war Japanese foreign policy has viewed relations with the U.S. almost entirely within a bilateral framework and has swung back and forth between dependence and rejection without discerning the U.S. global strategy and East Asia policy."[65] The authors urge adoption instead of a new "proposal/coaction style of policy" with the United States, "which features friendly assertiveness on the basis of Japan's own foreign policy principles and global strategy."[66] Specifically, they urge the government to press the United States to introduce a no first use policy on nuclear weapons, to use the Russia card and multilateral diplomacy to constrain China, and to shape U.S. policy on Taiwan and Korea. As we will see in subsequent case studies, this trend in thinking has gained momentum throughout the 1990s.

The third effort to capture the foreign policy agenda was Prime Minister Obuchi's 1999 blue ribbon panel entitled "Commission on Japanese Goals for the 21st Century." The commission's January 2000 final report paints a picture of an increasingly liberal and civil society in Japan, urging the government to improve the way citizens interact with the state and with the public domain through a series of reforms in regulation, the tax code, and the voting age. In examining Japan's foreign policy, the commission reviews the dashed hopes and growing angst of the first decade of the post–Cold War era:

> There has been considerable swing back and forth in the sense of direction in Japanese foreign policy. On the one hand, in the first half of the 1990's with the first Clinton Administration's increasing pressure on Japan and resulting bilateral economic friction, and the breakdown of the U.S.-Japan summit meeting, Japanese bureaucrats and business leaders increasingly grew weary of the United States and called for a return to the home ground of Asia. It was an argument for switching from America to Asia—*datsubei nyūa*. On the other hand, after seeing Chinese and North Korean missile tests, it was clear to Japan that Asia is not so calm after all. If anything, there is recently a strengthening of opinion that Japan itself should overcome post-war taboos and consider capabilities and policies for the security of our own country, a development that has been seen as possibly leading to the return of nationalism.[67]

The commission argues that Japan must break the pattern of swinging between Asia and the United States and instead pursue "enlightened self-interest." But, the members argue, this debate about national interest must be "backed by a healthy realism."[68]

A "healthy realism"? This could mean many things. In international relations theory, realism is a school of thought that argues nations pursue relative gains in power in an essentially anarchic international system.[69] While this school of realism tends not to focus on variations in states' strategic culture, it is clear that Japanese strategic culture is increasingly sensitive to relative power relations, particularly vis-à-vis China. Realism also could be defined in contrast to *idealism* in the formation of foreign policy.[70] Here again, the powerful idealism of Japanese pacifism, of Asianism, and of multilateralism is losing ground to a sharper-edged and somewhat narrower definition of national interest in Japan's foreign policy debate and a clearer recognition of the importance of security policy. A third definition of realism could be that Japan is reassessing its foreign policy to reflect a more "realistic" assessment of national economic resources and the need to get more "bang" for

Japan's shrinking diplomatic "buck." This reassessment certainly is evident in MOFA's strategy paper *Challenge 21*. Finally, the members of the prime minister's commission could be reflecting their own calls for Japan to continue defining its role as a "global civilian power," allied with the United States but expressing a vision for Asia. This definition flows from them their warning that Japan's experiences since the end of the Cold War could lead to greater nationalism and the hope that the Japanese will retain a healthy realism about the costs of a return to the militarism of the past.

By all four definitions Japan has already moved toward a greater realism regarding national security and identity. The changes in the Japanese worldview described in this book are the result of material circumstances—the decline of relative Japanese economic power assets and the rise of Chinese power in Asia—colliding with the aspirations of a new generation and the steady transformation of domestic Japanese political and economic institutions. While the nation-state has declined in importance with the rise of regionalism in Europe, in Japan (and in most of Asia, for that matter) the nation-state is finally arriving—just as economic malaise and Chinese hubris raise questions about Japan's weight and security in the international system.

Two things are particularly striking about this process. The first is the continuing resilience of the Yoshida Doctrine's broad parameters. The second, however, is how much Japanese foreign policy has been shaped since the Cold War by material changes in what is arguably a benign strategic environment. After all, Japan's ally retains primacy; China's power remains in check; and Japan's economy holds a comfortable lead over other national challengers for the spot of number two. Given the changes in Japan's strategic culture and *weltenshuaung* in this comparatively benign, though uncertain, setting, one can imagine the impact on Japanese foreign policy of more serious shifts in the power structure of international relations. As noted historian Kenneth Pyle argues, echoing Carol Gluck's theme about change in Japan, "once the structure of its external environment becomes clear, Japan is likely to accommodate itself to the new order of things. Moreover, if the past is a reliable guide, it will accommodate with a speed that will surprise those who look only at its present immobilisms."[71]

We return to such variables in the concluding chapter, after an examination of the changing nature of Japan's domestic political institutions and more detailed case studies on the "small changes" in contemporary Japanese foreign policy.

CHAPTER TWO

Domestic Institutions
and Foreign Policy

An Era of Uncertain Political Realignment

Japanese foreign policy has been described as "reactive," "minimalist," "situational," and "too little too late."[1] These characteristics reflect the parameters of strategic culture described in the last chapter, but they must also be understood as the external manifestation of a political and bureaucratic system that managed for almost four decades to maximize economic growth while maintaining domestic stability and egalitarianism. This chapter introduces those institutions and explains how they are shaping foreign policy in the post–Cold War period. The process of political realignment now under way in Japan is irreversible and should eventually lead to a new equilibrium and a clearer articulation of Japanese foreign policy. For the foreseeable future, however, the main effect will be greater political intrusiveness and fluidity in foreign policymaking, a steady weakening of the institutional barriers to security policy, more assertive responses to external threats to Japan's international position, and increasing collisions among Japan's competing international agenda.

The chapter first reviews the traditional role of domestic politics in Japanese foreign policy, considers the impact of current political realignment, and then examines each institutional actor in more detail.

The Impact of the "1955 System" on Foreign Policy

The Japanese domestic political economy is changing. But the institutions of power—the LDP, the bureaucracy, and big business—cling stubbornly to their positions of preeminence. The LDP has deep roots;

it ruled uninterrupted for thirty-eight years after the party was formed in 1955. Today the so-called 1955 system that kept the party in place is crumbling, but the institutional impact on foreign policy lingers.

Under the 1955 system the LDP maintained power with a simple formula of economic growth and alignment with the United States. The party was divided into half a dozen powerful factions, but this factionalism only reinforced its strength by increasing competition among the conservatives for voter loyalty in the multiseat districts of Japan's more powerful lower house and by providing a rotating premiership among faction leaders that satisfied the voters' occasional desire for change without causing them to look outside the LDP. Ideologically, the LDP was united by its anticommunism, but broad differences existed within the party on the issues of remilitarization, constitutional revision, and economic reform. These differences tended to be individual rather than factional, which prevented divisive policy issues from splitting the party, while providing maximum opportunity for co-opting the opposition's policy proposals and appealing to a broad majority as the catch-all party. In contrast, the opposition Socialist Party became increasingly wedded to a rigid ideological position (opposing constitutional reform, nuclear energy, and any remilitarization) and lost credibility as anything other than a "brake" or protest vote against the LDP's excesses—a role that kept it from seizing a majority in the Diet but always gave it substantial seats in order to block the LDP's excesses. Other middle-size opposition parties stole some of the Socialists' votes beginning in the 1960s, but these parties (the Clean Government Party, or *Kōmeitō,* and the Democratic Socialists) were too closely identified with specific interest groups to compete nationally against the LDP. The electoral system further disadvantaged the opposition parties by giving more voting power to conservative rural districts (sometimes a ratio of three-to-one in representation for rural over urban districts).

The LDP vote-gathering machine was backed by a competent and respected bureaucracy that insulated the ruling party's powerful constituencies (farmers, construction, etc.) against external economic threats. The effectiveness of the bureaucracy's formal and informal barriers against foreign penetration was evident in the consistently low level of foreign direct investment into Japan throughout the postwar period. The bureaucracy also reinforced conservative rule by maintaining a public policy that maximized the distribution of technology and productive capacity across horizontal industrial sectors while minimizing social dislocation that would be caused by the failure of major employers. In turn, the bureaucracies each maintained relative autonomy over internal personnel decisions, and individual bureaucrats enjoyed immense power and prestige even after retiring (often through *amakudari,* or "descent from heaven," into a second career under the ministry's family of regulated or semipublic corporations). Finally, the political and bureaucratic legs of the "iron triangle" were complemented by the cohesion of socioeconomic alliances in vertical and horizontal *keiretsu* groupings, by sectoral cartels, and by the labor unions' close affiliations with their parent firms.

The model of Japan's domestic political economy should by no means be seen as monolithic or static. But whether described as a "developmental state,"[2] "patterned pluralism,"[3] or "reciprocal consent,"[4] the general characteristics of the model are consistent and help to explain Japan's remarkable economic success and social stability in the first four decades of the postwar era. These same characteristics also help to explain the passive and dysfunctional aspects of Japanese foreign policy in the postwar period:

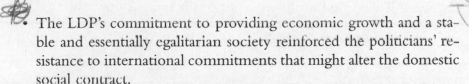

- The LDP's commitment to providing economic growth and a stable and essentially egalitarian society reinforced the politicians' resistance to international commitments that might alter the domestic social contract.
- The bureaucracy's vertical stove piping and strong autonomy of individual ministries (*tatewari gyōsei*) delayed the process of consultation and consensus-building for foreign policy. This assured that Japanese diplomatic initiatives or crisis response were often too late to make a difference. Even as Japan's economy "internationalized" with the appreciation of the yen in the mid-1980s, bureaucratic divisions on foreign policy continued as otherwise indifferent ministries became active in foreign affairs to protect their constituent interests.
- The LDP's strong factions constrained prime ministers (who were usually faction leaders themselves) from taking decisive action in foreign affairs and weakened the party's ability to articulate a guiding foreign policy vision, beyond the flexible principles of the Yoshida Doctrine.
- The multiseat election districts meant that an LDP politician could win with as little as 15 to 20 percent of the vote in a district. This encouraged the politicians to cater to specific economic interests and discouraged debate on national issues such as foreign policy. In Tokyo, this handicapped aspiring faction leaders who focused on foreign affairs and led to the promotion of faction leaders who

could deliver the most votes, posts, and political financing that would help individual politicians back in their districts. Aspiring faction leaders or new candidates in the districts might sometimes use foreign policy issues to secure an initial cadre of loyal supporters and to challenge the mainstream power brokers, but faction-climbers usually succeeded best when they shed divisive ideological issues. As a result, those who rose to the tops of the factions were often least versed in foreign affairs. An increasingly regimented seniority system in the factions worked against younger, more internationalist politicians.

- The Socialists' role as Greek chorus for pacifism and the Constitution discouraged the LDP from pursuing divisive foreign and security policy initiatives—particularly since these issues were often the only leverage the Socialists had to hold up otherwise popular LDP budgets in the Diet.

- The public was satisfied with the LDP's ability to distribute the benefits of economic growth and usually suspicious of assertive foreign policy proposals that emanated from either the left or the right of the political spectrum, since these were often designed as challenges to the status quo—a status quo that worked well for most people.

There were positive elements to the 1955 system as well. Japan's foreign policy in this period was remarkably consistent, if not glamorous. Steady political leadership allowed the Foreign Ministry to increase overseas development assistance and host nation support for U.S. forces without significant domestic objection. Nationalism and demagoguery were generally contained by a disciplined LDP leadership eager to avoid ideological splits that might strengthen the opposition's hand. The Japanese people maintained an idealistic, if passive, view of foreign affairs. On balance, however, the 1955 system frustrated Japanese diplomacy, as Japan remained unappreciated internationally, its fate left to others, and its leadership unprepared for sudden crises.

The Collapse of the 1955 System

Today, the 1955 system continues to shape Japanese foreign policy formation. But the system itself is dead. Major organs began failing in 1985 after the Plaza Accord and the rapid appreciation of the yen led to an asset bubble in the Japanese economy. For the first time, economic growth cut loose from the moorings of egalitarianism. As land prices skyrocketed, the gap widened between landowners and those salaried workers who had to rent or buy housing. Meanwhile, LDP politicians grew increasingly wealthy as they used their influential positions to win preferential insights into the real estate and stock markets. Corruption scandals erupted with increasing regularity, most spectacularly with revelations that LDP kingpin Kanemaru Shin had been given a shopping cart full of gold and unmarked bonds by the president of the Sagawa-Kyūbin shipping company (in exchange for help avoiding Transport Ministry regulations on its drivers). Corruption in the interest of local districts or political protégés was expected under the 1955 system, but personal aggrandizement was becoming an unacceptable new feature of the bubble years.

Socioeconomic cohesion also became frayed as the high yen drove Japanese manufacturers abroad. *Kūdōka* (or the "hollowing-out" of Japan's domestic manufacturing base in the 1980s) separated end producers from their subcontractors. When those subcontractors began to move offshore to keep up with their clients, the smallest subcontractors and parts suppliers were left behind to wither on the vine. Meanwhile, new service sector corporations like Recruit and Sagawa-Kyūbin began crowding in to the old boys' network of the established manufacturing and banking firms in Keidanren (the Federation of Economic Organizations). These new firms poured money into the LDP factions in order to catch up in influence to the existing corporations and to win some regulatory wiggle room. At the same time other high-tech firms, such as Kyōcera, Sharp, and Sega, were booming outside of the influence of MITI and the economic ministries. With growing pluralism in the industrial sector, the business community was unable to discipline the LDP, as it had during the earlier Lockheed scandals in the 1970s. The politicians had too many diverse sources of income from local construction companies and new service sector firms to be intimidated by the threats of the old-line manufacturing firms in Keidanren. The political machine continued to gorge itself even as it alienated the public and big business.

The social contract was further undermined by changing demographics. Urbanization changed the rules between the government and the governed. Japan went from a 50 percent farming population at the end of World War II to a 6 percent farming population in 1990. Urbanization weakened the sinews between Diet politicians and local voters—particularly the intervening influence of local politicians—and strengthened the impact of the media. Media was also diversifying. Television interview shows and weekly magazines were crowding out the traditional political reporting of the major dailies. Even within the dailies, the political section was being scooped by the city page as the political reporters became too cozy with the politicians they were covering. Further social pressure was brought as an aging society demanded more from the government's welfare budget and provided less revenue through income taxes. This led the government to institute a regressive 3 percent consumption tax in 1989, which only further exacerbated the gaps in living standards and the people's frustration with the LDP.

The 1955 system was created in the bipolar image of the Cold War confrontation between communism and the West. By the time the Cold War ended in 1989, however, the Japanese political system had become distorted. Ideological division no longer constrained the voters or the politicians' choices. All that was required to kill the beast was a shock to its system. There were two shocks: the 1991 Gulf War and the collapse of the Japanese economic bubble. In the past, the conservatives had responded to external shocks by introducing new social policies that would compensate the victims and re-establish the legitimacy of the LDP's "mandate of heaven." By 1991, however, compensation would no longer guarantee popular support for the LDP. There were too many tough choices between the various constituencies of the catch-all party. A minimalist response could not prevent defections from the conservative mainstream.

The most important defection was by Ozawa Ichirō, then a senior lieutenant in the largest LDP faction led by former Prime Minister Takeshita Noboru. Takeshita was a supporter of Prime Minister Miyazawa Kiichi, who had promised to introduce political reform in June1993 after the LDP had been buffeted by the collapse of the economy and a series of political corruption scandals. When Miyazawa backed away from this promise under pressure from the other faction leaders, Ozawa split away from the LDP with forty-three of his supporters, promising to reform the government from outside the party. Other smaller groups of LDP politicians also began splitting away from the party. Defections were not new, and most political commentators expected the party to compensate by wooing politicians back in to the government with posts or by forming a coalition with one of the small centrist parties. To almost every commentators' amazement, however, Ozawa and his defectors seized the majority in the Diet with an eight-party coalition under Hosokawa Morihiro (another former LDP member) that included every opposition party other than the LDP and the Communists. For the first time in forty-three years, the conservative LDP was in the opposition.

But the LDP existed for one reason only—to rule. Like a beached whale, the conservatives knew they could not survive in the opposition for long. After enduring the anti-LDP coalitions of Hosokawa Morihiro (August 1993 to April 1994) and Hata Tsutomu (April 1994 to June 1994), the LDP orchestrated a cynical power-sharing arrangement with their former rivals in the Socialist Party and a small group of LDP defectors under the Harbinger Party banner and came back into power in June 1994 in a government nominally headed by Socialist Prime Minister Murayama Tomiichi. Divided by ideology but united by a desperate longing for the status quo and access to the levers of power, the newly renamed Social Democratic Party and the LDP cooperated until May 1998, when the Socialists—reduced by elections and their transparent cynicism to only fourteen seats in the lower house (from a peak of close to one hundred)—abandoned the LDP and returned under Doi Takako to their previous position of ideological opposition. For the LDP, this defection no longer mattered. The party retained power by building new coalitions and working relationships with other opposition parties. The government of Hashimoto Ryūtarō (January 1996 to July 1998) passed banking legislation by cooperating initially with the opposition Democratic Party and then the Kōmeitō (CGP). The government of Obuchi Keizō (July 1998 to April 2000) then formed a coalition with Ozawa's Liberal Party in January 1999 and with Kōmeitō later in the year. Mori Yoshiro continued this coalition pattern into the new millennium.

But while these maneuvers restored LDP rule, they could not arrest the unfolding process of political realignment. The 1955 system died after the Cold War and the contours of a new system are only just coming into focus.

Regime Shift

With the coalition juggling act, the LDP maintained a grip on power through the end of the 1990s and into the twenty-first century, aided by the public's deep anxiety about the economy and continued aversion to risk. But the days of long-term stable LDP rule are gone, for at least six reasons.

1. *New electoral rules.* The brief interregnum of Hosokawa led to new election rules that pulled the plug on the 1955 system. Under these rules, the traditional multiseat arrangement of 511 seats divided into 130 districts was replaced with a combination of 300

single-seat districts and 200 seats drawn from eleven regional lists (later reduced in 2000 to 180 seats). Reformers hoped that the need to win with a plurality would foster debates on national issues within each district, since politicians can no longer win with only 15 to 20 percent of the vote in a district. That has not happened yet, but two things are evident from the reforms. First, the single-seat districts increase the possibility for large national realignment if cleavage issues force choices more important than traditional patronage; and second, now the LDP has even more difficulty holding on to seats. In the June 2000 Lower House election, the LDP emerged for the third election in a row under the new system without a stable majority in the Diet. The party won 60 percent of the single seats with only 41 percent of the popular vote and was devastated in suburban and rural areas where fifteen former cabinet members went down in defeat. Further volatility is unavoidable, because the policy choices facing the government are too hard.

2. *Too many hard choices.* The LDP's simple formula of anticommunism and pro-economic growth is now full of contradictions. Achieving full potential economic growth now depends on restructuring and deregulation in sectors that traditionally supported the LDP. The fissures between potential winners and losers in this process is reinforcing the socioeconomic cleavages within the party. In 1998 senior LDP and Democratic Party of Japan (DPJ) politicians split over whether the ailing banking sector should be revitalized through financial injections or allowed a "hard landing." In 1999 and 2000 the YKK generation of the LDP (Yamazaki Taku, Katō Kōichi, and Koizumi Jun'ichirō) battled with the Obuchi cabinet over whether to emphasize fiscal stimulus or fiscal responsibility, as Japan's stimulus packages created debt at 130 percent of GDP. As the society ages, even more difficult choices will have to made with even fewer resources. Even if the LDP remains the largest political party, the zero-sum nature of public policy decisions will undermine efforts to remain a broad catch-all party.

3. *The crushing weight of coalition politics.* The LDP will be forced to rule through coalitions for as long as it holds some power. The Upper House—with its larger floating vote—has moved beyond the party's control. The Lower House cannot be held with any certainty either, at least not without a partner. For the LDP, that partner has become the Kōmeitō, with its millions of loyal voters throughout the country. Yet the general public deeply distrusts the

LDP's alliance with Kōmeitō because of the latter's ties to the religious organization Sokkagakai. The LDP is therefore in a catch–22 situation: It cannot win *without* Kōmeitō, but it cannot expand or reestablish its broader base *with* Kōmeitō. If, on the other hand, the LDP drops Kōmeitō for a coalition with the smaller Liberal Party, Mr. Ozawa will insist on a distinct rightward tilt in Japanese national security policy, which would also exacerbate fissures within the party.

4. *A credible opposition.* Hosokawa's anti-LDP coalition government demonstrated, if fleetingly, that the opposition can rule in Japan. That was unthinkable when the Socialists were the largest opposition party. With the emergence of the Democratic Party of Japan, however, the LDP faces a serious threat. A *Nihon Keizai Shimbun* poll in 1998 at one point showed the two parties in a dead heat, in spite of the LDP's stronger infrastructure and political machine.[5] Ultimately, in the June 2000 race, the DPJ expanded by 32 seats to gain 127—an impressive gain, but not enough to unseat the LDP. The problem is that the DPJ's membership is even more diverse than that of the LDP, ranging from former conservative LDP politicians to former Left-wing Socialists. In addition, a DPJ government would lack strong support from the business community. Nevertheless, even if the DPJ collapses on internal policy disagreements and metamorphoses into another center-Left coalition or party, its potential for seizing power will continue as long as the single seat election system is in place—and its ranks provide fodder for the creation of new alliances or parties should the LDP split up.

5. *A traumatized bureaucracy.* The Japanese bureaucracy no longer commands the respect of the people, and this hurts the governing party. With mismanagement of the economy and a series of unprecedented corruption scandals extending even into the powerful Ministry of Finance, the bureaucrats have lost the confidence of the media and the politicians. Without the bureaucracy, the politicians cannot prepare legislation, let alone implement it. But the intrusion of the press and the politicians into the policymaking process will only increase.[6]

6. *A more affluent and liberal society.* In the 1955 system the LDP ruled with the help of gerrymandered districts that strengthened the voting power of rural districts, but Japan's demographics and values have changed. With affluence and lost confidence in government, urban and suburban voters are demanding more than

redistribution and compensation from the politicians. These voters, according to LDP Upper House member Takemi Keizō, want a more civil society and more civil self-determination.[7] Tamamoto Masaru, a keen observer of the Japanese sense of identity, notes that after years of skepticism, the Japanese public is finally undergoing a "silent revolution" and creating a more "liberal Japan."[8] The LDP machine has had difficulty connecting with these floating voters in the urban and suburban districts. In the 1998 Upper House election, for example, the party did not win a single seat in the urbanized districts of Kanagawa, Saitama, Aichi, Kyoto, Osaka, and Hyōgo. To appeal to these voters, the party will have to detach from the "old economy" constituencies that help it retain power.

While these six factors point to the difficulties of continued LDP rule, however, they offer only broad hints at what might come next. In that sense, as political scientist Ōtake Hideo points out, Japan is really still in the process of "dealignment" with "realignment" yet to come.[9] Similarly, T. J. Pempel argues that Japan is in the middle of a "regime shift" and that the new political regime will be shaped by larger changes in the political economy of Japan that are still under way:

> The shifts currently taking place in the Japanese regime are the result, I argue, first of alterations in the international political economy and the difficulties Japan's prevailing regime had in dealing with them, and second of endogenous changes within Japan's own demographic profile that eroded many of the power arrangements of the old system and that weakened the glue holding the old regime together. This dynamic combination of exogenous and endogenous changes has been the causal core of the restructurings currently taking place within Japan. The consequence is almost certain to be the creation of a new regime that will be based on revised socio-economic coalitional arrangements, modified political institutions, and uncharted directions for public policy.[10]

New Coordinates for Politics and Foreign Policy?

If it is clear that Japan is embarked on a regime shift, however, it is far from clear when or where the system will reach a new equilibrium. In the broadest terms of public policy, Japan is being pulled in different, contradictory directions. On economic policy, the tension is between restructuring/deregulation/fiscal responsibility on one hand and fiscal stimulus/protection/deficit spending on the other. In terms of foreign policy, the tension is between maintenance of a civilian power focus versus a greater focus on political/military role.[11] These tensions are illustrated in figure 2.1.

The norms and institutions of the 1955 system regime and the basic conservatism of the Japanese people all weigh heavily toward the lower left corner of the x/y axis shown in figure 2.1. However, the pressures of economic globalism, endogenous demographics, and international security threats all pull public policy toward the riskier environment of the upper right-hand corner of the axis—the zone of reluctant realism. Of the major political parties, the Communists and Social Democrats sit stubbornly at the bottom of the left-hand corner and Ozawa's Liberal Party stands defiantly at the upper right. However, the members of the two major parties—the LDP and the DPJ—are spread all over the chart and overlap in many areas. In other words, the major political parties are still not divided along clear public policy lines.

How then will a new regime equilibrium be established? Despite declining socioeconomic cohesion in Japan, the split between winners and losers in the economy may not prove consistent enough across election districts to force a national political cleavage. Politicians are increasingly being divided over "hard" versus "soft" landings for uncompetitive banks and the question of fiscal stimulus versus fiscal responsibility. However, the general population remains too risk-averse to embrace the advocates of austerity in a way that would lead to political realignment along economic lines. That could change as the national finances continue to hemorrhage in the effort to prop up all the uncompetitive banks and related sectors, such as construction. Or it could change if the economy declines in a way that makes the "hard

Figure 2.1 Tensions in Japanese Economic and Foreign Policy

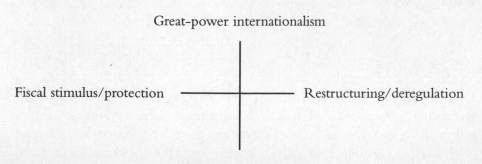

landing" either inevitable or possibly more attractive than the gradual disintegration of the status quo.

Foreign and security policy issues could also force a sharper political realignment, but here again, there is no clear public policy division among the largest parties. In addition, foreign policy remains a second- or third-order priority for most politicians—a useful tool for forging informal alliances or "study groups" across party and factional lines, but too divisive to attract a broad political following within any party other than the smaller Liberal and Communist parties. That would change, of course, if a major external security crisis pushed foreign and security policy issues to the top of the political agenda and forced politicians to choose sides based on deeply held ideological convictions—if, for example, a Korean contingency forced the government to introduce a new round of emergency and defense legislation, or a Chinese attack on Taiwan forced a sharper debate about economic relations with the mainland.

In many respects, the most distinctive cleavage in Japanese politics today is generational. Anecdotally this becomes clear to anyone who travels through the halls of the Diet or deals with the Japanese government. In polling on certain issues, such as constitutional revision, it is even more striking. *Yomiuri* found in surveys of Diet members in 1997, for example, that 90 percent of politicians under 50 favored constitutional revision, compared with 50 percent for those over the age of 50.[12] Youth, it turns out, is a weak point for the LDP. In order to keep senior politicians in place, the party has turned away conservative younger politicians. They are going to the DPJ instead, where Hatoyama has taken on constitutional revision to win their support. Thus the Constitution could become an issue that forces a new round of political realignment. And the splits may be generational as much as ideological.[13]

Of course, the new generation's common views on the constitution and Japan's international role do not mean that their ascendance will lead to the complete end of history or ideology in Japanese politics. While there is unity in the desire to move beyond the past immobilism, passivity, and deference to China and the United States—represented most by the constitutional debate—that still leaves unresolved the strategy and role Japan will adopt in response to new changes in the international security environment.

How long will a new political equilibrium and clearer architecture of national strategy take? Some, including Ozawa Ichirō, have argued that it is only a matter of time. They point out that the 1853 arrival of Commodore Perry's Black Ships in Edo Bay was the shock that killed the old Tokugawa Shōgunate, but it was not until 1889 that the new Meiji regime established a Constitution. If the Gulf War and the collapse of the economic bubble in 1991 were the modern black ships, and if it takes another thirty-five years for a new equilibrium to emerge, then Japan will be in a state of flux through the second decade of the twenty-first century. Nevertheless, even if decades are probably not required, it will probably take several election cycles with the new electoral system before the political parties sort themselves out by policy and ideological orientation.

In the meantime, Japan's foreign policymaking process will be subject to all of the uncertainties of political dealignment and realignment, even as the currents of the old regime continue to flow. The cartelization of decision making within the LDP and the bureaucracy will continue breaking down, reducing the power of the political *kuromaku* (kingpins) and *kagemusha* (shadow warriors), and introducing a new fluidity and individualism into foreign policymaking. Mid-level politicians and officials will be uncertain where future power centers lie, either laying low or gambling on one policy direction or another.

These patterns are already evident in the way that political and bureaucratic institutions are coping with the end of the old regime. They explain both the emerging strategic direction and the continuing dysfunctionality of Japanese diplomacy. We review them by institution next.

The Political Parties and Foreign Policy

The Politicians

Under the 1955 system the politicians typically exerted influence on foreign policy in four ways. First, of course, under a parliamentary system they formed governments and became prime ministers and members of the cabinet.

Second, through the policy caucuses—or *zoku*—within the party the LDP politicians began guiding policymaking across the board *before* decisions reached the relevant committees of the National Diet. At first the *zoku* grew around agriculture and the annual interagency fight over the government's official rice price in the 1970s. From there the *zoku* quickly sprouted around other policy areas with important rural constituencies and simple pressure points where the politicians could increase government expenditures—construction, postal services, and welfare, for example. By the 1980s the leaders of these *zoku* (Hata Tsutomu and Katō Kōichi in agriculture and Ozawa Ichirō in construction) became key players in the bilateral diplomacy of trade disputes with the United States, serving as power brokers between domestic interest groups and external actors. In the early 1980s smaller *zoku* also began forming around policy areas that required somewhat more expertise, including defense and foreign affairs. The foreign affairs *zoku,* for example, lobbied for the ODA budget, while the defense *zoku* actively solicited U.S. pressure on Japan to increase defense spending. With time, the *zoku* became institutionalized enough that Japanese political correspondents and scholars could trace their membership and informal promotion schedule.[14] Typically, the *zoku* were affiliated with a corresponding government ministry, operated around committees in the LDP's Policy Affairs Research Council (PARC—the party's policymaking organ), were managed by a small steering group of senior (fourth term or higher) politicians representing all of the factions, and relied on the bureaucrats to prepare legislation. For the bureaucrats, the *zoku* provided reliable centers of power to coordinate legislation and policy across faction lines (since each faction was represented in the leadership of the zoku) and a useful source of pressure on the always stingy Ministry of Finance Budget Bureau.

Third, and closely paralleling the *zoku* were Diet members' leagues (*giin renmei*), which brought together politicians with a particular interest in key bilateral relations (the Diet members' League for Japan-PRC Relations, etc.). These bipartisan groups were often ceremonial, but in some cases played important roles in advancing relationships where the Foreign Ministry was constrained—for example, with China before normalization in 1972 and with Taiwan after that. The Diet members' leagues played an important role within foreign policymaking, because the issues of diplomacy were too diverse to expect cohesion and consistent support from the foreign affairs *zoku,* which was always a looser grouping than the corresponding *zoku* for agriculture or even defense.

Finally, key faction leaders and opposition politicians attempted to broker diplomatic deals and maintain ties to unrecognized regimes—often against the wishes of the Foreign Ministry. This phenomenon increased in the 1980s and 1990s. Typical examples on the LDP side include Kanemaru Shin's effort to jump-start normalization with North Korea in 1990 and Ozawa Ichirō's attempt to cut an aid-for-islands deal with Moscow in March 1991.[15] For its part, the opposition party leadership maintained countervailing ties with the ideological opponents of the LDP's foreign allies in the Cold War. The Socialist Party sent numerous delegations to Beijing before normalization in 1972 (often to chastise imperialism and the West), for example, as well as to Pyongyang. The smaller Clean Government Party also globetrotted for world peace, though not with the same socialist ideology.

Many of these patterns of political intervention continued even after the process of political realignment began in 1993, but with some important differences. The *zoku* and factions, like all political institutions in Japan, now have far less cohesion and discipline. First, the introduction of single-seat districts has meant that politicians no longer receive the same benefit from establishing behind-the-scenes influence in one policy area that affects only a fraction of their electorate and they needed factions less at a local level since their races were not against other LDP members. (Factions still do count, though, for election of the LDP president and apportioning of cabinet and party posts.) In addition, the effectiveness of the *zoku* has been undermined by competing demands within sectors of the economy that once had greater common purpose. Finally, the *zoku* have less discipline and cohesion as the LDP has lost its monopoly on policy expertise and policymaking. Many *zoku* politicians defected to the opposition in 1993, and within the ranks of the opposition Democratic Party are numerous younger politicians with strong expertise on banking, defense, and other policy areas. The demands of coalition government also force the LDP to open up and negotiate much more in the policymaking process. The LDP attempted to integrate the Social Democratic Party into the Policy Affairs Research Council in 1995 through "consultative committees" (*renraku kaigi*), but has had to resort to much more ad hoc policy coordination in subsequent arrangements with other opposition parties.[16]

This does not mean that the *zoku* are less important. Certain *zoku*, such as commerce, have lost cohesion as their client base has diversified. But other *zoku*, such as fisheries and agriculture, have become even more powerful and intransigent as their constituencies have fought for survival and the bureaucracies have weakened vis-à-vis the politicians. The common denominator among all of the *zoku*, as one veteran *Yomiuri* political reporter has put it, is that they have gone from "orderly groupings to disorderly clusters of special interests."[17] Instead of arbitrating among interest groups, zoku now lie in ambush, waiting to defend their narrow interests.

As we will see, the fisheries caucus almost single-handedly scuttled Kim Dae Jung's effort to improve Japan-ROK relations in 1997, and the agriculture *zoku* forced the Ministry of International Trade and Industry (MITI) and the Ministry of Foreign Affairs (MOFA) to accept humiliating isolation at a 1998 APEC summit designed to accelerate the opening of regional agricultural markets. Other *zoku*, however, have emerged from the ashes of 1993 to exert a more positive influence, most notably the defense *zoku,* which played a key role in brokering the U.S.-Japan agreement to revise the Defense Guidelines in April 1996. The foreign policy *zoku,* which was never terribly strong under the 1955 system (because there was so little pork or relevance to election district interests), has also become somewhat more dynamic, issuing an activist foreign policy charter for the party in 1997 and championing the cause of indigenous intelligence satellites in 1998.[18] However, the activism in the foreign affairs and defense committees of the LDP reflects the energy and expertise of entrepreneurial junior politicians rather than a new organizational cohesion in the *zoku* themselves. This has been particularly true as the media has focused on security issues— a magnet for ambitious younger politicians eager to jump past their more cautious seniors.

With a loosening of both the faction and *zoku* hierarchies, younger politicians within *zoku,* as well as politicians from outside the *zoku* and even outside the LDP, are exerting more influence on the policymaking process. A typical example was the effort of the thirty- and forty-year-old Policy Generation X (*seisaku shinjinrui*), who briefly commandeered banking reform legislation in the LDP PARC in 1998 out of frustration with the old guard's cautious approach to reforming and recapitalizing the heavily indebted banking sector. These politicians included a former Bank of Japan official and others with significant expertise and a willingness to buck the system by taking their case on national television shows. They were aided and abetted by mid-level MOF officials equally frustrated with their bosses' inaction. Eventually, senior leaders of the old finance *zoku* (*ōkura zoku*) co-opted the young turks, but not before they made their impact on the legislation by bypassing the usual deliberative councils of the PARC and going directly to the director general of the LDP. In many ways the activism of the younger politicians and bureaucrats is reminiscent of the militarists' putsches in the 1930s, after the revered senior statesmen of the Meiji Restoration had passed from the scene. Fortunately, the young turks of the post-1955 system are media-savvy technocrats, and though many are nationalistic, they are hardly militarists.

Expertise will steadily continue to count for more and hierarchy for less, particularly with changes in the Diet deliberation rules forced by Ozawa Ichirō under the power-sharing arrangement between the Liberal Party and the LDP in January 1999 and implemented in October. Under the new rules, only political appointees (minister or vice minister) may answer questions in the Diet, and there will be an increase in the number of political appointees (vice ministers) within most bureaucracies. For the old guard, who were used to having the bureaucrats answer detailed questions for them, this spells the end of seniority as the sole determinant of who occupies cabinet posts in the ministries of foreign affairs, finance, or international trade and industry. And it will continue to erode the bureaucrats' control of information. Before this rule change, technocrats were already dominating the post of parliamentary vice minister in the Foreign Ministry, where they shocked senior career officials by writing speeches for the minister and preparing their own talking points for negotiations with foreign governments.[19] Ozawa had pledged to replace even the senior bureau directors in the ministries with political appointees. That proposal was scratched, but it indicates the direction many politicians wish to go.

With declining public confidence in the bureaucracy, politicians are clamoring for greater ownership of the instruments of government. When the government introduced legislation in 1998 to implement the revision of the 1978 U.S.-Japan Defense Guidelines, the DPJ, CGP, and Liberal parties all insisted on an amendment requiring the Diet to give some form of prior approval before the government could implement contingency plans. At one point, the DPJ proposal for the legislation argued that the Diet should be allowed to actively change the contingency plans in a crisis if members are not satisfied with them.[20] Many in the LDP agreed but held their fire because of the strong insistence by JDA and MOFA that such "prior approval" conditions would undermine the credibility of Japan's supporting role.[21] For their part, LDP politicians have insisted on greater access to indigenous intelligence information, particularly since the North Korean launch of the Taepodong ballistic missile over Japanese airspace in August 1998. As was mentioned, that launching led the LDP Foreign Affairs Commission to recommend deployment of an indigenous satellite capability, a move supported by many in the opposition and eventually adopted by the cabinet in November 1998.

From the perspective of the Foreign Ministry, the politicians' activism in foreign affairs is a mixed blessing. As one senior MOFA official noted with a mix of consternation and admiration:

> The politicians are becoming too educated. The defense and foreign affairs committees of the LDP are more fluid. We now have to coordinate with every member instead of just working with a few key leaders. And now that the politicians are writing more and more of the tactical wording of documents and legislation, we can't explain the logic of the policy

to the public ourselves. The public will start to get inconsistent messages from the government.[22]

The shift is relative, however, and politicians continue to be constrained in their policymaking roles by the paucity of independent information, their small staff sizes, and the continuing view of a majority of voters that constituency service should be the first priority. The bureaucracies have been on the defensive, but they still have greater access to the information needed for policy formation.

The Political Parties

In the current midway point of political realignment, the parties do not have clearly opposing policy platforms (except for the Communist Party on the far Left and the Liberal Party on the Right). In terms of foreign policy, this leads to political battles over tactics rather than strategy—or more *souron sansei, kakuron hantai* (agreement with the general principle but disagreement on specifics). A brief survey of the major opposition parties' foreign policy positions in 1998 demonstrates why. We begin with the opposition and end with the LDP.

The Democratic Party of Japan (Minshutō). The largest opposition party was expanded in March 1998 to include defectors from Ozawa's New Frontier Party and former members of the Social Democratic Party, the Democratic Socialist Party, the Harbinger Party, and Hosokawa Morihiro's Japan New Party. Given the Socialists' close ties to public sector labor unions, the close ties of the former LDP members to agricultural and other conservative constituencies, and the Harbinger and New Party's roots in urban and suburban Japan, the DPJ has some difficulty agreeing on a common foreign policy front. In interviews throughout 1998 and 1999, most senior party officials argued that they were "still studying" the party's position on foreign affairs. Deep divisions remain on fundamental questions of constitutional reform, defense policy, and deregulation. To paper these over and establish a common ideological front, the party's first leader, Kan Naoto, emphasized the populist themes of decentralization, independence from the bureaucracy, and transparency. In terms of foreign affairs, the party echoed these themes by calling for "a more mature relationship with the United States," UN-centered policy, an emphasis on multilateral security regimes in the Asia-Pacific region, maintenance of Japan's exclusively defensive military doctrine, and enactment of emergency legislation with proper oversight from the Diet.[23] Tactically these themes lead to some differences with the government, but primarily over process (i.e., the role of the bureaucracy versus the Diet and the issues of transparency). Kan was defeated for party presidency on September 25, 1999, by Hatoyama Yukio, who campaigned on a platform that included constitutional revision and more autonomous defense. While resistance to this rightward drift continues within the DPJ, the party is increasingly overlapping on foreign policy and defense with the LDP, with the DPJ highlighting tactical differences with the government over process and transparency rather than new coordinates for Japan's international role.

The Liberal Party (Jiyūtō).   Under the direction of Ozawa Ichirō, the architect of the "normal nation" vision for Japan, the smaller Liberal Party enjoys greater ideological cohesion than any party other than the Communists. Under the themes of "free," "fair," and "open" (written phonetically from English to emphasize their universality and normality), the 1998 Liberal Party Basic Policy document pushes for an assertive foreign and security policy. The striking difference from other parties is the Liberals' call for active and expanded participation in UN peacekeeping, including the use of force under UN collective security.[24] Most members also harbor a preference for constitutional revision. On their activist view of security policy, the Liberal Party members overlap with many of their former colleagues on the right of the LDP, and this is both the party's great strength and its great weakness. In certain circumstances, the Liberal Party might attract ideologically motivated conservatives to defect from the LDP, but the LDP might just as easily lure power-hungry Liberals back into the government party. This dilemma led Ozawa to highlight UN peacekeeping and other ideologically charged policy issues when he agreed to form a coalition with the LDP in January 1999, but his tactics ultimately failed and he left the coalition in frustration with half of his party staying behind in April 2000.

The Kōmeitō (CGP).   The Kōmeitō, or "Clean Government Party," draws its strength from the modern religious organization Sōkagakkai. The Sōkagakkai puts relatively few policy constraints on the party, other than demanding maintenance of religious freedom, protection of the lower-middle-class shop owners and workers who tend to be its loyal members, and adherence to the broad idealism of the organization's leader, Ikeda Daisaku. In addition, the Women's Department (Fujinbu) and Youth Department (Seinenbu) of the Sōkagakkai have pacifist traditions that discourage the CGP politicians from pushing an aggressive security policy agenda. These tensions and predispositions are reflected in the CGP's 1998 Basic Policy Outline, which the party prepared after separating from Ozawa Ichirō and other members of the Shinseitō and returning to the scene as the "New" CGP. The Basic Policy Outline stresses the theme of "humanism," which for foreign policy means an emphasis on "soft power." The CGP platform emphasizes nuclear disarmament and multilateralism in Asia (themes that echo the Democratic Party's platform) and the establishment of "independent foreign policy from the United States" but based on "partnership with the United States"—again, a theme reminiscent of the DPJ. On the other hand, the CGP also emphasizes PKO and collective security under the United Nations, including full membership in the UN Security Council. And like the DPJ, the CGP supports expanded defense cooperation with the United States, but only if the "break" of prior Diet consultation is introduced.[25]

The Communist Party of Japan (JCP).   The Communists have been the most ideologically consistent of Japan's political parties, and this has helped them to attract support from those disaffected voters on the Left who previously would have protested against the LDP by voting for the Socialists. Even the Communists have lost some of their ideological furvor, however, offering in the spring of 1998 to soften their rigid opposition to the Self Defense Forces and finally recognizing the JSDF in 2000.

The Social Democratic Party (SDP).   The Socialists were badly mauled by the voters after changing their ideological stripes in 1993 in order to join the Hosokawa coalition. Even more cynical from the voters' perspective was the Socialists' shift even farther to the Right when the party formed a coalition with the LDP in 1995. When Socialist Prime Minister Murayama Tomiichi checked into the hospital suddenly during the June 1994 Naples G-7 summit, sarcastic politicians joked that he "accidentally came out with a sex change operation," mocking the prime minister's dramatic change in policy. The dozen or so SDP members who remained in the Lower House after 1998 elections returned to a pacifist platform comparable to their pre-1993 position, but without the numbers to be effective. The SDP once relied heavily on the labor vote, but the labor unions' central federation now resists throwing power behind any one party, either SDP or DPJ, and this spells further doom for the former Socialists.

Figure 2.2   Genealogy of Japanese Political Parties (1955–2000)

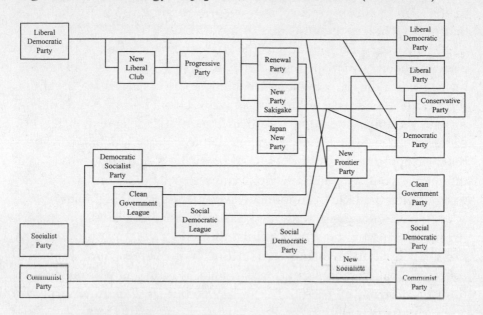

The Liberal Democratic Party

And that leaves the LDP. Its basic policy platform has remained within the same parameters since the end of the 1955 system. However, with the process of political realignment and the fluidity added by the new electoral system, ideological divisions are beginning to play a subtle but potentially more important role in political alignments within the party. Indeed, political scientist Kabashima Ikuo found in a detailed survey of the ideologies of the major parties in 1999 that while there is a steady move to the center Right by all parties (other than the JCP and DSP), within the LDP there are two distinct "peaks" on international issues. This lack of ideological solidarity within the LDP is still not enough to make the factions replacements for the parties, he argues, but it does suggest the prospect for future splits within the party along public or foreign policy lines.[26]

Traditionally, the LDP factions have been split between "mainstream" groups close to the center of power and those "antimainstream" factions seeking to work their way to the center. The "mainstream" factions since the 1970s centered on the Tanaka faction (later, Takeshita, then Obuchi, then Hashimoto faction), which is also known as the Keiseikai. In the early years of the LDP, this mainstream/antimainstream split was most pronounced and reflected to some extent the old policy views of the parties that had come together to form the LDP. Over time, this policy flavor faded. However, with the demise of the 1955 system, the mainstream/antimainstream split is again beginning to reflect the difficult policy choices the government must make.

The first sign of this trend was the challenge by Kajiyama Seiroku for party presidency in September 1998. Kajiyama eventually lost to the mainstream and Keiseikai leader, Obuchi Keizō. But Kajiyama—also from the Keiseikai—ran as an insurgent candidate, championing a hard landing for the economy and more assertive foreign and defense policies. He gathered 102 votes, which was not enough to defeat Obuchi's 225 votes, but his support came from across factional lines and included a large number of younger politicians from vulnerable suburban districts where tolerance for the LDP's economic management was ebbing quickly.

In the months after Kajiyama's failed challenge against the mainstream Prime Minister Obuchi skillfully lured the antimainstream factions led by Kamei Shizuka and Kōno Yōhei away from Kajiyama (offering quality cabinet and party posts), isolating him from politics until his death in mid-2000. But in November 2000 another group of anti-mainstream political leaders challenged the mainstream and Keiseikai again. This time it was Katō Kōichi and Yamazaki Taku who threw their support behind a no-confidence resolution against the LDP-led government of Mori Yoshirō. That attack on the mainstream also failed. But like Kajiyama before them, Kato and Yamazaki attacked the government's addiction to fiscal stimulus packages and the LDP's aversion to restructuring.

There is no question that, in spite of the failure of Kajiyama and then Katō, further attacks on the status quo from within the LDP will increase in the future until finally the party is forced on to the next level of political realignment. The choices the LDP has to make in public and foreign policy are becoming more difficult and the policy divisions within the party more pronounced. Moreover, Keiseikai itself has run out of credible leaders. The faction is powerful, but it is old, grey, and losing touch with the mainstream of Japanese society itself.

It is increasingly evident from internal LDP politics even at this juncture how the party could split along new lines in the future as difficult policy choices intensify. The factional lineage of the LDP is illustrated below in figure 2.3.

The Bureaucracy

Under the 1955 system, it was often said that Japan suffered from third-rate politicians but benefited from first-rate bureaucrats. The quality of

Figure 2.3 The Liberal Democratic Party Faction Genealogy (1995–2000)

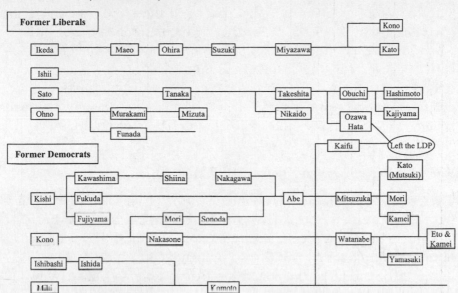

the civil servants in Japan is high, but the bureaucracy has hardly been insulated from the strong winds of change in the political world, in Japan's own political economy, and in the international system. Political realignment has complicated the bureaucrats' policymaking process and exacerbated interministerial conflicts (which must be arbitrated by the politicians). Changes of coalition governments have led to political purges against senior bureaucrats loyal to the previous regime. The loss of socioeconomic cohesion has weakened the bureaucrats' levers of influence. The collapse of the Japanese economic model has undermined their prestige and morale. The media and nongovernmental organizations are following the politicians and encroaching on bureaucratic control of information and policy decisions. And the external shocks of the Gulf War, the North Korean threat, and the rise of China have challenged their old modus operandi.

It is possible that a new equilibrium in political realignment and the emergence of clearer political platforms will lead to more centralization of decision making and the bending of the bureaucrats to a national mandate. Hints of this sort of impact from political realignment on the bureaucracy are already evident. In 1994, for example, a senior MITI official, Naitō Masahisa, was forced to resign by the Hosokawa cabinet for being too loyal to politicians of the previous LDP regime.[27] Later Saitō

Jirō, the administrative vice minister of MOF, came under intense LDP scrutiny during MOF scandals in 1995 because he was considered to have been too cooperative with Ozawa and the Hosokawa and Hata governments in 1993–95.[28] As party structures solidify, these trends could increase, eventually reinforcing centralization in foreign and security policymaking under the prime minister.

For now, though, each bureaucratic institution is in transition, wedded to old client areas but struggling to redefine new strategies that will safeguard national power and well-being in a time of uncertainty.

The Ministry of Foreign Affairs (MOFA)

There was a saying in prewar politics that "the Heike clan, the navy, and the Internationalists always lose" (*Heike, kaigun, kokusaiha wa kanarazu makeru*). In the postwar era the Japanese foreign ministry has suffered all of the complications and death by a thousand cuts of their counterparts in the U.S. State Department and the British Foreign Office. With internationalization of the Japanese economy in the 1980s other ministries began encroaching on their turf. Trade disputes and international standards brought the domestic-oriented Ministries of Posts and Telecommunications, Construction, and Agriculture Forestry and Fisheries into the international negotiating process. Even worse, it inspired these other bureaucracies to establish offices (usually as "think tanks") in Washington and other major world capitals. Initially, MOFA responded by ceding certain routine economic decision making to these other ministries. MOFA also created new divisions, such as the Atomic Energy Division and the Oceans Division, to maintain control or leverage in important new international economic negotiations. It also instituted more active "domestic diplomacy" in the 1980s to manage the economic negotiating process better.

As Japan increased its international profile in security and foreign affairs under Nakasone in the 1980's, MOFA also had to skirmish with the Ministry of Finance (MOF) and MITI for control of the growing official development assistance (ODA) account and with the Japan Defense Agency (JDA) for management of the U.S.-Japan Alliance and the allocation of growing defense budgets.[29] There is continuing debate about whether MOFA has succeeded in steering ODA away from industrial policy orientation of MITI, but as Japan's ODA has increasingly been dispersed through multilateral institutions, it is MOF's influence that has grown.[30] The JDA has also steadily increased its influence on security policy at MOFA's expense since the end of the Cold War.

Throughout Japan's internationalization, MOFA has had to manage growing responsibilities and interagency confrontations with a base of personnel and technical resources that barely expanded. In 1985 MOFA had 3,883 employees distributed among 110 embassies and 62 consulates abroad. By 1992, after the dissolution of the Soviet Union, MOFA had 173 embassies and many more consulates, but only expanded by 16 percent to 4,522 personnel.[31] The ODA bureaucracy has also been small. In 1990 there were only 1,490 aid-related personnel in Japan, compared with 3,522 in the United States to handle an aid program of comparable size.[32]

Throughout the 1990s MOFA has also been subjected to increasing media criticism for failing to articulate a clearly independent Japanese foreign policy. This domestic criticism and a poor crisis management and diplomatic response to the Gulf War led MOFA to embark on a major restructuring program in 1993. The two most significant changes were the reconfiguration of the United Nations Bureau into a Comprehensive Foreign Policy Bureau and the recasting of the Analysis Bureau into a better-equipped Information Analysis Research and Planning Bureau. The Comprehensive Foreign Policy Bureau has also had the effect of diminishing the importance of the "American factor" in foreign policy decision making, though MOFA remains the champion of the U.S.-Japan relationship in the Japanese government. In order to strengthen the independent and strategic dimensions of Japanese diplomacy, the new bureau combines a long-range policy planning function with short-term crisis management—a difficult balancing act, to say the least. The new organization contains within it the division for UN activities as well as the political/military divisions for multilateral dialogue, arms control, and disarmament.[33] But officials in the Comprehensive Foreign Policy Bureau report that they have instituted a matrix system with divisions in other bureaus that allows streamlined decision making on both short-term crises and long-term policy planning directives.[34] Overall, the new bureau appears to have reduced the "clientitis" that led to huge clashes between the North American Affairs and Asian bureaus, often requiring ultimate arbitration by the administrative vice minister himself.

The Ministry of Finance (MOF)

As the "ministry within the ministries," Japan's MOF has traditionally exerted unparalleled influence over all aspects of Japan's public policy, including foreign affairs. The core of MOF's influence lies in two of its functions: the budget bureau, which holds the carrot of expenditures; and the tax bureau and associated National Tax Agency, which hold the sticks of revenue collection and audits. From these core functions, MOF enjoys broad influence in diverse areas of the Japanese government. Ex-MOF officials frequently serve as governor of the Bank of Japan, administrative vice minister of the Defense Agency, prefectural vice governors, and presidents of special corporations. In addition, there are usually more than two dozen former MOF officials in the Diet, a number twice as high as former MITI officials and the negligible numbers of former MOFA officials (four in 1998).

MOF's direct role in foreign affairs is managed by the International Bureau. The International Finance Bureau (now simply "International Bureau") is one of the newest of the ministry's eight bureaus, created about the time Japan joined the Organization for Economic Cooperation and Development (OECD) and the IMF in 1964. The bureau is responsible for exchange rate policy, liaison with international financial institutions such as the IMF and World Bank, and financial policy toward developing countries. In fact, MOF officials dominate the Japanese representation in many of these international financial institutions. MOF also has some responsibility for management of the G-7 (now G-8) summits. This has led to frequent clashes with MOFA, which has increased its role as the summits have become less economic and more political.

Despite its enormous structural advantage, however, MOF has seen its own turf in public policy nibbled away since the collapse of the 1955 system. Initially, the coalition government of Hosokawa relied heavily on MOF expertise and influence.[35] However, the continuing liquidity trap of the Japanese economy and the arrest of senior MOF officials on charges of bribery and corruption in 1997 and 1998 led to a rapid decline in the ministry's public image and stature. "Ministry of Failure" was the growing criticism in the press in 1998. The banking and securities bureaus no longer command the same level of fear and respect among the financial sectors they regulate. MOF power has been further curtailed by the establishment of a quasi-independent counterpart to the U.S. Security and Exchange Commission (the Financial Supervisory Agency), by the "Big Bang" deregulation of financial markets, and by the growing independence of the Bank of Japan.[36] Agencies such as JDA have also exerted greater independence from MOF, as the expectation grows that future vice ministers will come from within the ranks of the agency and not laterally from MOF or another ministry. This has led to a change in the culture of the ministry. As one mid-level official described the ministry's shell-shock in late 1998: "most of my colleagues are proceeding with their jobs like automatons, the rest are either push-ing their seniors for major reforms, or looking at new careers in poli-tics or the private sector."[37]

There is one area where MOF is clearly energetic and ambitious, however, and that is in its push for a larger Japanese role in the manage-ment of the international financial system. Senior MOF officials have made high-profile proposals such as the Asian Monetary Fund and con-tinue to engage actively in the international debate over future "archi-tectures" for the international financial system.[38] Their efforts are hampered, however, by the ministry's inability to execute restructuring of the banking and financial sectors at home.

The Ministry of International Trade and Industry (MITI)/ Ministry of Economy, Trade, and Industry (METI) (after 2000)

As the master of industrial policy, MITI (new METI) once stood at the center of the developmental state model of the Japanese economy. With the appreciation of the yen and the move of Japanese manufacturing offshore in the 1980s, MITI's direct role in the economy was con-strained, but with this same internationalization, MITI actively ex-panded its role in foreign policy. With the consolidation of all bureaucracies into twelve ministries in December 2000, MITI's name changed to METI (the Ministry of Economy, Trade, and Industry), sug-gesting further expansion and ambition in international policy for the masters of industrial policy.

MITI/METI plays a direct role in Japanese foreign policy primarily through the International Trade Administration Bureau (which handles trade insurance, foreign exchange, and import/export promotion) and the International Trade Policy Bureau (which handles international trade negotiations and World Trade Organization, G-8, and APEC policy). As its leverage over domestic sectors of the economy has declined, so has MITI's assertiveness in shaping the international trade agenda increased. MITI pushed hard behind the scenes for the establishment of APEC in the early 1990s—initially against the resistance of MOFA, which was concerned with its diplomatic prerogatives and relations with the United States. MITI officials also champion the cause of multilateralism and the WTO, in part to resist direct bilateral U.S. trade pressure, but also to ex-pand the ministry's mission in international affairs.

As one senior MITI official told the author of an article in *Bungei Shunjū* in July 2000, "since MITI's role is not absolutely vital to Japan's national role like MOFA's or MOF's, or the National Police Agency's, we are forced to rethink our purpose as times change—making us the most robust ministry today."[39] In 1998 MITI established a new Economic Policy Unit within the minister's secretariat with responsibility for strategic planning well beyond MITI's traditional scope of industrial policy. The new brain trust includes the best and brightest of MITI's mid-level officials and prepares position papers on issues ranging from the global financial system, to Japan-ROK relations, to the road map for administrative reform.[40] MITI officials were particularly active behind the scenes in preparing the administrative reform package for Prime Minister Hashimoto in 1997 and succeeded in pushing a plan for realignment of ministries that would expand their own role in international economic policy. MITI also pushed hard for bilateral U.S.-Japan and U.S.-ROK cabinet level meetings (MOFA, MITI, MOF) and for similar quadrilateral meetings with the European Union, Canada, and the United States. These proposals have frequently raised the ire of MOF, which wants to guard its exchange rate coordination role, and MOFA, which wants to guard its diplomatic agenda.

Like MOF, however, MITI's growing activism in foreign policy and aspirations for management of the international economy are hamstrung by its inability to deliver credible deregulation or restructuring of Japan's excess capacity at home. In fact, from 1992 to 1993 MITI regulations actually increased in number.[41] The newly renamed METI cannot control certain sectors that obstruct its international trade policy agenda, such as agriculture or banking, and five of its eight bureaus remain closely aligned with the basic industrial sectors of the economy that the internationalists wish to deregulate.

The Japan Defense Agency (JDA)

The JDA now controls an enormous defense budget that ranks second in the world by some calculations, but the agency and the uniformed personnel of the Japan Self Defense Forces (JSDF) are strictly confined in their political and policymaking roles. The major roadblock against JDA and JSDF political influence is Article Nine of the Constitution and the continuing pacifist undercurrents in Japan's public debate on security. The JDA also holds second-tier status in institutional terms. The JDA director general, though nominally a member of the cabinet, is a "minister of state" rather than a full-fledged "minister of defense." The administrative vice minister of the agency has been seconded from either MOF or the National Police Agency with only one exception. Major bureaus of the JDA have often been run by external bureaucrats, including the Accounting Bureau, which is often run by a MOF official, the Equipment Bureau, which is usually run by a MITI official, and the Counselor for Foreign Relations, who is from MOFA. MOFA also holds primary responsibility for managing the security relationship with the United States through the Security Treaty Division of the North American Affairs Bureau.

Despite these constraints, however, the JDA and the JSDF enjoyed increasing legitimacy domestically as bilateral security cooperation expanded with the United States in the face of the direct Soviet Union military threat in the 1980s.[42] Since the end of the Cold War, the JDA role in foreign policy has increased even more significantly, a boom symbolized by the agency's shining new headquarters in Ichigaya. There are four explanations why.

First, the successful dispatch of a Maritime Self Defense Force minesweeping flotilla to the Gulf in 1991 and a Ground Self Defense Force peacekeeping construction battalion to Cambodia in 1992–93 established the JSDF as a prominent tool in Japan's diplomacy. PKO and humanitarian operations have since expanded to include Mozambique, the Golan Heights, and Honduras. The JSDF now also engage in joint training with regional navies (including Russia in 1997 and the ROK in 1999).

Second, the JDA and the JSDF have entered into more central roles in the management of the U.S.-Japan Alliance, pushing with the LDP defense *zoku* for revision of the bilateral defense guidelines in 1995 and 1996 at a time when MOFA was still cautious about taking the issue to the Socialists then in government. The clarification of the regional focus of the U.S.-Japan alliance in April 1996 inevitably brought the JDA into a larger role in regional security policy (Article Six of the U.S.-Japan Security Treaty), where before the agency had focused largely on cooperation with the United States for the defense of Japan against direct attack (Article Five). New systems, such as Theater Missile Defense, also brought the JDA into the regional and international debate on arms control and nuclear strategy, a realm previously dominated by MOFA.

Third, the clear threats represented by North Korean and Chinese missile tests and growing unease about the stability of the region have increased the public's interest in security policy and support for the JSDF and the JDA.[43] Uncertainty about region's future security architecture has also led to broader political support for the JDA and the JSDF to engage in dialogue and defense diplomacy with the region's other militaries, leading to closer security consultations with the ROK military in particular.

Fourth, the technical expertise and information available to the JDA and the JSDF has increasingly allowed them to trump MOFA and the intelligence arms of MITI and the National Police in the important bureaucratic war over information. The JDA's new Japan Defense Intelligence Headquarters (JDIH), established in 1997, enjoys a close relationship with the Defense Intelligence Agency in the United States and tends to closely guard its intelligence findings. Interestingly, the JDIH is led by a three-star general, a departure from the civilian bureaucrats' past practice of maintaining strict control in civilian agencies. The establishment of a smoother internal JDA-JSDF working relationship has contributed to the agency's overall clout.

There is every reason to expect the role of both the JDA and the JSDF to incrementally increase within Japan's bureaucratic system. The most pronounced but subjective evidence is the high quality of the younger and mid-level JDA officials. As one MOF official who had hoped to transfer to JDA put it:"with excellent staff coming up through the ranks, JDA will no longer have to accept vice ministers from MOF in the future."[44] In fact, the Finance Bureau and Procurement Bureau have begun placing JDA officials in the top posts. The JDA control of personnel further solidified with the consolidation of the Finance Bureau with the Equipment Bureau in 2001. For some time into the future, however, the older guard at JDA will continue to exert a cautious restraint on the "young turks" and restraint on the agency. When members of the LDP pushed for the JDA to become a ministry under the administrative reform proposals prepared under the Hashimoto cabinet in 1997, for example, it was the senior bureaucrats within the JDA who objected most strenuously.[45] The emerging generation is far more confident and ambitious.

The Business Community, Think Tanks, and Media

Zaikai—Big Business

The business community in Japan has had a central role in defining Japan's interaction with the world, as might be expected from a nation that depends so heavily on external trade. Nationally, big business is organized into four organizations: the Federation of Economic Organizations (Keidanren); the Japan Association of Corporate Executives (Keizai Dōyūkai); the Japan Chamber of Commerce (Nihon Shōkō Kaigisho); and the Japan Federation of Employers' Association (Nikkeiren or Nihon Keizai Dantai Rengōkai), which was absorbed by

Keidanren in 2000. Of these, Keidanren plays the largest role in foreign policy. With its 800 member firms and 110 industry associations, it is the "high temple" of the business community. Keidanren hosts or cooperates with a series of bilateral private-sector business councils, such as the Japan-Russia Economic Cooperation Committee, that play an important supporting role in bilateral economic negotiations with Japan's major trading partners.

Keidanren's mission has shifted in the same fundamental way as METI or MOF. Traditionally, Keidanren was wired into the political process in large part because of its direct donations to the LDP (and parallel corporate donations to individual politicians), but the organization halted its direct funding for the LDP after the collapse of the 1955 system. This weakened the business community's direct impact on the political process. Even before the end of its direct financial support for the LDP, Keidanren faced a pluralizing membership with competing views of economic policy, while the LDP politicians were turning to political funds from sectors not controlled by the traditional big-business groupings.[46] Moreover, issues in the "new" economy cut across all corporate and bureaucratic lines. The Internet, for example, falls under the jurisdiction of at least five different ministries.[47] In search of a new mission, Keidanren headquarters has focused on national economic strategy in much the way METI has. In 1998 Keidanren established a think tank (the Twenty-first Century Public Policy Institute) to chart long-term economic policy goals for Japan. The institute has championed deregulation and structural reform, leaving behind some of the more conservative members of its parent organization. The institute has also focused on foreign and security policies, joining the larger intellectual ferment over Japan's future role in international society.

The Keizai Dōyūkai is an association of individual business executives that has always had more flexibility than Keidanren to push for new directions in policy. Keizai Dōyūkai has promoted liberalization in agriculture (which is not represented in the group) and has pushed for deregulation, a reflection of the membership's international business focus.[48] In 1996 Keizai Dōyūkai prepared a major report on security policy, calling for greater participation in peacekeeping, a strengthening of the U.S.-Japan alliance, and consideration of reinterpreting the Constitution to allow the right of collective self-defense.[49] This was followed in 1998 by a similar report on security from the Kansai Keizai Dōyūkai, which represents industrial leaders from Osaka and environs, traditionally a more pacifist and liberal intellectual community.[50] While not directly active in the organs of foreign policymaking like Keidanren, the

Keizai Dōyūkai has nevertheless moved forward the national consensus on security policy.

The role of Keidanren and Keizai Doyukai in the foreign policy process in Tokyo is complemented on the ground by the activism of Japanese firms—and especially Japanese trading companies—in the far corners of the globe. Before either MITI or MOFA had extensive intelligence-gathering functions abroad, Japan's major trading companies were well established across the globe. Itōchū, Mitsubishi Corporation, Mitsui Busan, Marubeni, and other corporations maintain large research and analysis sections both at corporate headquarters and abroad. With significant financial resources and long-standing contacts, these organizations are often better integrated into the economic policy debates of host countries than the Japanese embassies and frequently play active roles in arranging Diet member visits, providing back channels on trade negotiations, and introducing new political and economic developments to uninformed Japanese officials. Most trading companies have internationalized in personnel and corporate identity and cannot serve as an arm of Japan's diplomacy, but they continue to constitute an important source of indirect information and influence.

Think Tanks, Parapublic Institutions, and Nongovernmental Organizations

Japanese diplomacy has rested on semiofficial or "second-track" organizations for several decades. METI maintains the largest such organization with the Japan External Trade Relations Organization (JETRO) and the smaller affiliate Manufactured Import Promotions Organization (MIPRO). These external organizations (*gaikaku dantai*) allow METI to maintain an analytical and logistical presence abroad without having to rely on MOFA. Other ministries have established their own institutional diplomacy through similar schemes. Examples include MOF's Japan Center for International Finance (JCIF) and the Construction Ministry's Research Center for Construction and Engineering (RICE).[51] MOFA has also utilized external organizations to facilitate second-track dialogue and negotiations on subjects not appropriate for official dialogue. Retired ambassadors and visiting scholars at the ministry's Japan Institute for International Affairs (JIIA) have moved Japan's diplomatic agenda forward with all the major nations in Northeast Asia through meetings that mix scholars and officials.

The resources and influence of the government-sponsored research institutes highlights the paucity of independent think tanks in Japan.

Japanese politicians frequently complain that they are constrained in policymaking by the lack of independent sources of information. Scholars in and out of Japan have long called for new independent institutions to chart Japan's future and provide information for a more open debate on policy.[52]

In the 1990s the growing competition for information from politicians and the media and the proliferation of international second track networks such as CSCAP (the Council on Security and Cooperation in the Asia Pacific) and PBEC (the Pacific Basin Economic Council) have given new life to independent research institutions in Japan. In foreign policy, the most noteworthy are the National Institute for Research Advancement (NIRA), the Okazaki Institute (headed by a former ambassador), the Institute for International Policy Studies (founded by former Prime Minister Nakasone), the Hiroshima Peace Institute (host of the Tokyo Forum in 1999), the Japan Forum on International Relations, Inc. (founded on the initiative of Dr. Ōkita Saburō, the former foreign minister, and now headed by Chairman Imai Takashi and President Itō Ken'ichi), the Research Institute for Peace and Security (a major institute for foreign affairs experts in academia), the Tokyo Foundation (backed by the Sasakawa Foundation), and Keidanren's Twenty-first Century Public Policy Institute. All of these think tanks have some ties to the government and none exhibit the same influence as some of their counterparts in the United States, but the larger political and societal trends in Japan suggest that they will continue to grow in importance.

Equally important has been the growing role of nongovernmental organizations (NGOs) in Japanese diplomacy.[53] Large parts of Japanese ODA are now implemented through NGOs. The NGO project subsidy increased dramatically, by 523 percent, between 1990 and 1998.[54] Grant assistance for grassroots projects also increased nineteen times since it was introduced in 1989.[55] In the treaty to ban anti-personnel mines in 1998, Japanese NGOs actively shaped the perceptions of politicians and the media and eventually won Japanese support for the treaty, against the advice of many security experts in MOFA and the JDA. NGOs were also active on the ground in East Timor in late 1999 at a time when Tokyo was unwilling to dispatch the JSDF. This recent phenomenon has emerged for three reasons. First, Japanese NGOs have been empowered to work on issues such as combating the international spread of AIDS by their American counterparts—particularly through the U.S.-Japan Common Agenda, which seeks bilateral government support for such efforts. Second, the nongovernmental movement in Japan has shifted from Left-wing antigovernment activities (often supported by the Communist or Socialist parties) toward a more cooperative relationship with government. Finally, the Diet bowed to public pressure and passed a new nonprofit organization (NPO) law in March 1998, which lowers the financial barriers to nonprofit status and reduces bureaucratic control. NGOs and NPOs are still constrained by unfavorable tax status and by the bureaucrats' continuing efforts to control their activities informally. Nevertheless, this new dimension of foreign policymaking and implementation will probably continue to expand in the future.

Extreme Groups

In spite of the demise of bipolarity in Japanese politics, there are still extreme organizations on the Right and Left that have retained their stubborn institutional continuity throughout the post–Cold War era. On the Left, these include groups such as Chūkaku-ha and other antimilitarists and pseudoanarchists that influence Japanese security policy primarily through protests at U.S. bases and nuclear power plants. Their ranks are graying rapidly and their numbers dwindling, though, and no new far Left organizations are rising in their wake.

More persistent and able to rejuvenate themselves are the groups on the Far Right, the so-called Uyoku, best known to Tokyoites for their gray or white sound trucks that travel the roads blaring loud martial music and castigating Russia, China, the United States, or anyone else who impinges on Japanese national sovereignty or dignity. There is no evidence that the ranks of the Uyoku have grown, but the various groups on the Right (groups like Nihon Seinensha, the Japan Youth League) have managed to continue raising enough funds through extortion (being paid *not* to blare martial music in certain areas) and sympathetic donors to keep in steady operation even through the postbubble years. The Uyoku's close ties to the LDP have frayed with political realignment, but that has also made it more difficult for conservative politicians to control these groups when they interfere in foreign policy by raising lighthouses on internationally contested territories or protest outside embassies.

Mass Media

Japan's largest daily newspapers (*Asahi, Yomiuri, Nikkei, Mainichi,* and *Sankei*) were as much accomplices of the 1955 system as the political parties and the bureaucracy. But as noted earlier, the newspaper reporters' close relationship with the politicians began breaking up in the 1980s as television news programs, city page editors, and weekly magazines began scooping the political sections on stories about LDP corruption and scandal. Today television news commentators, such as Tawara Sōichirō and Kume Hiroshi, terrify politicians and bureaucrats with their ability to mobilize popular opinion against an individual political figure or government policy. And the same power of television has empowered younger telegenic policy experts within the ranks of the LDP and the opposition.

For their part, the dailies have increased their focus on both Asia and security issues. *Sankei* and *Yomiuri* (the paper with the largest circulation) have always been more conservative and pro-defense. But recently the government and LDP's greatest critic on the Left—the *Asahi Shimbun*—has also been highlighting the dangers of North Korean and even Chinese behavior. An intense battle is under way for the soul of *Asahi* between the realists in the political and economic sections and the idealists in the city page and Kansai region, but, as in Japanese politics, the realists tend to dominate the next generation of leadership. In addition, a new generation of magazines blossomed in the 1990s—magazines such as *Foresight, Sapio,* and *Seiron*—that dissect foreign and defense policy in detail, and often with a dose of sensationalism and nationalism.

In short, the media has played an ever larger role in amplifying the external shocks and pressures the Japanese system has felt since the end of the Cold War. This growing influence on foreign policymaking has everything to do with the unbundling of the 1955 system and the fluidity in Japanese politics. Therefore, as Kent Calder warns: "The very salience of the mass media in Japanese decision-making today no doubt heightens the potential importance of any dramatic events overseas in the day-to-day policy calculus in Tokyo and could well be a force for substantial and rapid foreign policy transformation in the future, in response to overseas developments."[56]

Centralization and Decentralization— The Prime Minister's Office and Administrative Reform

The Prime Minister's Office—Old Weaknesses and New Strengths

The core weakness in Japan's traditional foreign policy structure lies in the Prime Minister's Office (newly reorganized into the Cabinet Office in 2001).[57] On paper, the prime minister should have power as the head of state. As Shinoda Tomohito notes in his study of the office: "As head of the cabinet in which the Constitution vests executive power, the Japanese prime minister leads the executive branch. He remains a member of the Diet and representative of the majority in the legislative branch. Through the cabinet's authority to appoint judges to the supreme court, he has some influence over decisions made in the judiciary branch. The prime minister, therefore, influences all three government branches and seemingly wields enormous power over government operations."[58]

In addition, in foreign policy, Japan's larger profile in international relations, and the increase in G-8, APEC, ASEM (Asia-Europe Meeting), and other summit meetings, all provide a prime minister with the external prestige and *gaiatsu* (external pressure) he needs to consolidate his influence vis-à-vis the bureaucracy and the other faction or coalition party leaders. But for the most part, the Japanese prime minister is at best a first among equals, forced to coordinate all his policies with faction or coalition partners. In many cases, the prime minister is only a pawn, put in office because his very weakness serves the other faction leaders' interests. (Kaifu Toshiki and Uno Sōsuke were so.)

Moreover, the Prime Minister's Office itself is also woefully understaffed, compared with the British Prime Minister's office and certainly the White House. The senior secretaries for external relations, security, and economic affairs are all seconded from MOFA, MITI, MOF, National Police Agency, or other ministries and exist to control the prime minister as much as to serve him.

The Prime Minister's Office also suffers from a lack of centralized information and analysis. The Cabinet Information Research Office (now Cabinet Intelligence Office) is supposed to synthesize information for the cabinet, but lacks authority over other ministries' intelligence arms or data collection capabilities of its own. The JDA's Japan Defense Intelligence Headquarters, MOFA's Information Analysis, Research and Planning Bureau, and the Public Security Investigative Agency all often stovepipe information for turf reasons, with the result that the prime minister rarely receives an integrated intelligence assessment. Prime Minister Hashimoto and his chief cabinet secretary, Kajiyama Seiroku, reportedly relied on private Internet newsletters and drinking sessions with reporters for up-to-date intelligence.

Finally, the prime minister does not have clearly established authority to deal with national emergencies. Conservative LDP politicians have been pushing for years for a national emergency legislation (*yūji hōsei*) that would give the prime minister emergency legislation over local governments and bureaucracies in the event of military crises or natural disasters. The legislation has never moved forward, however, because of the historical experiences of martial law in the 1930s and 1940s.

In short, as Shinoda notes, while the prime minister is vested with certain powers in the Constitution, his "direct authority over the executive is surprisingly limited."[59]

Nakasone was the first prime minister to attempt structural improvements in his office's ability to conduct foreign affairs and security policy. In 1986 he introduced an independent Cabinet Councillors' Office on External Affairs, a Cabinet Security Affairs Office, a Cabinet Information Office, and two other domestic offices as well as a crisis management office, which he utilized throughout his tenure. However, these same innovations proved useless during the 1990 Gulf crisis, because then Prime Minister Kaifu refused to rely on them. In the 1990s further crises highlighted the poor state of readiness of the Prime Minister's Office. When a major earthquake struck Kobe in January 1995 and the doomsday religious cult Aum Shinrikyō attacked the Tokyo subway system with sarin nerve gas in March 1995, Prime Minister Murayama Tomiichi's inept response led to calls for improved crisis management from all the major political parties (even the Socialists) and the media.[60]

In response to these crises, the Hashimoto cabinet established a crisis response room in the Prime Minister's Office and launched a series of interagency study groups on crisis management. The revision of the U.S.-Japan Guidelines in 1997 also fit within this larger effort at improved crisis management, but even the new Defense Guidelines are of limited utility without full emergency authority for the prime minister in a crisis. The North Korean Taepo-dong missile launch in August 1998 added more momentum to the centralization of emergency powers and facilitated the establishment of a cabinet Intelligence Council (Naikaku Jōhō Kaigi) to coordinate the Cabinet Security Affairs and Crisis Management Office (Naikaku Anzen Hoshō-Kiki Kanri Shitsu) to streamline cabinet coordination in a crisis. The LDP pushed for further crisis management legislation in 1999, focusing primarily on coordination in emergencies among civilian ministries, and leaving the more difficult task of legislating new emergency powers to the prime minister for a later day.[61]

Administrative Reform

While Nakasone and Hashimoto were the two prime ministers who pressed hardest for new capabilities in the Prime Minister's Office, their most significant achievement in strengthening the government's capacity to address national priorities lies in their active advancement of administrative reform. The first Provisional Commissions for Administrative Reform (Rinchō) was established in 1962. Subsequent "Gyokakushin" were organized through the 1980s and 1990s. The Rinchō recommendations charted a road map for privatizing NTT and the Japan National Railroads and implementing deregulation and decentralization of regulatory authority to local governments. Also central to the administrative reform process was the strengthening of the Prime Minister's Office. Under Nakasone, administrative reform led to the establishment of the Management and Coordination Agency (Sōmuchō) with authority over general bureaucratic issues such as personnel, statistics, and administrative inspections. Hashimoto's Administrative Reform Council (Gyōsei Kaiku Kaigi), which he personally chaired, recommended a wholesale reordering of the bureaucracies in its final report in December 1998. Based on the Hashimoto plan Japan consolidated the government from nineteen to twelve ministries and placed budgetary and emergency response authority in the Cabinet in 2001.[62]

The centralization and decentralization themes of administrative reform run up against three powerful obstacles in Japan. The first is the Japanese political culture's mistrust of centralized authority in one office, a legacy not only of the experience of prewar militarism, but also one passed down from the Meiji oligarchy. The second obstacle—at least to decentralization—is the massive debt in local and prefectural governments and the growing consolidation of corporate headquarters in Tokyo as firms downsize. The third obstacle, to both decentralization and centralization, is the pervasive structural influence of the Ministry of Finance.[63] It is not a coincidence that the most active supporters of administrative reform have been former police officials such as Gotōda Masaharu, the main rivals of the MOF for power and influence in postwar Japan.[64]

Ultimately, administrative reform that will strengthen the Prime Minister's Office is more likely to be implemented in a meaningful way after the process of political realignment results in lasting party structures. Cohesive parties with strong leadership will want to strengthen their administrative hand by pulling power away from the bureaucracies and toward the Prime Minister's Office. Not all changes must wait, however. Even in the midst of political realignment, the external pressures on Japan are pushing toward a centralization of emergence au-

List of Ministries and Agencies of the Government of Japan, as from 6 January 2001

The list of Ministries, etc. (i.e., Cabinet Office, Commission and Agency headed by a Minister of State, and Ministries) as from 6 January 2001 is as follows:

Cabinet Office [Naikakufu]
  National Public Safety Commission [Kokkakoan-iinkai]
  Defense Agency [Boeicho]
Ministry of Public Management, Home Affairs, Posts and
  Telecommunications [Somusho]
Ministry of Justice [Homusho]
Ministry of Foreign Affairs [Gaimusho]
Ministry of Finance [Zaimusho]
Ministry of Education, Culture Sports, Science and Technology
  [Monbukagakusho]
Ministry of Health, Labour and Welfare [Koseirodosho]
Ministry of Agriculture, Forestry and Fisheries [Norinsuisansho]
Ministry of Economy, Trade and Industry [Keizaisangyosho]
Ministry of Land, Infrastructure and Transport [Kokudokotsusho]
Ministry of Environment [Kankyosho]

Source: "List of Ministries, etc. as from 6 January 2001," in *January 2001: Central Government Reform of Japan* (Tokyo: The Headquarters for the Administrative Reform of the Central Government, 2000) (http://www.kantei.go.jp/foreign/constitution_and_government/list_0106/list_as_0106.html).

thority, as demonstrated by the reforms implemented after the North Korean missile launch of August 1998.

Conclusion: Ripe for a New Regime?

The forces of change that knocked the LDP out of power in 1993 are still colliding with the forces of conservatism and continuity that brought the party back in a year later. Nevertheless, the process of political realignment is irreversible. The 1955 system is over. The transition to a new equilibrium has only begun. Though no one is certain what is coming, the impact on Japanese foreign policy for the near term is already evident.

First, the institutions of Japanese policymaking—the factions, parties, *zoku,* associations, bureaucracies, and organizations—are all less disciplined. As Columbia University's Gerald Curtis puts it, Japan has moved from politics based on interest groups to politics based on special interests.[65] These special interests are exerting themselves more forcefully and decisively as the larger interest groups lose their ability to impose discipline within. As we will see, these special interest groups have skewed Japan-China and Japan–North Korea relations in ways that the LDP and the MOFA cannot control. This also explains the new impact of nongovernmental organizations in Japanese foreign policymaking. The foreign policy process is less hierarchical, less predictable, more entrepreneurial, and more driven by media.

Second, the declining autonomy and confidence in the bureaucracy has meant that unpopular foreign policy is much harder to promote within Japan. The emphasis on "national interest" in Japanese foreign policy reflects this basic fact; it is becoming relatively easier to argue against external pressures than to manage an increasingly complex and unpredictable decision-making process internally. The weak standing of the LDP reinforces this trend. As prime ministers struggle to hold together coalitions and maintain volatile public support, they are less able to take unpopular stands on foreign policy issues and more vulnerable to special interest pressure and media criticism. This has made Japanese foreign policy alternately immobile and highly reactive to external developments, depending on the domestic pressures.

Third, there is no mandate for the articulation of a clear foreign policy strategy. Particularly among the younger generation of politicians, there *is* a growing consensus on constitutional revision, the need for a more independent diplomatic identity, and the need to diversify diplomacy beyond economic power. However, aspiring leaders in both the DPJ and the LDP are still trying to form broad enough coalitions to rule, and security and foreign policy are not an effective magnet to do that. Even reform itself carries risks as a theme, since so many politicians in the LDP still rely on construction and agriculture and so many DPJ voters need labor. Political leadership in Japan still requires leaders to act with ambiguity, in large measure because the Japanese people are still ambivalent about many of the changes occurring in their society. The changing patterns of foreign and security policy are therefore *not* being trumpeted with strategic concepts or doctrines.

Finally, the institutional constraints on Japanese security and foreign policy have weakened. The Left no longer obstructs defense policy the way it did when the Socialists were more powerful. The leadership of both the LDP and the DPJ agree on the need for a more robust security and diplomatic presence in the world. Institutional rigidities exist because the LDP has less power to coordinate. The government is risk-averse in foreign affairs because of the volatility of support for the ruling coalition. But this same environment of weakened institutions would also be more permissive to significant departures in security policy if Japan were confronted with major external threats to its position.

Japan's relationship with China is, therefore, worth careful monitoring.

CHAPTER THREE

Japan-China Relations

Introduction

Nothing marks Japan's shift toward reluctant realism more definitively than the changing relationship with China.[1] Throughout the postwar period Japan maintained a policy of constructive engagement toward Beijing. This strategy was established by Yoshida Shigeru, who predicted that Japan and the West would eventually wean China away from Moscow by providing an alternative to dependence on the Soviet Union. In Yoshida's view, a prosperous China would inevitably become friendly with Japan and the United States.[2] At the core of his strategy was a faith in the principles of economic interdependence with China and in Japan's own growing mercantile power.

Yoshida's approach was hotly debated between the pro-Taipei and pro-Beijing groups within the ruling LDP, but his assessment of Sino-Japanese relations was largely prescient. Beijing began splitting with Moscow by the 1960s, and shortly after President Nixon's visit to China in 1972, the Japanese government normalized relations with the mainland. With time, Sino-Japanese economic ties deepened, particularly after the Cold War. Trade between Japan and China grew from $18.2 billion in 1990 to $62.4 billion in 1996. Over the roughly the same period, Japan's foreign direct investment into China expanded from $438 million in 1989 to $4.5 billion in 1995. The consensus behind Yoshida's formula for China relations deepened, and confidence in a close Sino-Japanese relationship shaped Japan's vision of a post–Cold War diplomacy in Asia.

But Yoshida's predictions were only partly correct. Greater trade, aid, and investment could not fully insulate Sino-Japanese relations from the turbulent developments of the 1990s. First the end of the Cold War opened the prospect of tenser bilateral relations because Japan and China were no longer indirectly aligned against the Soviet Union. Then the shocks of the Gulf War and the collapse of the Japanese economic bubble undermined Japanese confidence, while the interruption of stable long-term LDP rule opened the Japanese foreign policy process to greater pluralism and unpredictability. And eventually Chinese power and ambition became more visible in Asia.

The impact of these changes was not felt in the bilateral relationship for several years, however. Ironically, the crisis created by the Chinese government's massacre of student protesters in Tienanmen Square in 1989 created an artificial honeymoon in Sino-Japanese ties. After initially suspending yen loans to Beijing[3] in tandem with other Western sanctions to protest the incident, Japan was sucked back in to the vacuum created by China's international isolation a year later. In June 1991 Tokyo resumed aid; China responded by inviting Emperor Akihito for a historic visit in 1992 while heaping praise on Japan's regional security role when the JSDF was dispatched to Cambodia for peacekeeping. Heartened by this new Chinese attitude, Japanese intellectual leaders began writing of the new "Asianization of Asia."

By the middle of the decade, however, the real impact of the collapse of the Cold War structure was being felt directly in bilateral relations. Prime Minister Hosokawa Morihiro and Foreign Minister Hata Tsutomu began setting a new tone in the relationship in 1993 when they pressed Beijing publicly for greater military transparency.[4] Subsequently, an angry Diet then forced the Foreign Ministry to suspend $75 million in grant assistance after China ignored Japanese warnings and continued with a string of nuclear weapons tests in 1995.[5] Then in 1996 the Taiwan Straits crisis, the reaffirmation of the U.S.-Japan alliance, and an emotional dispute over the Senkaku (Diaoyutai) Islands sent Sino-Japanese relations to a postwar low. These punctuated changes in official relations were accompanied by a sea change in attitude toward China demonstrated in Japanese public opinion polls and newspaper editorials over the same period.[6] The Japanese and Chinese foreign ministries tried to turn the tide with a celebration of twenty-five years of relations in 1997, but a disastrous visit to Tokyo by Jiang Zemin in December 1998 only solidified the new view of China. In the space of only a few years, Japan's fundamental thinking on China shifted from a faith in economic interdependence to a reluctant realism.

The shift is relative, however. A strict realist policy based on balance-of-power logic would have Japan pursuing relative gains at the expense of China. Japan would cut off all aid and investment and generally take policies to retard China's economic growth. This Japan has not done. Instead, Japan's China policy is moving forward at two levels. At one level Tokyo continues to provide massive economic assistance in the form of yen loans, with only slight decreases in ODA (matching the pace of Japan's overall aid budget). At another level, however, Tokyo is actively seeking to counter Chinese political influence in Asia while hedging against the prospect of longer-term Chinese threats. This synthesis of engagement and hedging was well expressed in an LDP foreign policy paper in 1997: "Ultimately, China's future rests in its own hands—including how stably it will develop. Therefore, even as we seek to preserve and enhance our amicable relations with China, we must maintain a close watch on the direction China is headed and be prepared to cope with a variety of contingencies."[7]

There is still a strong consensus in Japan that friendly relations must be maintained with the People's Republic of China (PRC). There is also a continuing search for economic, technological, and diplomatic tools to shape the growth of the Chinese economy and Chinese foreign and security policy in directions that are beneficial—or at least not harmful—to Japan. However, this traditional strategy of engagement is now tempered by a suspicion of Chinese motives, doubts about Japanese capabilities to effect change in China, and a desire to use multilateral and bilateral security networks to balance, and even contain, Chinese influence.

This chapter illustrates these changes with five vignettes in post–Cold War Sino-Japanese relations:

1. The 1995 Chinese nuclear tests, which exposed the limits of Japan's economic influence on Chinese behavior
2. The 1996–97 Senkaku dispute, which highlighted the changing domestic politics of China policy in Japan
3. The Sino-Japanese contretemps over strengthening of the U.S.-Japan alliance in 1996–97, which revealed the post–Cold War bilateral defense dilemma between Tokyo and Beijing
4. The 1998 Jiang-Obuchi summit, which demonstrated how much the divergent Chinese and Japanese treatment of history would obstruct future cooperation
5. The changing patterns of Japanese trade and investment in China from 1995 to 1999, which suggested that Japan's relative economic influence on Beijing is on the decline

The chapter concludes by examining the implications of this emerging Sino-Japanese relationship for the U.S.-Japan alliance.

The First Shock Wave: China's Nuclear Tests

Aid and Security

At the core of Japan's traditional policy of engagement toward China has been foreign aid. China experts in the Japanese Ministry of Foreign Affairs often comment that Tokyo's bilateral economic assistance has grown from the "seed to the roots and the trunk" of bilateral Sino-Japanese relations. After opening contact with Beijing in 1972, the United States was barred by legislation from providing aid to Communist countries. This opened up an enormous role for Japan. Beginning with the 1978 Japan-China Treaty of Friendship, Japan agreed to provide large five-year loan packages to China.[8] By the 1990s these yen loan packages accounted for half of China's total economic assistance from abroad. For Beijing, the yen loans were seen as mandatory reparations for Japan's subjugation of China during the war. In Tokyo, however, economic assistance had meaning as the centerpiece of broader economic interdependence and as insurance against future political or military confrontation. Beneath these diverging views of economic assistance lay even broader gaps in each nation's assumptions about the other. These gaps were exposed by a series of nuclear explosions deep in the Chinese interior—the first shock wave in Sino-Japanese relations after the Cold War.

Beijing Explodes Bombs . . . and Tokyo's Complacency

On May 15, 1995, China conducted its forty-second underground nuclear explosion in Lop Nur, a remote desert area south of Mongolia. While the existence of Chinese nuclear weapons was hardly shocking, the timing of the test stunned Tokyo. Prime Minister Murayama Tomiichi had only just asked the Chinese premier, Li Peng, for a moratorium on testing during a visit to Beijing the same month, reminding his Chinese hosts of the Japanese people's intense feelings about nuclear weapons. If Japan's economic interdependence with China had teeth, this was an issue that mattered. But as it was, the nuclear tests proved just how limited economic investment and years of yen loans and foreign aid were as constraints on Chinese military behavior. Indeed, the Lop Nur test generated an intense debate in Japan about whether economic tools should be used as sticks against China at all. There was a consensus within MOFA and MITI that Japan should move from multiyear loan agreements to annual negotiations with China in order to increase Japanese leverage. However, interrupting aid was seen by many in the government as too heavy a stick to use on China, even in response to nuclear testing.[9] On the other hand, since 1991 MOFA had been bound by an ODA charter that specifically required Japan's aid policy to give full consideration of a recipient's military expenditures and the possible development, production, import, or export of missiles and weapons of mass destruction.[10] This charter had been created precisely to demonstrate Japan's readiness to use aid as a strategic tool after the Cold War, but thus far it had been applied only to distant and not terribly powerful Burma. Would it now be applied to the "root and trunk" of Sino-Japanese relations?

MOFA went back and forth on this question after the Lop Nur test. On May 15 Vice Foreign Minister Saitō Kunihiko called in the Chinese chargé Wu Dawei in Tokyo, and warned specifically that Japan's 1991 ODA charter might require an aid cut-off in response to the Chinese tests. Foreign Minister Kōno Yōhei then backed off from this threat in testimony to the Diet two days later. However, his suggestion that Japan would not—and in fact could not—use aid to demand better behavior from Beijing provoked a firestorm from within and outside of the government. The political pressure on Kōno and MOFA was intense. Senior politicians from all three coalition parties were calling for suspension of yen loans to punish China. On the Left of the coalition Sakigake and the Socialist parties were motivated by antinuclear sentiment. On the Right, the LDP was pushing for a more assertive Japanese stand toward Beijing for reasons of national pride.[11] Even the *Asahi Shimbun* warned that, given China's clear violation of the principles articulated in the ODA charter, "Japan's diplomacy is being questioned."[12] As one anonymous senior MOFA official told the *Yomiuri Shimbun,* "we cannot leave the situation as it is."[13]

Outflanked on both the Right and Left in a far more fluid political environment, MOFA and the government eventually compromised with the coalition partners on a symbolic suspension of $75 million in grant assistance, exempting medical equipment and flood relief.[14] Beijing was unimpressed, however, and conducted further nuclear tests in August and September of 1995. With the Taiwan missile tests in March of the next year and worsening tensions over the Senkaku Islands, LDP calls for a suspension of the yen loans grew louder. Senior Chinese officials reacted with indignation, arguing that suspension of the yen loans would constitute "interference ~~wow~~ in China's internal affairs" and pointing to Japan's obligation to continue paying reparations, "particularly on the 50th anniversary of the end of World War II.")[15] Beijing's claim that the loans were not Japan's to suspend further raised the ire of the LDP. Vice Minister of Foreign Affairs Hayashi Sadayuki warned the LDP that the yen loans were still "the main pillar of Japan's China policy."[16] But MOFA officials also recognized that continued Chinese nuclear testing might leave little choice but to reconsider the yen loan packages.

Then on July 30, 1996, China set off its last nuclear test at Lop Nur and announced its readiness to join the Comprehensive Test Ban Treaty (CTBT). The immediate crisis passed. The yen loans survived. However, Japan's faith in the power of economic interdependence and Japanese ODA was badly shaken. It was now clear to the Japanese public that China saw little obligation (giri) because of economic assistance just as it was clear to China that Tokyo could no longer manage anti-China sentiment within the Diet. The LDP's senior China hand, Gotōda Masayoshi, tried to warn his Chinese audience in a speech in Beijing that summer that the Japanese people had "connected China's nuclear tests with its potential for becoming a major military power." Gotōda was alarmed by the strong anti-China sentiment that had suddenly emerged within his own party and the opposition, particularly among younger members.

"If Sino-Japanese relations continue like this," he cautioned, "things will be rough."[17]

The Senkaku Dispute

Diverging Elites

Gotōda was speaking to his Chinese hosts as the last of a dying breed of elder statesmen who had managed the normalization of relations with Beijing since 1972. These were men whose views of China had been forged in the 1937 to 1945 Sino-Japanese War; men who equated Japan's militarism with its mistreatment of China; men who wanted to make amends. Prime Minister Tanaka Kakuei had been a sergeant in the Kwantung Army and developed a particularly close relationship with the leadership in Beijing after he normalized relations with the People's Republic as prime minister in 1972. Tanaka's pursuit of stable ties with Beijing was also the result of his hard-headed pragmatism. As a leader of the most powerful faction in the LDP, he and other elder statesmen in the party wanted to avoid ideological splits among younger Diet members comparable to confrontation between the pro-Taiwan Asia-ken group and the pro-Beijing Asia-Africa ken group in the late 1960s.

Gotōda's warning to the Chinese in 1996 stemmed from his knowledge of the changing ties between Japanese and Chinese elites. Generational change and unfolding political realignment had removed some of Beijing's closest supporters from the ranks of the LDP leadership. In 1996 Prime Minister Hashimoto Ryūtarō and opposition leader Ozawa Ichirō were both products of the Keiseikai (Tanaka faction). But neither had the same emotional or political ties to Beijing that their mentor, Tanaka Kakuei, had. Indeed, observers in Beijing tended to view both men has dangerous nationalists, since Hashimoto headed the World War II Veterans War Bereavement Association (Izokukai) and Ozawa was author of a best-selling book calling for Japan to become a "normal nation." Other influential Diet members active in China policy included Takemi Keizō, a former professor at Tōkai University fluent in Mandarin and weary of the old way of doing business with Beijing. These "hawks" and new China hands, were counterbalanced by political inheritors of the Yoshida school, including Kato Koichi, a former diplomat who served in Hong Kong, and Hayashi Yoshirō, chairman of the Japan-China Friendship League. However, even those advocating a softer line toward China lacked the commitment to relations with Beijing of the previous generation.[18] The breakdown of China's network in Japan extended to the Left as well, where the *Asahi Shimbun*—once an amplifier of Chinese criticisms of Japanese nationalism—led the editorial attack on China's nuclear tests.[19]

Tokyo's fraying elite ties with Beijing were being paralleled by a quiet but growing affinity for Taiwan among the newer generation of Japanese politicians. The original Taiwan lobby was motivated by the ideology of the Cold War. After the Cold War, Japan's Taiwan connection lost some of these elite fraternal ties, similar to what occurred in relations with Beijing. But there was a critical difference. Taiwan became a democracy and shared not only a comparatively benign colonial legacy with Japan, but now a value system as well. Taiwan's president, Lee Teng Hui, enjoyed broad popularity in all the major parties in Japan for his fluent Japanese language skills (he attended Kyōto University) and his flattering view of Japan's historical legacy in Asia. When the People's Republic Embassy in Tokyo attempted to establish a "parliamentary exchange" to lure younger politicians away from Taiwan, the endeavor backfired.[20] The same Japanese participants who had met fellow politicians in Taipei were treated to lectures on the wrongs of Japanese history by Chinese Communist Party (CCP) officials in Beijing. This affinity for Taiwan has not been operationalized in Japan's formal foreign policy—Tokyo maintains a strict consistency in its "One China" policy—but the quiet Japan-Taiwan connection increasingly began to worry Beijing in the 1990s.[21]

Finally, the political changes in Japan since 1993 have loosened the LDP's control of the Far Right groups that championed anticommunism during the Cold War. Though not necessarily larger in numbers, these groups are in many respects less constrained. This vocal nationalism weighed heavily on those like Gotoda who were concerned about Chinese behavior transforming the politics of Sino-Japanese relations in Tokyo.

In short, new electoral rules and political realignment in Japan added a further fluidity to the politics of diplomacy toward China—a fluidity that surprised the Foreign Ministry and the Chinese in the attacks on foreign aid after China's nuclear tests and later allowed the cork to fall off the bottle of nationalism during a dispute over some uninhabited rocks less than 100 miles off Okinawa.

Diaoyutai or Senkaku?

In 1895 the Meiji government sent a ship from Okinawa to explore a collection of eight islands and reefs near Taiwan that were called the Senkaku Islands in Japanese and the Diaoyutai in Chinese. The ship reported back that the islands were uninhabited and apparently unclaimed by Imperial China. In 1895, after Japan's victory over China in the Sino-Japanese War, the Meiji government issued a cabinet resolution claiming the Senkaku Islands as Japanese territory. The islands appeared to have little importance and were even used for fighter bomber practice by the U.S. Navy during the occupation of Japan after the war. But the islands took on new value in 1969 when UN geologists issued a report stating that considerable reserves of oil and natural gas might lie around them. With the prospect of oil reserves, Beijing formally announced its own claim to the Diaoyutai in 1970, arguing that Chinese vessels had first charted the islands in 1534. The Japanese Foreign Ministry formally rejected this position, arguing that China had never established a presence on the islands and pointing out that the United States had implicitly recognized Japanese sovereignty by transferring "administrative control" over the islands with the return of Okinawa to Japan in 1971.

While the diplomats in Beijing and Tokyo traded historical and legal arguments over the islands, however, the political leaders on both sides were always careful not to allow the territorial issue to become emotional or nationalistic. During his visit to Japan in 1978, Chinese leader Deng Xiaoping announced that the territorial issue should be put off for the future so that Tokyo and Beijing could focus on jointly developing the islands' resources based on the spirit of the new Japan-China Friendship Treaty. This formula for depoliticizing the Senkaku issue held for over a decade. In 1991, for example, when Right-wing LDP politicians threatened to land on the islands to plant the Japanese flag, the Prime Minister's Office and the LDP leadership persuaded them to desist.[22] Other potential clashes over fishing rights around the islands were also quickly averted by quiet, behind-the-scenes negotiations between Tokyo and Beijing.[23]

However, by the middle of the 1990s, this formula was strained to the breaking point. First the rules began to change with the opening of the UN Convention on the Law of the Sea (UNCLOS) in November 1994. Intent on establishing its territorial claim in the context of UNCLOS, Beijing had passed a territorial seas law in 1992, which opened the islands to Chinese oil exploration and asserted that force might be used to protect China's claim. By 1995 Chinese oil exploration vessels were regularly reported around the islands, and in February 1996 Foreign Minister Ikeda confirmed that a Chinese rig was seen drilling for oil near one of the islands. These incursions were played up in the Japanese press—particularly in the conservative Sankei Shimbun—and they amplified the impression of a belligerent China already created by the nuclear testing. MOFA protested through official channels, but by this point these sorts of official channels were no longer sufficient to contain a bilateral confrontation.

In July 1996 the Right wing again took the Senkaku's problem back into their own hands when six members of the Japan Youth Federation put up a lighthouse on one of the islands. Beijing protested that Tokyo had broken the formula for nonpoliticization introduced in 1978 and demanded that the Japanese government stop the Right-wing groups as it had done six years earlier.[24] But Tokyo's response was very different this time. The Chinese nuclear tests had worn down the already frayed China hands in the LDP and MOFA, and politicians in Tokyo were far less willing to respond to Chinese complaints about the Senkakus than they had been in 1991. Even if the LDP had been inclined to control the Right wing, it was far less able to do so since the collapse of the 1955 system. Even within MOFA, where China experts wished to avoid confrontation, the general mood was not one of conciliation. If anything, there was rising sentiment within the China school that they should no longer be China's "puppet."[25] Beijing did not receive the response it expected. The government's spokesman, Chief Cabinet Secretary Kajiyama Seiroku, told the press on July 18 that there was some danger of a diplomatic incident, but added: "I personally don't think we should say this and that about something being constructed legitimately with permission from the Japanese landlord."[26]

Emboldened by the hesitation in Tokyo and the implicit support of many in the LDP, the Right-wing Japan Youth Federation escalated the situation by placing a war memorial on the islands in August. Then in September the group was allowed back to the islands to repair its lighthouse. The Japanese Transport Ministry refused to officially recognize the lighthouse, but it also claimed that the Rightists were acting within the law, based on permission received from the islands' elderly landlord. It was, after all, Japanese territory, they maintained. Protests in Taiwan and Hong Kong increased, and there were even demonstrations in China, where the government usually attempted to control such spontaneous activities for fear that an anti-Japanese movement might turn against the ruling Communist Party.[27] Chinese charges of resurgent Japanese nationalism were further fueled by Prime Minister Hashimoto's "personal" visit to the Yasukuni War Memorial Shrine on July 29. Despite warnings of "serious damage" to Sino-Japanese relations from Beijing, however, the Japanese government did not back down—indeed, the Maritime Safety Agency sent seventeen cutters to repel protest boats sent from Taiwan and Hong Kong. Even MOFA officials who were eager to prevent further damage to bilateral relations recognized that stopping the Rightists from visiting the island would have given legitimacy to Beijing's claims and weakened Japan's negotiating position. In any case, the ruling LDP would allow no backing down in the face of Chinese pressure, an intention clearly signaled in the party's 1996 campaign platform, which claimed that the Senkakus would remain Japanese territory despite Beijing's pressure.[28]

The stiffening of Japan's position on the Senkakus was not just the result of its inability to control the Right wing, of course. The Japanese government was also legitimately concerned about the growing nationalism it perceived in China, including Beijing's 1992 claim that force could be used to defend the islands, a theme repeated in statements by the commander of the People's Liberation Army's Academy of Sciences in September 1996.[29]

From the U.S. perspective, this escalating confrontation over the Senkaku Islands was a sideshow. Few in the U.S. government thought that Japan and China would ever resort to force to resolve the confrontation, and the Clinton administration's first priority was to diffuse the tension as quickly as possible)by demonstrating strict U.S. neutrality on the territorial issue. However, the administration had completely missed the Japanese public's sudden and unprecedented sense of insecurity about China. Thus, when MOFA privately—and the *Sankei* and the *Yomiuri Shimbun* publicly—pressed for a symbolic statement that the United States would support Japan if China used force to seize the Senkaku Islands, the State Department responded that the U.S.-Japan alliance did *not* apply in this case. In fact, the United States was obligated to defend territory administered by Japan—which the islands were, according to U.S. records from the return of Okinawa in 1971. But the administration's extension of neutrality on the territorial issue to neutrality *in the event of Chinese use of force* seemed safe, since military confrontation was so unlikely. Under growing domestic pressure and fearful of an anti-alliance backlash in the LDP and the press, MOFA put its diplomatic efforts into high gear in Washington to clarify the U.S. defense commitment.[30] Eventually, senior Defense Department officials stepped in and unilaterally told the Japanese government and the Japanese press that the United States was still obligated to defend the Senkakus against attack according to the Security Treaty.[31] For the time being, the Senkaku issue quieted down, but it was striking that after decades of maneuvering to avoid entrapment in a U.S. confrontation with mainland China, Tokyo was for the first time urging a harder line than Washington.

In September 1997 Prime Minister Hashimoto finally reached an agreement in Beijing to set aside the issue of ownership of the Senkaku Islands and to establish a 200-mile-wide "joint management zone" that would allow fishing in the area by both nations and coordinated utilization of resources. However, Chinese warships and research vessels increased their activities around the islands, ignoring Japanese Maritime Safety Agency requests to clear the area.[32] U.S. officials had been puzzled by the Japanese Foreign Ministry's repeated insistence on an ironclad defense commitment on the islands when the possibility of Chinese hostilities was so remote. But the Japanese government and the Japanese press were becoming far more attuned than Washington to the activities of the Chinese navy and the emerging test of wills with Beijing. It was precisely to avoid a confrontation—to discourage the nationalists in Japan from calling for a unilateral military capability to deal with the Senkaku Islands—that MOFA was so adamant about clarifying the U.S. commitment.

Tokyo had another concern as well. During this same period the United States and Japan were engaged in the process of reaffirming and strengthening their bilateral alliance. Tokyo needed that reaffirmation to increase its diplomatic leverage vis-à-vis Beijing, but it also needed proof in the Senkaku dispute that the United States would not abandon Japan after asking Tokyo to play a more active role in regional security—a role that now appeared likely to spark a Chinese backlash.

The Guidelines, Taiwan Theater Missile Defense, and the New Defense Dilemma

A Shift in the Trilateral Structure of Security Relations

During the Cold War Sino-Japanese security relations were calculated almost entirely within the context of the U.S.-Japan alliance. But while Japan's formal relations with Beijing had to wait until a shift in U.S. China policy in 1972, Tokyo clearly diverged from Washington on the question of whether China represented a military threat. If anything, the legacy of World War II convinced the majority of Japanese political leaders that a hostile relationship with Beijing was contrary to Japanese interests.

Fear of entrapment in a U.S. military confrontation with China over Taiwan or Southeast Asia therefore led successive Japanese governments to deny full military cooperation to U.S. forces, even as Japan reconstituted its own Self Defense Forces.

The United States squeezed an official expression of support from Japan for the U.S. defense commitment to Taiwan only once—in the 1969 Nixon-Satō communiqué—when negotiating pressure to secure the return of Okinawa led the Japanese government to concede that "maintaining peace in Taiwan region is also an important element in Japan's national security."[33] Beijing's reaction was predictably negative, and officials in MOFA and the JDA spent the next decade retreating from any hint of a commitment to helping defend Taiwan. When the United States and Japan negotiated the first Guidelines for Defense Cooperation in 1978, Washington tried again to lock in a commitment of Japanese support for the defense of Taiwan and South Korea. However, Tokyo was concluding a Treaty of Peace and Friendship with Beijing at the time and was not about to enlist for missions that would provoke a Chinese backlash. The U.S.-Japan Defense Guidelines were completed with detailed agreements on bilateral cooperation for the defense of the Japanese archipelago against direct attack, but planning for cooperation in regional contingencies was left for another day.

For the most part, however, Washington tolerated Japan's conscientious objector status in the containment of China. As was noted in chapter 1 Japan's primary role in U.S. military strategy was to host U.S. bases, and Tokyo won the support of its ally by providing ever larger amounts of financial support, while not questioning too closely how U.S. forces in Japan were used. In fact, Tokyo put only one restriction on U.S. deployments from Japan when the government bowed to Diet pressure, on February 26, 1960, to define the "Far Eastern" clause of the treaty (Article VI)[34] as the area north of the Philippines. This insulated Japan from the unfolding conflict in Indochina (though U.S. forces continued to operate indirectly from Japan throughout the Vietnam war), and it left both Taiwan and Korea theoretically within the scope of permissible direct operations by U.S. military forces in Japan. Later not only the bases but also the JSDF capabilities themselves came to be seen as a military asset for U.S. strategy, particularly after the Soviet military expansion in the Far East in the late 1970s. Japan was not prepared politically to expand the security role of the JSDF, but the location of the Japanese archipelago near the Soviet Far East meant that Tokyo could obstruct a Soviet breakout by focusing on the self-defense missions already stipulated in the Defense Guidelines. Japan built up its forces in the 1980s for its own defense against direct attack, but with each new minesweeper and F-15, the Soviets' ambitions in the region were further thwarted.

This arrangement served China's interests as well. Behind their fierce rhetoric against the alliance in 1951 and its revision in 1960, Chinese leaders always recognized that the U.S.-Japan alliance contained the return of militarism in Japan. With the Sino-Soviet split in the 1960s, and with the growing Sino-Soviet confrontation in the 1970s, the U.S.-Japan alliance also contributed to China's strategic objectives by containing the Soviets' Far Eastern forces. As Washington played its "China card" against Moscow in the late 1970s, Japan made an even clearer tilt toward Beijing, including a transparently anti-Soviet "anti-hegemony" clause in the 1978 Peace and Friendship Treaty with Beijing.

At the end of the Cold War, however, this framework for sustaining mutually reinforcing security ties with Washington and commercial ties with Beijing began to unravel. First, Tokyo came under increased pressure to support U.S. forces more explicitly in conflicts like the Gulf War and later in the showdown with North Korea over Pyongyang's suspected nuclear weapons program in 1994. There was also a growing consensus in Tokyo that Japan should pursue a more normal defense policy, particularly after the demise of the Socialist Left removed one major obstacle. China had applauded Japan's participation in peacekeeping in Cambodia in 1992 and had not criticized the U.S.-Japan alliance in decades. In Tokyo there was therefore some optimism that

Beijing might not fear an incrementally strengthened alliance or more active Japanese security policy. Tokyo was wrong.

The Defense Guidelines and Taiwan

The changes in Japanese defense policy in the mid-1990s—while alarming from Beijing's perspective—followed a logical and incremental progression from Japan's previous approach to the alliance. The first step came when Socialist Prime Minister Murayama approved revision of Japan's basic force structure guidance, the 1976 National Defense Program Outline (NDPO), in November 1995. The revision had begun under Hosokawa in 1993 in order to streamline the JSDF for post–Cold War missions, but by 1995 the JDA was also using the NDPO revision to clarify Japanese support for UN peacekeeping and for U.S. operations in "situations that arise in the areas surrounding Japan"—the missing pieces from the 1978 Defense guidelines.[35] The changes in the NDPO were followed in April 1996 by the U.S.-Japan Security Declaration, in which President Clinton and Prime Minister Hashimoto "reaffirmed" the importance of the alliance and promised to revise the bilateral 1978 Guidelines so that they too addressed cooperation in "situations that arise in the areas around Japan."

The timing of the Clinton-Hashimoto Security Declaration was fateful. President Clinton had originally planned to sign the declaration with Prime Minister Murayama the previous November on the heels of the annual APEC summit, but the president stayed home to attend to a domestic budget crisis with the Congress. When he did travel to Japan in April of 1996, the atmosphere had changed significantly and what might have been a modest bureaucratic achievement instead took on the character of a new strategic initiative. Two intervening events accounted for this. First, Murayama was replaced by Hashimoto, marking a change from the Socialist's pacifism to the LDP and a politician with a long interest in defense policy. Second, and probably more important, China launched a series of missile tests across the Taiwan Straits and held military exercises in March 1996 in an effort to intimidate Taipei before elections and signal the People's Liberation Army's readiness to use force if necessary to prevent Taiwanese independence.[36] In response to the Chinese missile tests, the United States deployed two carrier battle groups to the area, while Japan protested Chinese actions and joined Australia and the United Kingdom as the only allies expressing "understanding" of the U.S. deployment. In fact, Japan took on considerably more risk than Canberra or London, since one of the two U.S. carriers was the Yokosuka-based USS *Independence*—a fact not lost on Beijing or ignored in subsequent Chinese criticism of Japan. Privately, Japanese diplomats in Beijing told the press that the missile tests showed the Chinese were "no better than Yakuza gangsters."[37]

The Chinese saw the U.S.-Japan Security Declaration as a response to the Taiwan Straits incident—which in a sense it was, since Murayama had not yet approved the Defense Guidelines revision for the original draft of the document in November, while Hashimoto had no difficulty convincing his cabinet to include the revision *after* the Chinese missile tests.[38] China's response was tough. Beijing charged that the Security Declaration had expanded the alliance by referring to Japan's role in the "Asia-Pacific region" rather than the "Far East," the language used in the original 1960 treaty. Beijing also argued that the alliance was now deliberately being aimed at China and intervention in the Taiwan Straits; and if that was not the case, Japan should explicitly *exclude* Taiwan from the newly revised guidelines. While the United States and Japan thought that they were reinforcing the status quo, Beijing thought the alliance was being redirected against China.

U.S. and Japanese officials attempted to reassure Beijing that the Security Declaration and the new Defense Guidelines were not aimed at China and ultimately served Chinese interests in a more stable Asia-Pacific region. Officially, Tokyo and Washington argued that the regional contingencies being addressed in the review of the guidelines were situational, not geographical.[39] Japan also explained that the review was taking place within the current framework of Japan's Constitution and the existing defensive missions of the JSDF. Privately Japanese officials made it clear through the press that the original impetus for revising the guidelines was the tense situation on the Korean Peninsula and not the crisis in the Taiwan Straits.

However, these efforts at transparency and reassurance were hampered by the fact that the United States and Japan had refused to rule in or out any specific scenario or geographic location around Japan, including Taiwan. Confusion ensued. When the LDP secretary general, Katō Kōichi, promised his counterparts during a visit to Beijing in August 1997 that Taiwan would not be *included,* he forced his rival, Chief Cabinet Secretary Kajiyama, to respond the next day that Taiwan could not be *excluded.*[40] The new guidelines were released in September 1997 without mentioning Taiwan, but since that time the Chinese government has used Kajiyama's statement to argue that Taiwan is included in the guidelines. When the North American Affairs bureau director of Japan's Foreign Ministry told the Diet on May 22, 1998, that the guidelines would not exceed the geographic definition of Article VI of the Security Treaty, he was forced to resign by Prime Minister Hashimoto. Hashimoto had told the Chinese that there was no geographic definition, and the director general had made the mistake of reminding the Diet that the government's standing interpretation of Article VI of the treaty included Taiwan.[41]

From Tokyo's perspective, these attacks marked a change in China's policy toward the alliance. If China saw a reaffirmed U.S.-Japan alliance as inimical to its interests—in contrast to Beijing's previous tacit support for the alliance—then there was good reason to worry about long-term Chinese intentions. In addition, Beijing's demand that the guidelines exclude Taiwan suggested that China views military action in the Taiwan Strait's as an internal matter with no bearing on Japanese security. While Japan maintained a strict policy of recognizing only one China, the Chinese assertion that a conflict in the Taiwan Straits had no regional implications was an unacceptable premise. Finally, it became clear by September 1997 that Beijing was focusing its pressure almost entirely on Japan and avoiding high-level criticism of the guidelines in relations with the United States.[42] The efforts at transparency and clarification had not exactly led to confidence building.

Theater Missile Defense

A very similar dynamic was repeated in the debate over theater missile defense (TMD). Japan first embarked on a joint study of missile defense requirements with the United States in 1994 after several years of U.S. prodding for Japanese participation in this major program. TMD, though costly and uncertain in terms of technical feasibility, had the support of Japanese industry, the JDA, and MOFA, as an alliance-enhancer, a technology-driver, and a buttress for the U.S. nuclear deterrent against North Korean and Chinese ballistic missiles. Like the Defense Guidelines review, joint work on TMD was seen in Tokyo and Washington as stabilizing and reinforcing the status quo against new threats; but once again Beijing saw the development as aimed at undermining Chinese security.

Conspicuous Chinese objections to Japanese participation in TMD began in 1995 and have been as strenuous as the objections to the revised Defense Guidelines. Beijing argued from the beginning that U.S.-Japan TMD cooperation undermines China's nuclear deterrent and might be extended to the defense of Taiwan.[43] The problem with this logic from Tokyo's perspective was that Japan possesses no nuclear weapons, and therefore China's concern about its ability to maintain a nuclear strike capability against Japan suggests that Chinese missiles not only target Japanese territory, but that China's policies of "no first use" and "no use against nonnuclear states" do not apply to Japan. Ironically, the Chinese objections to TMD only heightened Japanese concerns about a Chinese ballistic missile threat that had been a secondary concern after North Korea in the initial discussions over TMD.[44]

China's verbal battle to obstruct TMD cooperation in Japan was dealt a serious blow in August 1998 with the North Korea Taepo-dong missile launch. Washington and Tokyo had privately agreed to collaborate on research on the missile interceptor for the Navy Theater Wide system (a major step beyond the joint "study" of requirements started in 1994) and were delayed only by MOFA's concern that the announcement not undercut the visit of Jiang Zemin to Tokyo that fall. With the Taepodong launch, however, diplomatic deference to China fell quickly by the wayside, and the United States and Japan announced joint development in October 1998, a month before Jiang's visit. Politicians and officials in Tokyo still have many questions about TMD. Will it work? Will it undermine the Anti-Ballistic Missile Treaty? Will it be affordable? However, Chinese objections alone are no longer enough to derail TMD and could even enhance its support in Japan.

A New Defense Dilemma?

The predictable trilateral security dynamics of the 1970s and 1980s are over. Tightly constrained and asymmetric U.S.-Japan military cooperation is no longer credible in Washington or Tokyo. The Chinese tolerance for the U.S.-Japan alliance has waned. And Japanese planners now assume that Chinese military assets could pose a potential long-term threat to Japanese interests. Ironically, all of this became clear as both China and Japan sought to reestablish what they saw as the status quo: China by launching missiles to discourage Taiwanese independence, and Japan by reaffirming the U.S.-Japan alliance. These are the ingredients for a classic defense dilemma, as each side perceives the other's effort to protect itself from change as a new threat. Fortunately, the Sino-Japanese defense dilemma is largely cushioned by the overwhelming presence of the United States in the region and by Japan's continuing reliance on the U.S.-Japan alliance.

At another level, however, efforts to establish confidence and avoid a bilateral defense dilemma have been complicated by the diverging views on historical problems between Japan and China.

The History Question: Losing Traction

War Guilt as Diplomacy

At the base of the postwar structure of Sino-Japanese relations lies the legacy of the Sino-Japanese War of 1937 to 1945. The Japanese yen loan program, the domestic political consensus on China policy, and even the complementary Chinese and Japanese security policies of the Cold War era all rested on a common understanding that Japan had to make amends for the past. The war defined the legitimacy of the Chinese Communist Party, which had resisted the Imperial Japanese Army, and empowered Beijing to pass judgment on the direction of postwar Japan. When LDP leaders worshipped at the Yasukuni War Shrine or called for dramatic increases in defense spending, the Japanese media would amplify Chinese criticism to demonstrate the dangers of remilitarization. The legacy of the past gave Beijing a powerful card in Japan's domestic debate. Beijing has been unwilling to yield that card until it can be convinced that militarism is dead forever in Japan.

In Japan, however, there is increasing apology fatigue. A new generation of Japanese leaders no longer instinctively understand why China has the right to obstruct Japan's aspirations for influence. While they recognize still the necessity of dealing with the past, they are resentful of what they see as cynical Chinese manipulation of the history card in bilateral negotiations over issues unrelated to history. After fifty years of democracy, they believe Japan is a different country. They are ready to apologize for the past, but only if they can put it behind them and move forward.

Japanese leaders have attempted to move beyond the history problem with Beijing by expressing remorse and self-contemplation on a number of occasions. For example:

- In 1982 Prime Minister Nakasone Yasuhiro told the Diet that Japan must acknowledge the "strict international criticism that Japan invaded" other countries.
- In 1989 Prime Minister Takeshita Noboru told the Diet Budget Committee that "it is a fact that Japan brought great destruction on neighboring countries and peoples" and that "it cannot be denied that Japan invaded these countries."
- In 1990 Emperor Akihito gave a speech urging that the "unhappy past of this century . . . never be repeated again."
- In 1990 Prime Minister Kaifu Toshiki expressed "full acceptance of the fact that Japan invaded" the other nations of Asia.

- In 1992 Prime Minister Miyazawa Kiichi noted in a speech that Japan must "demonstrate deep reflection and regret."
- In 1992 Emperor Akihito, in his historic visit to China, told his Chinese hosts that he "deeply deplores" the historical actions of Japan against China.
- In 1993 Prime Minister Hosokawa Morihiro argued that Japan must again express feelings of "deep reflection and remorse for all of the pain and suffering caused to so many people in the past by Japan's aggressive war and colonization."
- In 1994 Prime Minister Murayama Tomiichi repeated this call for "deep reflection and remorse" in his opening speech to the Diet.
- In 1995 Prime Minister Murayama visited the Marco Polo Bridge, where fire fight began between Japanese and Chinese soldiers which triggered eight years of full-scale conflict between the two countries until Japan lost World War II. Murayama "prayed for Japan-China friendship and eternal peace."
- These expressions of deep reflection and remorse were repeated by Prime Ministers Hashimoto and Obuchi in 1996, 1997, and 1998.

Yet none of these tortuously negotiated and considered expressions of remorse ever ended the history problem with China. From Beijing's perspective, each one almost made things worse since negotiations with the Japanese government over the exact wording often revealed the extent to which many Japanese leaders did not share the sentiments expressed. Moreover, the preceding list of apologies is offset by a depressing lit of *mougen* (gaffes) by senior Japanese leaders over the same period. A short list would include the following:

- In August 1986 then Education Minister Fujio Masayoshi was fired after he argued that Japan did not commit "murder" in Nanjing according to international law.[45]
- On April 24, 1988, Okuno Seisuke, then director general of the National Land Agency, was forced to resign after telling a press conference that Japan was forced into the war to help Asia resist "white aggressors."[46]
- In May 1994 then Justice Minister Nagano Shigeto was forced to resign after telling *Mainichi Shimbun* that the Nanjing massacre was a "trumped-up story."
- In August 1995 then Education Minister Shimamura Yoshinobu was censored by the chief cabinet secretary for arguing at a press

conference that the question of Japanese culpability for World War II was a matter of personal interpretation.[47]

• The Chinese press and premier Li Peng were highly critical of the Japanese government's weak official apology on the fiftieth anniversary of the end of the war because the debate revealed such mixed sentiments among Japanese politicians. Even Prime Minister Murayama's own speech expressing deep remorse for Japanese actions did not assuage Beijing.[48]

At the same time, however, Beijing has also failed to see the extent to which the Japanese government's repeated efforts to express remorse have brought closure on the history issue for a new generation of Japanese.[49] In quantitative terms, these *mougen* have decreased over the past decade, but each new statement only confirms a deepening Chinese suspicion that Japanese "militarism" is being reborn. Indeed, Chinese perceptions of Japan worsened in the second half of the 1990s. A survey taken in 1996 by the Institute for Reform of the Economic System in China after the Taiwan missile tests in 1996, for example, found that the nation Chinese people disliked most was Japan (47 percent), followed by the United States at (37.7 percent). The divergence on the history problem is particularly striking among younger generations of Chinese. While younger Japanese are increasingly eager to move beyond the history problem, younger Chinese may be taking an increasingly hard-line view. In 1996 the China Youth Report conducted a survey of 100,000 youths in China averaging age twenty-five on the question of Japan-China relations and found that only 15 percent felt "proximity" with Japan, and only 14 percent thought Japan-China relations were good, while 42 percent did not have a "favorable" impression of Japan. Interestingly, an overwhelming majority of the youths named wartime premier Tōjō Hideki as the most famous Japanese. Japan did not get many points for economic cooperation either, with 45 percent of the youths responding that the main purpose of Japanese investment into China is to occupy the Chinese market. (Only 4.5 percent believe that Japanese companies want to contribute to the economic development of China.) Keio University China scholar Kojima Tomoyuki attributes the negative view of Japan among the younger generation to the persistent teaching of Japan's wartime invasion of China in Chinese textbooks.[50]

The Past Collides with the Future: The 1998 Jiang–Obuchi Summit

This growing divergence in Japanese and Chinese views of the history problem was illuminated in November 1998 during Chinese President

Jiang Zemin's official state visit to Japan. This was the first official visit of a Chinese president to Japan,[51] and fell just one year after the twenty-fifth anniversary of the normalization of relations between Japan and China. After tensions over the nuclear tests, the Taiwan Straits, the Senkaku Islands, the Defense Guidelines, and TMD, the foreign ministries of both countries were looking for a way to put relations on a more positive footing. The historic occasion of Jiang's visit appeared pregnant with opportunity. But in the end it would only reinforce the mistrust emerging between Beijing and Tokyo.

In preparation for the summit, the Japanese and Chinese foreign ministries discussed the inclusion of Japan's "deep remorse" (*hansei*) and "heartfelt apology" (*owabi*) in the joint declaration that would be signed by Obuchi and Jiang. This same formula had worked in the Japanese joint declaration with South Korean President Kim Dae Jung two months before, as we will see in the next chapter. However, Kim had accepted the Japanese apology as the "final word" and had agreed to move forward with a new Japan–Republic of Korea (ROK) relationship. Jiang, in contrast, rejected his diplomats' formula and argued that there should be no "final word" on the history issue. Without closure, Japan's MOFA could not win domestic political support for a joint declaration that included the word "apologize." Moreover, the LDP refused to support any reference to the "Three No's" on Taiwan (no support for Taiwan's independence, for membership in international organizations, or for two Chinas)—another demand from Beijing that President Clinton had endorsed during his visit to Beijing that June.

With the history problem boiling over, expectations that stability could be reestablished to Sino-Japanese relations quickly began to evaporate. Jiang grew visibly angry and frustrated at his hosts' unwillingness to apologize. During the official dinner with Emperor Akihito on November 26, he wore a Mao jacket to contrast with the imperial splendor in the palace and lectured his host on the history problem during the formal toast. That photo was on the front page of every newspaper the next day. Politicians and political commentators were shocked at the Chinese leader's "rudeness."[52] In his summit session with Prime Minister Obuchi the next day, Jiang broke from the pre-agreed agenda to give a lengthy expression of his dissatisfaction with Japan's treatment of the history issue and Taiwan.[53] Meanwhile, throughout the summit Jiang complained to the Chinese press about the dangers of Japanese remilitarization in interviews that were instantly reproduced in the Japanese media.

Obuchi refused to yield on the history question and won broad praise at home for his firm stand. The *Asahi* and *Mainichi* and the more conservative *Yomiuri* and *Sankei* either remained silent or expressed support for the government's position. Many LDP politicians skipped the state dinner held for Jiang, choosing instead to attend a speech by Korean Prime Minister Kim Jong Pil in Kyūshū at the same time. Even the business leaders in the Japan-China Business Association expressed support for the government's firm stand.[54] The only notable dissenter was the chairman of the Japan Communist Party, who expressed dissatisfaction with the Japanese government's statement on history during a meeting with Jiang that symbolized the renewed ties between the two countries' Communist parties. Yet this Communist connection only further reinforced the impression that the Chinese leadership was out of touch with contemporary Japan.

The centerpiece that the foreign ministries had planned for the summit still held impressive contents. The Japan-China Joint Declaration on Building a Partnership of Friendship and Cooperation for Peace and Development contained an agreement for up to 390 billion yen for twenty-eight projects during the remaining two years of the Fourth Yen Loan Package. In addition, Obuchi expressed his deep remorse (*hansei*) for "the serious distress and damage that Japan caused to the Chinese people through its aggression against China." But Obuchi stopped short of the heartfelt apology (*owabi*) that Jiang had wanted and that Kim Dae Jung had received. It was only one word, but its absence spoke volumes.[55]

In the weeks before the summit, China scholars in Japan had called for a "new era in Japan–China relations."[56] After the visit, as one China scholar put it: "the traditional pro-China school has been eradicated by China's behavior."[57]

The Declining Saliency of Economic Tools

In the midst of tensions over domestic politics, security policy, and history, economic interdependence between China and Japan remains a powerful force. According to MOF, total trade between the two countries grew from $18.2 billion in 1990[58] to $66.2 billion in 1999[59] while Japanese foreign direct investment into China rose from $438 million in 1989 to $4.5 billion in 1995.[60] (This number fell to $1.1 billion in 1998.[61]) These economic activities have created important sinews between Japan and China that were not in place during the Cold War.

Yet even in business relations, business as usual is over. Despite the explosion of trade and investment since 1989, three major problems emerged by the end of the 1990s to suggest that Japanese economic influence on China and China's economic influence on Japan may have peaked for the time being.

First, there is rising pressure for a decrease in the yen loans. As the LDP Foreign Affairs Commission warned in 1997: "It is highly likely that China will catch up to and overtake Japan economically by around the year 2010. When this occurs, the purpose of the yen credits program, conceived 30 years earlier, will have been fulfilled. Therefore, the time has come to initiate a comprehensive reassessment of Japan's assistance to China, including discussions of whether or not yen credits should be continued."[62]

Within years, that warning became reality. In July 2000, MOFA established a private sector study group to review the yen loan policy to China with an eye to establishing a new framework for the loans that would maximize Japanese leverage (by shortening the duration of the loans, for example) and sustain some level of domestic political support for continuation and refocusing of the loans.[63] That domestic support is proving more difficult, however. With growing Chinese military activities in the Senkaku area, mounting evidence that Beijing provided technical assistance to North Korean and Pakistani missile programs, and Chinese use of ODA to enhance its own influence in Asia and the Third World, the LDP's Foreign Affairs and Defense committees began drafting new stricter guidelines for aid to China in the summer of 2000.[64]

Second, Japanese foreign direct investment in China is likely to decrease in relative importance to the Chinese economy. The number of FDI projects (on a contract basis) decreased 43 percent in 1994, 22.2 percent in 1995, 33.7 percent in 1996, and 14.3 percent in 1997.[65] From 1995 to 1998 the amount of new Japanese FDI to China decreased from $790 million to $190 million.[66] Japan-China Economic Association research suggests that this trend accelerated with the economic crisis in Asia, but the economic crisis is not the only factor. Japanese firms have grown frustrated with uncertainty about Chinese exchange rate policy, diminishing returns on investment, and repeated experiences with harmful Chinese regulations. Most damaging has been China's refusal to honor a pledge to dismantle tax structures that favor domestic producers by placing a 17 percent value-added tax on sales from foreign affiliates.[67] As Tanaka Naoki of *Keidanren* notes, "the reality is that not many companies are making levels of profits that are commensurate with the level of investment being made in China and it is this current reality that is inducing a review of the investment being made in China."[68] In 1998 Japan's investment into China (excluding Hong Kong and Taiwan) was still higher than that of the United States or the European Union, but Japanese business leaders expect that U.S. investment into China will surpass Japan's in the future.[69]

Finally, Japanese economic relations with China have been affected by rivalry at the strategic level. The Japan–China Economic Association annual business executive forums in Beijing began to turn sour in 1995 when the Chinese side warned that Japan's suspension of grant aid after the nuclear tests would have a negative impact on Japanese economic interests in China. Li Peng told the delegation headed by Toyota chairman Toyoda Sōichirō that "the damage China received as a result of Japan's aggressive war cannot even be compared to Japan's level of aid."[70] In 1996 the Chinese side claimed that Japan's nationalism on the Senkakus "would affect business relations."[71] By the twenty-fifth anniversary celebration of Japan–China business ties in 1997 members of the Japanese delegation expressed frustration to the press at the heavy-handed Chinese approach.[72] Japanese business executives argue that working-level relations with local authorities or businesses often proceed well, only to be frustrated by decisions taken in Beijing to reverse Japanese advances for political or strategic reasons.[73]

The net effect of these changes on Japan's political and economic relationship with China is still uncertain. Officials at the Japan–China Economic Association maintain that the contradictions between the Chinese Communist Party's strategy of containing Japan and the desire for Japanese investment at the local level cannot continue. Either the Chinese side will emphasize the strategic issues because it has confidence in the draw of its market, or China's economic problems will lead to a more conciliatory posture toward Japan in order to attract FDI. What these same officials acknowledge is that the experiences from 1995 to 1998 have led to a convergence of opinions on China in the business community, the government, academia, and the media. As one executive at the Japan–China Economic Association put it: "Now that we have come to understand China better, everyone realizes that country's immense problems and possibilities."[74]

Terms of Engagement

From Beijing's nuclear tests in 1995 to Jiang Zemin's history-laden summit in Tokyo in 1998, the Japanese approach to China shifted reluctantly toward a greater realism. The pillars that held the structure of Sino-Japanese bilateral relations in place during the Cold War all crumbled to a significant extent. Japanese domestic politics came unhinged and pressure from both the Left and the Right of the Diet forced an unprecedented suspension of grant aid. Japanese and Chinese security policies stood in stark contradiction for the first time with the Taiwan Straits crisis and the guidelines review. The atrophying of elite ties between the two countries allowed nationalists to set the agenda for the Senkaku dispute. Dissonance grew between new generations of Chinese and Japanese leaders over the historical issue. Economic interdependence continued to grow, but the relative influence of Japanese economic tools may be in decline.

Economic Engagement

At the same time, however, it is important to account for what has not changed in Sino-Japanese relations. For one thing, the yen loans—the "root and trunk" of Sino-Japanese relations—have survived repeated attacks from the Diet. Despite some calls for a policy of relative gains vis-à-vis China, and despite the likelihood that the yen loans will decrease in both absolute numbers and relative impact to the Chinese economy, Japan simply cannot walk away from China's economic development. A politically unstable China would threaten Japan's fundamental interests as much as a cohesive and hegemonic China would. And as a *Keidanren* report warned in 1994, the most troubling near-term threat from China is not military or political at all, but rather the danger that unbridled Chinese economic growth could cause competition for energy supply as well as increased pollution and environmental degradation.[75] For some time to come, Tokyo will have to use its own funding to address these internal Chinese problems as a matter of Japanese self-interest.

China's excessive reliance on potentially unsafe nuclear power plants and fossil fuels presents a particularly serious problem for Japan. The Japan-China Energy Exchange Association estimated in 1993 that China would require 1,392 MTOE (million tons oil equivalent) by 2010. Japanese nuclear energy experts warn that if the China Nuclear Corporation's plans for increasing nuclear capacity tenfold to meet this new demand are realized, Japan would face the possibility of "multiple Chernobyl-style accidents" in which "radioactive clouds will first hit Japan and then spread around the world."[76] China's burgeoning interest in fast breeder reactors has also alarmed Japanese energy authorities, who now support the concept of an ASIA-ATOM organization (modeled on the EURATOM) in order to strengthen the prospects for inspection and control of China's future recycling programs (and to give greater legitimacy to Japan's own troubled program).[77]

In the 1980s Japan's grant aid and Overseas Economic Cooperation Fund (OECF) spending in China was devoted almost entirely to large-scale infrastructure projects. When acid rain from China began falling on Japan in the early 1990s, however, the focus of assistance was quickly rechanneled to cover environmental protection. The change in emphasis was marked with the establishment in 1991 of the $100 million Japan–China Friendship Environmental Protection Center in Beijing.[78] The portion of grant aid and concessional loans addressing environmental programs in China has steadily increased ever since. Of Japan's $5.52 billion Fourth Yen Loan Package (1996 to 1998), $2.25 billion were energy focused, and fifteen of the forty projects under the package were environmental.[79] Environmental projects also accounted for the bulk of projects in the final phase of the Fourth Package (1999 to 2001). Through the Green Aid Plan, MITI has leveraged ODA to encourage Japanese industry associations to cooperate on large-scale environmental projects in China. Japanese interest has also focused on pipeline projects inside China that would enhance interdependence and discourage China from embarking on a naval modernization program aimed at securing natural resources.[80]

Concerned about Chinese political stability, the Japanese government has also begun refocusing its yen loans on development of the Chinese interior. In 1997 the Japan-China Economic Association marked its twenty-fifth anniversary (dating to normalization in 1972) with a major symposium in Beijing for economic officials from the interior provinces of China. The final installment of the Fourth Yen Loan package also focused on projects in the Chinese interior. In part this was driven by Beijing's strategy to use Japanese aid to compensate for the lack of private investment in the interior regions, but Tokyo also has an interest in preventing destabilizing gaps in wealth within China.[81] Disintegration of China is one of the worst scenarios considered in Tokyo.

Japan's effort to integrate the China into the global economy has also continued, in spite of a new tensions on other fronts. Japan quietly supported Chinese participation in the G-7 summits in the early 1990s and formally proposed China's participation in the Naha Summit in Okinawa in July 2000 (which Beijing rejected). Japan has also pushed for China's early admission in the World Trade Organization, reaching agreement in July 1998 on the accession protocols during Prime Minister Obuchi's visit to Beijing. Tokyo has an interest in using the WTO to pry open Chinese markets and also to prevent China from undermining the global trading regime. As the 1997 report on WTO compliance by the Industrial Structure Council (an advisory body of MITI) notes "China's accession to the WTO, followed by implementation of its commitments for lowering tariff rates, elimination of trade restrictions, and improvements in its trade and economic systems, should benefit both Japan and the global economy significantly."[82] For Japan, a China outside of the WTO denies "means for either WTO members or China to resolve trade disputes between them other than to try to do so bilaterally."[83]

Japan—despite increased hedging—is still betting on economic interdependence and the peaceful integration of China in the global economy.

Rivalry

However, it is what is new in Sino-Japanese relations since the end of the Cold War that is most striking—and that is the pronounced rivalry and hedging that have emerged since the middle of the 1990s. Increasingly, Japanese diplomacy has been energized by the effort to engage, constrain, and outmaneuver China in East Asia.

At first the Japanese response to growing tension in relations with China was to push for greater dialogue and transparency. Since Sino-Japanese relations had remained friendly for the first few years after the Cold War, there was confidence in Tokyo that Chinese suspicion of the Senkaku problem, the guidelines, and history could be resolved with a simple clarification of Japan's position. For example, a 1995 nongovernmental blue ribbon commission on China policy urged "straightforward dialogue" with China on security issues, including a "frank discussion of historical questions."[84] The 1997 LDP foreign policy strategy paper also argued that "Japan must be candid with China and must not hesitate to press for more open sharing of national defense information or to request peaceful negotiations when problems do arise."[85] As *Nihon Keizai Shimbun* correspondent Ina Hisayoshi noted skeptically at the time, "there is an illusion that everything will be resolved by engagement."[86]

Nevertheless, MOFA has wielded the sword of dialogue with gusto. Bureau director–level security policy talks began with China in March 1996, with MOFA officials registering concerns about the Taiwan Strait's crisis and China rebutting with a list of territorial and historical grievances. In 1997 at the ASEAN Regional Forum (ARF) meetings in Jakarta, representatives from the Chinese and Japanese foreign ministries began crossing swords over TMD, Taiwan, and the guidelines.[87] Then in April 1998 Kyūma Fumio made the first visit to China by a JDA director general in eleven years.[88] Other efforts to expand direct military–to–military talks have proven less successful, primarily because of Chinese resistance (though China did finally agree to an exchange of ship visits in October 2000). As we will see in the chapter on multilateral diplomacy, these confrontations in bilateral and multilateral forums have continued, but Japanese officials still view any Chinese engagement on security issues as a positive development—even if solutions are not found.

Tokyo has also pushed for other "minilateral" forums to bring its case to China. After the Chinese criticisms of the U.S.-Japan Security Declaration in 1996, for example, Japanese officials and academics began proposing a U.S.-Japan-China trilateral dialogue. In 1997 the LDP Foreign Policy Commission and the *Asahi Shimbun* editorial pages both called on the government to initiate a trilateral security summit with Washington and Beijing.[89] Tokyo proposed a trilateral meeting to the United States in September 1997, but Washington was cautious and Chinese Foreign Minister Qian Qichen formally rejected the idea.[90] Eventually a trilateral scholars' forum was approved by Beijing.

Beijing's rejection of Japanese proposals for trilateral summits created transparency, if not confidence-building. The Chinese emphasis on bilateral Sino-U.S. dialogue at the expense of Japan sent an early signal of Beijing's intentions to contain Japan's political influence and profile in East Asia. Subsequent Chinese responses to Japanese diplomatic initiatives have only reinforced evidence of Beijing's strategy:

- In July 1997 the Japanese Finance Ministry's proposal for an Asian Monetary Fund was formally rejected by Beijing. Japanese MOF officials noted that working-level talks with Chinese officials went well, but at the senior level the Japanese initiative was rejected by Beijing for strategic reasons.[91]
- In April 1998 the Chinese quietly rejected Prime Minister Hashimoto's proposal for a four-way security summit with China, Russia, the United States, and Japan. The Japanese government hoped to leverage support for Russian membership in APEC for Russian pressure on China to agree to a regional security summit. Moscow could not deliver.[92]
- In June 1998 Beijing rejected Tokyo's proposal for a meeting of the permanent five members of the UN Security Council plus Japan and Germany to address the Indian and Pakistani nuclear

tests. The State Department brought the idea to China, which rejected it outright. The *Nikkei Shimbun* commented on China's attempts to prevent Japan from raising its profile in political and security affairs.[93]

- In July 1998 the Chinese Central Bank governor, Dai Xianglong, attacked Japan's economic policy, claiming that the "depreciation of the yen increases pressure on East Asia" as it struggles to extricate itself from the crisis.
- In February 2000 China rejected Tokyo's invitation to join the G-7 meeting in Okinawa.
- Beijing continues to withhold endorsement of a larger role for Japan in the United Nations, including any form of permanent membership on the Security Council.

The pattern of Chinese containment of Japanese diplomacy was made all the more problematic in this period by Beijing's effective enlistment of an often unwitting Clinton administration. The Asian Monetary Fund proposal was opposed by the U.S. Treasury Department, and this placed China and the United States on the same side against Japan. President Clinton's June 1998 China visit further reinforced the impression of Sino-U.S. containment of Japan when Clinton joined Jiang in criticizing Japan's economic policies during a press conference in Shanghai.[94]

With the limited success of multilateral diplomacy, Japan has reached out to strengthen bilateral relations with the countries that surround China. The 1997 LDP strategy paper articulated this strategy in unambiguous terms: "Not only must we make the Japan-U.S. alliance a key dimension of our China policy, but we must also strengthen the cooperative countries, South Korea, and Australia—nations which also have reason to be concerned about China's future course."[95]

Subsequent chapters go into more detail about Japan's bilateral relations with the other nations of East Asia. For now, suffice it to say that largely because of competition with China, Japan has pursued rapprochement with its historical enemy, Russia; launched a new initiative toward Central Asia; proposed strategic dialogue with Association of Southeast Asian Nations (ASEAN), New Zealand, and Australia; and, of course, reaffirmed the U.S.-Japan alliance. Beijing has accused Japan of pursuing a policy of containment, but as one JDA official describes the strategy, it is only "soft containment."[96]

And the diplomatic chess game with China in the region has only just begun.

Japan's China Diplomacy and U.S. Interests

The patterns of bilateral relations that emerged in Japan's China policy in the mid to late 1990s are likely to continue for the foreseeable future. To begin with, they are clearly the result of institutional and normative changes in Japan. In addition, China shows no sign of relenting on its pursuit of expanded influence in the region at the expense of Japan. Moreover, Japan is not yet forced to choose between its policies of strategic rivalry and economic interdependence because China does not yet pose an immediate military threat to Japan that would force a policy of containment or the "pursuit of relative gains." And because the strategic uncertainties with China are long-term issues, Japan has generally been able to avoid confrontation over more dangerous short-term problems where China is willing to use force. In Taiwan policy, for example, Japan has done nothing to promote Taiwan's independence or international stature and has approached the guidelines review purely in the context of self-defense. Finally, Japan has benefited from a generally reliable forward commitment from the United States. As long as the U.S. strategy toward China is also a mix of engagement and balancing, Japan's own course is fairly clear.

However, two questions linger. First, will the United States and Japan remain in tactical step on China policy over the near term, and, second, how will Japan respond if major changes do emerge in the Sino-U.S. relationship—if the current state of strategic flux in Asia takes a clear new direction?

The question of U.S.-Japan approaches to China is a near-term problem. It is apparent from the case studies in this chapter that the process of maintaining closely coordinated U.S. and Japanese approaches to China has not always been smooth, in spite of the growing unease in both countries with demonstrations of Chinese power and assertiveness. There are at least four reasons for this.

First, Japan continues to view its relationship with China as a special tie that should not be determined exclusively by Washington. Tokyo is particularly concerned about American volatility on issues related to human rights and Taiwan. As the junior partner in the alliance, Japan for decades guarded its China policy against entrapment in the U.S. containment strategy. Later Japan turned to China to define its own Asian identity and relative independence from the United States. Even today—in the midst of the greatest competition in Sino-Japanese relations in decades—Tokyo still sometimes tries to play the "China card" in relations with Washington. The China card has become a weak one for Japan's diplomacy toward the United States, but old habits die hard.

Second, U.S.-Japan policy coordination on China is undermined by the U.S. penchant to ignore Japan in its own China policy formation. The 1972 "Nixon shock" was the most dramatic example of the United States keeping Japan in the dark about its China diplomacy, but examples of "Japan passing" continue. The U.S. misstep on the Senkaku dispute, President Clinton's decision to criticize the Japanese economy during a press conference in China, the coincidental convergence of Chinese and U.S. objections to Japanese initiatives such as the Asian Monetary Fund—these all erode Tokyo's confidence in sharing its limited sources of leverage on China with the United States. Apprehension about abandonment by the United States undercuts policy coordination as much as fears of entrapment. If anything, the impact of "Japan passing" is more significant today than it was in Nixon's time, since Japan has moved toward a more independent strategic assessment of its security concerns with China.

Third, the domestic politics of China policy in both countries have become far more fluid and unpredictable. The State Department has collided with the Pentagon and the Congress over China the same way that MOFA has lost control of its China account to the Diet and the media. Domestic U.S. pressures on human rights and trade do not coincide with Japan's domestic pressures on territorial issues and history. Coordination of diplomacy is always more difficult in liberal, pluralistic democracies—particularly in cases where the country in question has sparked a fundamental domestic debate about foreign and security policy.

Finally, U.S.-Japan coordination on China policy is difficult because, in spite of the close U.S.-Japan alliance, this remains a three-legged triangle. Beijing has often taken steps, such as the 1996 Taiwan Straits missile tests, that push the United States and Japan closer together. At other times, however, Beijing has found it necessary to make tactical shifts in its overall strategy of keeping Japan down while developing a bilateral modus vivendi with the United States. After Sino-U.S. relations worsened in 1999 in the wake of the Kosovo campaign and failure to reach bilateral agreement on WTO accession, for example, Beijing temporarily softened its stance toward Japan. Nevertheless, a visit to Tokyo by Premier Zhu Rongji in October 2000 helped to take some of the sting out of Jiang's early trip, even though Zhu's efforts were undermined by a People's Daily front paper article criticizing Japanese "militarism" immediately after his departure from Tokyo. These tactical changes in direction open gaps between the United States and Japan, which is in part why Beijing employs them.

There will therefore continue to be fluidity in the U.S. and Japanese approaches to China, in spite of common strategic goals between Washington and Tokyo. Coordination would be easier if the United States and Japan had a simple policy of containment, but China has two potential futures, and Washington and Tokyo should not foreclose the more positive of those futures by crafting a strategy of containment just for simplicity's sake. Instead, senior policymakers in both countries must recognize that the United States and Japan are engaged in a competition for power with China as well as a game of engagement and integration. In that competition, the U.S.-Japan alliance is a powerful asset, not only in the military role of deterring contingencies, but also as a diplomatic asset to enhance negotiating leverage. It is therefore in U.S. and Japanese interests to work harder to reduce the opportunities for China to drive any wedge in the alliance. That means more active consultation, dialogue, and coordination of policy on issues ranging from WTO accession to arms control negotiations and multilateral diplomacy as it relates to China.

And what if there is a change in Sino-U.S. relations? The dynamics of Sino-Japanese relations since the Cold War are not predictive of the future, but do suggest several outcomes. First, if the United States reversed its policy of forward engagement, it seems likely that Japan would expand its active efforts to balance and constrain China in compensation. While this would occur primarily in multilateral and bilateral diplomatic settings, there should be little doubt that Japan would also strengthen its unilateral military capabilities to manage potential Chinese threats to Japanese sea lanes and the home islands.

If the United States and China came into open conflict over Taiwan, on the other hand, Japan would face its nightmare scenario. Ultimately, the Japanese response would depend on the justness of the fight. A unilateral provocation of China by expanded U.S. support for Taiwanese independence, for example, would likely lead to Japanese efforts to constrain the United States and would leave open to question Japanese support in a contingency. On the other hand, in the case of an unprovoked Chinese use of force against Taiwan, Tokyo would be more likely to support a robust U.S. response, preferring diplomacy to force but ultimately backing force. These are obviously subjective judgments in part, but it is clear from the impact of Chinese military actions since the Cold War that Japan's political culture does change in response to newly perceived threats and that Tokyo is no longer passive in the face of such challenges. No matter what the U.S. response to a Taiwan contingency, therefore, it is safe to predict that Japanese constraints on military preparedness will be weakened.

The key is to avoid a confrontation in the Taiwan Straits in the first place. Closer U.S.-Japan coordination can contribute to that goal. The U.S. policy on Taiwan is strategic ambiguity and tactical clarity—that is to say, it is not certain how the United States would respond to the use of force by China, but it is clear that the United States has interests and could respond in a robust manner if necessary. A strong U.S.-Japan military alliance reinforces that policy. The United States and Japan should be clear that the alliance does not exist to protect Taiwanese independence, but that the alliance is prepared to deter and if necessary defeat any actions that threaten the vital interests of the alliance. A firm U.S.-Japan alliance complicates and deters any Chinese consideration of the use of force in the Straits without provoking Chinese preemptive action. At the same time, closer U.S.-Japan coordination on Taiwan issues (and closer U.S. coordination with other allies as well, for that matter) has a mutually constraining effect that helps to mitigate against dangerous changes in the status quo. The United States exacerbated the Taiwan situation by first breaking its pledge to China and allowing President Lee Teng Hui to visit the United States and later compensating with support for Beijing's "Three Nos" on Taiwan. By comparison, Japan has been far more consistent in its One China policy. A closer calibration of U.S. Taiwan policy with allies like Japan might have avoided the unpredictable and ultimately provocative nature of the U.S. approach to Taiwan in the 1990s.

It should be clear to U.S. policymakers that Japan is also now playing a dual game of hedging and political-economic engagement with China. Since U.S. and Japanese actions have more of an impact on each side's respective China policies, each side should be working harder to coordinate approaches. With time, economic integration may smooth the rough edges on China's relations with both the United States and Japan, but that event is not certain. Until it is, the United States will have to work with Japan as a real strategic partner in the region.

CHAPTER FOUR

Japan and the Korean Peninsula

Introduction

Japan's relationship with the two Koreas since the end of the Cold War has also been marked by the shift toward reluctant realism, but the colonial legacy and the very proximity of the peninsula have amplified domestic political factors and complicated the formulation of a coherent Japanese strategy for its neighbors to the West.

At one level Japan's approach to the Korean Peninsula reflects a growing sensitivity to the importance of both North and South Korea as independent strategic actors in Northeast Asia since the end of the Cold War. Japanese relations with the Republic of Korea (ROK) in the South have steadily improved as the direct North Korean threat to Japan has increased and Japanese ties to China have become tense. With the revision of the Defense Guidelines and the establishment of the Korean Peninsula Economic Development Organization (KEDO), Japan has taken its first explicit role in the security of the peninsula, while direct political and military coordination with Seoul are rapidly expanding. The growth of bilateral Japan-ROK trade has also contributed to strategic convergence between the two countries, particularly after Japan contributed billions of dollars to help rescue the South Korean economy (and vulnerable Japanese banks) during the 1997–98 Asian financial crisis. Japan and South Korea have also succeeded in resolving contentious historical and fisheries issues. These positive trends and accomplishments culminated in Obuchi Keizō and Kim Dae Jung's declaration of a New Japan–ROK Partnership for Twenty-first Century in October 1998.

At the same time, however, Japanese policymaking toward both Koreas remains fluid and inconsistent. With large Korean communities in

Japan, a legacy of thirty-five years of colonial rule, and direct economic competition in fisheries, electronics, steel, and other sectors, Japan has important domestic constituencies and attitudes that shape Korea policy in ways that often contradict national strategic objectives. There are patterns in Japan-ROK relations that could, in a different strategic context, drive Japan and South Korea further apart. A dramatic downturn in Asia's economic recovery, sudden reunification of the peninsula, or changes in U.S. security posture in the region are all variables that could bring enormous volatility to Japan-ROK ties.

To make sense of the change and continuity in Japan's policies toward the Korean Peninsula, this chapter traces three strands in the Japan-Korea relationship that converged in the Obuchi-Kim summit in October 1998, but could well have resulted in renewed antagonism. These are: (1) management of the North Korean problem; (2) bilateral disputes over fisheries, territorial claims, and history; and (3) bilateral responses to the economic crisis. All three strands are closely interrelated, but disaggregating each demonstrates the variables that will determine whether Japan-ROK ties continue to improve and whether Japan–North Korea normalization is possible. But first, some historical context.

A Dagger Aimed at the Heart of Japan

For four centuries Japan-Korea relations have been marked by more antagonism than cooperation. Alignment between the two countries occurred only when Korea was annexed by Japan (1910 to 1945) and when the Cold War forced the two nations into parallel alliances with the United States. As one South Korean scholar has characterized the historic pattern of relations:

> For four hundred years since the Hideyoshi invasion of Korea, there has been no love lost between these two proud and energetic peoples. Although Japan moved ahead of Korea through early modernization in the nineteenth century, and ruled Korea for thirty-five years, in the twentieth century, Korea never accepted nor recognized Japan's "superiority." . . . In contrast, the Japanese have contended that the Koreans are ungrateful for the contributions they have made to Korea's modernization, while asserting that South Korea also benefits from the American-Japanese military relations.[1]

The gulf in attitudes between the Japanese and Korean peoples has led numerous observers on both sides of the Japan Sea (the East Sea in

Korea) to proclaim the other side "so near and yet so far."[2] In geostrategic terms, however, the Japanese always viewed the Korean Peninsula as dangerously near. It was through Korea that the Mongols launched two unsuccessful attempts to invade Japan, leading Meiji oligarch Yamagata Aritomo to call the peninsula "a dagger aimed at the heart of Japan" that must never fall under foreign domination. Determined to maintain Yamagata's "line of maximum advantage" on the peninsula, Japan entered into a strategic competition with China in the 1890s for influence over Korean modernization (which Japan wanted to accelerate)—a contest that led to war in 1894. The1904–5 Russo-Japanese War in Manchuria was precipitated as the line of maximum advantage spread north and west to protect Japan's new hegemony over the peninsula. Then in 1910 Japan annexed Korea outright. The next thirty-five years saw the systematic attempt to eradicate the separate Korean cultural identity and the forced conscription of the Korean people in Japan's war effort. It also saw significant—though highly distorted—economic modernization in Korea.

After defeat in World War II, Japan no longer had the resources or the political latitude to control the peninsula, but the line of maximum advantage was maintained at the 38th parallel by the U.S. system of bilateral alliances in East Asia. Though Japan and the Republic of Korea scrupulously avoided direct security cooperation during most of the Cold War, the two alliances had an implicit linkage from the beginning. The Korean War gave birth to the U.S.-Japan alliance, the reconstitution of Japanese military and conservative political forces, and the recovery of Japanese heavy industries.[3] For Japan, the U.S.-ROK alliance stood to deter threats to Japan through the peninsula. For Korea, the U.S.-Japan alliance "contained" Japan, while providing bases for operations in the defense of the South. Each alliance partner therefore remained highly sensitive to the steps that the United States took with the other. The Japanese government, for example, voiced great concern at President Carter's plans for troop withdrawals from the Korean Peninsula and eventually took steps through the 1978 Defense Guidelines to ensure that Washington would not be tempted to reduce its defense commitment to Japan during the period of détente.[4]

During the Cold War the United States tried to build on these implicit strategic linkages to strengthen the Japan-Korea leg of the trilateral relationship, but with little success. On the Japanese side there was fear that entrapment in U.S. strategy for the Korean Peninsula would jeopardize Japanese sovereignty and the domestic consensus behind the pacifist principles of the Constitution and the Yoshida

Doctrine. Consequently, the Japanese government moved steadily away from committing itself to a role in the defense of South Korea in the decades after the Korean War, when Japanese infrastructure and personnel were utilized by the U.S. military occupation authorities— often without Japanese government control. Prime Minister Satō Eisaku broke the trend once during his 1969 summit with Richard Nixon when he acknowledged in the joint communiqué that the security of the Korean Peninsula is "essential to Japan's own security." However, as was noted, his statement was part of a trade-off in exchange for the return of Okinawa from the United States, and the Japanese government made great efforts in the wake of the communiqué to bury the explicit Japanese connection to Korean security as deep as possible.[5] In 1972, for example, Foreign Minister Kimura Toshio of the Tanaka cabinet asserted that there was no threat to South Korea or Japan from the North, and Prime Minister Satō reminded reporters that "a communiqué is not a treaty."[6] Thus, the Japanese government resisted all U.S. attempts to include specific language about Korea or even the Far East in the 1978 Defense Guidelines.[7]

On the Korean side, the tone was set by Syngman Rhee's openly hostile Japan policy from 1948 to 1960. In spite of the combination of South Korea's desperate need for economic relations with Japan, Tokyo's desire for a resolution of wartime responsibility, and heavy U.S. pressure, normalization of relations between Seoul and Tokyo took two decades to complete. Japan initiated talks in 1953, but the process stalled because the chief Japanese negotiator insulted his counterparts by arguing that Korea had benefited from Japanese occupation and annexation.[8] Talks did not resume again in a substantive way until 1958. In 1961 the new military government of Park Chung Hee pressed for normalization and stronger economic ties with Japan as U.S. economic assistance declined. Kim Jong Pil, then head of the Korean Central Intelligence Agency (KCIA), reached a draft agreement with the Satō government on normalization in 1963, but opposition to Park's military government from Korean democracy activists and Japan's Socialist Party stalled the signing for two more years. When a treaty establishing basic relations was finally signed in 1965, Japan agreed to provide $500 million in reparations but made no official apology for the war or annexation—an omission that would plague bilateral relations for decades. Meanwhile, Japan was able to conclude a bilateral fisheries treaty that established Japanese fishing rights in the Japan Sea/East Sea, while denying South Korean jurisdictional claims to islands between the two countries. The 1965 Treaty of Basic Relations also confirmed the South as "the only lawful government in Korea." However, this did not prevent Tokyo from annoying its ally in Washington and undermining its cooperation with Seoul by frequently pursuing contacts with North Korea well into the 1980s.[9]

After normalization, Japan's trade with South Korea exploded from $180 million in 1965 to an average of $1,765 million per year between 1971 and 1975.[10] Closer security and political relations did not begin to converge with this trend until the early 1980s, however, as growing Soviet military power in the Far East began reinforcing a common threat perception in both Seoul and Tokyo. Japan's recognition of the North Korean and Soviet military threats was finally articulated in the Defense White Papers of the early 1980s.[11] As the pressure of the new Cold War strengthened the Reagan administration's relations with the governments of both Chun Doo Hwan and Nakasone Yasuhiro, the Japanese and Korean leaders pursued a more proactive partnership with each other. Nakasone made the first state visit by a Japanese prime minister to the Republic of Korea in January 1983. Based on the groundwork of Itōchū counselor Sejima Ryūzō, who acted as the Prime Minister's special emissary, Nakasone announced a $4 billion loan package agreement with the Chun government and helped convince Chun to release opposition leader Kim Dae Jung from prison (Kim had been kidnapped from a Tokyo Hotel in 1973 and was a high profile figure for the Japanese media). In Seoul, Nakasone also moved bilateral relations forward by noting the need for "a penitent attitude regarding the past."[12] Chun reciprocated with a state visit to Tokyo the next year. United by closer security relations with the United States and a strong personal relationship between Chun and Nakasone, Seoul and Tokyo began a tentative exploration of indirect security contact in the mid-1980s through "rolling" (separate but sequential) bilateral exercises with the United States, such as RIMPAC, and joint training between USAF units from Korea and the Japan Air Self Defense Forces.[13]

The Nakasone-Chun summits established a precedent that was built on throughout the 1980s and into the early 1990s. In 1990, for example, Japanese Prime Minister Kaifu Toshiki agreed in his summit with South Korean President Roh Tae Woo to coordinate all Japanese policy toward the DPRK and to proceed with normalization talks with the North at a pace acceptable to Seoul. With this reassurance established in Seoul, Japan opened normalization talks with Pyongyang in 1991. Subsequent Japan-ROK summits were noted for their informal setting and detailed substance.[14] In 1993 Hosokawa Morihiro made his first official visit as prime minister to Seoul, where he tried for a new breakthrough in bilateral relations by offering a personal apology for Japan's subjugation of Korea. His counterpart, Kim Young Sam, reciprocated by promising a "new era of Japan–ROK ties."[15]

But Japan and Korea were not yet ready for this new era. As political scientist Chong-Sik Lee notes in his account of Japan-Korea relations through the 1980s, the generally positive trajectory set by normalization in 1965 and the Nakasone-Chun summits in the 1980s masked unresolved bilateral issues: "In their eagerness to pursue their respective aims, both sides pushed aside their historical animosity and emotional conflicts. Detractors were unwelcome, and Japanese and South Korean leaders made no attempt to build a bridge of genuine understanding."[16]

The 1990s presented difficult tests to the Japan-ROK relationship: an unpredictable and increasingly dangerous North Korea; a return to the unresolved and highly political issues of history, fisheries, and territories; and the challenge of financial collapse. By 1998 Seoul and Tokyo emerged from these trials with what diplomats on both sides called "real normalization"—but not before passing through some of the best and worst chapters in the two countries' postwar relations.

Managing the Threat from North Korea

One factor that should provide common cause between Japan and South Korea, but instead has often fueled mistrust between Seoul and Tokyo, has been Japan's diplomacy toward the North. This factor in Japan-ROK relations became particularly complex after the end of the Cold War, when Japan hoped to capitalize on thawing conditions in Northeast Asia to improve ties with the North. At that time, the Kim Il Sung regime in Pyongyang was becoming isolated from its sponsors in Moscow and Beijing and was ready to seek new infusions of foreign exchange and technology from Japan. Meanwhile, Seoul's *nordpolitik* and pursuit of ties with Moscow and Beijing had removed the South Korean brake on Japan-DPRK normalization. And Japan was cash rich.

Instead of improving, however, Japan's relations with North Korea went from bad to worse. By the end of the 1990s, the modest diplomatic pipeline between Tokyo and Pyongyang was clogged, the Japanese government was expanding security cooperation with Seoul, and Japanese politicians had to be pressed by American and South Korean officials to maintain a policy of engagement with Pyongyang. In 2000 Japan attempted a new approach to normalization talks with Pyongyang, but by that time the lessons about the North Korean threat were deeply ingrained within Tokyo's worldview. The story of the collapse of Tokyo's modus operandi for relations with Pyongyang in this period is at the core of the Japan's shift toward reluctant realism and the changing nature of Japan-ROK ties.

Elusive Normalization

In 1990 normalization with North Korea looked like a political winner for the power brokers in the LDP. Despite years of Cold War confrontation, Japan had maintained informal ties with the North. The 160,000 members of the pro-Pyongyang General Association of Korean Residents in Japan (Chōsen Sōren) were sending an estimated $600 million per year in remittances to the North.[17] Paralleling the private remittances, Japan and North Korea engaged in about $500 million per year in trade throughout the 1990s—an amount that was growing in relative importance to the North as "friendship trade" to the Communist bloc dried up.[18] There were already considerable political funds flowing to the LDP and JSP politicians from the Japanese pachinko industry (which was largely rooted in the North Korean community in Japan), with a potential windfall in contributions from Japanese companies for those politicians who managed the billions of dollars in reparations that might be paid to the North once normalization occurred.[19] Normalization would also form a useful tool for stabilizing LDP relations with the opposition JSP, which was pro-Pyongyang, and showing new strength in the Diet. And finally, in an extra bonus of media attention, a new overture to the North might succeed in releasing the Japanese captain and the engineer of the cargo ship Dai-18 Fujisan Maru, who had been held by Pyongyang since the North had found a defecting North Korean soldier on board in 1983.

With all these objectives in mind, LDP kingmaker Kanemaru Shin organized a mission to Pyongyang in September 1990. The delegation included Tanabe Makoto, vice chairman of the JSP, thirteen government officials, and thirty-six journalists. In Pyongyang, the Kanemaru mission signed a three-party declaration, issued by the LDP, the JSP, and the North Korean Workers Party (KWP), that "strongly urged" their respective governments to start negotiations toward diplomatic normalization and called for Japan to "fully and formally apologize and compensate the DPRK for thirty-six years of Japanese occupation and forty-five years of abnormal relations after World War Two."[20] Kim Il Sung had made a powerful impression on Kanemaru, urging him in private meetings that excluded the Japanese Foreign Ministry to stick closely with his North Korean "yellow skinned" friends against the "white skins."[21] Japanese journalists accompanying Kanemaru saw tears in his eyes as he emerged from meetings with the North Korean leader.

The next month Pyongyang released the two Japanese seamen, clearing the way for the Japanese Foreign Ministry to open formal negotiations with North Korean representatives in Beijing.[22] The normalization talks began in January 1991 and lasted two years, with eight rounds of talks in Beijing, Pyongyang, and Tokyo. MOFA approached the process determined to prevent Kanemaru's enthusiasm for the North from damaging relations with Seoul and Washington. Tokyo announced at the start of the talks that it would stand by four principles: no damage would be allowed to Japan-ROK relations; no "indemnity" would be paid to Pyongyang; North Korea must accept inspections by the International Atomic Energy Agency (IAEA); and Japan would not allow the negotiations to interfere with ongoing negotiations between Pyongyang and Seoul. Pyongyang put its faith in Kanemaru and stood by its guns, insisting that it was owed indemnity for its wartime and postwar struggles against Japan and that the nuclear issue would be negotiated only with Washington.[23]

It was not an auspicious beginning for the normalization talks. Kim Il Sung tried to sweeten the deal by offering to visit Japan after normalization was agreed upon, but the North demonstrated little other flexibility and had few remaining cards to play.[24] Meanwhile, South Korea backed away from its earlier endorsement of an improvement in Japan-DPRK ties. Kanemaru's promise of huge reparations to the North had threatened to undermine Seoul's own negotiating strategy, and the South Korean government was warning Japan to go slow.[25] Even more problematic was Pyongyang's intransigence on the question of its budding and unmonitored nuclear program, which caused the talks to be suspended several times in the summer of 1991.

Some new hope for reenergizing the normalization process emerged in December 1991, when North and South Korea completed the Agreement on Reconciliation, Nonaggression and Exchanges and Cooperation and a parallel nonnuclear accord. Bejing's move to normalize relations with Seoul in August 1992 also improved the external conditions for a return to Japan-DPRK normalization talks. However, these external developments proved less important to Japanese policymaking than the emergence of yet more damaging news in the Japanese press about North Korean provocations. The specific problem was North Korean kidnapping of Japanese civilians. Kim Hyon-hui, a North Korean commando who had been caught after planting a bomb that killed

115 people on a Korean Air passenger plane in 1987, confessed to reporters that she had been taught to impersonate a Japanese tourist by a Japanese woman with the Korean name of Lee Un-hye. Kim said that this Japanese woman had been abducted directly from Japan by North Korean commandos. Soon the relatives of other missing people along the Japan Sea coast began pressing the Japanese government for a full accounting of their own cases. By 1992 Japanese police investigations of missing persons along the Sea of Japan coastline pointed to North Korea's intelligence service as the likely abductors—not only of "Ms. Lee," but of other persons as well. The Japanese public was shocked and the Japanese media had a powerful front-page story. (The National Police Agency concluded in 1997 that ten people had been "missing."[26])

Pyongyang refused to cooperate on the issue, and the Japanese Foreign Ministry, facing intense domestic pressure, walked out of the talks on November 4, 1992.[27]

Changes in domestic Japanese politics further undermined the prospects for normalization. Kanemaru urged the Japanese negotiators on, vowing that he would risk his entire political life to achieve his vision of normalization with the DPRK. By the time the talks collapsed in November of 1992, however, the domestic political equation that had allowed the Kanemaru mission in the first place was no more. In 1992 Kanemaru fell from power and was arrested for tax evasion in the Sagawa Kyūbin scandal. The next year his own lieutenant, Ozawa Ichirō, defected to the opposition and brought down the LDP government. Sakigake (New Harbinger Party) founder Takemura Masayoshi and the LDP's Katō Kōichi assumed some of Kanemaru's role in managing relations with the Chōsen Sōren and Pyongyang, but quickly found it to be a political liability and backed away. Other LDP politicians, such as Nonaka Hiromu, maintained a quiet link to the North through their local constituencies, but avoided high-profile exchanges with Pyongyang. On the other side of the aisle, Tanabe's Socialist Party had lost half its seats, with further contraction to come. Meanwhile, the Chōsen Sōren pipeline to both Pyongyang and the domestic Japanese political parties was shrinking as bankruptcies spread in the pachinko industry and a new generation of North Koreans born in Japan lost their ideological fervor for Pyongyang.[28]

In addition to the collapse of the domestic formula for managing policy toward Pyongyang, the direct North Korean threat to Japan was visibly increasing. In March 1993 North Korea abandoned the Non-Proliferation Treaty (NPT). Then in May of that year, the North test-launched a Nodong–1 SCUD-type missile with the range to strike

Japan. The Japanese Foreign Ministry maintained that the Nodong should not be added to the list of Japanese demands on North Korea in the normalization process, but members of the LDP were alarmed and demanded that the government take the missile threat more seriously.[29] Kanemaru's visions of normalization and growing Japanese influence on the peninsula were steadily being replaced by a nightmare of escalating confrontation.

The Nuclear Crisis

North Korea's nuclear and missile development programs quickly sucked Japan into the security equation of the peninsula in a way Tokyo had managed to avoid since the Korean War. In early December 1993 a U.S. National Intelligence Estimate was leaked that concluded North Korea had already developed one or two nuclear weapons.[30] The assessment was disputed within the U.S. government, but there was little doubt in Tokyo that if married with the Nodong missiles, nuclear bombs would be intended for use against Japan, rather than South Korea. As North Korea dragged its feet about IAEA inspections in January 1994, the Clinton administration prepared to deploy new Patriot batteries to South Korea, and the South Korean Defense Ministry threatened to resume the bilateral U.S.–ROK military exercises that had been on hold for several years. When the North Korean government began unloading the fuel rods at its Yongbyon nuclear reactor in May 1994, Washington felt it had no option but to confront Pyongyang directly with the threat of blockade and the implicit use of force.[31]

With tensions over Pyongyang's nuclear program mounting, the U.S. military command in Korea began preparing for the possibility of hostilities with the North. The Clinton administration was ready to impose new sanctions, including military blockade, and Pyongyang had already signaled that any such move would be seen as a declaration of war. The United States would require Japanese help to cut off the Chōsen Sōren remittances to North Korea, to enforce any naval blockade, to assist with the evacuation of noncombatant personnel, and to provide rear area logistical support for the hundreds of thousands of U.S. troops that would pour through Japan to reinforce the South if tensions escalated. Under the UN Status of Forces Agreement, Japan had already given the UN command a de facto green light to send forces through six major U.S. bases in Japan in response to North Korean hostilities. But this time Washington expected much more of Japan.

In Tokyo, Prime Minister Hata Tsutomu's coalition government was gasping for oxygen after losing its majority in the Diet with the sudden defection of the Socialists in April 1994. Hata was ready to act in support of U.S. sanctions, but his government was ill prepared. The Japan Maritime Self-Defense Force (JMSDF) commander informed the U.S. Navy that Japan probably could not provide ships for surveillance and minesweeping unless Japan was directly attacked or the United Nations provided an appropriate mandate. The National Police and Finance Ministry reluctantly agreed to close Chōsen Sōren financial institutions and to prevent travel to the North, but they warned that these steps would not stop all money flows to Pyongyang and would lead to violent protests from the North Korean community in Japan. MOFA and the JDA held a series of crisis planning meetings with their counterparts in the Pentagon, State Department and U.S. Forces Japan, but it became apparent to U.S. officials that their interlocutors would not have the legal authority to support U.S. war plans without new legislation that the Socialists would attempt to block.[32] The fight over the legislation would likely force Hata to form a new coalition with the LDP, the party he had left to reform politics, the party he had told the press for months that he "detested." In anticipation of Hata's problems, the LDP's Hashimoto Ryūtarō, convened his own internal study group to examine crisis legislation and prepare for the party's return to government. Conservatives in the LDP and Hata's coalition saw an issue that might bring them together in a pro-defense national emergency cabinet, and Hashimoto wanted to be at the helm.

In the end, Japan and the entire world were spared a military confrontation with Pyongyang by the intervention of former President Jimmy Carter, who brokered a deal with Kim Il Sung in Pyongyang in June 1994. The LDP did enter the government, but in a coalition under Socialist Premier Murayama Tomiichi and not with Hata. The LDP and the JSP stood at polar opposites on security policy, but as many in the Japanese press quipped, "Jimmy Carter made the Murayama administration possible." Nevertheless, the North Korean nuclear crisis of 1994 left a searing impression in the psyche of many in the Japanese political world. After Japan's poor performance in the Gulf War and now a near miss in Korea, a new generation of political leaders like Hashimoto and Ozawa agreed that the nation had to strengthen its crisis preparedness. In addition, North Korea's repeated threats to turn Seoul into a "sea of fire" during the crisis deepened the Japanese public's recognition of the potential for missile or commando attacks against Japan in a future confrontation.[33]

In the diplomacy that flowed from former President Carter's deal with Kim Il Sung, Japan was pulled further into the security affairs of the Korean Peninsula than at any other point since World War II. First, based on Carter's intervention, the Clinton administration negotiated an arrangement with North Korea in which the United States would "undertake to make arrangements for the provision to the DPRK of a light water reactor (LWR)" that could not be used to produce nuclear weapons, as well as "[d]eliveries of heavy oil . . . to offset the energy for-gone due to the freeze of the DPRK's graphite-moderated reactors." Pyongyang, in turn, declared its intention to freeze and eventually dis-mantle its graphite-moderated reactors and related facilities and move toward full normalization of political and economic relations with the United States, and to improve ties with the South and "strengthen the international nuclear nonproliferation regime."[34] Based on this 1994 U.S.-DPRK Agreed Framework, the United States asked Japan, the ROK, and the EU to join in the Korean Peninsula Energy Develop-ment Organization, which would construct the two LWR. MOFA con-vinced an initially reluctant LDP to do so by arguing that participation in KEDO was the best way for Japan to play a more active role in ad-dressing the North Korean threat. As the Japanese deputy director to KEDO put it in 1996, from Japan's perspective the organization was es-sential "to stop North Korean nuclear weapons development, to reduce tension on the Korean Peninsula, and as a model for U.S.-ROK-Japan cooperation."[35]

Throughout the response to the North Korean nuclear crisis and the formation of KEDO, Japanese and South Korean officials also began co-ordinating their policies toward Pyongyang in a way they never had be-fore. The United States prodded this coordination in order to implement its own policies, but in Tokyo and Seoul officials also saw the value of informal behind-the-scenes teamwork.

In other ways, however, Japan found itself cut out of the diplomacy on the peninsula. When President Clinton and South Korean President Kim Young Sam met on Cheju Island in April 1996, they proposed Four Party talks to bring together China, the DPRK, the United States, and the ROK to work toward a permanent peace treaty on the penin-sula to replace the armistice that had ended the fighting in 1952. Kim and Clinton promised to consult with Japan and Russia, but neither was included in the negotiations. Moscow was profoundly dissatisfied, but the Hashimoto government accepted this backseat role and expressed official support for the Four Party process. The Japanese side recognized that the Four Party talks brought together the parties to the Korean War armistice (plus Seoul, which had refused to sign at the time) and that establishment of a permanent peace treaty on the peninsula would open the way for broader diplomatic initiatives involving Japan in the future. Tokyo was also sensitive to Seoul's concerns about Japanese interference in North-South negotiations and expected that Japanese security interests in the talks would be coordinated through the U.S. side, since the U.S.-Japan alliance had also been "reaffirmed" with the joint security declaration in Tokyo immediately after the Four Party talks proposal.

These expectations were dashed, however, as North Korean provocations toward Japan continued over the next few years and U.S. attention to Japanese security concerns appeared to wane. In 1996, though, Japan still saw room for another try at normalization talks with Pyongyang. That was where Tokyo focused its initial efforts after the diplomacy prompted by Jimmy Carter's trip to Pyongyang.

A Second Try at Diplomacy with Pyongyang

Though Kanemaru had passed from the political scene, the launching of KEDO and the new Four Party talks gave new impetus to Japan's own dialogue with North Korea. In March 1995, just after the KEDO project was launched, the three political parties in Japan's coalition government (LDP, SDPJ, and Shintō Sakigake) signed an agreement in Pyongyang with the Korean Workers Party calling for a resumption of normalization talks without any preconditions. Several months later the Japanese government announced it would give 500,000 tons in food aid to the North after Pyongyang agreed to also request assistance from the South and not just Japan.[36] Tokyo agreed to go slow on talks with the North after South Korean President Kim Young Sam expressed concern in a summit with Hashimoto in January 1997 that a new round of Japan-DPRK talks might complicate the Four Party talks. But as one senior MOFA official later told *Yomiuri Shimbun,* "Japan must have its own place for negotiating with North Korea" and must "engage actively in the problems of the Korean Peninsula."[37]

Once again, however, direct normalization talks with Pyongyang crashed before they even got off the ground. Negotiators still could not keep ahead of the growing Japanese media focus on North Korean misdeeds, not only the kidnapping cases and Nodong missiles, but now also the fate of 1,800 Japanese wives of North Korean citizens and the status of Japanese *Yodogō* hijackers in asylum in the North. (*Yodogō* was a JAL airplane hijacked by a radical Left-wing students in the late 1960s.) Working-level representatives from the North and the Japanese foreign ministries agreed in Beijing in August 1997 to reopen formal negotiations as soon possible, but the Japanese side insisted that the DPRK must address the alleged kidnapping of Japanese citizens by North Korean commandos and *Yodogō* hijackers.[38] Pyongyang, desperate for food aid, allowed fifteen carefully screened wives to visit Japan in November 1998 and made symbolic gestures to an LDP delegation about investigating the Japanese charges on kidnapping.[39] This was enough to free up $28 million in Japanese emergency assistance through the UN World Food Program, but not nearly enough to jump-start normalization talks. Opposition to normalization with North Korea hardened in the LDP, while the Japanese government scrambled to address each new bilateral problem before it pushed Japan-DPRK relations into a deeper hole. When U.S. officials began quietly warning Japan in the spring of 1997 that the North was developing an even more powerful ballistic missile, the Japanese government downplayed the assessment lest it do even more damage to diplomatic efforts toward Pyongyang.[40] The U.S. warning proved only too accurate, however.

The Taepo-dong Launch

On August 31 North Korea launched a three staged ballistic missile named Taepo-dong directly over Japanese airspace. Stunned, despite warnings from the United States, Tokyo unilaterally suspended its already fruitless negotiations with the DPRK in Beijing[41] and announced that it would suspend all food aid for the North and financial support for KEDO.[42] Angry LDP politicians called for even harsher responses. LDP Secretary Mori Yoshirō, who had led the Japanese delegation to Pyongyang the year before, warned that "a war could have broken out."[43] The party's Policy Affairs Research Council began investigating measures to cut off Chōsen Sōren remittances to the North.[44] Some LDP political leaders argued that Japan should have the right and the capability to counterattack in such circumstances.[45] As an assessment of the missile crisis in the Japanese journal *Foresight* concluded, the Taepo-dong launch demonstrated for the first time "the real possibility of direct attack on Japan" by North Korea.[46]

The shallow state of U.S.-ROK-Japan coordination on North Korea policy was now revealed. The trilateral coordination during the nuclear crisis and the formation of KEDO had been ad hoc and largely directed from Washington. Now, rather than coordinate policies on Korea, Washington and Tokyo made unilateral decisions and threatened even more extreme unilateral steps. U.S. frustration with the volatility of Japanese politics mounted, while Japanese faith in the U.S. defense commitment was shaken.

In the end, the Clinton administration called Japan's bluff. Immediately after Tokyo announced its suspension of KEDO funding, a U.S. official told reporters on background that Japan's tough rhetoric would not stop the LWR project.[47] Washington knew that in a test of wills over how to respond to the North, Tokyo would have to back down. By suspending talks in Beijing and payments to KEDO, Japan had cut off its only direct negotiating channels with the DPRK. Moreover, Japan could not let KEDO die without putting its own security and international reputation at risk. It was a choice, Secretary of State Madeline Albright cautioned her counterpart Kōmura Masahiko shortly after the Taepodong launch, between "peace and war."[48]

MOFA officials knew they had a weak hand for sustaining a tough line on North Korea. Still, they expected that Washington and Seoul would at least keep the DPRK waiting before moving forward with KEDO. The Taepo-dong launch occurred only hours before the KEDO board of directors was preparing to sign its cost-sharing agreement in New York on August 31; under Japanese pressure the board had postponed the signing indefinitely.[49] Tokyo wanted the North to sweat. In direct bilateral U.S.-DPRK negotiations concluded on September 5, however, the U.S. side moved in a completely different direction from Japan, agreeing with Pyongyang to "accelerate" the LWR schedule for KEDO in exchange for a North Korean commitment to discuss the missile problem.[50] MOFA officials were furious. The State Department later added oil to the fire by announcing that the Taepo-dong launch was, in fact, a failed attempt to launch a communications satellite and not a military weapon. Technically, this was accurate, but it was irrelevant since future payloads could just as easily be warheads. The Obuchi government in Tokyo viewed the U.S. assessment as further undermining Japan's tough stance toward Pyongyang.

Under heavy pressure from Washington and Seoul, the Obuchi government eventually signed the KEDO cost-sharing agreement on November 10, 1998, pledging to contribute U.S. $1 billion to the LWR project (an amount eventually approved by the Diet in July 1999).[51] However, the Taepo-dong crisis catalyzed growing dissatisfaction within the LDP and MOFA with both the U.S. and Japanese formulas for managing the North Korea problem. Japan's direct negotiating pipe to the North had clogged; the Four Party formula was not addressing Japanese security concerns, particularly about missiles;[52] direct U.S.-DPRK negotiations were showing symptoms of "Japan passing"—and all of this while North Korea was demonstrating a willingness and a capability to inflict direct damage on downtown Tokyo. Japanese options were limited. It was clear that abandoning KEDO or attacking the Four Party talks would only undermine relations with the United States and the ROK and increase instability and the potential North Korean threat to Japan. Instead, Japanese diplomacy was pressed toward other outlets.

First, Tokyo attempted to utilize the multilateral card. Japan's UN ambassador submitted a resolution to the Security Council condemning the DPRK launch on September 10. The resolution did not pass, but with U.S. support the Security Council president issued a statement on September 15 noting that the DPRK missile launch ran "counter to the promotion of confidence among the countries in the region."[53] Then in his UN General Assembly speech later that month, Prime Minister Obuchi called for a Six Party forum for Northeast Asia. The timing was vague and MOFA officials did not follow up with specific requests to the other states in the region, but the desire of Japan to play a new and larger role in the Korean security dialogue was clear. Japan also pressed for greater representation of its concerns in the Four Party talks. When the talks reopened in October to establish two subcommittees, for example, MOFA Vice Minister Yanai Shunji told reporters that Japan was examining how to play a role with Russia in the subcommittee on tension reductions.[54] Most of these steps were symbolic, but they put the United States and the region on notice that Japan had aspirations for a new and even larger role in the diplomacy of the peninsula.

The second thing the Taepo-dong crisis increased was Japanese hedging. The missile launch consolidated political support in Japan for passing the implementing legislation for the U.S.-Japan Defense Guidelines and therefore played an indirect role in bringing together a conservative coalition of the LDP and Ozawa's Liberal Party. (As noted earlier, many saw the North Korea crisis as the key to a conservative realignment since the nuclear crisis of 1994.) The Taepo-dong experience also cleared the way for the Japanese government to announce its participation in research on joint theater missile defense with the United States in October 1998, despite concerns about costs, feasibility, and Chinese objections.[55]

Not all the hedging was aimed at North Korea, however. The LDP and many in MOFA were dissatisfied with a perceived lag in U.S. intelligence sharing on the missile launch and the signs that Washington might take the Taepo-dong threat less seriously than Tokyo did. Armed with broad political support and detailed technical plans from Mit-

subishi Electric Corporation (MELCO), the Obuchi cabinet announced its decision to develop an indigenous Japanese surveillance
satellite system of its own in November 1998.[56] That same month the
JDA released an independent intelligence assessment reaffirming the
government's original charge that the Taepo-dong was a purely military
program (and not designed to launch satellites). Privately, officials in
Tokyo made it clear that the Japanese satellite system was designed to
give Japan the means to judge future threats like the Taepo-dong independently. Japan's capacity for independent action against North Korea
was also showcased in March 1999, when the Obuchi government authorized the JMSDF to use live fire to halt intruding North Korean spy
ships—this was the first such engagement by the MSDF ever (only
warning shots were fired in an unsuccessful attempt to compel the spy
ships to surrender).[57]

The third and most significant new direction in Japanese diplomacy
after the Taepo-dong crisis was the deliberate institutionalization of political and security coordination with Seoul. Trilateral U.S.-Japan-ROK
diplomatic coordination had increased during the 1993–94 nuclear crisis and the establishment of KEDO. Meanwhile, trilateral defense dialogue moved from ad hoc unofficial sessions in the early 1990s to
regular official meetings in 1996 as the U.S. Defense Department and
JDA sought to explain the new Defense Guidelines to the ROK. The
JDA was initially cautious about the trilateral meetings, concerned that
they might complicate the guidelines process or spark questions in the
Diet about violations of the "collective defense" ban. After the Taepo-
dong launch, however, the Japanese government found new enthusiasm
for security cooperation with Seoul. Tokyo called a trilateral meeting at
the assistant secretary level the week after the launch, and the JDA
began consultations with the ROK Ministry of Defense on ways to
build a trilateral "joint defense framework" in the future. As early sym-
bols of this still-undefined framework, the JDA and the ROK Ministry
of Defense agreed to hold joint naval search-and-rescue exercises (SAR)
and to establish a bilateral hot line for crisis management.[58] A more
powerful symbol of the new shape of ROK-Japan security cooperation was the October 1998 Japan-ROK joint declaration, which
pledged to increase defense exchanges and consultations and to establish regular bilateral cabinet meetings.[59] Naval exercises and training
for SAR missions followed in August 1999, and hot lines were established for the key security establishments of the two governments. As
Victor Cha, a leading analyst of Japan-ROK relations, put it in 1999,
"what is distinct about [these] activities is that they represent the first

step in the evolution beyond pragmatic and transitory cooperation to a more deeply rooted and preplanned relationship."[60]

The Perry Process and One More Attempt at Normalization

The breakdown in U.S.-Japan-ROK coordination in the wake of the Taepo-dong crisis alarmed both Seoul and Washington. Worse from the Clinton administration's perspective, Japan's frustration resonated with a Republican-controlled U.S. Congress that was also dissatisfied with what critics saw as the administration's accommodating approach to Pyongyang. In October 1998 a task force of senior U.S. experts sponsored by the Council on Foreign Relations wrote President Clinton urging him to appoint a senior coordinator to review Korea policy before it broke down completely.[61] In the House Appropriations Committee, where funding for the heavy fuel oil commitment of the Agreed Framework was stalled because of the Taepo-dong launch, this proposal became the centerpiece of congressional legislation that eventually approved continued funding for the administration's policy toward North Korea. On November 12, 1998, the State Department announced that former Secretary of Defense William Perry had been appointed the senior coordinator for Korea policy. One of the first tasks he undertook was to rebuild the frayed trilateral coordination with Seoul and Tokyo. Perry consulted closely with senior Japanese officials in conducting his review and as he traveled to Pyongyang in May 1999 to sound out North Korean interests in improved relations. When the review was completed and Perry made his final report on October 12, he proposed a new approach to Pyongyang beginning with the United States lifting certain economic sanctions in exchange for a North Korean moratorium on missile testing.[62] Perhaps even more important, Perry recommended that the administration formalize his own efforts at trilateral coordination with Seoul and Tokyo by establishing the Trilateral Coordination and Oversight Group (TCOG) at the undersecretary level.[63] The TCOG was formally launched in Hawaii in April 1999.

With smooth U.S.-Japan-ROK trilateral coordination reestablished and U.S.-DPRK relations moving forward, officials in Tokyo began reassessing their own diplomacy with Pyongyang. Under his "Sunshine Policy" for broad-based engagement with the North, South Korean President Kim Dae Jung had been openly advocating Japanese normalization with the North—a marked departure in tone from Kim Young Sam and his predecessors. MOFA officials and Korea experts in Tokyo also recognized the self-inflicted wound caused by the September 1998 decision to cut off talks with the North in Beijing. With Seoul and Washington both moving forward, MOFA convinced the Obuchi government that Japan could not afford to sit out the newest round of diplomacy with North Korea.

In January 1999 Prime Minister Obuchi announced his determination to reopen diplomacy with the North in his opening speech to the 145th session of the Diet.[64] In August of that year the DPRK outlined the terms for normalization with Japan in announcements made during the forty-ninth anniversary of North Korean independence. According to Pyongyang, Japan would have to abandon a policy of hostility toward the North, offer a sincere apology for the past, and offer compensation for the past. In December 1999, after several delays caused by North Korean provocations, former Prime Minister Murayama led a sixteen-member Diet delegation to Pyongyang to lay the groundwork for a resumption of talks. In Pyongyang, Murayama agreed with Kim Young Sun, the secretary of the Central Committee of the Korean Workers Party, to resume negotiations within the year. Meanwhile, Nonaka Hiromu, who by this time had emerged as the LDP's top North Korea expert because of the large North Korean community in his district, called publicly for full diplomatic ties by the end of 2000.[65] Following Red Cross talks on humanitarian assistance and a Japanese agreement to deliver 100,000 tons of food aid in exchange for a North Korean "investigation" into the kidnapping incidents in March 2000, the talks on normalization resumed in April of that year.[66]

Japan appeared to earn a new opportunity to make progress with the North after Kim Dae Jung's historic summit with North Korean leader Kim Jong Il on June 13–15. In Tokyo, the summit was seen as bearing both the prospects for peace and the dangers that Japan would again be isolated from the diplomacy of the peninsula—particularly because of China's prominent behind-the-scenes role and South Korean pressure for Japan to move forward. But even after the North-South summit led to Pyongyang's first participation in the ARF and a face-to-face meeting in Bangkok between Japanese Foreign Minister Kōno and North Korean Foreign Minister Paek on July 26, North Korea poisoned the waters by demanding historical apologies and compensation before it would move forward.[67]

Numerous obstacles lie in the path of Japan-DPRK normalization. North Korea clearly wants Japanese reparations, but the Japanese government will have difficulty agreeing without a resolution of the kidnapping cases and the missile problem. Such a resolution would involve a fundamental change in North Korean behavior that does not seem likely at this point. The North would have to acknowledge the kidnapping (assuming the victims are still alive), and this in turn would spark an even greater backlash in the Japanese media. The missile situation is even more difficult. The Taepo-dong launch moratorium lasts only as long as North Korea is satisfied with U.S. concessions. Meanwhile, the North continues to receive help developing the missile from Pakistan and elsewhere. And the moratorium does not cover the 100 or so Nodong missiles already developed by Pyongyang. Still, as one veteran North Korean watcher put it, "even getting from reverse to neutral in Japan-DPRK relations is good news for MOFA."[68]

Resolving Bilateral Japan-ROK Tensions

In spite of the strategic convergence between Tokyo and Seoul forced by North Korean actions, numerous bilateral issues plagued Japan-ROK relations in this same period. Indeed, part of the breakdown in U.S.-ROK-Japan coordination after the Taepo-dong launch occurred precisely because of these areas of bilateral mistrust between Japan and South Korea. The manner in which Seoul and Tokyo overcame these problems, turning from nationalist confrontation to unprecedented cooperation in security and political affairs, gives room for optimism about the future course of Japan-ROK ties. But these episodes also point to the potential for further disruptions in Japan-ROK relations. Each of these problem areas—specifically, the territorial and fisheries disputes and the treatment of history—merits further examination.

Territorial Disputes and Fisheries Negotiations

In 1996 Japanese and South Korean preparations to ratify the United Nations Convention on the Law of the Sea (UNCLOS) led to competing claims to a small group of islands situated between the two countries. Strategically insignificant in themselves, the Takeshima (in Japanese)/Tokdo (in Korean) Islands became crucial markers of each nation's exclusive economic zone (EEZ) under the UNCLOS rules. Closely related to the territorial problem was the revision of the 1965 bilateral fisheries pact, for which negotiations began in 1996. The negotiating process for both issues brought out the worst patterns in Japan-Korea relations. Historical animosities were inflamed, insults were traded by national leaders, and politicians warned hysterically of armed conflict. But by the time of Kim Dae Jung's October 1998 visit to Japan, the issues were largely, if not completely, settled.

The Takeshima/Tokdo Islands were first claimed formally by Japan in 1905, but Korean dynasties as far back as the sixth century have exercised jurisdiction and Seoul has effectively administered the small chain of islands since 1953. When the South Korean government began building a wharf on one of the islands in February 1996, the Japanese Foreign Ministry formally protested, sending the confrontation into high gear. The South Korean side responded to the Japanese territorial claims by beefing up planned military exercises around the islands on February 15.[69] South Korean President Kim Young Sam appeared on national television to demonstrate his commitment to defending the islands, an event that further inflamed Korean and Japanese public sentiment. Meanwhile, nationalists in Japan took their sound trucks to the streets of Tokyo to denounce South Korean arrogance.[70] Both governments then rushed to make formal EEZ plans that would include the islands. (The Japanese EEZ law passed the Diet in July; the Korean law passed the National Assembly in September.)[71] Kim Young Sam and Hashimoto met on the wings of the March 1–2 Asia–Europe Meeting (ASEM) in Bangkok and used the opportunity to turn down the flames, but the competing claims remained unresolved and the problem reignited in the negotiations over a new fisheries treaty that began in May.

When Japan and the ROK concluded the original 1965 fisheries pact, each side had agreed that its maritime territory would be limited to twelve nautical miles off the coast. By 1971, however, large South Korean fishing boats were operating around Japanese waters. Seoul agreed in 1980 to police its own fishermen operating in those waters, but the Japanese fisheries industry brought constant complaints about South Korean violations to the government and the LDP fisheries caucus. By 1996 frustration was boiling over in coastal ports and in the Diet in Tokyo. The Korean fisherman also had their complaints, particularly after Japan unilaterally extended its territorial waters in January 1997 and the Japanese Maritime Safety Agency began seizing South Korean fishing vessels it accused of violating Japanese waters in the summer of 1997.[72]

Throughout this period, U.S. officials asked Japan to avoid confrontation with Seoul over the fisheries dispute, and South Korean president-elect Kim Dae Jung sent a special envoy to Japan in January 1998 to promise a more conciliatory approach under his new administration. Despite these gestures, however, the Japanese government decided to let the treaty lapse for one year, with the knowledge that failure to resolve the dispute by 1999 would lead to an automatic nullification.

Why did Japan allow such a confrontational approach, given the strategic imperative of maintaining strong ties to Seoul as the threat from Pyongyang and rivalry with Beijing were mounting? The Japanese Foreign Ministry wished to resolve the dispute amicably, but domestic politics confounded their efforts. For one thing, elite ties between Seoul and Tokyo had frayed with political realignment in both countries. Kim Dae Jung's coalition partner, Kim Jong Pil, had negotiated the original draft of the ROK-Japan normalization treaty in the 1960s and had a long history of connections with the LDP. However, Kim Dae Jung's party did not have such strong ties at the elite level, although many Japanese did remember Kim from the famous incident in 1973 when he was kidnapped by the KCIA in Tokyo.

Thus within Nagatachō (Tokyo's "Capitol Hill") the logic of the dispute centered almost entirely on domestic considerations. The LDP fisheries caucus was headed by Satō Kōkō, whose district in Hokkaidō had been hard hit by economic competition from Korean fishermen. Satō was a difficult man for Hashimoto or the LDP to control. He had been forced to resign from the cabinet because of lingering controversy over his arrest in the famous Lockheed scandal of the 1970s, and therefore was not inclined to cooperate with either the Hashimoto or Kim government. Before 1993 someone like Satō might have been controlled by the leader of his faction, but by 1997 the LDP factions were growing weak and undisciplined. Even when former Prime Minister Takeshita Noboru attempted to put together a compromise based on a "joint postponement" of the talks until Kim Dae Jung established a new government, he failed.[73]

In his February 1998 inaugural speech, Kim Dae Jung announced his intention to improve relations with Japan, and one of the first acts of his new foreign minister was to reinitiate talks on the fisheries dispute.[74] More important, the South Korean side invited Satō for direct talks in Korea in June before formally reopening the negotiations.[75] It was his first trip to Seoul, and Satō was treated as an honored guest by Kim Dae Jung and Prime Minister Kim Jong Pil. The Korean side also reestablished voluntary fishing limits off Japan, which had been lifted when Tokyo unilaterally suspended the treaty in January. Satō and the fisheries caucus began to soften.[76] On the eve of the Kim Dae Jung visit, Satō huddled in Tokyo with leaders of his fisheries caucus and their South Korean counterparts. The two sides were close to an agreement but had deadlocked on where the fishing zones would be separated. Late in the evening on September 24, Prime Minister Obuchi intervened, inviting the negotiating parties to his official office (the kantei) where he patiently worked with the two sides until a settlement was reached early in the hours of the twenty-fifth.[77] Under the agreement, the line between each country's fishing area was drawn at 135.30 degrees east longitude, a midway point between the boundary that each country had been claiming. Current catch limits were also maintained for three years.[78] Satisfied, Kim Dae Jung signed the agreement in Tokyo on October 7.

The successful resolution of the fisheries issue was influenced by exogenous factors, such as the North Korean Taepo-dong launch and Japan's diplomatic maneuvering vis-à-vis China, but at its core it was handled where the problem originated—in the domestic political arena. The LDP was satisfied because the party's hard line forced the Korean side to compromise on the demarcation line. But ultimately that hard line could have led to increased confrontation with the ROK, had it not been for Kim Dae Jung's sustained commitment to strengthening ties with Tokyo and Obuchi's personal intervention at the last minute. As it was, the South Korean opposition almost defeated the new treaty in the National Assembly because the territorial issue remained unresolved.[79] The resolution of the impasse was a near miss—highly contingent on the personality of Kim Dae Jung—that demonstrated how far Japan-Korea ties had come and how many potential areas for bilateral confrontation remain beneath the surface in each side's political system.

Toward Closure on the History Issue

In the midst of the fisheries negotiations, one of the key Japanese players almost scuttled the talks with controversial statements to the press about Japan's historical relationship with South Korea. Agriculture, Forestry, and Fisheries Minister Nakagawa Shōichi, a young nationalist LDP politician from Hokkaidō and one of the key negotiators in the fisheries talks, was also the founder of a group of young Japanese Diet members dedicated to the drafting of more patriotic history textbooks in Japan's public schools.

Frustrated with the pace of negotiations with the South Koreans, on July 31, 1998, Nakagawa responded to a reporter's provocative questions about the history issue by arguing that the government should stop highlighting negative aspects of Japan's past in history textbooks.[80] He touched on one hot-button issue in particular—expressing skepticism about accounts that the Japanese Imperial Army had maintained forced prostitution of so-called comfort women from Korea for the front-line troops.[81] The Foreign Ministry nervously held its collective breath. Japan-Korea normalization talks had collapsed for ten years over similar statements in 1953 by a leading Japanese negotiator and accounts of

Nakagawa's statement would undoubtedly appear in the Korean press the next day.

Who were the comfort women? The story itself is tragic. Young women from Korea and Taiwan were recruited—either forcefully or for money, depending on whom one believes—to serve in brothels organized near the front lines by the Japanese army. Shamed by their desperate situation, few women came forward after the war to make claims against the Japanese government, and Tokyo therefore ignored the problem at an official level. However, as questions about the comfort women began surfacing in the Japanese Diet in 1990, the problem could no longer be ignored. Initially the Japanese government maintained that the women were recruited and controlled by private firms and were therefore not the responsibility of the Imperial Army or the current Japanese government. However, in 1992 documents were discovered in the Defense Agency archives that demonstrated the Imperial Army's role in recruiting and controlling the comfort women stations during the war, and Tokyo had to change its line of argument. In 1993 Chief Cabinet Secretary Kōno Yōhei issued a report acknowledging the responsibility of the Imperial Army and offering his "heartfelt apology and deep remorse" to all those affected.[82]

Nationalists in the LDP objected, however, and would not allow the government to offer compensation to the victims or to declassify remaining archival records that would allow a full accounting of individual cases. Kōno's own deputy, Ishihara Nobuo, denied in subsequent Diet testimony that Kōno's statement had any legal or factual bearing beyond the testimony of a few of the "comfort women."[83] Instead, the Japanese government established a private Asian Women's Fund (Jōsei no tame no Ajia Heiwa Kokumin Kikin), which distributed $17,000 and a private letter from Prime Minister Hashimoto to each of seven victims in Seoul in January 1997. The Kim Young Sam government immediately protested the Japanese side's inadequate handling of the issue and demanded Japanese government compensation.[84] Japan would not respond. Once again Kim Dae Jung stepped into the breach as the newly elected president, arranging in April 1998 for the Korean government to compensate individual victims and dropping the ROK government's demand for official Japanese compensation.[85] Still, the problem festered in the Korean and Japanese press, and Nakagawa's statement threatened to reopen the controversy with his explosive comments.

To the amazement of the Japanese press and the delight of the Foreign Ministry, however, almost nothing happened after the Nakagawa bombshell. The Kim Dae Jung government made no formal protest, as was typical in the past in such circumstances, and the Korean president ignored the issue when he called Prime Minister Obuchi to congratulate him on his inauguration the day after the news hit. Meanwhile, Nakagawa continued to play a central role in the fisheries negotiations as a leader in the LDP fisheries caucus, and he was with Satō Kōkō throughout all of the staged kabuki of the final negotiating session in the Prime Minister's Office. Instead of becoming a problem in the bilateral relationship, he became a key player in finding the solution.

The Nakagawa flap demonstrated once again the ability of the Japanese and Korean governments to manage even the domestic problems associated with their troubled past—when they have a common purpose. Kim Dae Jung's tolerant response to Nakagawa set the stage for a direct approach to the overall history problem between the two governments.

Japan had struggled with the apology problem for decades without any more success in Korea than in China. In 1984 Emperor Akihito expressed "regret" for the past ("*makoto ni ikan de ari*") in a state dinner for visiting President Chun Doo Hwan, sentiments his successor Akihito repeated in future state visits from the ROK. Prime ministers also expressed their personal remorse beginning with Nakasone's call for "a penitent attitude regarding the past" during his visit to Seoul in January 1983 and continuing through Hosokawa's statement of "deep remorse and heartfelt apology" at Kyongju in November 1993.[86] However, the Japanese government had never been able to muster domestic political support for a national statement of apology in a joint official document.

Kim Dae Jung's state visit to Tokyo in October 1998 presented just such an opportunity. The two governments went to work on a draft joint declaration that would feature a formal Japanese apology based on a formula Kim Dae Jung proposed. Japan would apologize and Korea would accept that apology once and for all while expressing appreciation for Japan's international role. When the formula was put on paper and floated in Nagata-chō in the weeks before Kim's visit to Tokyo, nationalist politicians from the LDP and the Liberal Party raised strong objectives, but in the end only nineteen Diet members signed a petition urging the government not to apologize.[87] The domestic path was clear in both countries for an official statement of closure on the historical problem. And the October 8 joint declaration did just that, stating as follows:

President Kim Dae Jung expressed appreciation for Japan's contributions to and the Japanese role in the international community, including the

United Nations, and expressed expectations that these kinds of contributions and role will be increased in the future.

Prime Minister Obuchi regarded in a spirit of humility the fact of history that Japan caused, during a certain period in the past, tremendous damage and suffering to the people of the Republic of Korea through its colonial rule, and expressed his deep remorse and heartfelt apology for this fact.[88]

The resolution of the apology issue in the October 1998 Obuchi-Kim summit was critical to the summit's success and the credibility of the men's joint declaration on a new partnership. As the director of MOFA's Korea Division noted in a postmortem in the ministry's journal *Gaikō Forum* in December, the Japan-ROK joint declaration established the "real" normalization between the two countries that had not been possible after 1965.[89] And in contrast to the 1965 normalization process, the summit enjoyed a significant level of support in both countries. In South Korean opinion polls conducted in Japan the weeks after the summit, 80 percent of the Japanese responded that the two countries had at last reached closure on the history issue, and over 70 percent pointed to "bilateral cooperation for international peace and security" as the most important dimension of the joint declaration.[90] In South Korea, leading editorials in the major dailies applauded the joint declaration and Japan's apology, while reminding readers that some issues, such as the sovereignty of Tokdo and the fate of the comfort women, still needed work.

The Japanese apology contrasted sharply with the summit meeting with Chinese leader Jiang Zemin two months later, as we saw in the last chapter. What accounted for the success of Japan and Korea in managing the history issue? Kim Dae Jung set the tone early, offering to invite the Japanese emperor to Korea and declaring, as president-elect, to then Foreign Minister Obuchi in March 1998, that Korea should acknowledge Japanese contributions in exchange for Japan acknowledging its history. After taking office in February 1998, Kim took other steps to ease the way for an apology from Japan: unilaterally compensating comfort women, referring officially to Akihito as the "emperor" for the first time in ROK history, and agreeing to lift the long-standing ban on Japanese cultural imports into Korea (including TV, movies, *manga* cartoons, and popular songs).[91]

The international context also mattered. The growing North Korean threat to Japan and unease with rising Chinese influence led to a new strategic appreciation of the importance of Japan-ROK ties in Tokyo.

Moreover, in contrast to China's approach to the history problem, South Korea accepted the Japanese apology and responded with expressions of support for a larger Japanese role in the United Nations and the region. The initiative and patience displayed by Kim Dae Jung also made a strong impression in Tokyo (and led Japanese in opinion surveys to list him third after British Prime Minister Tony Blair and U.S. President Bill Clinton as the most popular world leader).[92]

In addition, the subtle ties that had grown between the Japanese and South Korean people as citizens of two advanced industrial democracies grew throughout the 1990s, in spite of the ban on Japanese cultural imports to South Korea and the lingering historical problems. In part this connection flowed from informal nongovernmental networks. In part it was also a matter of generational change gradually overriding some of the divergent teaching of history between the two countries. As the Brookings Institution's Kongdan Oh puts it, "the South Korean people have progressed from sentiments of *han-il* (resisting Japan), to *ban-il* (anti-Japan), to *kuk-il* (overcoming Japan), and eventually *chi-il* (knowing Japan)."[93]

Economic Relations: Competition and Interdependence

Another critical factor behind the gradual establishment of political cooperation between Japan and South Korea in the three decades after normalization was the growing economic relationship between the two countries. Japan has become South Korea's second largest trading partner, after the United States, and Korea's leading source of investment. At the same time, the economic relationship has been asymmetrical and often contentious, given persistent trade imbalances in Japan's favor and increasingly fierce export competition between the two countries in steel, shipbuilding, semiconductors, and consumer electronics.[94]

The eruption of South Korea's currency crisis in late 1997 had the potential to exacerbate these tensions in bilateral economic relations. The Japanese devaluation of the yen was seen by many in Seoul as one of the causes of the collapse of the won that year. Moreover, the refusal of Japanese banks to roll over South Korean debt in December 1997 was the specific trigger of South Korea's currency reserve crisis. In addition, as the crisis spread, Japan's failure to stimulate its own economy denied South Korea its best hope to export its way out of the economic crisis without overloading the U.S. market.[95]

By the time of the Kim-Obuchi summit in October 1998, however, the economic crisis was acting as a greater force for mutual dependence and cooperation than acrimony and conflict between Japan and Korea. South Korea's financial crisis revealed the Japanese banks' high level of exposure in that country. Japan accounted for over one-third of all foreign bank claims on South Korean debt in 1997, and, ironically, some of Japan's strongest banks at home were the most exposed in Korea. Many in the Japanese Ministry of Finance feared that if South Korea's financial system collapsed, Japan's banks could go down with it. MOF barely hesitated before pledging US $10 billion to South Korea as part of the initial IMF package ($21 billion from the IMF, $10 billion from the World Bank, $4 billion from the Asian Development Bank, and $20 billion from the G-7 countries, half of which was Japanese).

The IMF crisis also accelerated trends toward greater mutual economic opening by ending many of the government-chaebol (industrial conglomerate) policies that had kept Japanese companies from investing in key sectors of the Korean economy. As Yonsei University professor Ahn Byung-joon pointed out in the pages of the *Munhwa Ilbo* in January 1998, Tokyo decided on an early release of $3.3 billion earmarked for the bailout but "announced support only after securing promises from Seoul that South Korea would open its own markets and implement structural changes in the economic system."[96] Though Japan was not subject to the same stringent IMF requirements for restructuring, the process of deregulation in Japan (incremental though it may be) will likely open the Japanese market to greater South Korean imports and investment.

Kim Dae Jung was inclined to improve relations with Japan even before the economic crisis hit, but Japanese financial assistance to South Korea in late 1997 clearly eased his task at home. Under the 1998 Kim-Obuchi joint declaration, Japan's Export-Import Bank (now the Japan Bank for International Cooperation) signed a memorandum of understanding with Korea's Ministry of Finance to provide an additional $3 billion in untied loans for small to medium-size South Korean firms. The two leaders also signed a new tax treaty, removing preferential tax treatment for South Korea and establishing preferential system of incentives through 2003 to encourage Japanese investment in the ROK.[97] Japan's Keidanren and the Federation of Korean Industries followed the summit with an agreement to coordinate a reduction in overlapping capacity between the two countries and to explore the creation of a bilateral free trade zone in the future. This was an ambitious agenda with an uphill battle for implementation, but few would have endorsed such a bold vision of cooperation before the economic crisis.[98] Indeed, by March 1999 the Japanese and ROK governments had agreed on a series of steps to harmonize standards, promote mutual investment, and generally consolidate their growing economic partnership.[99]

At the same time, however, some seeds of potential future economic confrontation were also sewn with South Korea's financial crisis. A further depreciation of the yen will put increased pressure on South Korean exports and could undermine Seoul's program for economic recovery. And long-term depreciation of the yen is one possible scenario as Tokyo seeks to retire its own massive banking sector debt. On the other hand, a strong yen relative to the won could erode Japanese competitiveness in third sectors and spark frustration against South Korea in Japan.[100] For the foreseeable future, however, the net effect of Japanese bank exposure in Korea and Seoul's requirement for foreign direct investment and loans will serve to reinforce political cooperation between the two countries. That positive tone of cooperation and growing mutual economic dependence is certainly the one being embraced by the majority of business and government leaders in the two countries.

Conclusion: The U.S.-Japan-ROK Triangle

If the contemporary history of Japanese relations with the two Koreas teaches Japanese diplomats and foreign analysts anything, it is to not make predictions about the future of those relations. Still, as this chapter demonstrates, certain trends in Japan's diplomacy toward the peninsula are building, other patterns are being repeated, and some variables have to be watched.

Trends

The first trend apparent in post–Cold War Japan-ROK/DPRK relations is Japan's growing readiness to play a role in the security and diplomacy of the peninsula. After three decades of avoiding the Korea clause in the 1969 Satō-Nixon communiqué, Japanese politicians and diplomats now freely acknowledge that "the security of the Korean Peninsula is essential to Japan's security." Though the new U.S.-Japan Defense Guidelines are not scenario-based, there is no doubt that they could apply to the Korean Peninsula. And while KEDO is ostensibly an energy organization, there is no doubt that through it Japan is participating in the most important confidence-building measure on the peninsula. Many in Tokyo are eager to expand their security portfolio in Korea to include increased trilateral U.S.-Japan-ROK security consultations and a new six-power forum to complement the Four Party talks.

With Japan's growing focus on the threats emanating from the Korean Peninsula, its leadership has also developed a clearer recognition of the importance of strategic convergence with Seoul. That is not to say that domestic Japanese politics cannot easily upset this strategic perception, as they did with fisheries and immediately after the Taepo-dong launch. Nevertheless, there is clearly an unprecedented level of political support in Japan for enhancing bilateral security and political cooperation with Seoul based on the agenda outlined in the Kim-Obuchi joint declaration. This support derives not only from the growing North Korean threat to Japan, but also from a recognition of mutual economic interests, a sense of progress on the historical issue, and strategic unease about China.

And just as Japanese relations have improved dramatically with South Korea, they have deteriorated with North Korea. In part this is due to changes in Japanese politics and the eroding pipeline of money and communication between Japan and the North. The North Korean community in Japan is losing money and interest in supporting Kim Jong Il. The Socialist Party has collapsed. LDP politicians who deal with the Chōsen Sōren in their districts have only tactical concerns with North Korea and lack Kanemaru's clout to achieve a strategic breakthrough in relations, though Nonaka assumed some of that role beginning in 1998. Meanwhile, the Japanese media and public have a growing list of grievances against North Korea (missiles, kidnapping, harboring terrorists, etc.) that Pyongyang is unable to address without considerable damage to its legitimacy. However, the fact that relations are improving with South Korea does not in itself mean that Japanese relations cannot also improve with North Korea. In fact, it is in part because of Kim Dae Jung's prodding that Japan made another attempt at normalization with North Korea in April 2000. More could follow from the June 2000 North-South summit.

Recurring Patterns

At the same time, certain patterns in Japan's relations with the Korean Peninsula have remained disturbingly consistent since the end of the Cold War. For one thing, Japanese security concerns vis-à-vis North Korea continually diverged from those of the United States and South Korea. In the 1960s and 1970s, the Japanese government maintained that the North Korean threat to Japan was not significant, but Seoul was alarmed by the threat from Pyongyang. With the Taepo-dong launch the positions reversed: the Japanese government argued that the new North Korean missile threat was highly significant, but Seoul was not alarmed. In the 1970s Japan was able to benefit from U.S. and ROK deterrence against North Korean aggression. In the 1990s Japan was able to benefit from U.S. and ROK engagement of North Korea. Despite expanded security coordination with Seoul and Washington, in short, the three capitals still have different thresholds for the North Korean missile and nuclear threats, and the danger of divergence remains.

A second recurring pattern that may not improve given the increased fluidity in Japanese politics is the continuing penchant of Japanese politicians to foment trouble on the historical issue. In spite of the progress made with Japan's expression of deep remorse and heartfelt apology to Korea in 1998, there is no shortage of nationalist politicians who will continue to fight for a more patriotic presentation of history in Japanese textbooks and movies. This impulse has passed to a new generation in Japan, just as the teaching of Japan's brutality has been conveyed to a new generation in Korea. It will continue to complicate bilateral relations, though perhaps with a lower level of national attention than before. Nevertheless, South Korea's tolerance for these outbursts is only marginally lower after the formal Japanese apology in 1998.

Finally, it should be remembered that in spite of the deft maneuvering in 1998, the problem of determining which country has sovereignty over Takeshima/Tokdo remains unresolved. This territorial issue in itself is insignificant, and one major benefit of sovereignty (determining fishing zones) was temporarily neutralized by the compromise in the new fisheries agreement. Nevertheless, the issue lies dormant only until nationalism over other issues raises it in a different context.

Variables to Watch

Whether the positive trends listed earlier can defeat these recurring patterns in Japan-ROK relations will depend on several variables.

- *Leadership.* It is possible that Japan and South Korea could have achieved closure on the apology issue and the fisheries treaty or avoided hysteria over Takeshima/Tokdo if Kim Dae Jung had been elected president in 1992 instead of Kim Young Sam. "Kim Dae Jung's commitment to improving relations, and Obuchi's reciprocation, were critical factors in the new trajectory set by the 1998 joint declaration. Different leaders in Seoul and Tokyo might not be as inclined to contain clashing constituencies between the two countries.

- *The Japanese economy.* A Japanese economic downturn would undermine South Korea's return to economic growth and could lead to calls within Japan for protection against Korean competition. A devaluation of the yen will press South Korean exports and could raise tensions. Unequal market opening and aggressive Japanese FDI could cause a backlash in Korea.

- *China.* The general convergence in Japan-Korea relations and security cooperation does not apply to China. Japan is motivated to improve relations with South Korea in large part because of uncertainties about China, but Seoul does not share the same level of unease about Chinese power. Regional crises—in Taiwan or the disputed Spratley islands, for example—would exacerbate this difference.

- *The U.S. commitment.* Some scholars argue that Japan-ROK security relations have improved when the strategic presence of the United States in the region is in doubt. This may have been so in the 1970s, but the obverse is not therefore accurate. Certainly in the post–Cold War era, Japan-ROK policy coordination has tended to deepen only when there is a trilateral or multilateral effort led by the United States, such as KEDO or the defense trilateral meetings.[101]

- *Unification of the Korean Peninsula.* This is the 500-pound gorilla of variables in the Japan-ROK relationship. It is often asserted that Japan fears the unification of the Korean Peninsula. This view is particularly strong in South Korea. On the thirtieth anniversary of the normalization of Japan-ROK ties, for example, 43 percent of Koreans surveyed answered that unification of the peninsula would have a bad influence on Japan. In the same survey only 17 percent of the Japanese respondents felt the same way.[102] It makes sense that the elimination of the threat of war on the peninsula would be seen as a good thing for Japan and that peaceful reunification would therefore be an outcome preferable to the lingering prospect of destructive conflict. The reason Japan appears to be a status quo power on the Korean Peninsula is not because unification has negative implications for it, but because the possibility remains that the process of unification could threaten its interests. This would be particularly true if a nuclear Korea emerged—or one aligned with China against Japan. Even a unified Korea that sought full independence from the United States would be destabilizing from a Japanese perspective. However, we cannot assume from the troubled history of Japan-Korea relations that Japan would necessarily obstruct unification or come into conflict with a newly reunified Korean Peninsula. If anything, the pattern of Japan's relations with the peninsula in the 1990s suggests that Japan could play a critical and positive role in the process of reconciliation and reunification of the two Koreas.

The U.S. Role

The "strategic triangle" of choice for most analysts of East Asian security tends to be the U.S.-Japan-China triangle. However, U.S. strategic objectives in the region also hinge on the triangle that links the United States, Japan, and the ROK. Closer Japan-ROK cooperation will enhance U.S. efforts to maintain forward presence, manage diplomacy and potential crises on the Korean Peninsula, and integrate China as a cooperative partner in the region. In contrast, distant Japan-ROK relations would complicate all of these U.S. objectives. Moreover, hostile Japan-ROK relations, particularly in the context of Korean reunification, would have a spillover effect on Sino-U.S. relations and could return the region to the great-power rivalry over the Korean Peninsula that ruined the last century.

What steps should the United States take to enhance U.S.-Japan-ROK trilateralism? Japanese scholar Kimiya Tadashi has noted that Washington has an indispensable role in resolving the "high politics" (i.e., the strategic issues) in Japan-Korea relations, but cannot resolve the problems of "low-level politics," such as economic cooperation and war liabilities.[103] Nevertheless, a common purpose in the strategic issues of high politics will create the proper political environment for resolution of other bilateral problems between Seoul and Tokyo.

In general, U.S. policy has succeeded in maintaining a common strategic direction in U.S.-Japan and U.S.-ROK relations since the end of the Cold War. However, the architecture of the diplomacy on the Korean Peninsula is an obstacle to trilateralism. Japan will provide $1 billion to the construction to KEDO and would likely be the single largest external provider of capital for the reconstruction and reunification of North and South Koreas. Japan also has central national security interests at stake in the Four Party talks, including missile proliferation, sanctions, and terrorism. However, Tokyo is not integrated directly in the negotiating process and must rely on briefings from Washington and

Seoul to understand what is transpiring. Meanwhile, as a party to the 1953 armistice agreement, Beijing is a central player in the Four Party talks—yet Beijing is not a cooperative partner in KEDO or in the multilateral provision of food aid to North Korea.

The establishment of the Trilateral Coordination and Oversight Group (TCOG) by former Secretary of Defense William Perry in April 1999 was an important step toward rectifying this situation. The United States can take further steps to strengthen strategic cooperation on a trilateral basis with Japan and the Republic of Korea. The United States should strengthen the TCOG's function in coordinating diplomacy while simultaneously accelerating trilateral defense talks and joint exercises. Since TCOG focuses on near-term diplomatic coordination, there is also a need for a parallel policy planning process to address longer-term issues related to the costs and conditions of the reunification of the peninsula. Second-track dialogue can also play a useful role in addressing postunification scenarios for Japan-U.S.-ROK cooperation.[104] In addition, the United States should support the establishment of a Northeast Asia forum (Six Party talks). Though the objections of North Korea and disinterest of China are significant obstacles, Seoul and Tokyo (and Russia, for that matter) are ready for such an endeavor, and Washington should throw its support behind the idea once again. These steps are particularly important given the potential for a far more fluid diplomatic and strategic environment around the peninsula following the June 2000 North-South summit.

Ultimately, these steps do not require dramatic reorganization of government or changes in policy, but they will go a long way toward preparing the U.S.-Japan and U.S.-ROK alliances to interact with each other as the division of the Korean Peninsula reaches its denouement. Seoul should always take the lead on North-South reconciliation, and there is no doubt that the United States has significant security interests on the peninsula and should maintain dialogue with China on these. But Japan's attention to its security interests on the peninsula has clearly increased, and U.S. diplomacy ignores these at its own risk.

CHAPTER FIVE

The New Eurasia Diplomacy

Energy and Geopolitics in Russia, Central Asia, and the Caucasus

Introduction

In the early twentieth century, Sir Halford Mackinder advanced a strategic theory known as Eurasianism that posited that the earth will be forever divided into two naturally antagonistic spheres: land and sea.[1] For the sea powers, he argued, the greatest threat was hegemonic dominance of the Eurasian landmass by a hostile power. It was the geopolitics of Eurasianism that drove British and Russian strategy in the nineteenth and early twentieth Centuries. With the collapse of the Soviet Union and the end of the Cold War, the United States, China, and Turkey all rushed to establish a business and diplomatic presence at the heart of the Eurasia as well. The latest aspirant to this "Great Game" has been Japan.

From about the time Mackinder advanced his theory of Eurasianism, Japan's relationship with Russia has been trapped in mutual animosity and mistrust. The 1904 Russo-Japanese War, the Soviet invasion of Manchuria the week before Japan's surrender in 1945, and Moscow's continued occupation since the war of Japan's Northern Territories all led Japanese diplomats to warn their Western counterparts well into the 1990s that the Russian threat to Japan would transcend the ideology of the Cold War and the collapse of the Soviet Union. By 1996, however, the Japanese approach to Russia began changing dramatically. In March of that year Prime Minister Hashimoto dispatched Foreign Minister Ikeda Yukihiko to Moscow to explore ways to improve ties. In April Usui Hideo made the first visit of a Japanese Defense Agency director general to Moscow. In July 1997 Hashimoto announced a new Russia policy before a group of Japanese business executives in which he outlined the principles of "trust, mutual benefit, and long-term perspective" as the pillars for bilateral relations with Moscow. Then in a summit meeting with Russian President Boris Yeltsin in the Siberian city of Krasnoyarsk in November, the two leaders unveiled the Hashimoto-Yeltsin Plan for economic cooperation. Later they spoke separately of completing a peace treaty by 2000 to address the unresolved issues from World War II. As Russia policy began to shift, Hashimoto turned his eyes farther to the West, articulating a comprehensive vision for a Eurasian strategy that would make Japan a diplomatic player from Sakhalin to the Caucasus.

What accounts for Japan's change of course? The tempting answer would be that Tokyo is simply pursuing economic interests—in this case energy—as it always has in the postwar period. Certainly Japan has a long-term interest in accessing Russia's vast gas and oil resources, but the obstacles to investment in Russia are considerable and Japanese industry is cautious about advancing too far or too fast. More significant have been the geostrategic and ideational changes illuminated in the previous chapters. With rising Chinese power and fluidity in the Northeast Asian security environment, Japan had no choice but to improve relations with Russia to prevent the emergence of a Sino-Russian alignment in the Eurasian landmass at Japan's expense. In addition, Japan had to improve relations with Russia because U.S.-Russian relations in the mid-1990s warmed so quickly that a tough stance toward Russia no longer reinforced U.S.-Japan security ties—indeed, it only increased the dangers of abandonment. And for Hashimoto, who was looking for a card to demonstrate Japan's proactive diplomacy to domestic and foreign audiences, Russia seemed ideal. Indeed, Japan needed Russia, just as Russia needed Japan, to reinforce its own geostrategic presence and weight in East Asia at a time of uncertain economic power and regional influence.

However, Japan's new "Russia card" has its limits. Russia's growing economic and political problems and the reemergence of tension between Moscow and Washington have greatly complicated Japan's efforts to strengthen ties with Russia. Ironically, in 2000 Japan stood as the only provider of new major economic assistance to Russia, just as in the early 1990s it once stood alone resisting economic aid to Moscow. Nevertheless, despite these complications, Japan has embarked on a new approach to Russia and Central Asia that reflects a strategic perspective going well beyond narrow economic interests. It is a policy that recognizes, in the words of the Foreign Ministry's 1998 annual *Diplomatic Bluebook,* "Eurasian diplomacy from a Pacific perspective."[2]

This chapter examines this new Eurasia diplomacy, reviewing the evolution of post–Cold War diplomacy with Russia, the shift in policy in 1996–97, the energy ties between the two countries, and Japan's diplomatic foray into Central Asia and the Caucasus. The chapter then concludes with observations on the Russia factor in U.S.-Japan relations.

Historical Background

Three Centuries of the Northern Threat

Japan's Eurasian diplomacy and improving ties with Russia stand in striking contrast to centuries of antagonistic relations between Moscow and Tokyo. As early as 1635, the Tokugawa government was mapping the four islands in the Northern Territories (Etorofu, Kunashiri, Shikotan, and the Habomai group).[3] By 1791 Tokugawa scholars such as Hayashi Shihei were commenting on the emerging Russian threat from the north.[4] Over the next 150 years, Japan solidified its claims to the islands and its rivalry with Russia through treaties and war. In 1855 the Japan-Russia Treaty of Trade and Friendship (the Shimoda Treaty) confirmed Japan's sovereignty over Etorofu, Kunashiri, Shikotan, and the Habomai group. In 1875 Japan established its rights over the Kurile Archipelago as far as the Kamchatka Peninsula in the Treaty of St. Petersburg. By the end of the nineteenth century, Russian pressure for a warm-water port in the Far East and the Japanese drive for hegemony over Manchuria and protection of the Korean buffer led to the 1904–5 Russo-Japanese War, which ended in Japanese victory and control over the southern half of Sakhalin Island. At times in the past Moscow and Tokyo were driven to establish cooperation for strategic reasons, to be sure. For example, in 1916 Russia and Japan signed a treaty to cooperate against Germany in the context of World War I. But by 1919 Japan was participating in the Siberian intervention and shifting back to its traditional anti-Russian, and now anti-Bolshevik, position.

In the closing days of World War II, the Soviet Union retook all of its lost territories with a sudden attack on an already mortally wounded Japan. The sneak attack struck the Japanese people as an act of betrayal, since Moscow and Tokyo had signed a nonaggression pact at the beginning of the war.[5] Japanese citizens taken on the northern Territories were forcibly repatriated or sent to Soviet labor camps together with hundreds of thousands of military and civilian prisoners taken in

Manchuria and Northern China. Over 60,000 died in Soviet captivity; many of the living were not returned to Japan until as late as 1956. Japanese enmity toward the Soviet Union was further reinforced by Moscow's refusal to sign the 1951 San Francisco Peace Treaty.

Despite this deep enmity toward Russia, however, some Japanese political leaders saw advantage in stabilizing ties with Moscow in order to win more freedom of action in the complex relationship with the United States. When Hatoyama Ichirō became the first LDP prime minister in 1955, one of his first acts was to attempt a restoration of relations with Russia. Hatoyama traveled to Moscow in 1956 to negotiate a peace treaty and to secure the return of the Northern Territories. Ultimately he failed in both objectives, primarily because the Japanese government was unwilling to sign a peace treaty without resolving the territorial issue, and Moscow was unwilling to return all the territories. However, Hatoyama did succeed in reopening bilateral diplomatic and trade relations with Russia, and Moscow offered to return half of the territories—the Habomai group and Shikotan Island—once a peace treaty was signed. Conservatives in Japan were unwilling to accept a partial settlement, and Washington, concerned about the extent of Hatoyama's attempted rapprochement with the Soviets, pressed Tokyo to hold out for the return of all occupied territories.[6] When Japan and the United States signed the U.S.-Japan Security Treaty in 1960, Soviet Premier Nikita Khruschev rescinded the 1956 offer and the first window to resolve the Northern Territories problem was closed.[7]

In the 1970s, as U.S.-Japan relations entered a period of uncertainty following the 1969 Nixon Doctrine, the opening to China, and the beginning of détente, Japan once again moved to secure its strategic position by improving relations with Moscow. In 1973 Prime Minister Tanaka Kakuei traveled to Moscow and attempted to entice the Soviets into signing a peace treaty by offering economic aid and help developing gas and oil reserves in Siberia. The Soviets did not oblige, but Moscow did finally acknowledge in the joint communiqué that a bilateral peace treaty would have to follow "resolution of unresolved issues" between the two countries.[8] Meanwhile, the Japan Export/Import Bank (now the Japan Bank for International Cooperation, JBIC) signed a series of agreements to finance the first Sakhalin oil and gas development projects with the Soviets in 1974. In spite of the unresolved strategic issues, MITI and Japanese trading companies were eager to establish a toehold in Sakhalin and Irkutsk, particularly after the oil shock of 1973. However, the Sakhalin projects produced more frustration than gas for Japan over the next two decades, as the Soviet side failed to approve development or to repay the initial loans.[9]

Tanaka's efforts in the early 1970s to improve Russo-Japanese relations were very much against the overall tide of domestic Japanese politics and international relations in the Cold War. The Soviet occupation of the Northern Territories provided a unifying theme for the LDP's anticommunism and was particularly important to LDP politicians battling for elections in the economically underdeveloped Hokkaidō and Tōhoku regions of northern Japan. The Soviet invasion of Afghanistan in 1979 further soured the Japanese public's view of Moscow, in addition to presenting a clear and present threat as the Soviets deployed Backfire bombers in the Far East, ballistic missile submarines in the Sea of Okhotsk, and new MiGs and ground forces on the Northern Territories. The expanded Soviet threat provided the basis for MOFA, JDA, and their allies in the LDP to push through defense budget increases that averaged 6 percent in the 1980s, as well deepening U.S.-Japan defense ties. Advocates of a more activist Japanese security policy had leveraged the Soviet threat to make great gains in this period—and rightly so, given the Soviets' behavior.[10] But these same officials and politicians were loath to drop the Soviet threat after the Cold War ended. The Japanese government argued that the Russian threat, like the Russian occupation of the Northern Territories, transcended the end of bipolar ideological competition and the collapse of the Soviet Union.

However, as Mikhail Gorbachev opened a new chapter in relations with the West through the peaceful unification of Germany in 1989, and then as Boris Yeltsin came on the scene in 1991 as the leader of a newly democratic Russian Federation, Japan increasingly found itself isolated in its hard-line policy toward Moscow. Gorbachev tried to set a new tone with Tokyo by returning to the original 1956 offer to return two of the islands. The last Soviet leader also sweetened the pot by acknowledging at a summit in Tokyo in April 1991 that, in principle, all four islands should be part of discussions for a permanent peace treaty. Japan, under Western pressure, particularly from Germany, and ready to test Gorbachev's intentions on the territorial issue, responded with 1 billion yen in December 1990 as "emergency humanitarian" grant aid. Japan also decided to provide aid totaling $2.5 billion in October 1991, including a $500 million loan for food and medical supplies and their transport.[11] On the whole, however, Tokyo remained skeptical about Gorbachev and perestroika.

After Yeltsin came to power in 1991, Japan's reticent policy toward Moscow came under further pressure from the Western camp. At the 1992 G-7 summit, the major Western powers agreed to provide $24 billion in aid to Russia, despite Japanese efforts to scale down the package. Under European pressure to increase its own economic assistance to the Newly Independent States, Japanese Foreign Minister Watanabe Michio attempted in a visit to Moscow in early 1992 to leverage economic assistance for the return of the Northern Territories on a "flexible" timetable, but Yeltsin complained about this naked use of economic pressure and rejected the Japanese overture.[12]

Nonetheless, by this time it was apparent to officials in Tokyo that Japan needed to adjust its Russia policy in order to avoid even greater isolation from the other G-7 members. The rapid decoupling of former Soviet client states that occurred in the early Yeltsin years appeared to offer some promise that a new approach to Moscow might yield compromises on the Northern Territories. Indeed, Yeltsin himself sent a letter to Prime Minister Miyazawa in February 1992 in which he referred to Japan as a "potential alliance partner," and in May 1992 the Russian president claimed that he wanted to sign a peace treaty with Japan during 1993.[13] Sensitive to both Washington's warming relationship with Yeltsin and the potential opening to strike a new deal on the Northern Territories, in 1992 Tokyo began delinking economic aid from political discussions with Moscow and stopped pressing for references to the Northern Territories in the G-7 communiqués after the Munich summit.

These steps set the scene for a historic state visit by Yeltsin to Tokyo in October 1993, where the Russian president and Prime Minister Hosokawa agreed in the Tokyo Declaration that the territorial issue should be resolved based on: "1) historical and legal facts; 2) a joint agreement signed by both countries; and 3) the principles of law and justice."[14] Tokyo followed that declaration with a $5 billion proposal for economic assistance that would focus on energy and environmental development in the Russian Far East.[15] Moscow responded by agreeing with a Japanese-led multinational consortium on the exploration and development of the Sakhalin I Gas and Oil project in November 1993, and then signed a contract with a U.S and Japanese consortium for development of a second oil and gas site at Sakhalin II.[16]

Ultimately, however, the Tokyo Declaration failed to produce enough momentum for a resolution of the Northern Territories issue. Part of the blame lay with the Japanese government, which refused to yield on its basic political demand that Russia return all of the Northern Territories. In addition, there was little push from the Japanese business community, which remained skeptical that the domestic investment environment in Russia would improve any time soon, or from conservatives in the LDP, who still clung to the Russian threat to explain defense policy and motivate nationalist support on the right. Russia also was to blame. Finally, before making a trip in October 1993, Yeltsin had canceled his visit to Tokyo several times. The cancellations offended the Japanese hosts and raised questions about the Russian commitment to improved relations. Yeltsin's ability to deliver on his promises was also in doubt, given the growing challenges to his authority on territorial issues in the Russian Duma after nationalist forces ascended in December 1993 elections.[17] In addition, German unification had an impact on Japan-Russia territorial negotiation. After unification, which gave the final stroke on Gorbachev's political leadership, territorial concessions to foreign powers were deemed as an act of betrayal in Russian politics.[18] When Foreign Minister Hata visited Moscow in March 1993, he found it difficult to extract any reaffirmation of the Tokyo Declaration. For the next few years after that, Japan-Russia relations returned to stalemate—until the geostrategic plates of Eurasian international relations shifted once again.[19]

A New Russia Policy

The Shift

The Japanese rethinking about the strategic importance of ties to Russia in Northeast Asia was sparked by developments in another region: Eastern Europe. With the expansion of the North Atlantic Treaty Organization (NATO) in 1997, the other G-7 countries determined that Russia should be handed concessions in other areas. Specifically, they wanted Moscow invited to the G-7 summits. On the eve of the March 21 Clinton-Yeltsin Helsinki summit, Clinton telephoned Hashimoto to ask for Japan's "understanding" of an expansion of the G-7 to include Russia. The president explained that it was in the mutual interests of the United States and Japan to integrate Russia in the world economy and to avoid a Russian backlash against NATO expansion. Japan's modus operandi on Russia once again came under external pressure.

As the most hawkish prime minister since Nakasone, Hashimoto might have been expected to bridle at Clinton's plans for including Russia in the G-7. Certainly on trade and other issues Hashimoto had developed a reputation for standing up to U.S. pressure. Moreover, as a former national leader of Izokukai, the World War II veterans' association, Hashimoto was well aware of the continued antagonism toward Russia in the Right wing of the political spectrum. However, Clinton's call also catalyzed quiet rethinking of Russia policy already under way in MOFA, MITI, and the Prime Minister's Office itself. As MITI minister in the Murayama cabinet (June 1994 to January 1996), Hashimoto had overseen the creation of a plan for expanding Japanese trade and investment with Russia in large part to balance the Japanese business community's rush to invest in China in the early 1990s.[20]

Hashimoto was also looking for a bold new diplomatic initiative to mark his tenure as prime minister. Precisely because he could speak to the Right wing, he seized on the potential for a breakthrough on the Northern Territories. Animated by the chance to reclaim the islands, key conservative actors such as Suetsugu Ichirō, a representative of the Council on National Security Affairs (Anzen Hoshō Mondai Kenkyūkai) and a chairman of Steering Committee of Japan-Russia Friendship Forum 21, lined up in favor of a new approach to Russia.[21] In some ways, this new euphoria for a deal may have been as unrealistic as the Right's earlier intransigence on the Northern Territories—but that only became apparent later. The main point in the spring of 1997 was that Japanese domestic politics seemed particularly well configured for a bold move on Russia policy and the Northern Territories with Hashimoto in the lead.[22]

The prime minister's response to Clinton was therefore positive. He told the president that Japan did not want Moscow included in economic consultations at the summit, but he agreed that Russian participation in the political discussions would be a positive step.[23] After the call, Hashimoto pressed the bureaucracy to come up with a new formula for Russia policy that balanced Japanese concerns on the Northern Territories with the geostrategic considerations he had discussed with Clinton and had been considering himself for some time.

MITI was an eager accomplice, and MOFA, despite its traditional hard line on Russia, also came around. The announcement of a Sino-Russian Strategic Partnership by Jiang Zemin and Yeltsin only weeks after the U.S.-Japan Joint Security Declaration in April 1996 had caused veteran Russia hands in MOFA to reconsider Russia policy in new geostrategic terms. As Professor Hasegawa Tsuyoshi argued at the time:

The quickness with which Russia and China have forged a "strategic partnership" makes Japan nervous. The volatile situation in North Korea, the most serious security threat to Japan, requires cooperation with Russia. It has finally dawned on the Japanese political leadership and Gaimushō officials that continuing stalemate in Russo-Japanese relations would not be in the best interests of the country.[24]

Prime Minister Hashimoto also focused on this geostrategic factor in an interview with Funabashi Yoichi in July 1998, saying:

> Japan may lose if we play the same game as China: the realpolitik game. China has been very skillful at this game since the days of the Three Dynasties Rivalry. Japan should not attempt to play such a dangerous game in the present context of Japan-U.S.-China trilateral relationship. Japan needs to transform this trilateral game into quadrennial one by bringing Russia in the game. Russia is certainly an important partner for Japan.[25]

Small tests of the political and security relationship with Russia in 1996 had also gone well. On April 29, 1996, Usui Hideo signed a series of confidence-building measures with Russian Defense Minister Grachev in the historic first visit of a JDA director general to Russia.[26] The first of these confidence-building measures, a port visit to Vladivostok by three MSDF vessels in July,[27] received positive press inside Japan, including an endorsement of warmer ties with Moscow by the conservative editorial pages of the *Sankei Shimbun*.[28] The political environment in Russia improved as well, after Yeltsin won reelection in June and promised to return to the progress hoped for in the 1993 Tokyo Declaration.[29] And Yeltsin's granting of sovereignty over the Crimea to Ukraine suggested that the reelected Russian president might have the power also to manage politically charged territorial issues in the Far East.[30]

By the time Clinton telephoned Hashimoto in March 1997, therefore, MOFA and MITI were separately converging on the idea of improving relations with Moscow already. In that sense, the loss of G-7 support for Japan's position on the Northern Territories was less of a shock than a nudge in a new direction that key figures in the Japanese bureaucracy had already largely accepted. In May 1997 Tokyo formally dropped its objection to Russian participation in a G-7 meeting, though continuing to insist that Russia be excluded from discussions on exchange rates, financial markets, and other macroeconomic issues.[31] When Russian Defense Minister Igor Rodionov visited Tokyo the same month, he gave clear signals that Tokyo's move would have geostrategic dividends, noting—in contrast to the theme of the April

1996 Sino-Russian Strategic Partnership statement—that "the U.S.-Japan Alliance is essential to the security of Asia."[32]

At the Denver summit in June 1997, Hashimoto took further steps to signal a new approach to Russia. In a side meeting with Yeltsin at the summit, he promised to hold annual meetings with the Russian leader. Yeltsin, in turn, endorsed Japan's permanent membership in the UN Security Council (without being specific on the terms). The two also discussed an expansion of Japanese economic investment in the Russian Far East, including possible Japanese participation in the major gas project at Irkutsk.

Despite this progress, however, Hashimoto's new approach to Russia was not winning his government the credit he expected, either in Japan or on the world stage. MOFA officials were particularly irked that in Hashimoto's bilateral session with Clinton at Denver, the U.S. president again pressed Japan to improve relations with Russia—something Japan had just done. A U.S. offer to mediate in the Northern Territories dispute was even more disconcerting, since it suggested Japan was incapable of managing its own interests with Moscow. Clearly, Japan's new policy was not sufficiently understood or appreciated.[33]

Hashimoto again turned to the bureaucracy to come up with a clear statement on Russia policy—this time in the form of a major policy speech. MITI officials under Isayama Takeshi, the deputy director general of the International Trade Policy Bureau, pushed for an emphasis on the energy connections between Japan and Russia, but MOFA modified the speech to put these connections in a geostrategic context.[34] As MOFA's senior Russia hand, Tamba Minoru, put it, "some explained Japan's effort to move closer to Russia based on economic factors relating to oil and natural gas, but if you ask me, that is only one factor. In my mind was a geostrategic approach."[35] Ultimately, neither bureaucracy expected energy to drive relations with Russia without a strategic rationale behind it. When the prime minister delivered the speech before the Keizai Dōyūkai on July 22, 1997, the centerpiece of his speech was Mackinder's geostrategic concept of Eurasianism. Henceforth, the prime minister declared, Japan would steer a "new course" with Russia based on the three principles of "trust, mutual benefit, and a long-term perspective."[36]

A Peace Treaty by 2000!

From that point, the Russo-Japanese bilateral relationship made rapid improvements. Yeltsin and Hashimoto met in Krasnoyarsk, Siberia, in

November 1997, after which MOFA officials made the stunning announcement that they intended to complete a new peace treaty by the year 2000. At the "no-necktie summit," the two leaders also announced a six-point Hashimoto-Yeltsin Plan to help the Russian economy. Tokyo also officially endorsed Russian membership in APEC. The next month Moscow and Tokyo suddenly resolved long-standing and contentious negotiations over fisheries, and in February of 1998 Foreign Minister Obuchi promised $1.5 billion in loans to Russia.[37]

Hashimoto's visit to Krasnoyarsk was followed by Yeltsin's visit to Kawana, Japan, in April 1998. At Kawana Hashimoto proposed an international border demarcation that would give Japan sovereignty of the four islands while Russia retained some form of administrative control and economic assistance from Japan.[38] Yeltsin countered with a proposal for tax incentives and other measures to encourage joint investment in the territories before resolution of the sovereignty issue. The two leaders concluded with a confirmation that they would make their best efforts to conclude a peace treaty by the year 2000.[39]

In the end, little was actually resolved at the Kawana meeting in terms of the Northern Territories problem. This should have been a sign that momentum would soon run out of the Russo-Japanese new relationship. Nevertheless, the Japanese side clearly relished its new Russia card. As a MOFA official observed after the summit in Kawana, "this [engagement policy] will have an extremely good impact on Japan's diplomacy toward China. Even if the Krasnoyarsk agreement leads to no peace treaty with Russia, it will still work as a plus for Japan's diplomacy." A *Tokyo Shimbun* editorial put it this way after the Kawana summit: "with China in the middle of the new U.S.-Japan-China-Russia quadrilateral international system, the Japan-Russia movement will be a plus in Japan's diplomacy toward China."[40] The same editorial noted that Russia diplomacy would pay off in Japan's bid for a UN Security Council seat and in other areas where Tokyo was trying to raise its diplomatic profile and China was an obstacle.[41] The potential security dimension of Japan's closer ties to Russia were further symbolized in pilot training conducted by the JSDF and Russian forces in February-March 1998,[42] and joint search and rescue in July 1998.[43] From the military threat that gave political momentum to the JSDF in the 1980s, Russia was now the partner that added political legitimacy to a regional security presence for Japan after the Cold War. In addition, the meeting at Kawana did lead to a new agreement on fisheries, Japanese support for Russian membership in APEC, an investment protection treaty, and a $1.5 billion JEXIM credit in partnership with the World Bank.[44]

Lost Momentum and Prospects for Future Relations

Of course, the Russia card is only as good as the progress in the Russo-Japanese relationship itself. By 1998 it was becoming evident that the enthusiasm of Krasnoyarsk and Kawana was unsustainable and that the goal of completing a peace treaty by the end of 2000 was unrealistic. Prime Minister Obuchi tried to keep up the appearance of continued progress during his November 1998 visit to Moscow, but his trip was reduced to a short ninety-minute meeting from which the two leaders issued the Moscow Declaration and agreed to establish two subcommittees: one on border demarcation and the other to study the possibility of conducting joint economic activities in the disputed area without prejudicing either side's legal claims. Meanwhile in the Duma, Yeltsin was coming under increasing criticism from Communists and nationalists, while polls showed over 70 percent of the Russian public opposed the return of the Northern Territories.[45] Popular support for improved relations was also a problem in Japan as well. An Asahi-Itar Tass poll taken on the eve of Obuchi's trip to Moscow showed that only 4 percent of the Japanese public had positive feelings about Russia, a sign that popular sentiment had not tracked with the changing strategy of the Japanese government.[46]

Japan tried to test Russian interest in a proposal for recognition of ultimate Japanese sovereignty of the Northern Territories in exchange for immediate economic joint development of the islands, but Moscow was evasive. Finally, in December 1998, the Russian ambassador to Tokyo confessed that his government did not expect to achieve a treaty until well after the 2000 deadline.[47] As Yeltsin's position weakened inside Russia, the prospects for resolution of the territorial and peace treaty issues dimmed.

Nor has the post-Yeltsin era offered new promise of a peace treaty. While as prime minister Vladmir Putin endorsed the idea of a peace treaty with Japan, he did little to move beyond Yeltsin's formula after assuming the presidency on December 31, 1999, when Yeltsin resigned. Worse, from Tokyo's perspective, Russia's growing strategic cooperation with China has redoubled in response to the Kosovo campaign in the spring of 1999, the U.S. move to develop National Missile Defense, and Russia's diplomatic isolation after the 1999 assault on Chechnya. Russian sales of Su–27 fighters, Mi–17 helicopters, anti-air and ship-to-ship missiles, and naval vessels (including Kilo-class submarines and the Sovremenny class destroyers, with their Sunburn cruise missiles)[48] have had a direct impact on Japanese security, while Beijing's common cause with

Moscow in criticizing missile defense has complicated Tokyo's own plans for TMD cooperation with the United States.[49] Concerned about the loss of its Russia card, Tokyo defied the other G-7 nations in 1999 by releasing a $375 million aid package to Russia—the only loans by the outside world after Russia's attacks on Chechnya and revelations that billions of dollars of IMF stabilization funds had been embezzled by Moscow oligarchs. Ironically, Japan again stood as the holdout in the G-7 on Russia policy—only this time as the one nation extending assistance.

In August 2000 MOFA officials finally conceded to the press that a peace treaty would be impossible by the end of 2000. Instead, Japan agreed to consider Putin's proposal at his July 23 summit with Mori for an "interim friendship pact" aimed at promoting bilateral ties until a formal resolution of the territorial issue permits a peace treaty.[50]

Prospects for Future Relations

Will Japan-Russia relations now return to the confrontation of the past? Probably not. In spite of growing complications in Russia's domestic politics, Japan is likely to continue pressing for improved relations with Russia, and Russia will likely reciprocate to some extent, for as Princeton's Gilbert Rozman explains, the two countries now need each other:

> Japan and Russia are great powers with unbalanced standing in the world order and an unfulfilled quest to return to "normalcy." They have shared the experience of fallen powers and are now searching for international support to boost their standing. The two countries matter for each other in at least three ways: 1) as symbols to each other of arrogance and lack of respect for legitimate great power aspirations; 2) as complementary economies with potential to contribute to both regional and national long-term needs; and 3) as parallel cases in some respects and contrasting cases in others in the struggle to adjust national ambitions and domestic capacities to suit the new world order that is taking shape.[51]

For his part, the Foreign Ministry's Tamba argues: "Our message to Yeltsin and the Russian people had a different meaning from the message we wanted to send to the Japanese people; it was 'Russia! Please join Japan in playing a more assertive role in the Asia Pacific Region.'"[52]

The Energy Connection

The change in Russia policy simply would not have occurred without a shift in the geostrategic thinking of people like Hashimoto and

Tamba. However, the initial impulse for improving relations did come in large part from MITI, based on long-term energy considerations. While the prospects for joint energy development between Japan and Russia are in some ways even more complicated than the prospects for settlement of the territorial issue, the matching of Japanese energy requirements and Russian energy resources could provide the glue needed to strengthen Japan's new Russia policy over the long haul.

For Japan, energy and geostrategy are closely linked, of course. After the experiences of the 1973 and 1979 oil shocks, a broad consensus emerged in Japan that vulnerability to oil supply shocks must be reduced as a matter of "comprehensive security." In April 1993 an influential MITI-affiliated report entitled "Energy Security and Environmental Problems" outlined a four-part strategy that anticipated the ministry's growing interest in improving relations with Russia. The report recommended that Japan:

1. Diversify and maintain friendly relations with energy suppliers
2. Establish independent energy development projects
3. Reduce reliance on oil and increase efficiency
4. Take measures to help prevent environmental disasters.[53]

In terms of diversifying and maintaining friendly relations with energy suppliers, Russia was a natural choice for MITI. MITI officials estimated in 1994 that Russia could meet up to 30 percent of liquid natural gas (LNG) and 5 percent of Japan's oil needs.[54] This same logic was behind MITI's 1994 plan for improving investment and trade with Russia.

However, Japanese industry has remained far more skeptical about the prospects for investment and energy development in Russia than MITI. Even as Yeltsin and Hashimoto were putting ink to their plan for economic cooperation in Krasnoyarsk in 1997, Japan-Russia trade had fallen to one-half of its 1989 "Cold War" level.[55] Past Japanese business experience in Russia has generally not been positive. In the 1970s, during the brief flowering of positive relations under Tanaka and détente, Japan invested $160 million for oil and gas exploration in Sakhalin. The money simply disappeared. Japanese industry groups, including the Keidanren-sponsored Japan-Russia Economic Council, complain of numerous obstacles to investment, including criminality, corruption, detrimental legal and tax structures, and uncertain power struggles between the Maritime Provinces and Moscow.[56] A survey by the Japan External Trade Organization (JETRO) found that in 1996, Japan did not have a single investment in Siberia larger than $1 million, while

U.S., Australian, Korean and Western European firms had doubled their investment in the Russian Far East from the 1995 level.[57] Russian Prime Minister Sergei V. Kirienko signed a series of investment insurance and joint venture agreements with the Japanese government in July 1998, which sparked interest among several Japanese trading companies in building hotels and restaurants in Russia, but as one official from Mitsubishi Corporation warned Kirienko, investment in larger-scale manufacturing in Russia "will take more time."[58]

Japanese diplomat Harada Chikahito was even more to the point in a 1997 International Institute for Strategic Studies (IISS) monograph about Russia:

> There are many obstacles to foreign direct investment. Russia has not yet developed a coherent legal framework with transparent rules for domestic and foreign investment or joint ventures. Duties levied against importers have been regularly increased leading to rampant corruption, custom rules are applied inconsistently. The Russian *mafya's* control of business, difficulties in obtaining accurate business information, and poor transport and other infrastructure are also powerful obstacles to investment.[59]

Oil and Gas Investment

These obstacles notwithstanding, Japanese corporations have invested in two oil and gas projects in the Russian Far East and are exploring three more:[60]

- Sakhalin One. This project for an estimated 2.5 billion barrels of oil and 421 billion cubic meters of gas was agreed upon in 1993 by SODECO (Sakhalin Oil and Gas Development Co., Ltd., Japan) (30 percent), EXXON (30 percent), and a Russian consortium (40 percent). The estimated cost is $15 billion. Based on a general agreement in 1975 with MITI.
- Sakhalin Two. This project for an estimated 1 billion barrels of oil and 392 billion cubic meters of gas was agreed upon in 1994 by the MMMSM Consortium (McDermott, Marathon, Mitsui, Shell, Mitsubishi) (20 percent), Shell Sakhalin Holdings (20 percent), Diamond Gas Sakhalin (owned by Mitsubishi—20 percent), and Russian Petroleum (50 percent). The estimated development cost is $6 to $10 billion. Based on a general agreement in 1991, to begin in 2003.

- The Irkutsk pipeline. Japan National Oil Corporation and ten Japanese utilities and trading companies agreed to do a feasibility study on the $10 billion Irkutsk-to-Beijing natural gas pipeline in October 1997, after Moscow and Beijing signed an agreement in June to develop the fields without Japan. The Irkutsk pipeline faces massive technical and political hurdles (including the possible routing of the pipeline through North Korea), but Tokyo could not afford to stay out of the project for strategic and longer-term energy reasons.
- Sakhalin Three and Four. Initial discussions have also begun on third and fourth reserve fields located in Sakhalin.

It is not certain how far these joint energy projects will progress. The projects with the greatest potential and existing commitment are Sakhalin One and Two. Each was expected to begin delivering gas to Japan by the year 2005. However, the main consumers, Japan's utility companies, claimed in March 1999 that they had sufficient contracts for natural gas through 2010 due to the Japanese recession and low oil prices.[61] Meanwhile, the utilities estimate that Japan might not need any of the 25 billion cubic meters of gas to be pumped from the Irkutsk pipeline until after the year 2020.[62]

Even with uncertain Japanese demand for Russia's LNG and oil, however, the Japanese government—and MITI in particular—will continue pressing industry to remain involved in the development of Sakhalin and Irkutsk's oil and gas fields. For one thing, longer-term energy strategy dictates that Japan wean itself from its high reliance on the Gulf for oil imports. Maintaining investment in Sakhalin and a foothold in Irkutsk secures an additional energy source for Japan, should market conditions or political stability in the Gulf shift. In addition, Japan has a clear interest in helping China meet its own growing energy requirements. The alternatives to Chinese imports of Russian oil and gas would be increased Chinese reliance on coal or nuclear energy, both of which threaten Japan's environment, or increased Chinese reliance on Middle East and Gulf oil, which might tempt Beijing to develop naval power projection into Japan's vital sea lines of communication. Finally, Japan has an interest in encouraging multilateral development of Irkutsk in order to reinforce economic cooperation in the region with itself as a central player.

In short, the energy and geostrategic considerations behind Japan's Eurasia diplomacy are inseparable. This is not simply because Japan's strategy is to secure its energy from Russia, but also—and perhaps more important—because energy development in Russia is a tool for Japan to reinforce regional cooperation and stability and its own diplomatic weight.

Proliferation and Environmental Concerns

One final factor must be added to the energy component of Japan's comprehensive approach to Russia, and that is the environmental and proliferation threat presented by Russia's aging civilian nuclear power plants and military nuclear weapons. As early as 1990 MITI and Japanese trading companies expressed interest in working with Moscow to improve nuclear safety and to help with the dismantling of nuclear weapons. Washington discouraged the latter, but the Japanese government did provide aid in 1993 for nuclear safety training to Russia after the Russian navy dumped radioactive nuclear waste in the Sea of Japan.[63] Supporters of Japan's controversial plutonium recycling program also focused on Russia as a target of assistance for clean and safe fast-breeder reactor development—and as a potential source of legitimacy for Japan's own besieged program.[64]

Cooperation in this area was limited until the rest of Japan's Russia policy began to turn around in 1997. U.S. concerns about Japanese involvement in Russian nuclear weapons–related programs also diminished somewhat in comparison with larger concerns about Russian "loose nukes." In May 1999 the Japan Nuclear Cycle Development Institute and the Russian Research Institute for Atomic Reactors agreed to a five-year pact to work together on developing ways to convert plutonium from dismantled warheads into nuclear reactor fuel.[65] The Science & Technology Agency (STA) began funding Russian experiments with conversion and use in civilian reactors of plutonium extracted from nuclear warheads. Japan burned about 44 pounds of MOX (mixed oxide fuels) from Russian warheads in Russian reactors in March 2000, a figure that will rise to 1.3 tons a year by 2010.[66] This combination of Japanese energy development and nonproliferation policy adds credibility to Japan's beleaguered plutonium recycling scheme and leverages Japanese technological strengths to national security purposes.

The Great Game in Central Asia

With this merging of energy, nonproliferation, and geostrategic thinking, Japan's eyes have traveled beyond Russia proper to Central Asia and the Caucasus. In his July 1997 speech, Hashimoto announced Japan's intention to play a more assertive role across this region: "Positive assistance by Japan for the nation-building efforts of these countries will most certainly have a constructive significance, not only for these newly independent states, but also for the peace and prosperity of Russia, China, and the Islamic states, and I am certain that it will expand the frontier of Japanese foreign policy to the Eurasian region at the dawn of the 21st Century."[67]

In his speech, Hashimoto conjured the images of the "Silk Road" that linked China and Imperial Rome through the Caucasus and Central Asia. It was a wise choice. *The Silk Road* was an extremely popular television documentary series in Japan in the late 1980s and the Japanese media quickly identified with the romance of this "new frontier" for Japan's foreign policy. If Hashimoto's declaration of Japan's participation in the "Great Game" of Central Asian diplomacy was largely romantic, however, it was also rooted in the same energy and geostrategic calculations that led to the shift in relations with Moscow.

Estimates about the size of the Caspian oil reserves vary widely, but most in MITI/METI and MOFA have latched on to the U.S. Department of Energy estimate that 179 billion barrels of oil, or 10 percent of world reserves, lie in Central Asia.[68] Hashimoto ended his Eurasia diplomacy speech with a call for Japanese business to take advantage of these oil and gas resources in the Caucasus and Central Asia. Japanese investment in the region's energy resources began in a modest way in 1992, the year after Armenia, Azerbaijan, Georgia, Kazakhstan, Kyrgyszstan, Tajikistan, Turkmenistan, and Uzbekistan became independent countries. Still, Japan's total imports from this entire region totaled only $235 million in 1997, a figure smaller than its imports from North Korea.[69] Investment picked up in April 1996 when the Itōchū Corporation took a 3.9 percent share in a consortium and later a 20 percent share in two oil projects in Azerbaijan. Sumitomo followed in October 1996 by joining Mobil in a project to develop the Tulpar fields in Kazakhstan. Later Mitsui Trading Company took a 15 percent share in the Kurdasi project in Azerbaijan. In 1998 Marubeni and Mitsubishi joined the rush, signing four contracts with Kazakhstan.[70]

Despite these "down payments" on future energy development, however, Japan and other nations face massive political, financial, and technical challenges in transporting gas and oil from the remote Central Asian and Caucasus regions to markets in Western Europe and Asia. There are four pipeline proposals, only one of which—the Baku-Ceyhan Main Export Pipeline—does not run through Iran or Russia. For strategic reasons, the Clinton administration threw its weight behind the Baku-Ceyhan pipeline in 1997. Japanese industry remains hopeful that the cheaper pipeline through Iran might become a political reality someday, but Tokyo has maintained neutrality on the pipeline choice, arguing only that it should be made based on economic principles.[71] Many would argue that those very economic principles may prevent the costly trans-Caucasus pipelines from ever being built.[72] In the meantime, the investments in the region's energy resources remain place savers that keep Japan abreast of China's aggressive energy diplomacy in the region and keep open Japanese options for participation in future projects.

Japan's foray into Central Asia and the Caucasus also parallels the geostrategic and diplomatic objectives of the new approach to Russia. As an analytical piece in *Sankei Shimbun* argued in February 1998, Japan's diplomatic and economic engagement of Central Asia and the Caucasus strengthens Japan's diplomacy vis-à-vis both Moscow and Beijing by making Japan a positive economic player in their own backyards.[73] This comprehensive strategic approach to engaging the region was articulated in a "Silk Road Action Plan" prepared by MITI, MOFA, and MOF at Hashimoto's direction and released on March 7, 1998. The action plan consisted of three pillars: "strengthening political dialogues, assisting with economic and natural resource development, and cooperation in facilitating nuclear nonproliferation, democratization, and stabilization for peace."[74] As part of the security pillar, in March 1999 MOFA hosted a conference on comprehensive strategy in Tokyo for representatives from the region as well as Turkey, China, Russia, and the United States.[75] Diplomatic connections were also energized by the first of what would be regular head-of-state visits to Japan by Presidents Heydar Aliyev of Azerbaijan in February 1998 and Eduard Sheverdnadze of Georgia in March 1999. Both leaders went home with considerable packages of aid and joint venture deals bringing greater focus on Japan's diplomacy in the region.[76] Japan has spread this largesse to other countries through investments in a "New Silk Road" project to link Central Asia and the Caucasus with transport and communications networks. In the long run, the Central Asia card may not provide much energy to Japan, but it does empower Tokyo to explore a larger diplomatic role in an area of crucial strategic significance to its powerful neighbors on the Eurasian landmass.

Conclusion: Japan's New Eurasia Diplomacy and the U.S.-Japan Alliance

The shifting terms of Japan's relationship with Russia through the first decade of the post–Cold War era echo patterns we saw in Japan's changing interaction with China and the Korean Peninsula. Indeed, the first conclusion one can draw from the emergence of Japan's new Eurasia diplomacy is that geostrategic considerations were the dominant factor in Japanese thinking. Certainly Japan's increasing isolation from the rest of the G–7 created pressure for a new approach to Russia and undermined Tokyo's traditional source of leverage in dealing with Moscow on the Northern Territories problem. But that *gaiatsu* does not explain the enthusiasm and deliberateness with which Hashimoto and his fellow travelers in MOFA and MITI embarked on their new Eurasia policy. Clearly they were motivated by concerns about balancing China and preventing a Sino-Russian alignment at Japan's expense.

Ideational factors interacted with these power considerations. Japan and Russia share a sense of uncertainty about their future roles in East Asia. Japan's situation clearly is not as desperate as Russia's, but both nations craved a position of influence and respect in East Asia that was denied them by the diplomacy of the Four Party talks on Korea and the rise of Chinese influence, particularly on the American diplomatic radar. The "boldness" of Japan's new approach to Russia marked Japan as a geostrategic player—a "normal" country capable of playing the "Great Game" alongside other major powers—even in the heart of the Eurasia landmass itself. Notably, it was Tokyo that initiated the new relationship—a contrast to 1956 and 1973, when Tokyo waited for Moscow to make the first move. At the same time, it must be noted that the ideational side of Japan's Russia policy also made it quite dysfunctional and ultimately less than successful. The Hashimoto government's euphoria for the Russia card and a clear resolution of the Northern Territories dispute led to unrealistic expectations, overinterpretation of minor Russian gestures, and bold pronouncements and deadlines that could not be met.

Of course, Hashimoto's bold move on Russia would not have been possible without the right domestic political constellation. Changes in domestic Japanese politics favored an improved relationship with Russia just as they led to increased friction with China. Hashimoto, the most Right-oriented leader Japan had seen since Nakasone had the domestic credibility to propose a closer relationship with Moscow. For nationalists within Japan, the increasing focus on anti–Chinese sentiment caused by episodes like the Senkaku dispute also eased the domestic pressure on Russia. It helped that from Russia there was little finger-pointing over history. Indeed, the Russian Duma stopped celebrating Victory Over Japan Day in 1999. The business community was also supportive, if not enthusiastic. There was long-term interest in investing in Russian energy resources, but the primary obstacles to that investment were related to domestic Russian political problems rather than the state of diplomatic ties between the two countries. Still, improved political relations certainly did not hurt from the perspective of business, and this left plenty of room for MITI to push the rest of the government to change its thinking about Russia. In the end, this mix of domestic interests gave Hashimoto enough flexibility to push a new approach. However, it was not enough to allow a compromise on Japan's basic demand for a return of all four islands. Editorials in the conservative *Sankei* and *Yomiuri* newspapers during the Krasnoyarsk and Kawana summits made this demand clear, even as they endorsed a more strategic approach to Russia. Moreover, the domestic political constellation of elite interest has not translated into depth of popular support for ties with Russia, as opinion polls demonstrate.

In terms of the U.S.-Japan alliance, it is worth noting that Eurasia diplomacy solidified only after the reaffirmation of the U.S.-Japan alliance in April 1996. True, Hashimoto was also responding to Clinton's request for help during NATO expansion, but Japan needed the confidence that it could defend itself with American help before Hashimoto could move forward. In short, U.S. pressure on Japan to improve relations with Russia mattered, but only after geostrategic circumstances in the region led key Japanese policymakers to the independent conclusion that they needed a new Russian policy and only after the United States provided reassurance of its commitment to the alliance.

Given the stalled progress on the Russo-Japanese peace treaty negotiations, it may be tempting for U.S. officials to offer mediation. The United States should approach this role with great caution, however. When the United States offered to broker a deal between Tokyo and Moscow in June 1997, the reaction from both sides was negative. In Tokyo there is still a view that the Northern Territories problem could have been resolved decades ago without U.S. interference aimed at keeping Japan from moving too closely to the Soviets during the Cold War. In addition, Eurasia diplomacy is still the "new frontier" of Japanese independent diplomacy, and the United States would be trampling on important national aspirations by pressing too hard for a central role on the Northern Territories problem. It should be remembered that U.S.-Japan relations began to sour at the beginning of the twentieth century when Theodore Roosevelt brokered the first Russo-Japanese peace treaty at Portsmouth in 1905. The Japanese people rioted in Tokyo because they were outraged by concessions forced in Portsmouth even though Japan won the war with Russia. Japan also won the Cold War, and the United States should consider carefully the implications of once again pressing Tokyo to concede to Russia at the beginning of the twenty-first century. As Hasegawa persuasively argues, Moscow and Tokyo have the diplomatic acumen necessary to reach a peace treaty as two mature nations.[77] The United States can therefore be most helpful in a quiet, behind-the-scenes supporting role.

At the same time, Tokyo's new Eurasia diplomacy could form part of a much stronger U.S. policy toward Russia. The expanding Soviet threat of the late 1970s and early 1980s provided the glue for closer U.S.-Japan military cooperation in the Reagan years. It is possible for the United States and Japan to form a similarly close partnership in helping Russia to build democratic institutions, reform the domestic economy, and dismantle the disintegrating Soviet nuclear forces left from the Cold War. Together, the United States and Japan could also enhance Russia's sense of belonging to the emerging Asia-Pacific community. Japan's new relationship with Russia, despite its numerous problems and likely future setbacks, still remains a positive force on Russian behavior, a useful expression of Japan's diplomatic potential, and a helpful complement to the United States' own objectives for relations with Moscow. Stable Western relations with Russia require recognition of Russia's role as not only a European power, but also an Asian power—and that perspective will be enhanced by Japan's new Eurasian diplomacy.

CHAPTER SIX

Japan and Southeast Asia

Introduction

Southeast Asia has been an important testing ground for postwar Japanese foreign policy. It was in Southeast Asia that the United States first pressed Japan to emerge from defeat and isolation after the war by providing reparations to help buttress the region against the threat of communism. And in the post–Cold War era, it is Southeast Asia where Japan has made its most pronounced attempt to establish a different identity from U.S. foreign policy.

This chapter uses three case studies to examine Japanese "independent diplomacy" (*jishu gaikō*) in Southeast Asia in the 1990s. The case studies are the Cambodian peace process, relations with Burma, and the response to the crisis in East Timor. In Cambodia Japan bridled at exclusion from U.S.-led peace talks and asserted an independent diplomatic role, backing it up with both money and troops. In relations with Burma, Japan again demonstrated its independence by siding with ASEAN's policy of engagement over Washington's policy of isolation. But in East Timor, Japan was hobbled by domestic politics and cozy ties to Jakarta, and lost the diplomatic initiative to outside actors.

Taken together, these case studies demonstrate that Japan's diplomatic focus in Southeast Asia is shifting from Washington to ASEAN and that Japan's calculation of interests in the region is shifting from economic issues to broader strategic concerns. This includes participation in regional multilateral forums like the Asia-Pacific Economic Cooperation (APEC) meetings and the ASEAN Regional Forum (ARF), which will be explored in more detail in the next chapter. At the same time, however, the case studies reveal that Japan has still not developed a strategic role in Southeast Asia comparable to the United States or even China.

In the words of one diplomat from Singapore, "when it comes to key political or strategic decisions, we still consider Washington's position first and then Beijing's. Tokyo is a distant third, not much different from Canberra."[1]

Why the difficulty? First, as we shall see, the region is not yet ready for Japan to play an independent security role, particularly if it invites a reaction from China. Second, Japan's economic influence is limited by the fact that Tokyo is willing to use it only as a "carrot" and rarely as a "stick," since Japanese investment has created mutual vulnerabilities and dependence with the region. Third, despite a growing penchant for independent approaches to the diplomatic problems of Southeast Asia, Japan still relies on the United States as the final guarantor of stability in the region. And finally, ASEAN itself has begun to lose cohesion in the wake of the financial and domestic political crises of the late 1990s.

Nevertheless, the examples of Cambodia, Burma, and East Timor do suggest that Japan's relationship with Southeast Asia will continue to broaden beyond economics and that this relationship will be characterized by competition with China for strategic influence and competition with the United States for an independent identity. While this does not mean that U.S. and Japanese strategic objectives themselves are diverging, it does serve as a warning that U.S. policymakers will have to prepare for a more independent Japanese political role in Southeast Asia, but one that should be based on common strategic goals if not identical approaches.

Background: From Aid and Investment to "Comprehensive" Relations

Japan's diplomatic return to Southeast Asia after World War II began in the early 1950s, when the State Department urged reluctant officials in Tokyo to provide war reparations to the region to forestall Chinese Communist expansion. Five decades later Japanese officials were in Washington, urging the Clinton administration not to isolate the regimes in Burma and Cambodia over human rights issues, lest China expand its influence in the region.[2] For the most part, Japan's postwar relations with Southeast Asia have been dominated by economic interests, but Japanese diplomacy in Cambodia, Burma, and East Timor in the 1990s marked a deliberate attempt to establish "comprehensive" relations with ASEAN—that is, relations that include both economic and security dimensions. The road from reluctant payment of war reparations to the enthusiastic pursuit of strategic relations provides the setting for our three case studies.

Growing Economic Ties

From initial reparations payments of $1.5 billion between 1955 and 1977,[3] Japan's economic relations with Southeast Asia have grown to $2.4 billion in aid 1998,[4] $3.9 billion in investment 1998,[5] and $100.5 billion in trade 1999.[6] In addition, under the New Miyazawa Initiative announced on October 3, 1998, Japan agreed to provide another $12.5 billion to the Southeast Asian countries.[7] Well before talk of "comprehensive" relations, this economic dynamism defined Japan–Southeast Asian relations—and it was beneficial to both parties. At first, the nations of Southeast Asia provided gas, oil, timber and rubber to the Japanese economy as they had during the war. Then the rapid appreciation of the yen in 1985 coincided with a drop in commodity and oil prices that threatened the region's traditional exports. With the increase in Japanese FDI and aid brought on by yen appreciation, Thailand, Malaysia, and Indonesia began nurturing competitive manufacturing sectors. In 1985 manufactured exports exceeded agricultural exports in Thailand for the first time, and in Indonesia the export of manufactured goods caught up to oil and gas exports a few years later. In Malaysia, Japanese FDI accounted for 27 percent of all manufacturing by 1996.[8] (In 1997 this number fell to 18.86 percent.)

By the 1980s this close aid and investment relationship encouraged officials in Tokyo to start thinking about a more explicit economic leadership role in the region. In 1987 MITI released *The New Asian Industries Development Plan,* which proposed to coordinate private Japanese investment and ODA in the region. In 1988 Prime Minister Takeshita launched the ASEAN–Japan Development Fund.[9] In 1992 Prime Minister Miyazawa argued that Japan should lead an economic bloc in Asia that includes ASEAN and Korea to "outdo" North American or European blocs.[10] And as we will see in chapter 8, Japan claims to have provided over $80 billion to help Asia recover from the financial crisis that erupted in 1997, and tried, with mixed success, to establish an emergency monetary fund for the region.

Japan's domination of economic policy in Southeast Asia has often been overstated, however. Japanese economic planning and theories of "flying geese" notwithstanding, the Southeast Asian economies have varied significantly from the Japanese model. To begin with, none of that region's economies has put in place the array of nontariff barriers and obstacles to investment that Japan used to perpetuate growth (and that South Korea emulated). Moreover, while there are various forms of state intervention in the economies of Southeast Asia, only Singapore has established a bureaucracy with the autonomy and integrity that characterize Japan's MOF or MITI. Elsewhere state intervention is a negative factor, more notable for graft and crony capitalism than strategic guidance. Finally, as we will see in chapter 8, before the 1997 financial crisis the central bankers of ASEAN were pegging their currencies more to the dollar and deutsche mark and much less to the yen. Thus, with the exception of Malaysian leader Mohammed Mahathir's "Look East Policy"—which is largely a rhetorical tool against the West—most Southeast Asians see a Japanese-centered trading bloc as a remote possibility.

Nevertheless, Japan has built economic relationships with the nations of Southeast Asia that have clearly surpassed those nations' economic ties to their former colonial masters and that rival their economic ties to the United States. Much more difficult has been the establishment of a political and strategic relationship with the region.

Toward Political and Security Ties

Throughout the first two decades of the postwar period, Japan kept its political relations with Southeast Asia at a modest level. In 1974 Prime Minister Tanaka Kakuei traveled to the region to test the waters for broadening relations beyond economic exchange. His motorcade was stoned. In 1977 Prime Minister Fukuda Takeo made another attempt to broaden political relations on the tenth anniversary of the establishment of ASEAN. Rather than highlight Japan's ties to former subject territories, Fukuda focused on ASEAN and the theme of regional integration in Southeast Asia. He established the Japan-ASEAN Forum for economic dialogue and offered a $1.5 billion aid package so that there would be something positive to discuss. More important, perhaps, Fukuda took great pains to emphasize that Japan no longer had hegemonic aspirations for the region. His three-part Fukuda Doctrine reinforced this theme, pledging that: Japan would never become a military power or produce nuclear weapons; that Japan would promote "heart-to-heart" contacts with the nations of Southeast Asia; and Japan would endeavor to support ASEAN and improve relations with Vietnam to contribute to regional peace.[11]

Japan put this third pledge into action by normalizing relations with Vietnam in 1973 and offering a $36.5 million grant to Hanoi in 1976.

However, Japan's proactive engagement of Vietnam came to an abrupt halt with the invasion of Cambodia in December 1978.[12] It was not until Hanoi's decision to withdraw from Cambodia and begin participating in a peace process a decade later that Japan had another chance to demonstrate its potential leadership in the region. In the early post–Cold War era, however, the strategic environment in Southeast Asia was far more fluid. The Soviets' strategic presence was rapidly declining. China was reasserting influence in the South China Sea and Burma. U.S. strategic attention to the region ebbed and flowed with contradictions among human rights, trade, and security objectives. ASEAN was beginning to demonstrate unprecedented cohesion and assertiveness. And in Tokyo there was a growing consensus that after the Cold War, Japan's profile in the region should move beyond investment and aid.

Beginning with active participation in the Cambodian peace process and the dispatch of JSDF peacekeepers to Cambodia in the early 1990s, Tokyo focused on establishing what MOFA officials began calling "comprehensive" relations with the newly energized ASEAN. A veteran of the Asian Affairs Bureau of MOFA recalls that 1996 was a watershed year as officials focused on how to use ASEAN as a "balancer" in the increasingly complex "U.S.-Japan-China triangle."[13] Prime Minister Hashimoto also sought to build a more explicit strategic relationship with ASEAN. In January 1997 he traveled to the region to propose a broader relationship based on closer, regular consultation at the cabinet level with ASEAN; expanded cultural exchange; and cooperation on transnational and environmental security problems. Explaining the significance of the Hashimoto Initiative, MOFA's journal *Gaikō Forum* in November 1997 argued that it was high time for Japan and ASEAN to move toward a closer political-security relationship.[14]

ASEAN's response was cool, however. Wary of being caught in the growing diplomatic competition between Beijing and Tokyo, the leaders of Southeast Asia turned the Japanese proposal into a forum that also included China and South Korea. Though not exactly what Tokyo had in mind, Japan nevertheless joined the first official ASEAN Plus Three meeting in late 1997. Meanwhile, Japan expanded its dialogue on political and security issues in other directions, sending the JDA director general to Hanoi in 1997 and subsequently engaging in exchanges with ASEAN over the more benign concepts of "human security"[15] and "transnational threats."[16] Although Japan's focus on ASEAN was dealt a blow by Southeast Asia's loss of cohesion in the wake of financial and internal political crises in the late 1990s, there is now a strong consensus in Tokyo that economic ties are no longer sufficient and that Japan has a national interest in relations with the region that encompass political and security relations as well.

The proving ground for this broader relationship in the 1990s came in Cambodia, Burma, and East Timor.

Cambodia: Test Case for "Independent" Diplomacy

Japan's role in the Cambodian peace process in the 1990s has been hailed by senior MOFA officials as a "turning point in Japanese foreign policy," a change from "reactive to proactive diplomacy," and a first step toward "independent diplomacy."[17] In Cambodia, Japan took the initiative in international peace negotiations, sent not only money but also troops, and successfully defied the United States on key issues. In large measure, Japan's actions have been vindicated by the reestablishment of some stability in Cambodia. But if that country proved a success story for Japanese diplomacy, it was a mixed success, and one that was not easily repeated elsewhere in the region.

The Peace Conferences

Peace in Cambodia seemed a remote prospect after the Vietnamese invasion of December 1978. Decades of war, genocide, and invasion had created implacable hostility among the warring factions: Hun Sen's Vietnamese-backed government in Phnom Penh, the Chinese-backed Khmer Rouge, and the Western-backed factions of Prince Sihanouk and Son Sann. As the Cold War ended, however, the geostrategic competition that had started the Cambodian conflict gave way to a more benign environment for the warring factions to begin negotiating a peace. The first tentative encounters occurred on the outskirts of Paris in late 1987 between Sihanouk and Hun Sen and were followed by a series of informal meetings sponsored by Indonesia. Based on these first contacts, France and Indonesia called for a formal peace conference in the summer of 1989. The warring factions and their external supporters agreed to meet in Paris.

Japan, which had been left out of all previous international peace conferences on Indochina, was invited not only to participate, but also to co-chair with Australia the Third Committee of the talks, which covered refugees and economic reconstruction. Conscious of the unfulfilled promise of the Fukuda Doctrine, MOFA put its best people on the job. And to Japan's credit, while the rest of the peace talks languished, the Third Committee actually produced draft agreements among the negotiating parties and blueprints for the reconstruction of Cambodia. In a sea of frustration and animosity, it was about the only substantive progress made in Paris.

Without resolution of the fundamental security issues dividing the warring factions, however, the Paris talks could not move forward. The peace process therefore shifted to the UN Security Council, where U.S. Secretary of State James Baker was attempting to organize a resolution to the conflict backed by the P-5 members (the permanent members of the UNSC: the United States, Russia, China, Britain, and France). Baker was notorious for his dismissive view of Japanese diplomats and politicians as small thinkers, and his focus on the great powers left Japan out of the key deliberations. As former Japanese Ambassador to Cambodia Imagawa Yukio recalls, "MOFA was forced to sit outside in the hallway and ask the U.S. for information on the proceedings."[18]

For his part, then Assistant Secretary of State Richard Solomon acknowledged that "the Permanent Five was easy relative to the complex processes of maintaining support from other international multilateral parties—especially Japan and Thailand."[19] "The core issue behind Japan's second rank status in the diplomacy was not US resistance to Japan's playing a frontline role, but the fact that Japan was not a permanent member of the UN Security Council. We made assiduous efforts to bring our Japanese counterparts [in]. . . . [B]ut this consultative process was insufficient for governments with serious interests in the outcome of the process, especially, those facing considerable domestic political pressures to be significant players. . . ."[20]

Baker's demotion of Japan humiliated MOFA and sparked a bottom-up rethinking of Japanese diplomacy toward Cambodia, beginning in the Asian Affairs Bureau and spreading eventually to the senior leadership of the government and the LDP. MOFA had three concerns. First, how could Japan give real meaning to its Southeast Asia policy beyond the economic cooperation and "heart-to-heart" diplomacy started with the Fukuda Doctrine? Second, how could Japan increase its diplomatic influence as the world's leading ODA donor (since Tokyo would inevitably be handed the bill for the Cambodian peace process)? And third, how could Japan demonstrate to the United States and the world the Japanese capacity to play a larger diplomatic role after the Cold War?[21]

The geostrategic and domestic political conditions were conducive to MOFA's desire to take a more assertive posture on Cambodia. China had been isolated diplomatically after Tienanmen and seemed willing to support Japanese diplomacy in Cambodia to win Tokyo's goodwill.

Russia was inward-looking after perestroika and the fall of the Berlin Wall and was growing distant from its Vietnamese ally. Vietnam was also tiring of the Cambodian conflict and suddenly announced its intention to pull out troops in September 1989, focusing national attention instead on the Doi Moi economic reforms. ASEAN was divided over Cambodia policy, with some countries, such as Thailand, favoring a new approach and others still wedded to support of the anti–Hun Sen coalition. The United States was also somewhat divided on Cambodia—opposed to Hun Sen because of the Vietnamese invasion, but uncomfortable backing an anti-Vietnam coalition that included the genocidal Khmer Rouge. More important, Cambodia was not a critical area for U.S. foreign policy, which meant that Japan had freedom to maneuver without angering key actors in the United States. Finally, Japan had a good intelligence on Indochina from diplomats such as Imagawa and little competition among or disagreement among domestic ministries or businesses. MOFA was confident it could carve a larger role for Japan in the peace process.

Years of investment and ODA in Southeast Asia gave Japan significant economic tools to work the Cambodia problem, but officials at MOFA decided that Japanese credibility depended on a willingness to do something that none of the other major powers could do given their own ties to different warring factions. Japan would have to reach out to *all* parties in the conflict as a neutral actor and honest broker. This would mean drawing somewhat away from the U.S. and ASEAN backed anticommunist forces and entering into direct dialogue with Hun Sen. Eventually MOFA hoped to broker direct talks between Hun Sen and Sihanouk that marginalized the Khmer Rouge and built a 50/50 power-sharing arrangement between the two major parties in the conflict. This assessment of the Cambodia situation was not unique. Thailand had already reached the same conclusion, and by July 1990 the United States would also abandon its one-sided support for the anti–Hun Sen forces, entering directly into negotiations with Vietnam. But in the winter of 1989–90, MOFA was confident enough in its own independence and flexibility to move ahead of the other players.

Japan Moves Alone

In February 1990 the director of the Southeast Asian Division in MOFA responsible for Indochina, Kōno Masaharu, traveled to Washington to explain Japan's new approach. Predictably, the State Department warned him not to send the "wrong signal" to Cambodia by undermining Baker's ongoing efforts to win UN Security Council support for a draft peace proposal. Mindful of U.S. concerns, even in the midst of a deliberate attempt at independent diplomacy, MOFA agreed to send only a "fact-finding" mission to Cambodia. Shortly after returning from Washington, Kōno was again dispatched, this time to Phnom Penh. After a week of meetings he reported back the facts that MOFA expected to hear—the Hun Sen regime had considerable support from the Cambodian people and must be at the center of any peace negotiation.[22] Japan had already decided to go its own way.

Japan invited the four Cambodian factions to Tokyo on June 5, 1990, in an effort to jump-start peace talks that had made no more progress in the Security Council than they had in Paris the year before. Thailand proved an invaluable ally. Constrained by ASEAN but eager to move toward a new arrangement with Hun Sen, the Thais pushed the warring Cambodian factions to participate in the Tokyo meeting. When the Khmer Rouge decided to boycott the meeting, angered that Sihanouk would be representing them, the Japanese press predicted failure. But even that wrinkle helped MOFA's cause by reinforcing the strategy of brokering direct talks between Sihanouk and Hun Sen. That strategy succeeded. Signing as "the Delegation of H. R. H. Samdech Norodom Sihanouk" and "the Delegation of H. E. Mr. Hun Sen," the two leaders agreed to a six-point communiqué addressing an early cease-fire and the establishment of a joint Supreme National Council.

The Tokyo communiqué was an important development. If only temporarily, it took the peace process out of the great-power arena in the Security Council and demonstrated the possibility for a settlement based on direct cooperation between Sihanouk and Hun Sen. This precedent added momentum to the UN effort, and in November 1990 the P-5 reached agreement on a draft peace document to end the fighting in Cambodia. Japan's diplomatic initiative was vindicated.

Empowered once again in the Cambodian peace process, Japan continued to intervene in the implementation stage of the draft accord. Even after the P-5 agreement, the warring parties in Cambodia still had to be convinced. Hun Sen was particularly resistant to parts of the agreement that would compel his forces to withdraw from areas that the Khmer Rouge might seize. The P-5, which should have been following up on the agreement with pressure on the warring factions to comply, was now fully engaged in the diplomacy of the Gulf War. Forward momentum on the Cambodian peace process came to a halt.[23] Once again Japan took the opportunity to seize the initiative. In February 1991 Tokyo proposed a compromise agreement on disarmament in which the United Nations Transitional Authority in Cambodia (UNTAC) would verify the successive stages of the military cease-fire and disarmament. The State Department was furious that Japan was tinkering with a delicate P-5 agreement, but Japan gradually convinced other parties to the talks to support the new position. Hun Sen was convinced to back the Japanese proposal while in Tokyo having his Soviet-made false eye replaced with a Japanese model. (One can only assume it improved his "vision.")[24] Eventually France and Indonesia, the co-chairs of the Paris talks, also agreed to modifications. In August all four Cambodian factions compromised around a new peace plan, based in large part on Japan's proposal. While other geostrategic factors were critical—particularly the Sino-Vietnamese decision to normalize bilateral relations—Japan remained ahead of the curve and influential in the process. Japan had defied the United States and led the P-5, and in the end its vision of the peace process largely prevailed—an impressive accomplishment even though Japan itself did more anticipating of the final outcome than actual leading.

Japan's success in the Cambodian peace process had everything to do with a willingness to put full financial, political, and, eventually, personnel resources behind its diplomacy. From the beginning Japan financed a substantial portion of the UNTAC budget (estimated at $1.9 billion from November 1991 to July 1993 alone).[25] In 1992 Japan resumed grant aid, which reached $61.34 million in 1993, or 61.3 percent of all assistance to Cambodia.[26] In 1993 Japan promised with France to write-off Cambodia's IMF debts.[27] And Japan hosted or chaired almost all of the major international conferences on Cambodian economic reconstruction, beginning with the Ministerial Conference on the Rehabilitation and Reconstruction of Cambodia (MCRRC) in 1992, which organized pledges of hundreds of millions of dollars in assistance. Japan was also proactive in its negotiating process, working not only through Washington, but directly with the Cambodian factions, China, and ASEAN. Finally, Japanese personnel played key roles on the ground. Akashi Yasushi was appointed head of UNTAC in 1992, and Japan's new PKO legislation gave Tokyo the legal basis to dispatch a JSDF construction battalion to Cambodia in June 1992. Japanese police and private citizens also monitored the Cambodian elections in 1993. Although Japanese police observers were withdrawn abruptly when two policemen were killed, and the JSDF activities were strictly limited and monitored from Tokyo, the Japanese soldiers and citizens generally performed well and added credibility to Japan's commitment.

Peace at Risk: The 1997 Putsch

All of these investments and Japan's credibility as an honest broker in Cambodia were put to the test when fighting broke out in Phnom Penh in July 1997 between the royalist Fucinpec forces and Hun Sen's Cambodian People's Party. The coalition government established with elections in 1993 had always been shakier than Japan would admit, and it was perhaps inevitable that "Second Prime Minister" Hun Sen would someday grab power by deposing "First Prime Minister" Norodom Ranariddh, the son of Prince Sihanouk. In response to the putsch, Japan temporarily froze its economic cooperation with Phnom Penh, but Tokyo began backtracking toward Hun Sen almost immediately. MOFA officials downplayed the notion that a coup had occurred, arguing that the constitutional system of Cambodia would remain intact, if only Ranariddh would return from exile for direct negotiations with Hun Sen.[28] U.S. officials responded that hundreds of Ranariddh's followers had been killed and that he could not be expected to expose himself to such danger. U.S. congressional criticism of Japan's position mounted, and over the summer and fall U.S. officials, including Special Envoy Stephen Solarz and Assistant Secretary of State Stanley Roth, were dispatched to Tokyo to press Japan not to resume aid.[29] In spite of this pressure, though, Japan's official reply from Prime Minister Hashimoto and Foreign Minister Ikeda was that "the United States and Japan will simply have different positions."[30]

In many respects, however, Japan's position in the wake of the putsch was not as divergent as Hashimoto's bravado toward Washington would suggest. In spite of its tough stance toward Hun Sen, for example, the United States also maintained humanitarian aid to Cambodia (about one-third of total U.S. assistance to that country). The biggest difference in U.S. and Japanese aid was in the much broader Japanese definition of what constituted "humanitarian" aid. (Japan, for example, funded bridge construction across the Mekong River based on "humanitarian" concerns.)[31] Moreover, MOFA officials once again detected indecision and discomfort about the administration's Cambodia policy within Washington. Japanese Embassy officials in Washington told *Sankei* that many in the Clinton administration recognized that without a Hun Sen–dominated government, Cambodia would be more susceptible to pressure from China.[32] Imagawa also argued that the United States and Japan, though divided over human rights, were quietly united by a concern that Cambodia not be driven "nearer to the Chinese side."[33] In addition, Japanese officials recognized that the Congress was forcing the administration to take a stand against Hun Sen on principle, but that the State Department was worried about U.S. isolation from ASEAN, France, and Japan, which were less concerned about punishing Hun Sen for overturning the 1993 election, as long as the status quo ante was established. Finally, there was a strong sense in MOFA that Secretary of State Albright had no game plan for resolving the crisis and little sustained attention to the region, leaving open an opportunity for Japan to demonstrate its own initiative and resolve.[34]

Japan again focused on direct agreement between the Royalist Fucinpec and Hun Sen factions as the solution to the crisis. MOFA proposed a new Japan plan shortly after the July 1997 crisis began in which Hun Sen would hold a trial for Ranariddh, who would then be pardoned by his father, allowing Ranariddh back into Cambodia for a resumption of the coalition government. The plan was classically Japanese, designed to save face for all parties while buying their cooperation with aid. Japan announced it would back the plan with a resumption of aid contingent on four conditions: renewed observation of human rights, reestablishment of constitutional government, observation of the 1991 Paris Peace Agreement that created the coalition government, and the holding of free elections.[35] Since Japanese aid accounted for 39 percent of Phnom Penh's budget, this formula carried considerable weight.

Eventually the Japan plan and the Four Principles became the basis for a resolution of the crisis. Pressed by the United States and isolated from ASEAN, which had postponed Cambodia's membership, Hun Sen relented in the spring of 1998 to hold new elections and allow the reestablishment of coalition government. The elections were held in July (and declared generally "free and fair" by UN monitors), and the new coalition government, led by a Cambodian Communist Party plurality under Hun Sen, was inaugurated in November 1998. The surrender of most of the Khmer Rouge leadership in the same period reinforced the sense of new stability in the country. True to its word, Japan announced in February 1999 that it would resume yen loans to Cambodian—the first in thirty-one years.[36]

For Japan—A Diplomatic Success Story

Over the course of the decade, then, Japan's Foreign Ministry seized on the Cambodian crisis as a testing ground for proactive and independent Japanese diplomacy. Its success in Cambodia rested on three important factors. First, Japan backed its diplomacy not only with financial resources, but also took on a share of the political and personnel risks involved. Second, Japan successfully anticipated changes in U.S. policy toward Cambodia, tacking at different times, but generally maintaining the same course as the sluggish U.S. ship of state. Finally, Japan hewed closely to the unfolding ASEAN position, relying heavily on the more nimble diplomatic prowess of Thailand and rarely challenging ASEAN openly the way it did Washington. These factors explain Japan's success, but also suggest that its Cambodia diplomacy may not be easily replicated in more strategic areas, such as the Korean Peninsula—or, as we will see, in East Timor.

Japan's Cambodia policy also had faults. For one thing, Japanese aid was used almost entirely as carrot rather than stick. As a result, much Japanese ODA money was funneled to corrupt leaders in Phnom Penh without careful monitoring.[37] Tokyo also let slide Hun Sen's numerous deceptions, choosing, for example, not to press for investigation of fraud and corruption in the July 1998 election (allegations that marred the general seal of approval provided by UN monitors). Overall, the comparatively looser conditionality placed on Japanese aid to Phnom Penh after 1997 gave critics in Washington and the region the strong impression that Japan's position had drifted from honest broker to Hun Sen partisan. The Japanese view of Hun Sen stood in particular contrast to that of the U.S. Congress, where some members compared the Cambodian leader to Adolf Hitler.[38] Suspicion of Japan's intentions was only reinforced by MITI's efforts to organize new Japanese foreign direct investment in the Cambodian textile sector in the immediate wake of the election.[39]

It would be a mistake, however, to conclude that Japan's Cambodia diplomacy was motivated primarily or even significantly by mercantile interests. The most striking motivation was ideational—MOFA's desire to demonstrate that Japan could play a leadership role in Asia as a "normal" country. And to the extent that Japan identified material interests in Cambodia, they were clearly strategic as well as economic.

A Separate Course on Burma

In the 1990s Burma continually frustrated and confounded Japanese diplomacy. Japan struggled to keep obstinate juntas in Rangoon from isolating themselves from the West or tilting toward Beijing. Rangoon reciprocated by undermining Japanese diplomatic initiatives with shootings, arrests, and canceled election results. After a decade of encouraging the West to be patient with the regime in Rangoon, Japanese diplomats are quietly acknowledging that there has been "no visible change in

Myanmar's [Burma's] policies."[40] There *has* been a change in Japan's policies, however. In working the Burma problem, Japan has steadily set a separate course from Washington and established closer diplomatic coordination with ASEAN. Driven initially by economic interests and ties to ASEAN, officials in Tokyo have come to view Burma as another important front-line state in the game of diplomatic maneuver with China and in Japan's search for a more independent identity in Asia.

Engaging a Stubborn and Isolated Regime

Burma was a major Japanese aid recipient from the opening of bilateral ties in 1954 until September 1988, when the military junta (the State Law and Order Restoration Council, or SLORC) seized power, massacring thousands of civilians during antigovernment demonstrations. The massacre forced Japan to suspend bilateral aid and join international economic sanctions against the regime. Privately, however, officials in Tokyo looked for ways to continue economic support for Rangoon without breaking openly from the United States and European Union.

The first opportunity to restore aid and investment occurred in 1989, when the SLORC announced that it would hold elections the following year. Without waiting to see the result, Japan moved quickly to recognize the SLORC as the legitimate rulers of the newly renamed Union of Myanmar and announced plans to resume limited aid. Encouraged by the SLORC's decision to temporarily release opposition leader Aung San Suu Kyi from house arrest, Tokyo also announced a first installment of $24 million in grant aid. MOFA explained that this "carrot" was designed to encourage further political liberalization in Burma.[41] Unfortunately, the carrot was not enough to prevent the SLORC from throwing out the results of the 1990 election when Aung San Suu Kyi's National League for Democracy (NLD) received 82 percent of the vote. Betrayed, Japan again put its proposal for a resumption of aid on hold.

A second opportunity to reestablish economic aid to Burma emerged in 1995 after the SLORC released Aung San Suu Kyi from house arrest. Tokyo announced that it would reopen financing for certain humanitarian projects on a "case-by-case" basis, focusing on "ongoing projects suspended since 1988."[42] MOFA reassured the United States that this move did not yet represent a full resumption of ODA to the regime in Rangoon, though there was strong pressure in Tokyo to move in that direction.[43] Once again, however, the SLORC undercut Japan's position, this time by barring Aung San Suu Kyi from leaving the country. MOFA was compelled to announce in May 1996 that for the fore-seeable future, only small-scale, grass-roots assistance through NGOs would be allowed in Burma.

Despite the continuation of case-by-case, grass-roots assistance, Japan more or less toed the Western line on ODA in this period. Grasping at small gestures by the SLORC had only backfired. Japan risked a con-tradiction of its 1992 ODA charter and a backlash from the United States and other leading ODA donors if it reopened full aid with no demonstrated progress from Rangoon. But aid was not the only diplo-matic tool Japan had for engaging Burma. On other diplomatic fronts, Japan's Burma policy began to unhinge from the United States.

The Tilt to ASEAN

When Prime Minister Hashimoto traveled throughout ASEAN in Jan-uary 1997 to propose broader strategic relations with the region, he was told that ASEAN was moving toward a decision to include Burma as a member. The United States and European Union had been imploring ASEAN not to accept the junta in Rangoon, but ASEAN governments responded that Burmese membership in ASEAN was critical to work "constructively" to moderate the SLORC's repressive policies, bring Burma into ASEAN to counter China's growing influence, and resist Western interference in Southeast Asian affairs. [44] These were all goals that resonated with Tokyo. The key for Hashimoto was to maintain a balance between Japan's alliance with the United States and sympathy for ASEAN's position. Hashimoto struck a middle ground. He ex-pressed understanding of ASEAN's position, but warned that Burma's membership not become a "smoke screen" for further human rights vi-olations in Burma. [45]

However, Japan's balancing act between ASEAN and the United States proved unsustainable as sympathy for Aung San Suu Kyi and re-vulsion of the SLORC grew in Washington. In April 1997 President Clinton declared Burma a pariah state and barred government credits and guarantees for U.S. trade and investment with Burma. Meanwhile, local governments across the United States were putting even stricter restrictions on companies doing business with Burma, including Japa-nese companies. As the gulf between ASEAN and the United States widened, Japan was forced to choose sides. It chose ASEAN. In June 1997 Prime Minister Hashimoto announced formally that Tokyo would support ASEAN's inclusion of Burma. [46] Hashimoto referred to the membership of the Union of Myanmar (the junta's official name for the country) and not Burma, a further indication of the gulf with Washington.

Since the decision to support Burma's membership in ASEAN, Tokyo has gradually returned to the issue of economic assistance. Prime Minister Obuchi promised Burmese leader Than Shwe in Manila in November 1999 that Japan would consider reextending aid to Burma on a "case-by-case" basis if Rangoon demonstrates some further willingness to institute political and economic reforms.[47] Japan continues to quietly urge moderation on the regime in Rangoon. However, having agreed to the principle of Burma's inclusion in ASEAN, Tokyo is coming under increasing domestic and regional pressure to provide economic assistance. The regime in Rangoon would not have to demonstrate much flexibility to win Japanese aid. For Tokyo its intransigence is maddening.

Explaining Japan's Stance in Burma

While Burma stands alongside Cambodia as an example of independent Japanese diplomacy in Southeast Asia, the decisions involved in Burma have been far more contentious, reactive, and difficult. Japan has been torn between conflicting interests.

On one hand, there are greater Japanese economic interests in Burma than in Cambodia. Japanese FDI in Myanmar in 1998 reached only $219 million, less than the $234 million invested by the United States and the more than $1 billion invested by Singapore.[48] But proven gas reserves and large forests in Burma have attracted the interest of Japanese trading companies. Marubeni Corporation president Toriumi Iwao led a high-level Keidanren mission to Burma in 1994 and chaired the first Japan-Myanmar Joint Business Conference in 1997.[49] On the financial services side, Daiwa Securities has been working with SLORC (renamed the State Peace and Development Council, or SPDC, in a bloodless internal coup in 1997) to establish rudimentary capital markets.[50] Japanese firms have also maintained a focus on Burma throughout the troubled 1980s and 1990s because of Rangoon's unpaid loans to Japan of over 80 billion yen.[51] While Japanese investment in Burma will remain a longer-term prospect (even with a restoration of democracy there are numerous regulatory problems), the domestic pressure on MOFA and the LDP from business is clearly more significant than in the case of Cambodia.

On the other hand, there is considerable political support in Japan for Burma's democratic opposition—a contrast to Cambodia. Aung San

Suu Kyi, 1991 Nobel Peace Prize laureate, is a far more compelling figure than Cambodia's effete Prince Norodom Ranariddh. The Diet
members League for Aung San Suu Kyi, led by Kosugi Takashi, includes
powerful politicians such as Hatoyama Yukio, leader of the Democratic
Party of Japan. MOFA's hand on Burma is also constrained by the principles of the 1992 ODA charter. And, of course, the United States
weighs heavily in Japanese thinking, in spite of the "independence" of
Japanese diplomacy. As one Japanese diplomat with long experience in
Rangoon has noted:

> Our strategy or approach toward Myanmar is defined slightly differently
> from that of the American government. However, the Japanese and
> American governments share the same goals for democratization and
> improvement of human rights. . . . America is politically and economi-
> cally the most important country for Japan, therefore, it is no wonder
> that some Japanese companies, particularly doing business in America,
> give careful consideration to business in Myanmar.[52]

Ultimately, the factor that probably tipped the scales in Japan's Burma
policy around 1997 was neither the U.S.-Japan alliance nor business interests in Burma, but the growing importance of Southeast Asia as a
strategic element in Japan's foreign policy. As we have noted, Japan has
placed great importance on supporting the cohesion of ASEAN and
therefore would not obstruct the achievement of Burma's inclusion in
the ASEAN 10. Japan has also been increasingly sensitive to Chinese influence in Burma. Japan's large gestures toward the SLORC have always
followed closely behind Chinese diplomatic inroads. Japan announced
its first partial resumption of aid shortly after Chinese Premier Lee Peng
visited Rangoon in December 1994.[53] After Beijing announced a 70
million yen loan to Rangoon and a new economic cooperation agreement in March 1997, Japanese officials grew alarmed that China's "aid
offensive" in Burma was aimed at gaining naval access to the Indian
Ocean.[54] Several months later the Japanese government announced its
formal support for Burma's membership in ASEAN. Privately, MOFA
Asian Affairs Bureau officials often describe their policy objectives in
Burma in terms of shoring up ASEAN against Chinese influence. And
MOFA has reason to worry. Closer strategic ties to Burma would offer
Beijing naval access to key shipping lanes from the Indian Ocean and a
wedge position within ASEAN. China has attempted to cement its influence in Rangoon through extensive military sales, to include tanks,
armored personnel carriers, F-7 fighters, and Hainan and Houxin
guided-missile attack boats. China has also helped Burma upgrade key

naval facilities and electronic listening posts along its strategic coast in the Indian Ocean.[55]

From a Japanese position, this strategic view of Burma should be consistent with the security interests of the United States. As with Cambodia, Japanese policymakers detect division and inconsistency in the U.S. approach to Burma. While the State Department and White House put a first-order priority on democracy and human rights in the 1990s, the Defense Department—particularly under Secretary of Defense William Cohen—took a more strategic and security-oriented view of Burma in the context of U.S.-China and U.S.-ASEAN relations. As National Defense University professor Marvin Ott warned in 1998, the costs of emphasizing moral issues with Burma above U.S. interests "are measured in an escalating heroin problem, a loss of strategic ground to China, and an estrangement from ASEAN."[56] Recognizing support in the United States for a strategic approach to Burma, MOFA has been fairly confident that its engagement policy will not undermine the U.S.-Japan alliance.

Finally, Tokyo's divergence from the United States in Burma flows from the Japanese frustration at not receiving full recognition as a strategic player in the region. Japan accounts for three-quarters of ODA to Burma, but most observers see Japan's influence in Rangoon declining relative to ASEAN or even Beijing. Understandably, Tokyo wants more influence for its money (again, no "taxation without representation"). If Japan followed the U.S. lead in isolating the regime in Rangoon, Japanese diplomatic influence in Southeast Asia would be that much weaker and Japan itself that much more isolated from ASEAN. The dilemma for Japan, of course, is that a policy of engagement without teeth is hardly "proactive," and Japan risks becoming as passive and reactive to ASEAN—or even Rangoon—as it fears becoming to the United States.[57]

Stumbling in East Timor

The third case study we briefly examine in this chapter is Japan's response to the humanitarian and political crisis in East Timor in the 1990s. This case study contrasts to the Cambodian and Burmese examples because Japan was so passive in the East Timor crisis, in spite of the fact that Japanese economic interests in Indonesia are exponentially larger than in the case of either Cambodia or Burma. Japanese NGOs and private citizens have certainly done good work in East Timor and the Japanese government has given hundreds of millions of dollars in assistance, but Tokyo lost its diplomatic bearings as Australia led a humanitarian intervention in 1999 to stop the slaughter of East Timor civilians by the Indonesian-backed militias. Why the passivity in East Timor? The answer suggests the limits of Japanese autonomous action in Southeast Asia.

A Focus on the Center, a Surprise at the Periphery

Japan has deep economic roots in Indonesia. Indonesia has been the largest recipient of Japanese ODA since 1987, averaging more than $2 billion per year in the 1990s, or 60 percent of total aid to Jakarta.[58] Indonesia is an important supplier of gas and oil to Japan, and much of Japanese ODA has gone into infrastructure that contributes to the development of those sectors. Private investment flows—$41 billion as of December 1997—have also reinforced Indonesia's exporting sectors.[59] Japan also has strategic interests in Indonesia, which has the largest population in Asia outside of China and is the heartbeat of ASEAN. With Japanese oil and imports flowing through the Straits of Malacca and Lombok, Japan desperately needs stability in the Indonesian archipelago.

Japan has virtually no economic or political interests in the former Portuguese colony of East Timor. But as East Timor has become a sore in Indonesia's relationship with the West, it has also become a problem for Tokyo. Japan's extensive aid and economic relationship with Indonesia first came under pressure from the West because of the separatist movement in East Timor in the early 1990s. When Indonesian troops gunned down more than 100 East Timorese in November 1991, the governments of the Netherlands, Canada, and Denmark all suspended aid. For Japan, however, East Timor was a marginal affair in the overall bilateral relationship with Jakarta. Japan expressed its concern about East Timor privately to Jakarta, but publicly announced that aid would remain unaffected.[60] Even after the establishment of the 1992 ODA charter, Japan continued to press for improved human rights in East Timor through low-key dialogue with Jakarta rather than with economic "sticks."

For a while, this low-key approach held, but the problem of political reform in Indonesia and with it the autonomy of East Timor suddenly became acute again with the financial crisis of 1997. As we will see in examining Japan's response to that crisis, Tokyo provided over $21 billion to Jakarta to stabilize the ruppiah (a figure that coincided with the $20 billion Indonesia still owed Japan). Japanese officials also pressed

President Suharto and his successor, B. J. Habbibie, to implement reforms pledged under the IMF bailout package. At the same time, Japan lobbied the IMF to soften conditionality on Indonesia where it affected political stability (interest rates, for example). Tokyo's focus was on stabilizing the economic and political situation in Jakarta. MOFA and MOF were concerned primarily about the stability of the Indonesian economy, and believed that stability and recovery would solve other problems at the periphery of the country. It came as a surprise, therefore, when Habibie suddenly announced in January 1999 that he would resolve the festering East Timor problem by approving a referendum on East Timor independence. A bigger surprise hit in September 1999. After separatists in East Timor won a landslide victory in the referendum, militias trained by the Indonesian military turned on them, massacring hundreds and razing the provincial capital of Dili. They committed these atrocities at a time when hundreds of international election monitors and aid workers had been sent into East Timor by the UN and NGOs. The once-peripheral problem of East Timor now became the core issue of Indonesia's relations with the world.

As Australia organized a humanitarian intervention to prevent further bloodshed in East Timor, the Japanese government stood in near paralysis. Prodded by Australia, Japan agreed on September 16 to provide $2 million to help finance the UN-authorized peacekeeping force. Once the situation stabilized with the insertion of a multinational force that also included Malaysian, Singaporean, Thai, and even Chinese forces, MOFA announced in December that Japan would provide another $100 million over the following three years for the reconstruction of East Timor.

What Japan did not do was to send its own peacekeeping forces. The Japanese government argued that the restrictions of the 1992 PKO law prevented JSDF participation. As LDP heavyweight Katō Kōichi explained, Japanese participation would have violated the PKO law because the peacekeepers were clearly advocates of East Timorese independence—a violation of the rule that peacekeepers remain neutral.[61] Of course, that did not stop other ASEAN nations from sending troops or the Indonesian government from approving the dispatch of PKO forces to East Timor. The technical obstacles to Japanese participation in the peacekeeping effort could have been overcome—indeed, probably would have been overcome—if it had been the United States leading the effort and not Australia. Japan could also have sent other forces, for example, such as police. But only three policemen were dispatched. The bottom line was simply that Tokyo had little enthusiasm for taking on the risk of East Timor peacekeeping.

An Unexpected Diplomatic Failure

Why such timidity after seven years of successful PKO operations in Cambodia and elsewhere? Domestic political factors were certainly important. The PKO law might have required some amendment, but Prime Minister Obuchi was in no frame of mind to push for those changes in the midst of his election battle for the LDP presidency or at a time when he was trying to strengthen the party's coalition with the more pacifist Komeitō Party. Beyond domestic politics, Tokyo was clearly also nervous about distancing itself from the regime in Jakarta. MOFA officials put "careful consideration" on Japan's "special relationship" with the Suharto regime and sought to maintain that connection with Habibie even as the crisis unfolded.[62] Even a strong LDP government may have been reluctant to take a lead in a military intervention that risked a political backlash from Jakarta, or encouraged separatism in Aceh and other Indonesian provinces. With over $40 billion invested in Indonesia and more than $20 billion in outstanding loans, Japan's potential influence on Indonesia was offset by mutual dependence with the regime in power.

This cautious stance hurt Japan and was criticized at home and abroad. For one thing, Japan's close ties to Suharto and his family came under scrutiny as democracy sprouted in Indonesia. After the referendum, East Timorese leaders complained publicly that Japan blocked efforts by the UN Commission on Human Rights to establish a formal investigation of violence in the province.[63] Charges also emerged that as much as $1.44 billion of Japanese loans in fiscal year 1997 went to infrastructure projects benefiting the Suharto family. Whether true or not, Tokyo responded to domestic and international criticism and changed its focus in 1998 to address the problems of the "poor and weak" in Indonesian society.[64]

Japan's back-bench status in the East Timor intervention also raised alarm in Japan about the saliency of its economic and diplomatic power in Southeast Asia. The failure to send peacekeepers led to an intense debate during the LDP presidential election. The media was generally critical of the passivity of Japanese diplomacy. Typical was a *Nihon Keizai Shimbun* commentary on October 18, 1999, which argued that Japan should have used its economic influence in Indonesia demonstrate diplomatic initiative, but instead "stood by passively until a military solution became necessary."[65] *Yomuiri* attacked the government for not taking the long-overdue step of revising the PKO legislation so that Japanese forces could have been on the ground in East Timor. And *Asahi* noted ironically that even after all of its economic and political investment in Indonesia, Japan was ultimately "unable to move within its own fortress walls."[66]

While indicative of the constraints Japan faces in Southeast Asia, however, the decision to keep JSDF and police personnel out of East Timor should not be interpreted as a major reverse in Japan's march toward broader participation in peacekeeping. Indeed, even as it refused to participate in the Australian-led peacekeeping operation, Tokyo dispatched a JASDF C-130 to West Timor to prepare for a possible military evacuation of Japanese civilians in the event the crisis worsened.[67] Moreover, due credit should be given to the two dozen civilian election monitors from Japan and the activism of Japanese NGOs in East Timor, all of whom took personal risks on behalf of democracy in the region.[68] Nevertheless, the East Timor case does suggest that Japanese "proactive" and "independent" diplomacy can quickly become bogged down in countries where Japanese economic stakes are deepest and ties to the power center too constraining.

Conclusion: Japan and U.S. Strategy for Southeast Asia

The case studies of Cambodia, Burma, and East Timor give a mixed message about Japanese diplomacy in Southeast Asia. Japan's diplomacy in the region is clearly becoming more independent. It reflects growing attention not only to economic interests, but also to strategic calculations. And it continues in many respects to be dysfunctional, inconsistent, and reactive. Given that U.S. foreign policy in Southeast Asia is also dysfunctional and inconsistent, however, it might be worth considering how Japan's enthusiasm for proactive diplomacy in the region can be harnessed to U.S. objectives. Japan is devoting more resources and attention to the region than the United States is, and U.S. policy should focus on this as an opportunity rather than a threat.

The Shift toward ASEAN

The first lesson from Japan's regional diplomacy in the 1990s is that Japan has moved toward a stronger relationship with ASEAN. This is true in terms of a relative shift in emphasis away from Washington and in terms of Tokyo's effort to establish comprehensive relations with

ASEAN that encompass both economic and security cooperation. Japan has been a strong supporter of the goal of ASEAN's expansion to the ASEAN 10. Japan has backed ASEAN solidarity in controversial issues such as Burma, pressing for action privately on a bilateral level, but always maintaining respect for ASEAN leadership in public and multilateral settings. [69] Increasingly, Japanese officials have also been concerned about the loss of cohesion in ASEAN—particularly as its core member, Indonesia, goes through a period of political and social disruption.

The United States should share this concern. Japan's tilt toward ASEAN in the 1990s has been caused in part by the U.S. tilt away from ASEAN over issues related to human rights and democracy. The United States has had the leeway to emphasize these normative issues precisely because the cohesion of ASEAN has prevented great-power competition from threatening U.S. strategic interests in the region. A weak and disjointed ASEAN might open up the region to such a power vacuum in the future, however. In the 1990s there was more sensitivity to this danger in Tokyo than in Washington. The United States should not abandon the ideals that animate its foreign policy in the region, but Tokyo and Washington should be united on the premise that ASEAN cohesion is an important strategic goal for both.

The Geostrategic Game

At the center of Japan's growing concern over ASEAN solidarity is a more straightforward focus on balance of power—or at least balance of influence—with China. The Hashimoto Initiative in January 1997 failed to produce a clearer strategic dialogue between ASEAN members and Japan, but Tokyo continues to press quietly for a strategic dimension to its relations with the region. In late 1999, for example, Tokyo considered a proposal with ASEAN members to establish joint multilateral "antipiracy patrols." ASEAN eventually countered with a more modest proposal for sharing data and "coordinating" patrols.[70]

A logical partner for Japan in this grand strategy is India. India has even deeper concern about China's potential military access to the Indian Ocean and shares with Japan a history of military cooperation dating to Japanese support for the Indian independence army in World War II. In fact, in the summer of 2000 Japan and India agreed quietly to begin bureau-director political-military talks on Asia.[71] Overall, however, a Japan-India alignment has been hampered by profound disagreements over India's nuclear weapons program and cultural and geographic distance. Nevertheless, strategic cooperation with India is a potential growth area for Japanese diplomacy.

Japan's Need for Independent Diplomacy

Having tasted the sweet success of independent diplomatic action in Cambodia and to a lesser extent in Burma, Japan now expects to pursue a "national interest"–based diplomacy in Southeast Asia. Indeed, in an era when Washington seems dismissive of Japanese power, officials in Tokyo point to Southeast Asia as an arena where Japan's potential as a diplomatic player is recognized. As we have seen, though, Japan has pushed an independent approach to the political problems of Southeast Asia only within broader strategic parameters set by the United States. In some cases—Tokyo's move toward Hun Sen in 1990, for example—Japan has moved in the expectation that the United States would follow. In both Cambodia and Burma, Japan took an independent approach, confident that its strategic objectives would resonate with many in Washington. In general, the lack of high-level attention to Southeast Asia in the United States has given Japan more diplomatic leeway. The Japanese need for an independent stance in the region should therefore not be read as anti-Americanism. As MOFA veterans of the Cambodia and Burma disputes with Washington have argued, Japan's initiative in Cambodia was not "Asianist" or "anti-American." "It simply means that if Japan puts forward money, it will also be voicing its opinion too."[72]

Another important lesson for U.S.-Japan relations, then, is that the United States must recognize Japan's expectation of a broader leadership role in Southeast Asia. That is not to say that ASEAN is ready for Japan to supplant the United States as the most important strategic actor in the region, or that Tokyo should write the script for U.S. policy. However, the U.S. script should include a leading role for Japan, beyond that of financial backer. U.S. policymakers who expect Japan to pay for U.S. initiatives without such a role can expect more cries of "no taxation without representation" from MOFA and the Diet.

Strengths and Weaknesses in Japanese Tactics

As we saw in East Timor, though, Japan's diplomatic acumen is not always up to the rhetoric of "proactive" and "independent" diplomacy. There were both strengths and weaknesses in Japan's diplomacy in the region. In certain respects, Japan developed a unique and effective pattern of diplomacy. First, Tokyo worked hard behind the scenes to broker a compromise among warring factions. In Cambodia, Japan's definition of the *otoshidokoro* (the point of compromise) helped to jump-start the peace talks in 1990 and reestablish elections after the 1997 putsch. In Burma, Japan had less success finding a formula between the SLORC and Aung San Suu Kyi, primarily because of the intransigence of the junta. In East Timor, Japan could have usefully played a brokering role, but only decided in December 1999 to host a reconciliation meeting in Tokyo of the East Timor factions—too late to have significant impact on the ground. In all three cases, though, Japan's capacity to broker among conflicting factions is a useful asset for the international community to have. In addition to its enthusiasm and energy for brokering talks in the region, Japanese diplomacy deserves credit for backing words with funds. This stands in contrast to the U.S. inability to back regional diplomacy in Southeast Asia with aid. Economic "carrots" enhanced Japanese influence with interlocutors in the region and gave Japan a leadership role in multilateral coordinating meetings such as the MCRRCC.

At the same time, however, Japan's diplomatic approach to Southeast Asia has suffered from contradictions. In order to define a role as "independent" broker in Cambodia and Burma, Japan had to maintain closer ties than the United States had to the disagreeable regimes in power (Hun Sen in Phnom Penh and the SLORC in Rangoon). Often Tokyo was playing two games of influence at once—one a struggle to moderate the behavior of the regimes in power and the other a struggle to resist U.S. pressure. Whenever Japan cut political or economic ties to Phnom Penh or Rangoon, it lost its means for independent diplomatic action. Engagement therefore became something of a prison for Japanese diplomacy, and Japanese diplomats increasingly found themselves slipping into positions of advocacy for the regimes Washington criticized and Japan ultimately hoped to moderate.[73] In that respect, Japan's "independent" diplomacy in Southeast Asia in the 1990s was not entirely different from Japanese "omnidirectional diplomacy" in the 1970s. A policy of good relations with all parties cannot be translated into real leverage without a price. This problem became even more acute in the case of Indonesia, where economic interdependence with the regime in power further paralyzed Japanese diplomacy.

Finally, it is clear in all these case studies that Japanese diplomacy was most successful where there were Japanese personnel on the ground. Just as the presence of peacekeepers enhanced Japanese credibility in

Cambodia in 1992, the absence of any JSDF personnel hampered Japanese diplomacy in East Timor in 1999.

Playing to Japanese and U.S. Strengths

U.S. policy toward Southeast Asia must therefore take into account Japan's expectation of leadership in the region, as well as an objective assessment of the strengths and weaknesses of Japanese diplomacy. Japan is clearly at its best when it brings a combination of money, ideas, *and* personnel to the problems of the region. Setbacks like East Timor notwithstanding, Japan is increasingly able to bring all three to Southeast Asia at a time when the United States is less inclined to do any of the three. The United States should therefore raise the hurdle of expectations for Japan's role in the region. Japanese financial backing has become indispensable in resolving crises such as Cambodia and East Timor, but Japanese peacekeepers, police, and NGOs should *also* be on the ground. And Japanese ideas—which ultimately proved successful in Cambodia—should be given full airing. The United States should press hard for Japan to share risk in the region, but should not expect results if Japan is not helping to shape the strategy from the beginning. Over the long term a carefully coordinated Japanese role in regional diplomacy will sustain broader U.S. leadership in the region—even if Tokyo and Washington adopt different tactics.

CHAPTER SEVEN

Multilateral Diplomacy

The United Nations, APEC, and the ASEAN Regional Forum

Introduction

The multilateral impulse has been strong in Japan's postwar foreign policy thinking, but in practice it has often been elusive. After joining the United Nations in 1956, the Japanese Foreign Ministry declared in the preamble of the *Diplomatic Blue Book* that "UN-centrism" would become a central pillar of Japan's world role, but the Soviet veto on the Security Council undermined any hopes of achieving collective security through the UN. Efforts to establish regional multilateral forums proved no more productive. Japan had resisted the Eisenhower administration's attempts to establish a NATO-style collective defense organization in Asia after the Korean War, and subsequent Soviet proposals for region-wide multilateral frameworks were seen as cynical efforts to limit U.S. influence in the region. Aside from the Asian Development Bank, even regional economic groupings proved difficult to establish. The Cold War, in short, was not kind to multilateralism in Asia. By 1958 "UN-centrism" disappeared from the preamble of the *Diplomatic Bluebook*.[1] While Tokyo continued incrementally to increase its profile in the UN and its ties to other Asian states, Japan had nowhere else to turn for its security other than the United States.

With the end of the Cold War, however, Japan's multilateral diplomacy was again liberated. The 1990–91 Gulf War experience was particularly important for Japan, as the UN appeared to reestablish a central role in international politics. While UN-centered diplomacy scarcely appeared in prime ministers' domestic speeches during the Cold War, it became an increasingly common *lietmotif* in the speeches of cabinet ministers from 1991 through 1994.[2] With the end of the Cold War, Japan also took an active role in the formation of new regional multi-lateral efforts in East Asia. Foreign Minister Nakayama Tarō called for a regional security forum centered on the ASEAN Post-Ministerial Conference in a speech in Bangkok in 1991, marking Japan as an early and enthusiastic supporter of what later became the ASEAN Regional Forum (ARF). The 1992 reorganization of MOFA established a new National Security Division within the powerful Foreign Policy Bureau, significantly increasing the bureaucratic resources available for participation in both the ARF and other first- and second-track multilateral security forums that proliferated in the 1990s. In the same period, MITI took a lead in the establishment of the Asia-Pacific Economic Cooperation forum (APEC) with the aim of reinforcing Japanese leadership in the process of regional economic integration. From the Left to the Right of the political spectrum, all definitions of Japan's future international role once again focused enthusiastically on multilateralism in the beginning of the 1990s.

By the end of the decade, however, the idealism and enthusiasm surrounding multilateral diplomacy began giving way to a more cautious realism. Whether aimed at collective security or regional integration, the multilateral impulse in Japanese foreign policy has been frustrated on all fronts. UN reform, which Japan supported since the 1980s and pushed in the 1990s in order to secure a permanent Security Council seat, has stalled. Expectations for regional security structures based on the ARF are also adjusting downward as that forum stumbles over the most basic efforts to establish transparency and confidence-building measures. APEC failed to play a central role in responding to the 1997–98 regional financial crisis and is increasingly being overshadowed by the World Trade Organization (WTO). And Japan's own skill at initiating these new regional institutions has not been matched by a skill at maintaining them or giving them meaningful agenda.

Nevertheless, multilateralism remains at the center of Japan's diplomacy—as it should. Regional and global institutions are becoming important components of Japan's China policy, because these institutions shape Chinese norms of international behavior and increase Tokyo's leverage on Beijing. Fickle U.S. leadership in the United Nations and in international arms control has also increased the importance of Japan's role in sustaining these international regimes. In addition, declining expectations of Japanese economic power are giving way to new calls for

Japan to compensate by demonstrating more political initiative in multilateral institutions.[3] At the same time, though, Japan is gradually having to recast its approach to multilateralism to fit a narrower definition of national interest and the prospect of declining financial resources.

The United States should support Japan's aspirations to play a larger role in multilateral organizations and forums. Japanese objectives in the UN and the ARF are largely supportive of U.S. goals. (Indeed, this has sometimes hampered Japan's ability to demonstrate leadership itself.) Bilateral differences between the United States and Japan have emerged in APEC, but both share an interest in strengthening trans-Pacific economic cooperation. Encouraging and supporting Japan's initiative in multilateral institutions can contribute to a more balanced, and therefore healthier and more sustainable, U.S.-Japan security alliance. Indeed, it would be a great loss to the United States and the world if a frustrated Japanese public lost its idealism about the United Nations or APEC and turned away from multilateralism. Unfortunately, U.S. policy in the 1990s probably did as much to feed this frustration as to encourage Japanese leadership.

This chapter examines Japan's multilateral diplomacy in the 1990s. It begins with an assessment of the attraction of multilateralism for Japan and then reviews the patterns of Japanese multilateral diplomacy in three areas: the United Nations, APEC, and the ARF (including a discussion of arms control and other dimensions of multilateral security). These are three distinct areas of diplomacy, but they reveal common problems—and common opportunities for U.S.-Japan cooperation.

The Attraction of Multilateralism for Japan

Multilateralism encompasses a broad range of institutions and linkages in international relations. Then Harvard professor Robert Keohane gave one straightforward definition in 1990 when he described multilateralism simply as "the practice of coordinating national policies in groups of three or more states."[4] Columbia University professor and UN advisor John Ruggie refined that definition in 1994 to focus on the establishment of institutions rather than mere policy "coordination," which also characterizes traditional bilateral relationships. Ruggie argued that "multilateralism is an *institutional* form that coordinates relations among three or more states on the basis of generalized principles of conduct: that is, principles which specify appropriate conduct for class actions. . . ."[5] In contrast, more recent definitions offered by Peter Katzenstein and Shiraishi Takashi and other constructivists move away from institutions altogether, arguing that in Asia the critical multilateral link derives not from formal structures but from informal economic, cultural, and political networks—often centered on Japan.[6]

One reason for the broad support multilateral diplomacy enjoys in Japan is this very diversity of interpretation and definition. Like the *tamamushi-iro* insect that changes color depending on one's position, multilateralism offers something important but different to every constituency within Japan's foreign policy community. In broad terms, multilateralism is compelling in Japan for seven reasons.

Idealism: Rejoining the Community of Nations

Japan's road to militarism and defeat in World War II began with withdrawal from the League of Nations and the rejection of multilateralism in the 1930s. When the UN Charter was signed on June 26, 1945, Japan was still at war with all of the signatories. Indeed, the UN Charter included specific reference to Japan in the "former enemies clause (Article 53, 77 (1) (b) and Article 107)," which state that "nothing in the present Charter shall invalidate or preclude action, in relation to any state which during Workd War II has been an enemy of any signatory to the present charter."[7] In the postwar period, entering the United Nations and erasing the "former enemies" image became critical to Japan's effort to redefine itself as a positive and contributing member of international society. With time, the goal of leadership in multilateral institutions has become part of Japan's agonizing attempt to move beyond its troubled past.[8]

Asserting an Independent Diplomatic Identity within the U.S.-Japan Alliance

As we have noted already, Japan faces a dilemma in its diplomacy between entrapment in U.S. policy and abandonment by the United States. Active participation in multilateral institutions established and led by the United States allows Japan to begin resolving this dilemma in three ways. First, Japanese leadership in the UN and other institutions increases Japan's value as an ally, a useful hedge against abandonment. As the Prime Minister's Advisory Panel on Defense (the Higuchi Commission) argued in its 1994 final report, Japan should increase its focus on multilateral security because the *Pax Americana* will increasingly "depend to a certain extent on actions of nations in a position to cooperate with the United States."[9] Second, by strengthening multilateral institutions such as the UN, Japan can compensate for flagging U.S. engagement, another useful hedge against abandonment. A report on multilateral diplomacy prepared by the bipartisan Asian Forum Japan in 1995 echoed this theme, arguing that Japan should develop a more "assertive" multilateralism to compensate for the "introspective mood gripping the United States."[10] Finally, Japanese influence in multilateral institutions such as the UN, APEC, or the WTO offers a hedge against entrapment, since these institutions can often constrain U.S. unilateralism.

Legitimizing Military Activities through Collective Security

The collective security mechanism of the United Nations has emerged as an important opportunity for the Self Defense Forces to demonstrate political and constitutional legitimacy and to expand their scope of operations. During the Gulf War, MOFA and pro-defense LDP politicians struggled to draft peacekeeping (PKO) legislation that would allow Japan to dispatch forces to the Gulf, but that effort failed. A subsequent bill, the International Peace Cooperation Law, did pass in June 1992 after constraints were placed on the participation of the JSDF in peacekeeping operations.[11] The successful deployment of Japanese forces to UN missions in Cambodia, Mozambique, the Golan Heights, and elsewhere in the 1990s opened a new horizon for the JSDF. It also refocused the expansionists in Japan's security community on the opportunities inherent in post–Cold War collective security actions. Most notable was a 1992–93 LDP special commission led by Ozawa Ichirō on Japan's role in the international community. In this commission Ozawa brought together prominent LDP hawks and advocates of constitutional revision with doves and internationalists to forge a consensus that Japan could play an expanded role in cooperative security actions because the Japanese Constitution is itself based on the UN Charter.[12] The 1994 Higuchi Commission report on Japanese Defense Policy reinforced this theme, as did Japan Defense Agency White Papers throughout the decade. Article Nine of the Constitution continues to limit the use of force by Japanese forces participating in UN collective security actions,[13] but that has allowed advocates of constitutional reform to co-opt UN-centrism as one of their most compelling arguments for an expanded security policy.

Nationalism of the Left: Escaping the Alliance

For the Left, multilateralism serves the opposite purpose. Rather than enhancing the role of the JSDF or supporting U.S. leadership in Asia, multilateralism is often presented as an escape from U.S.-centered security policy based on liberal idealist expectations about the future of East Asian international relations. The 1951 and 1960 U.S.-Japan security treaties both express the hope that the UN will eventually furnish Japan with a secure environment.[14] Many skeptics about the alliance in Japan take this goal seriously—arguing not for collective security, which might legitimize remilitarization, but instead for *cooperative* security, in which nations form institutions to peacefully resolve potential conflicts. This sentiment emerged in the editorial pages of the *Asahi Shimbun* during the 1995–96 reaffirmation of the U.S.-Japan alliance, for example. The *Asahi*'s editorial writers did not oppose the continuation or even strengthening of the alliance, but they did urge the government to use multilateral security dialogue as a balance to the bilateral security relationship with the United States.[15] The Democratic Party's flirtation with a "no base alliance" proposal in the late 1990s flowed from an even more concerted attempt to supplant the importance of the U.S.-Japan alliance. The DPJ recruited a team of intellectuals—many of whom were active opponents of the U.S.-Japan alliance in the past—to write a policy proposal that premised the withdrawal of U.S. forces on the creation of an East Asian multilateral institution based on the Organization for Security and Cooperation in Europe (OSCE).[16] It is quite clear in the pages of the group's report that the focus is on ending perceived asymmetries in the U.S.-Japan alliance rather than establishing effective multilateralism in Asia. As DPJ advisor Terashima Jitsurō has argued, "the world's largest debtor nation only defends the world's largest creditor nation" in order to keep "the cap on the bottle."[17]

Great-Power Realism: Constraining China

Japanese leadership in multilateral institutions also provides Japan with what one Japanese foreign correspondent has called a "new card to counter the military power cards held by China, the United States and Russia in the new power game of Northeast Asia."[18] For realists in Japan, this is particularly true in terms of managing the rise of Chinese power—even though they may be skeptical about the prospects for cooperative security in the region. National Defense University professor Nishihara Masashi represents this perspective when he argues that the ARF can at best discourage "potential adversaries" such as China from becoming "actual adversaries."[19] Former Ambassador Okazaki Hisahiko makes a similar point when he argues that Japan's permanent membership in the UN Security Council is necessary for an Asian balance of power against China's rise.[20] And as we noted in examining Sino-Japanese relations, MOFA officials prefer to say positive things to China bilaterally and tough things in multilateral settings. Confident in its own seniority in these settings, Japan is an strong supporter of Beijing's participation in the WTO, G-7, and other multilateral forums.

Focusing on Asia

Multilateral diplomacy can also reinforce Japanese regional leadership in East Asia. As the only Asian power in the G-7, Japan often seeks empowerment to represent regional interests in that global forum.[21] Within APEC, Japan is pushing for cooperation on energy, the environment, and other issues that might spur regional integration and secure its own energy resource requirements. With the ARF, Japan hopes to enhance regional confidence in the Defense Guidelines, peacekeeping, and other new security roles. But the history of Japan's multilateralism in Asia (the Greater East Asian Co-prosperity Sphere) makes most other Asian states wary of Japanese leadership. Indeed, this is one of the major obstacles to Japan's multilateral aspirations in the region. For this reason, Japan's softer cultural and economic "network" power in Asia has attracted the attention of senior Japanese policymakers. Prime Minister Hashimoto Ryūtarō attempted to build on these informal networks with a new Multilateral Cultural Mission to Southeast Asia in 1997.[22] Arguably, cultural diplomacy and the gradual emergence of a common "pop culture" in Asia have provided a better regional environment for Japanese diplomacy.[23] The problems are that this regional cultural integration is difficult to distinguish from *global* cultural integration, and soft-power networks do not translate into hard power or even coalition leadership for Japan.

Insulating Japanese Domestic Interests

One consistent motivation for Japanese participation in multilateralism from the prewar era to the present is a desire to protect domestic constituencies. Multilateral agreements inevitably entail some loss of sovereignty by the signing parties, and Japan has had to keep a close eye on trends in the UN, WTO, G-7, and other forums that might change trade rules or issue statements detrimental to its approach to economic policy. This has been true even in APEC and regional forums Japan helped to establish. As Michael Blaker has noted in his studies of pre- and postwar Japanese diplomacy, this anxiety about external pressure and the difficulty of coordinating an internal position have often led to a minimalist and reactive posture in important multinational negotiations.[24]

The diverse and often conflicting motivations behind Japan's multilateral diplomacy explain both why it remains so popular and why it is so often ineffective. As Japan has attempted to embrace a more active role in establishing and leading regional and global multilateral forums and institutions, the foreign policy elite is being forced to confront the inherent risk and loss of sovereignty inherent in real collective regimes—whether oriented to security or trade. This may lead to a decline in the popularity and mystique of multilateralism in Japan. It may also lead to a more effective Japanese approach. In any case, as an examination of the UN, APEC, and ARF suggest, it is gradually leading to a new realism about what such institutions can and cannot do for Japanese interests.

The Elusive Gold Ring:
Permanent UN Security Council Membership

All of the aspirations, contradictions and frustrations of Japan's multilateral diplomacy were embodied in Tokyo's quest in the 1990s for a permanent seat on the UN Security Council. The questions that emerged in pursuit of the UNSC seat are *the* fundamental questions about Japan's world role. As a permanent member of the UNSC, would Japan use force in UN-mandated collective security actions? Would Japan represent Asia, or simply continue its close alignment with U.S. foreign policy goals? Would Japan articulate a clear position on contentious issues, even at the risk of alienating trading partners?

Japan's International Civic Duty in the UN: How Much Is Enough?

These questions became acute after the Japanese government announced its candidacy for permanent membership in the Security Council in 1993, but they have complicated Japan's UN diplomacy from the moment Tokyo began lobbying to join the General Assembly back in 1952.

Tokyo's enthusiasm for rejoining the UN was tempered in 1952 by an intense debate in the Diet about whether membership in the UN might pull Japan into another Korean War. Despite idealism about the world body, after all, it was recognized that the United States dominated the UN and might use it to pull Japan into future conflicts. This fear almost caused the Japanese government to miss the opportunity for membership in the General Assembly, but MOFA eventually worked out a compromise position in which Japan would agree to accept its obligations under UN Charter "by all means at its disposal"—in other words, consistent with the Japanese Constitution. This cleared one domestic hurdle toward Japanese membership in the General Assembly, but the question of JSDF participation in UN activities continued to simmer as Japan came under pressure to contribute personnel to UN forces in Lebanon in 1958, in the Congo in 1960, and in subsequent UN missions elsewhere. Recognizing that Japan's credibility as a contributing member of the United Nations depended on resolving this issue, MOFA officials quietly prepared draft UN peacekeeping legislation in 1965 that would authorize JSDF participation in peacekeeping missions. The effort was premature, though, and MOFA abandoned the legislation after a press leak the next year caused a political firestorm.[25] For almost three decades after that, the best MOFA was able to do was send civilian election monitors to Namibia in 1989. The JSDF stayed home.

Japan's participation in the United Nations after 1956 also added a new wrinkle in alliance relations with the United States. As UN scholar Ueki Yasuhiro has pointed out: "Japan is often torn between a sense of dependence on the Western democracies, particularly the United States, and a desire for autonomy. The United Nations is one forum where all issues can be brought in and debated. Therefore, this dichotomy frequently manifests itself there."[26]

It was inevitable therefore that a significant issue would arise in the UN General Assembly that divided the United States and Japan. The event was the 1975 General Assembly resolution condemning Israel (the "zionism is racism" resolution). The United States voted against the resolution, but Japan, concerned about energy dependence and relations with the Arab states, abstained. This was the first high-profile case of "independent" Japanese diplomacy in the postwar era. Since then Japan has signaled differences with the United States by abstaining on a number of issues in the United Nations, mostly related to human rights and disarmament.[27]

More often, however, Japan's activities in the UN have supported the United States. In fact, Japan's first foray into a leadership role in the UN occurred in the 1980s as Tokyo pushed a reform agenda in order to lure a skeptical Reagan administration back to the traditional American leadership role in the organization. Japan was forced to take action in 1984, after a series of harsh attacks on the UN from Washington led to the isolation of the U.S. delegation in New York. When the Congress enacted legislation in 1985 mandating a freeze on certain U.S. contributions to the UN budget, Foreign Minister Abe Shintarō stepped in between the feuding parties and proposed an international "Wisemen's Group" to recommend reforms in UN management and budgetary practices. The group's recommendations (drafted with major input from Japan) provided political cover for the United States to begin resuming its payment of arrears—exactly what Japan intended.[28] From that point on, Japan took a more active approach on UN activities, influencing several important Security Council resolutions on the Iran-Iraq War and other issues.

Even as questions about peacekeeping, reform, and relations with the United States complicated Japan's UN profile, they also focused MOFA officials on the objective of permanent Security Council membership. Key officials began preparing an incremental path toward permanent membership in the 1980s by winning nonpermanent seats on the UNSC and promoting Japanese citizens to prominent positions in the UN bureaucracy. (Japan has had a record eight terms as nonpermanent UNSC member, thanks in large measure to U.S. diplomacy.) In 1987 Prime Minister Nakasone proposed at the Venice G-7 summit that Japan be given "quasi-permanent" status. Step by step, MOFA was laying the groundwork for permanent membership, waiting for a consensus at home and in New York that Japan's economic power merited greater recognition.

The Gulf War and the Push for a Permanent Security Council Seat

This incremental approach to UNSC membership ended abruptly with the crisis in Japanese diplomacy caused by the 1990–91 Gulf War. Under intense international pressure to support multinational forces in the Gulf, Japan raised taxes to pay for a $13 billion financial contribution, but since the country was unwilling to send personnel in harm's way, this massive financial contribution was dismissed by critics as mere "checkbook" diplomacy. Pressed to provide rear-area support to multilateral forces in the Gulf, MOFA convinced a reluctant Prime Minister Kaifu Toshiki to support a bill authorizing Peace Cooperation with the UN in 1990. The legislation was hastily drafted by the MOFA task force, mainly led by the United Nations Bureau[29] without full support from the JDA, the JSDF, or even MOFA's own senior leadership. Opposed even by the ruling LDP, the bill was eventually withdrawn.

Japan was finally able to dispatch minesweeping force to the Gulf in June 1991 to clean up unclaimed mines (not legally considered the use of force since hostilities had ended). The unprecedented dispatch of MSDF forces was a huge operational and political success and opened the way for another stab at a UN peacekeeping bill. Working more closely with the JDA and with more time for consultation with politicians, MOFA introduced a new bill in September 1991. This time the new International Peace Cooperation Law passed over the opposition of only the Democratic Socialist and the Communist parties. The legislation strictly limited the JSDF ability to use force, but it set the legal and political groundwork for Japanese participation in UN operations in Cambodia in 1992 and later in Mozambique, the Golan Heights, and other crisis areas. More important from MOFA's perspective, it cleared one important hurdle on the way toward permanent Security Council membership.

The humiliation of contributing $13 billion and receiving virtually no appreciation from the rest of the world brought particular hard criticism down on MOFA. As veteran UN diplomat and Japan scholar Robert Immerman has noted:

> MOFA was charged with a multitude of sins: failure to anticipate the Iraqi invasion of Kuwait; failure to assess the nature of the American response; failure to learn every detail of the deliberations of the Security Council's five permanent members (the "Perm Five") regarding a UN response; and—depending on the political position of the critic—failure either to prevent any Japanese involvement in the UN authorized enforcement action or, conversely, to move Japan into a more positive action in cooperation with its U.S. ally and Western friends.[30]

The intensity of this domestic criticism prompted MOFA to accelerate its incremental timetable for permanent Security Council membership. The Japanese public's frustration with international criticism during the Gulf War and the successful deployment of Japanese peacekeepers to Cambodia in 1992 eased political concerns that had impeded that effort before. The fiftieth anniversary of the United Nations in 1995 provided the target date for a new push by MOFA.

When senior MOFA officials began signaling to the Bush administration Japan's intensified interest in a permanent seat on the UNSC, Washington offered implicit support but warned that Tokyo would have to take the lead and make its own case. After the Clinton administration came into office in 1993, UN Ambassador Madeline Albright gave more public support for Japanese permanent membership, but again urged Japan to establish its own road map to get there. MOFA had no strategy in hand and no idea how to even begin the process, but in 1993 the General Assembly presented one when it created the Open-ended Working Group on the Questions of Equitable Representation and Increase in the Membership of the Security Council. In July of 1993 MOFA prepared a position paper for the working group declaring Japan's intention to fulfill the "maximum role possible" on the Security Council. *Asahi Shimbun* proclaimed the MOFA paper Japan's first "de facto declaration of candidacy for permanent membership on the UNSC."[31]

Meanwhile, a domestic political backlash began against the sudden move toward permanent membership in the Security Council. Prime Minister Hosokawa's special advisor, Tanaka Shūsei, a pacifist member of the Harbinger Party, spoke for many on the Left when he argued that permanent membership in the UNSC entailed too many risks and would reignite militarism. Though still divided by some internal disagreement over the importance and desirability of a permanent seat, MOFA countered with four arguments why it was time for a permanent UNSC seat for Japan:[32]

1. The UNSC needs a nonnuclear power.
2. Japan would have a voice in UN peacekeeping operations (an important new role for the JSDF).
3. Japan's large contributions to the UN budget (20.5 percent by the year 2000) should be matched by fuller political representation.
4. Japan would not have to develop military power or nuclear weapons comparable to the other UNSC permanent members.

Tanaka succeeded briefly in slowing Hosokawa's and the Japanese public's enthusiasm for a permanent seat, but under the Murayama cabinet in 1994, the coalition partners (LDP, Harbinger, and Socialist) agreed that the prime minister would for the first time officially ask for a permanent Security Council seat during his speech at the UN General Assembly. Japan's bid would be based on four principles:[33]

1. Japan would not participate in military actions.
2. Japan would become more involved in arms control, environmental and social welfare issues.

3. Japan would push for UN reforms.
4. Japan would lobby for deletion of the former enemies clause from the UN Charter (an outdated legacy of the UN's role in 1945).[34]

In the battle for Japanese public opinion, MOFA continued to score victories from that point forward. In 1994, 56 percent of respondents to a poll by the Prime Minister's Office favored Japan becoming a permanent member of the UNSC; that number increased to 64.4 percent in 1997, rose to 68.1 percent in 1998, and fell to 67.0 percent in 1999.[35]

Sisyphus on the Hudson: Japan's UN Dream Frustrated

In many respects, however, Japan's bid for a permanent Security Council seat may have peaked in 1994. The major obstacle has proven to be the complexity of Security Council reform itself. The Open-ended Working Group has been unable to agree on a concrete path for reform beyond a 1997 recommendation by the chairman, Malaysian ambassador Razali Ismail, that the UNSC be expanded from fifteen seats to twenty-four seats with five more permanent members added from major regions.[36] This recommendation received a cool response from the existing P-5 nations, including the United States, which was willing to see Japan and German become permanent members, but not under a major expansion of the UNSC. China has also quietly blocked Japanese permanent membership, although South Korea has expressed support for Japan's bid provided Tokyo has no veto power.[37] MOFA has thrown its support behind other proposals, such as rotating permanent membership, but none of the proposed reforms seems likely to win the necessary unanimous support from the current P-5.[38]

A second problem has been the declining importance of the UN in international security in the years since the Gulf War. Its success in Cambodia has not been matched in the Balkans, where NATO has proven the multilateral instrument of choice for the United States. Japanese officials have been uneasy with the UN's declining importance to U.S. foreign policy and have expressed their concern through official statements. When U.S. and allied war planes prepared a major strike on Iraq in February 1998, for example, Tokyo withheld statements of official "support" until the last minute because of the lack of a clear UN mandate for the attack. In contrast, there was a UN mandate for air strikes against Iraq under Operation Desert Fox that summer, and Japan was quick to offer a statement of support. In the Kosovo campaign in the spring of 1999, Japan expressed only "understanding" of the U.S.

action—this time because there was again no UN mandate for the use of force. As uncomfortable as Tokyo is with U.S. decisions to use force without UN mandate, however, the reality is that Japan's alliance with the United States is more critical to Japanese security than the UN is. And the declining importance of the UN to U.S. decisions on the use of force since the Gulf War has meant that the Security Council is that much less important to Japan—at least in terms of managing relations with the United States. As the independent Asian Forum Japan recognized in a report on multilateral strategy in 1995, "the UN's function with regard to security depends upon the United States."[39]

Finally, Japan's bid for a permanent UNSC seat has been dealt a psychological blow by the malaise of the Japanese economy in the 1990s. Although public support in Japan for a permanent seat has not declined, Japan's economic woes have made it more difficult for MOFA to convince other nations of the uniqueness of Japan's case. As Robert Immerman has noted, "Japan now appears to be waiting, rather than pushing, for U.N. change."[40]

Japan continues to play an important leadership role in UN efforts at arms control, environmental protection, and a range of social and economic issues. Japan hosts the United Nations University and in the late 1990s sponsored major UN conferences on African development assistance, peacekeeping, "human security," and disarmament. In addition, prominent Japanese citizens such as Ogata Sadako, the UN High Commissioner for Refugees, and Matsuura Kōichirō, the director-general of United Nations Educational, Scientific and Cultural Organization (UNESCO), highlight the continued importance of UN-centered diplomacy for the Japanese public. And prominent politicians, particularly Ozawa Ichirō, continue to argue that Japan's role in international security should be defined through the United Nations.

But even though the ideals of the UN continue to have a powerful hold on the Japanese people, the idealism has been tarnished. There is a danger that Japan's commitment to the UN may ebb. As UN expert Fukushima Akiko warns: "[The] skewed balance between Japan's role and contribution may antagonize UN sympathizers in Japan. Like the U.S. Congress, the Japanese Diet, faced with enormous budget cuts and lacking strong domestic support for the United Nations, may refuse to allow taxpayers' money to be used for the UN, which does not validate Japan's contribution by offering it a seat on the Security Council."[41]

In 1997 Foreign Minister Obuchi set just this tone in a speech warning that "there would be a problem with respect to fairness" if Japan's assessment were to increase without corresponding Security Council reform.[42] Japan's UN ambassador in 1999, Satō Yukio, also reportedly warned his interlocutors in New York that Japan's funding could be at risk if Japan did not receive a proportionate number of positions for its citizens on the UN staff.[43] These threats were backed in the Diet with 1999 legislation prepared by maverick junior member Kōno Tarō that sought to cut Japan's UN dues if reform were not undertaken.

Sensitive to this frustration, U.S. Ambassador to the UN Richard Holbrooke reiterated in September 1999 that the United States strongly supports Japan's permanent membership on the Security Council.[44] Lobbied steadily by Japanese Ambassador Satō, Holbrooke began shifting U.S. policy away from his predecessor's strong opposition to expanded membership in the UNSC beyond twenty—giving Japan more room to find support for its own membership and removing a potential irritant in U.S.-Japan relations even if actual reform of the UNSC remains almost as remote as ever.

The United States has an interest in seeing Japan's commitment to the United Nations continue. It is important not only because of Japan's status as the second largest contributor to the UN budget, but also because Japan shares many of the reform goals of the United States. But since a permanent UNSC seat seems less than likely for Japan, Washington and Tokyo will have to focus on other areas to enhance Japan's contribution, credibility, and credit at the UN. These may include personnel increases, support for Japanese candidates to senior positions, and ongoing U.S. support for nonpermanent Japanese membership on the Security Council.[45] For the foreseeable future, Japan's focus on reform and membership in the UNSC may well bear more frustration than fruit.

The APEC Experience

While reluctant to embrace multilateral security arrangements in East Asia during the Cold War, Japanese officials saw the advantages of forums for regional economic cooperation long before the fall of the Berlin Wall. As early as the 1960s and 1970s Japanese intellectuals such as Ōkita Saburō and Kojima Kiyoshi put forward bold proposals for the creation of a Pacific Free Trade Area. These proposals were carefully crafted to counterbalance any protectionism from European integration and U.S. trade policy, while reinforcing the open global trading regime represented by the new General Agreement on Tariffs and Trade (GATT) round.[46] These were not just pieces of paper either. Individual Japanese put these proposals into practice—Ōkita as organizer of the 1968 Pacific Trade and Development Conference and Japanese business leader Gotō Noboru as a founding member of Pacific Basin Economic Conference (PBEC). Finding common cause with Australia in this agenda for regional economic cooperation, Prime Minister Ōhira Masayoshi agreed with Prime Minister Malcolm Fraser in 1979 to a political formula for the establishment of the nongovernmental Pacific Economic Cooperation Council (PECC).[47] And in 1989 this same Japan–Australian combination pushed for the formation of the Asia–Pacific Economic Cooperation forum (APEC)—the region's most significant multilateral effort to date.

Tokyo's activism in the formation of APEC was motivated and enhanced by the unique Japanese position between East and West—its status as both a regional and a global player. But this same position has confounded Japanese diplomacy in the formation of an agenda for trade liberalization and integration in APEC. As APEC has moved toward more formal institutionalization, Japan has faced contradictory tensions. First, there has been the tension between open and closed regionalism. As a global trading power, Japan cannot tolerate the formation of regional trading blocs. Yet the rest of Asia looks to Japan for leadership primarily as a counterforce against the hegemonic influence of the United States and the GATT/WTO. Malaysia, in particular, has pressed Japan to demonstrate its credentials as an Asian "leader" by endorsing the East Asian Economic Caucus (EAEC), which excludes the United States, Oceania, and Canada.

The second tension has been between the trade liberalization agenda of APEC and the requirement for consensus within the organization and, even more problematically, within Japan. MITI recognized in the early stages of APEC that without an active agenda for regional trade liberalization, the group would lose its importance to regional economic integration, U.S.-Japan relations, and global trade negotiations. Yet ironically, domestic Japanese resistance to liberalization of sensitive sectors such as agriculture and wood products have gradually forced MITI and MOFA into the position of blocking the trade liberalization goal of APEC. Together, these two dilemmas have confounded Japanese diplomacy toward APEC and complicated the leadership role that Tokyo demonstrated early in the establishment of the forum.

Leading from Behind: Japan's Role in the Formation of APEC

Looking back to the formative years of APEC, however, Japanese leadership showed great promise. There is some controversy over how much of the initiative behind APEC was Australian and how much Japanese (and specifically MITI), but there is no doubt that Japan played an important role early on—particularly in the conceptualization of the forum. Australian Prime Minister Bob Hawke first proposed its formation in a speech in Seoul in January 1989, but as Funabashi Yōichi points out in his groundbreaking 1995 history of APEC, *Asia-Pacific Fusion,* Hawke's proposal was vague and gave no hint of any specific Australian plan for the forum. MITI, in contrast, had engaged in detailed planning for a regional economic grouping in the late 1980s and had been floating the idea informally in Australia and elsewhere at a lower level for months.[48]

No matter who deserves more credit for the birth of APEC, MITI and the Australian government were clearly united by their enthusiasm for its establishment. Both were highly dependent on U.S. forward engagement in Asia and the maintenance of open global trading regimes. Both were concerned about the potential for trading blocs in North American and Europe with the North American Free Trade Agreement (NAFTA) and the European Union. And both expected to see greater intraregional trade and investment in Asia.

For MITI, though, the problem was perhaps made more acute by the persistence of U.S.-Japan trade friction. MITI officials recognized that the large U.S. trade deficits of the 1980s would not be sustainable and that Japan had to encourage an expansion of intraregional trade to increase the absorption of U.S. goods. The strategy to do this was spelled-out in a series of documents, including the Economic Planning Agency's *Sekai to tomoni Ikiru Nihon* (Japan Living with the World), MITI's 1987 *New Asian Industrial Plan,* and the 1988 MITI *White Paper.*[49] In these pages, MITI argued that Japan would have to recycle surpluses to Asia in the form of FDI and ODA and open Japan to more Asian exports. The effect, of course, would not only be more regional absorption of U.S. exports, but also greater influence for Japan in global trade negotiations as Japanese FDI stock surpassed the United States in the region. (And it did, thanks more to the appreciation of the yen than to any deliberate planning by MITI. In 1986 the stock of U.S. FDI in Asia was greater than Japan's, but by 1993 U.S. FDI stock in the region was less than half of Japan's.)

MOFA, while in favor of regional integration, was initially more cautious about the formation of a regional organization that might appear to confront the United States or suggest Japanese domination of the region. But that changed after U.S. Secretary of State James Baker expressed an accommodating view toward APEC in a speech in June 1989 and after MITI began seizing the limelight at the first regional trade ministers' meeting in Canberra that November. Despite bureaucratic jockeying, both MOFA and MITI came to share the view that APEC should move forward gradually, based on consensus, a recognition of diversity, and open regionalism. Consensus and diversity were necessary to maintain smooth relations with ASEAN, and open regionalism (the application of APEC liberalization to non-APEC members on a most-favored-nation basis) was necessary to maintain smooth relations with the United States. As Foreign Minister Hata Tsutomu emphasized in a speech in 1993, APEC should reinforce global regimes like the GATT/WTO, but at the same time APEC should be process-oriented rather than results-oriented.[50] MITI and MOFA therefore focused efforts on those areas that would facilitate mutual trade and investment but not prove overly controversial. Areas such as energy cooperation and economic data sharing were ideal. At the same time, Japan supported the longer-term goal of trade liberalization, since MITI had seen this as a necessary measure to facilitate intraregional trade and jump-start the GATT round.

In the first few years of APEC, these various objectives were not in contradiction. Gradualism and consensus-building were still compatible with the longer-term goal of trade liberalization. The first step was to establish the forum and start talking. Meanwhile, the collapse of the Uruguay Round talks of the GATT in Brussels in 1990 and the growing fear of European protectionism added both a sense of urgency and common purpose to the APEC members' first meetings. At the 1991 ministerial meeting in Seoul, the members agreed to realize free and open trade and investment and to promote economic and technical cooperation. Much of the Seoul Declaration was aimed at promoting global free trade, which was a de facto warning to Europe to make progress on the GATT negotiations. At the next meeting, in Bangkok in 1992, the members of APEC agreed to expand their membership from fifteen to seventeen by including Mexico and Papua New Guinea, and also established a secretariat and an outside group of advisors, the so-called Eminent Person's Group. APEC also held two special meetings of trade ministers in Vancouver that year to discuss steps the forum could take to breathe life back into the Uruguay Round talks. In 1993 in Seattle, President Clinton elevated the importance of APEC by inviting the seventeen heads of state to a historic summit of Asia-Pacific leaders. Then in Bogor, Indonesia, in 1994, APEC reached what may have been its high-water mark in the 1990s as members agreed to realize "free and open trade and investment" for advanced economies by 2010 and all economies by 2020.[51] United by a common fear of Europe's impact on the global trade regime and a broad consensus about longer-term liberalization in Asia, APEC was tracking with MITI's original vision.

Japan Stumbles: Trade Liberalization versus Economic Integration

In 1995 it fell to Japan to host the APEC summit, and it was at this point that the contradictions in the Japanese approach to the forum first began to appear. The onus was on Tokyo to create an "action agenda" at the Osaka summit for implementing the longer-term trade liberalization goals the forum had enunciated in the Bogor Declaration. What should have been an opportunity for leadership soon became a burden. Tokyo found itself torn between ASEAN and the United States and hampered by its own domestic constituencies. MITI and MOFA emphasized the gradual, consensus-oriented approach to trade liberalization, but arguments about regional diversity were clearly also an excuse to exempt Japan's own uncompetitive agricultural sector from further liberalization. Japan tried to convince the United States to allow flexibility on the final dates for opening sensitive economic sectors, but Washington called for strict adherence to the Bogor Declaration without exception. Japanese initiative in the Osaka meeting was further hampered by the weak leadership of Prime Minister Murayama, who—in the words of Funabashi Yōichi—was "nowhere to be seen in the APEC process."[52] In the weeks leading up to the summit, the Japanese government appeared to be heading for a disaster. In the end, however, Tokyo was saved as each country—most notably China—volunteered an initial set of liberalization commitments.[53] Through luck and some skillful diplomacy, Japan prevented a rupture in APEC. The meeting ended with the announcement of an impressive-sounding Osaka Action Agenda, but it still remained unclear how the liberalization objectives contained in the Bogor Declaration would be realized.

At the next summit, in Manila in 1996, each APEC member promised to move beyond their initial commitments at Osaka to more comprehensive Individual Action Plans (IAPs) for liberalization. These were entirely voluntary, however, and the contents were largely summaries of ongoing liberalization already planned under the GATT round. Together, they became the Manila Action Plan (MAPA). Japan's IAP was perhaps the most impressive of the MAPA in quantitative terms, as Tokyo promised to accelerate Uruguay Round tariff reduction commitments on 697 nonagricultural items,[54] but for the most part, the members' commitments on liberalization were vague and the American, Canadian, and Australian desire for concrete results came into sharper confrontation with the developing countries' emphasis on diversity, flexibility, and consensus.

At the Vancouver meeting in November 1997, APEC did make more concrete progress on the trade liberalization agenda, but the momentum was partly illusory, since the difficult implementing decisions were postponed to the next year's meeting in Kuala Lumpur. In Vancouver APEC members agreed to liberalize trade in fifteen sectors, including nine "priority areas" worth $1.9 trillion (environmental goods and services, fish and fish products, wood products, medical equipment and instruments, telecommunications, energy, toys, gems, and jewelry and chemicals).[55] Members were asked to announce their Early Voluntary Sectoral Liberalization (EVSL) initiatives at the next meeting. Japan agreed, but insisted that each country could choose which products would be liberalized.[56] Meanwhile, the Vancouver meeting was overshadowed by the East Asian financial crisis, in which APEC ministers were able to play little role beyond an expression of support for the IMF approach to the crisis. The exposure of APEC's insignificance compared with global regimes like the IMF was shocking and called into question the exact purpose of the group. APEC's future identity was also complicated at Vancouver by the expansion of membership to twenty-one states, including Russia and several Latin American nations. APEC now represented half of the world's GDP, but did it really represent Asia? It is striking that Malaysia's Mahathir supported the expansion of APEC at Vancouver, precisely to dilute its importance and strengthen the prospects for an Asians-only grouping in the future.

At Kuala Lumpur in November 1998, members were expected to put the EVSL initiatives into practice. A showdown between the U.S. results-oriented approach and Japan's process-oriented approach to APEC could no longer be avoided. Clinging to the principle that each country could voluntarily choose areas in the EVSL to be liberalized, Japan stood almost alone in defiance of U.S. demands for a cut in tariffs on fish and wood products across the region. For the Clinton administration, this was not just a bilateral trade matter. Washington saw further Japanese market opening as a critical ingredient in the region's economic recovery. Indeed, the United States was attacking Japan for not living up to the vision of APEC originally set by MITI.[57] Japan also stood as the only member state demanding an exception to the EVSL process. Technically this exceptionalism was allowed in the APEC approach, but it threatened to undermine the effectiveness of the forum as a whole.[58]

The United States needed a strong statement from APEC on liberalization—particularly in agriculture—in order to strengthen the prospects for the new WTO round, which was scheduled to begin in Seattle in November 1999. For Japan, on the other hand, the U.S. demands for agricultural liberalization threatened the consensus-oriented rules of APEC—and the very stability of the Obuchi government in Tokyo. MITI and MOFA officials argued that tariff reductions on fish and wood products were not necessary, since Japan already had among the lowest tariff rates on fish and wood products in the world (4.1 percent for fish and 1 percent for wood products) and since Japan was by far the largest importer of both products in the world. MITI officials also complained that the U.S. position on APEC was volatile and unpredictable. As one MITI negotiator remembered, "the EVSL in Vancouver were negotiated primarily with the State Department, but in 1998 the U.S. Trade Representative (USTR) suddenly showed up with a whole new set of demands."[59]

Meanwhile, in Tokyo, prolonged economic malaise had given rise to new economic nationalism, while a hardening of positions in the LDP agricultural *zoku* (caucus) undercut the bureaucrats' flexibility in negotiations. The LDP and its agricultural *zoku* had been in the opposition during the Seattle meetings and had believed in the "voluntary" principle promised in subsequent discussions in Bogor, Manila, and Osaka. But with the tougher U.S. approach and the LDP's disastrous showing in July 1998 Upper House elections, the agricultural constituencies mobilized. MITI and MOFA both tried to control the agricultural interests but were not powerful enough to sway them. Nor was the Obuchi government. As a result, the LDP agricultural *zoku* set the entire scenario for Japan's negotiating position, even dispatching members to Kuala Lumpur to keep an eye on the MOFA and MITI negotiators. As one senior MITI official lamented to the *Sankei Shimbun,* "normally you have a compromise proposal in your back pocket, but this time there is nothing."[60] Even Foreign Minister Kōmura buckled before the agriculture *zoku,* warning that "if Japan swallows liberalization on agriculture, it will affect the very stability of the Obuchi government."[61]

When the APEC trade ministers met in June 1998 to prepare for the Kuala Lumpur meeting, the chairman's statement announced that trade liberalization would proceed. Japanese officials sensed their growing isolation in APEC, and the Obuchi government dispatched cabinet ministers throughout Asia to drum up support for Japan's position.[62] Talks with the United States, Australia, and New Zealand went nowhere. Seoul refused to help Japan block the liberalization agenda, but proposed an extension of the EVSL as a possible compromise. [63] In Southeast Asia Japan had somewhat more success. These nations hoped to see greater opening in Japan's agricultural, fisheries, and wood markets, but the generous Miyazawa initiative had also won goodwill for Japan in ASEAN, and many of the developing countries were concerned that the U.S. demands might undermine the APEC principle of voluntary liberalization. Japanese officials such as MITI minister Yosano Kaoru and former ambassador to the United States Matsunaga Nobuo called in all the chits won from decades of ODA to the region. Eventually the Japanese pressure worked. On the eve of the APEC meeting, the ASEAN trade and finance ministers announced their recognition of Japan's right to refuse forced liberalization in certain sectors. [64]

With reluctant ASEAN backing, Japan was able to escape the pressure for EVSL in agriculture, fisheries, and wood products at the Kuala Lumpur meeting. U.S. officials tried to convince ASEAN countries, South Korea, and China that Washington's only intention was to jumpstart regional growth with Japanese market opening, but the U.S. position was seriously undermined by Vice President Al Gore's aggressive attack on Malaysia's human rights record in his keynote speech at the summit. With one speech, the U.S. approach took on the unfortunate colorings of a debate on Western values versus Asian values. The United States came away from Kuala Lumpur with even less sympathy for its arguments about Japan.

For Japan, however, the Kuala Lumpur meeting was a pyrrhic victory. On behalf of small but powerful domestic constituencies, MITI and MOFA had all but destroyed their original dreams for APEC. First, Japan had not delivered on the vision captured in the MITI White Papers of the late 1980s of an open domestic market driving regional growth and integration. Second, Japan had undermined the role of APEC as a pathbreaker for global trade liberalization, particularly after U.S. officials vowed to bypass APEC and take the agricultural liberalization fight directly to the WTO. Finally, while Japan demonstrated diplomatic prowess in mobilizing support for defensive actions in APEC, it won no kudos for "leadership" in its debilitating fight with the United States, Australia, and New Zealand. In postmortems after the meeting, the Japanese press acknowledged the dilemma their country's diplomacy had created. *Yomiuri* lamented that APEC for the first time had ended a meeting with confrontation and a demonstrated inability to actually address trade issues. *Sankei* warned that the emergence of economic nationalism had undercut the integration process in Asia and even the future convening power of APEC itself.[65] And *Asahi* predicted that the WTO would now take over momentum from APEC, as the Asian forum grasped without focus for a new mission like civil society or education.[66]

Asahi's assessment was not far from the truth. In the tenth APEC meeting and the last of the twentieth century in Auckland, New Zealand, in September 1999, Japan and the United States rejoined their battle over trade liberalization—but this time in anticipation of the next round of the WTO scheduled to begin later that year. The United States pressed APEC members to accept a sector-by-sector focus for the WTO that would reduce industrial tariffs in addition to already man-dated negotiations on services and agriculture. Japan argued for a broader "comprehensive" agenda that would also include constraints on U.S. antidumping actions and unilateral "Super 301" trade retaliation. Caught in the middle again, the APEC leaders gave a vague endorse-ment to Japan's rhetoric of a comprehensive "single-package" approach without denying that the U.S. sectoral approach could fit within it.[67] Satisfied that the real battle over trade liberalization, antidumping, and Super 301 would be in the WTO, the United States and Japan left Auckland without initiating the kind of bruising battle that had dam-aged both countries' reputations the year before.

Whither Japan's APEC Strategy?

At the beginning of a new century, Japanese trade officials and diplo-mats are asking what purpose APEC can, in fact, fill. MITI officials hope to focus once again on the less contentious issues of cooperation on en-ergy, the environment, and economic data sharing. They point to the success of 1995 agreement to standardize and computerize customs procedures by 2000, the 1998 establishment of a foreign direct invest-ment forum, and other meetings aimed at reducing the costs of trade in the region. Japan also participates actively in a dozen working groups, such as the APEC Business Advisory Council and the Eminent Persons Group. These areas of cooperation can gradually contribute to the sense of an Asia–Pacific economic community. Overall, however, APEC re-mains "four adjectives in search of a noun"—particularly after the Kuala Lumpur meeting and the shadow of WTO.

Ironically, one area of diplomatic activity in the APEC forum where Japan is increasingly successful is security. When U.S. Secretary of De-fense William Perry speculated in 1995 that APEC might someday have a security dimension, he was criticized throughout Asia, including

Japan. Yet the highlights of the Auckland meeting were the discussions on the crisis in East Timor, the U.S.-Japan-ROK trilateral summit on North Korea's missile program, and the U.S.-China meetings on WTO accession. Two out of three issues were security-related, and one of those (Korean security) was largely initiated by Japan.

Meanwhile, both MITI and MOFA are demonstrating far less reticence about participation in other regional meetings that exclude the United States. "Asianists" like Ogura Kazuo in MOFA and Sakakibara Eisuke in MOF pushed for Japanese participation in informal Asian-only meetings from the moment Mahathir proposed the EAEC in 1990. Over the decade, Japan's participation in such forums has steadily expanded. In the early 1990s Japan participated in the ASEAN economic ministers meetings with South Korea and China. In 1994 MOF began holding sessions with ASEAN before the annual IMF–World Bank meetings.[68] In March 1996 Japan joined ASEAN, South Korea, and China in the first annual ASEM meeting with the European Union. And in 1997 Japan joined in the first annual meeting of the ASEAN Plus Three—a forum originally proposed by Tokyo to strengthen strategic cooperation with Southeast Asia, but later turned by ASEAN into a broader meeting that resembled the membership of Mahathir's original proposal for the EAEC.

The growing Japanese penchant for participation in such exclusive groupings clearly reflects differences with the United States over trade. Nevertheless, it would be a mistake to point to such meetings as evidence of a secular trend toward divergence between Tokyo and Washington for five reasons.

First, with the dilution of APEC and the growing evidence that regional organizations exist primarily for dialogue, Japanese participation in forums like ASEM is less threatening to the United States than it would have been in the early years of APEC. Forums like ASEM and the ASEAN Plus Three are not trading blocs by any stretch of the imagination. Instead, they are symbolic hedges against exclusive trading practices by other actors. Just as APEC's meetings sent a signal to Europe, the ASEM and ASEAN Plus Three meetings sent a signal to the United States about unilateral U.S. trading practices such as antidumping and Super 301.

Second, the meetings of the ASEAN Plus Three also reinforce the sense of Asian economic cooperation and integration drained from APEC by the fights over early voluntary liberalization and Japan's proposal for a regional monetary fund. Debt-swapping arrangements symbolized these, as will be explained in the next chapter on international finance. But as we shall see, these arrangements remained gestures rather than institutions.

Third, Japan's enthusiasm for establishing new forums still has as much to do with constraining China and gaining leverage on North Korea as balancing the United States. In the first Japan-ROK-China trilateral summit held on the wings of the ASEAN Plus Three meeting in 1999, for example, Tokyo wanted the discussion to focus on how China could control North Korea's missile and nuclear programs. Beijing refused, so the three leaders had a discussion about economic cooperation that was completely redundant with APEC. If MOFA had its way, there would be many other forums to maximize Japanese diplomatic leverage vis-à-vis China.

Fourth, it is important to note that Tokyo has complemented its multilateral economic diplomacy with efforts to establish bilateral free trade agreements with Singapore, South Korea, and Mexico—signals that closed regionalism is not the intent. The hedging represented by Tokyo's participation in the ASEM and ASEAN Plus Three meetings points to the continuing Japanese desire to maintain an open global trading system. Nevertheless, this tactic creates its own friction with the United States and other powers, and thus the tension between exclusive regionalism and open regionalism is still not resolved.

Finally, Japan's regional economic diplomacy must be contrasted with Japanese behavior in the WTO, which is increasingly legalistic. WTO norms are being used by Tokyo both to protect Japan from U.S. unilateralism—as with the Fuji-Kodak film dispute—and as a non-U.S. source of *gaiatsu* for restructuring the Japanese economy.[69]

For all these reasons Japan's economic diplomacy is likely to be increasingly aggressive and legalistic, using the regional card whenever possible, but not in a way designed to undermine global regimes like the WTO. In a sense, therefore, Japan's role in APEC will depend on how successful and relevant WTO remains. For the WTO also faces monumental challenges of its own. As former White House economic advisor Daniel Tarullo points out: "Much of the public debate will focus on whether trade agreements should impose trade sanctions on countries that do not enforce minimal labor or environmental standards. . . . This takes trade negotiations far beyond their original purpose of reducing tariffs. The ever-expanding scope of the trading system has also revealed its policy, political, and practical limitations."[70]

Just as APEC surged in importance in the early 1990s in the wake of stalled Uruguay Round talks, the forum may find a new purpose in the future if the WTO talks begun in Seattle in 1999 falter. But this time there may be many more fault lines within the APEC membership—between the U.S. and Japan over antidumping, for example, and between the developed and developing countries over labor and environmental standards. These cleavages will test Japanese diplomacy at a new level. The symbolism of APEC was enough in 1992 to affect global trade diplomacy. In the future, Japan will have to deliver substance.

The ASEAN Regional Forum and Security Multilateralism

Compared with the United Nations and APEC, Japan's diplomacy in regional security multilateralism has the most recent beginnings. Multilateral security proposals during the Cold War were primarily designed by the Soviet Union or the nonaligned bloc to constrain U.S. freedom of action in the region—something Japan could not tolerate. However, as other U.S. allies began calling for a regional security forum after the Cold War, Japan soon joined the chorus.

Leading from Behind II:
Japan's Role in the Formation of the ARF

In 1990 Australian Foreign Minister Gareth Evans proposed an Asian version of the Conference on Security and Cooperation in Europe (CSCE), building on the Australian lead in APEC. Canada soon followed. Then in July 1991 Japan dropped its earlier reticence on regional security multilateralism, and Foreign Minister Nakayama Tarō formally proposed a region-wide security forum in a speech to the ASEAN Post-Ministerial Conference in Bangkok. Japan's new foray into multilateral security policy fell flat, however. In spite of Tokyo's coordination of the issue with Washington beforehand, the Bush administration remained suspicious; nor was ASEAN eager to see Japan take a lead on security issues in Southeast Asia. With time, however, Japan's endorsement did add weight to the earlier Australian proposal and helped to soften U.S. opposition. What was ultimately required was ASEAN blessing; in June 1991 the ASEAN-ISIS (Institute of Strategic and International Studies) network approved the idea of an ASEAN Post-Ministerial Conference, paving the way for the ASEAN governments to eventually agree to the first formal ASEAN Regional Forum in Brunei in July 1994.[71]

In its early years, the ARF inspired hope among Japanese observers that a new East Asian regional security order might be established.

MOFA's expectation was that the ARF would be able to move forward from transparency measures, to actual policy coordination, and finally to collective action.[72] The second meeting in Brunei in 1995 suggested that such progress might be achievable. At that meeting Japan joined ASEAN in pressing China to soften its position on the territorial dispute over the Spratley Islands. Facing isolation, Beijing agreed with other claimants to follow UNCLOS rules and international law in resolving the dispute.[73] Japan, Australia, and other participants also used the Brunei meeting to condemn France for nuclear tests in the South Pacific, creating indirect pressure on China to stop its own nuclear testing.[74] Finally, in an agreement pregnant with possibility, the other participants in Brunei promised to further institutionalize the ARF process, moving forward from: confidence-building, to preventive diplomacy, and, finally, to conflict resolution—a path consistent with Japanese hopes and expectations.

However, subsequent ARF meetings failed to institutionalize the agenda articulated in Brunei, and Japanese diplomats and scholars increasingly found themselves tussling with Chinese counterparts over issues such as TMD and the Defense Guidelines in both formal ARF sessions and intersessional gatherings. Despite the diplomatic skirmishes with China, though, Japanese diplomats were still satisfied with the developments in the ARF. As Nishihara Masashi of the National Defense University noted in 1997, China may have become active in the ARF only to protect its own national interests, but it is better to have Beijing inside a forum where other participants share Japanese concerns about Chinese intentions.[75] Indeed, the ARF forum created sufficient pressure for Chinese agreement to publish a defense White Paper, a transparency step Tokyo had sought for several years.

Over the next few meetings, however, Japanese expectations for the ARF began to flag. Chinese resistance to confidence-building measures was only part of the problem.[76] ASEAN participants also began to turn inward after the financial crisis, concerned about sovereignty and the implications of transparency in a time of economic uncertainty. The expanding membership of the ARF also diluted the focus of the forum, just as it had with APEC. By the 1999 ARF session in Singapore, the participants were bogged down over conceptual definitions of "preventive diplomacy."[77] In second-track forums associated with the ARF, such as the Council for Security Cooperation in the Asia Pacific (CSCAP), somewhat more productive dialogue was possible, but even in these forums Chinese participants were closely linked to the government in Beijing, slowing forward momentum.

There is no doubt that Tokyo continues to invest energy in the ARF process in the hope of enhancing confidence-building and raising Japan's own diplomatic profile in the region. The ARF forums have also created opportunities for bilateral meetings and ad hoc coalition building, such as the trilateral meeting among the U.S., Japanese, and ROK foreign ministers to address the North Korean missile threat on the wings of the 1999 Singapore ARF meeting.[78] However, once-enthusiastic observers of the ARF process in Japan are now changing their views. On the Right, the frustration is reflected in a 1998 essay penned by Morimoto Satoshi of the Nomura Research Institute (NRI):

> Multilateral security cooperation dialogues such as ARF and ASEM had been developing significantly in recent years, but they have lost momentum as the economic crisis has continued. ASEAN had provided much of the impetus behind these dialogues and this leadership has waned as member nations have become focused on their domestic economic and political problems.
>
> As a consequence, the possibility of regional consensus and agreement on CBMs is becoming remote and the ARF process has stalled. At the same time observers argue that we must promote multilateral cooperation during critical times like these.[79]

On the Left, similar views are echoed by *Asahi Shimbun* editorial-page writer Shimada Kazuyuki, who lamented in *Gunshuku Mondai* (*Monthly Journal of Disarmament*) in October 1998 that the ARF has "failed to deliver expected results" and is "losing its convening power" as the participants and themes broaden and the ASEAN powers turn inward after the financial crisis. A firm believer in the importance of multilateral diplomacy, Shimada urged Japan to demonstrate greater initiative in revitalizing the ARF process.[80]

But how can Japan demonstrate greater initiative in a forum that operates on the rules of consensus and maintaining the comfort level for all participants? The limitations placed on the ARF by its Southeast Asian focus are not lost on Japan's Foreign Ministry, of course. Japan's major security concerns involve Taiwan and the Korean Peninsula, which the ARF has yet to—and perhaps cannot—address. With a view to supplementing the ARF, Foreign Minister Kōno Yōhei endorsed the notion of a Northeast Asian Security Forum as early as May 1994, and Foreign Minister Obuchi Keizō repeated this theme in 1998. However, neither proposal has come to fruition, primarily because North Korea refuses to participate, preferring instead to pursue bilateral relations with the United States and other countries, and China therefore resists such proposals as well. Over the longer term the Four Party talks on the Korean Peninsula may yield a peace treaty, and as South Korean President Kim Dae Jung has pointed out, that would pave the way for six-party talks in Northeast Asia. But in the near term, China is unlikely to decrease its own leverage in the Four Party talks by creating a forum where Japan has equal weight. Frustrated, Tokyo continues to search for forums that will allow security dialogue on Northeast Asia. The November 1999 Japan–ROK–China summit—far from being an anti-U.S. gathering—was just such a bid by Japan.

The ARF still has value to Japanese diplomacy, however. The forum provides a unique opportunity for one-stop shopping with all the region's foreign ministries and after July 2000 with North Korea. In substantive terms, however, the ARF remains at best a talk shop for Tokyo.

Japan's Role in Second-Track Security Dialogue

Japan has also maintained active participation in other multilateral security forums. These include KEDO, which has emerged as perhaps the most successful multilateral instrument of Japanese security policy. In addition, Japanese scholars like Morimoto at NRI and Fukushima at NIRA ably represent Japan in second-track forums such as the Northeast Asia Cooperation Dialogue (NEACD) and the Council for Security Cooperation in the Asia Pacific (CSCAP). Minilateralism has also taken hold, as Japanese think tanks team-up with second and third countries to address specific security issues. Examples include the MOFA sponsored Japan Institute for International Affairs link with the Institute of World Economy and International Relations (IMEMO) in Russia[81] and the Johns Hopkins University School of Advanced International Studies in the United States; or the Harvard, JIIA, Chinese Academy of Social Science trilateral meetings. These minilaterals allow for more discreet dialogue and greater focus on security issues of common concern. They are nonbinding and carry only limited governmental authority, but they are a start.

Arms Control and Nonproliferation

In addition, Japan attempted to make a greater mark in international arms control and nonproliferation since the 1990s. After embarrassing revelations in 1987 that Toshiba Machine Tool Company had violated export control rules of COCOM (the Coordinating Committee for Multinational Export Control)—helping the Soviets to advance their submarine construction—MITI and MOFA introduced some of the strictest export control legislation of any COCOM member. Japan has also been a reliable party to the Missile Technology Control Regime (MTCR) and the Chemical Weapons Convention (CWC). In May 1991, smarting from its poor diplomatic performance in the Gulf War, MOFA attempted to take a leadership role in establishing an international arms registry for the UN, championing the idea at the Kyōto Conference on Disarmament (which has been held annually in Japan since 1989). After modifying its proposal somewhat, Japan joined the United Kingdom and other European nations in 1992 to formally establish the registry under UN auspices.[82]

Ironically, Japan's multilateral diplomacy on nuclear proliferation has been less successful. As the world's only victims of atomic weapons, the Japanese have often assumed that their nation has a unique credibility on nuclear disarmament issues. Indeed, it should, but Japan's neighbors do not necessarily share this view, and Japanese intentions with regard to nuclear proliferation have often been interpreted as less than benign.[83] During negotiations over the indefinite extension of the Nonproliferation Treaty (NPT) in 1993, for example, the Miyazawa government dragged its feet on signing and forced other G-7 members to water down a June 1993 communiqué endorsing quick adoption of the new treaty.[84] This was not motivated by a desire for nuclear weapons so much as to maintain maximum diplomatic leverage on North Korea to join the NPT and also on the United States and other nuclear powers to reduce their arsenals based on Article VI of the treaty. Nevertheless, this idealistic agenda was lost on many outside observers, and Japan came under intense international criticism for hinting dangerously at its own nuclear option.[85]

Japan's nonproliferation diplomacy suffered from excessive idealism a second time in the wake of nuclear tests by India and Pakistan in May 1998.[86] After the tests, Tokyo froze new grants and yen loans consistent with the ODA charter—a significant bite since Japan was the number-one provider of assistance to India at the time.[87] Japan also introduced and cosponsored a resolution in the United Nations condemning the tests. But these steps were not enough; Tokyo wanted to play a "leading role in finding a new framework to keep nuclear arms from spreading." The Hashimoto government therefore proposed a nuclear nonproliferation forum that would address South Asian security concerns while calling on the permanent members of the UN Security Council to "strive for nuclear disarmament." Tokyo's gesture was an attempt to strengthen the case for Japanese participation in a June 4, 1998, P-5 meeting in Geneva on the South Asian tests—but the move backfired. Suspicious of Japanese intentions, the P-5 excluded Japan. As one U.S. official put it, the United States was eager to work with Japan, but "Tokyo's emphasis on Article VI echoed India's rhetoric and created unease in the Department [of State]."[88] Instead, MOFA established the Tokyo Forum, a track-two meeting that issued a report in July 1999 calling for greater action to reduce nuclear arsenals.[89]

In addition to the trap of excessive idealism, Japan has been unable to escape suspicions about its own plutonium recycling program. In the quest for greater energy security, Japan has been developing a special reprocessing plant (the Recycling Equipment Test Facility, or RETF), designed expressly to separate supergrade plutonium. In the eyes of many, Japan's pursuit of mixed uranium-plutonium oxide (MOX) and fast-breeder reactors suggests intent to develop nuclear weapons. Indeed, in 1968 the Security Research Council, a think tank sponsored by the Japanese Defense Agency, published a study that states, "Japan could make 20 to 30 nuclear weapons per year if its civilian nuclear reactors discontinued power generation and were devoted entirely to the production of fissile plutonium 239."[90] Japan's plutonium recycling program has come under renewed criticism after a fatal accident at the Tokaimura plant in 1999, but through bureaucratic inertia—rather than nuclear weapons aspirations—it lives on.[91] And as a result, Japan's own nonproliferation activism is less effective. Japan's nuclear energy industry backs some of the Japanese NGOs' activities on nonproliferation and has real energy requirements for further reactors, but it is in an uphill battle.[92]

Japan's diplomacy on nonproliferation and nuclear disarmament has also been undermined at times by U.S. policy—most notably when the U.S. Senate rejected ratification of the Comprehensive Test Ban Treaty in October 1999. The Senate's action and the administration's mishandling of the issue prompted Tokyo to dispatch Parliamentary Vice Minister Yamamoto Ichita to Washington to express disappointment to his former Georgetown University professor, Secretary of State Madeline Albright. Japanese adherence to the U.S. nuclear umbrella and self-restraint on nuclear arms is strong, but further tactical disagreements with Washington over nuclear arms control issues such as the CTBT could lead Japan to press for a more independent stance in multilateral arms control. In the lead up to the April 2000 NPT review in New York, for example, the Japanese delegation's position began gravitating toward the "New Agenda" countries led by South Africa, which are highly critical of the lack of cuts in the U.S. nuclear arsenal. Japan did not formally join the New Agenda in the NPT review, and actually helped, with Norway and Australia, to bridge the gap between the New Agenda Coalition (NAC) and the P-5. (Though again, Japan's primary role was in drafting papers that anticipated the resolution rather than in working the delegates.)[93] However, Tokyo's more independent and activist approach prompted the Clinton administration to establish a new bilateral Commission on Nonproliferation and Arms Control with Japan in March 2000 that would elevate consultations with Japan on such issues to the same level as NATO.

For the time being, MOFA resists proposals within Japan to join the New Agenda countries or to press the United States to adopt a "no first use" policy designed to jump-start nuclear arms control talks with China and Russia. Nevertheless, rumblings are increasing in academic and political circles that Japan should take more control of its nuclear arms control policy.[94] It is possible that these pressures, combined with U.S. inaction on the nuclear arms control front or further political realignment in Japan, could lead to more pronounced divergence between Tokyo and Washington on nonproliferation and arms control issues. Tokyo will be constrained by its reliance on the U.S. nuclear umbrella, the trap of idealism, and suspicions about the Japanese plutonium recycling program. But the bilateral divergence would still do harm to the U.S. and Japanese agenda for combating the spread of weapons of mass destruction.

Assessing Japan's Multilateral Diplomacy

What lessons has Japan learned from its experience with multilateralism after the Cold War, and what lessons should the United States take away?

Leading from Behind versus Leadership at the Front

To begin with, Japan's skill at "leading from behind" in the establishment of multilateral forums in Asia has not been matched by equal skill when Japan is at center stage defining the agenda. It is one thing for MOFA or MITI to propose the establishment of a forum like APEC, but implementing any significant liberalization through that forum brings out powerful domestic constituencies that can halt the bureaucrats' initiative. The hindrances to Japanese initiative are external as well. The consensus-oriented approach of a forum like APEC or the ARF places an inevitable brake on Japanese leadership, particularly when a legacy of mistrust of Japan remains in the region. Finally, as we have seen, Japan's balancing act between Asia and the United States undermines bold action, since Tokyo is constantly deducing its own position based on an assessment of where Washington stands vis-à-vis Seoul, Beijing, or Jakarta.

On the other hand, Japan has certain advantages in the multilateral arena that the United States does not share. For one thing, Japanese economic power counts. Japan's successful defense against U.S. pressure at the Kuala Lumpur APEC summit demonstrated the diplomatic influence gained from the 1998 Miyazawa Initiative (discussed in the next chapter) and years of ODA and FDI in East Asia. Granted, the Japanese goal of slowing EVSL for agriculture coincided with ASEAN concerns about maintaining the "diversity" rule for APEC, but it was still a uniquely partisan victory in a consensus-oriented forum. Japanese financial dues to the UN have also added firepower to Tokyo's push for UN reform, even if they did not lead ultimately to a permanent Security Council seat. Beyond economic power, Tokyo's tactical attention to forums such as the ARF and APEC far outstrips Washington's. In both forums Japanese diplomats, politicians, business envoys, and scholars have spun a web of contacts and consultation that the U.S. diplomats have not even tried to match. And even though Japan's position between East and West has created a dilemma, it does give Tokyo the opportunity to bring a certain amount of U.S. leverage to bear on Asia and Asian leverage on the United States.

The Advantages of Quiet U.S.-Japan Cooperation

Despite these tools, however, the bottom line for Japan has been that multilateral diplomacy has been most effective when Tokyo and Washington are cooperating and least effective when these two allies are in open competition. APEC and the ARF worked best for both Japan and the United States in 1995, when Washington was most engaged and least confrontational. In the UN, the reform agenda has made the most progress when Tokyo and Washington are in sync. (Indeed, in the 1980s Japan used the reform agenda to bring U.S. and Japanese diplomacy back into sync.) At the same time, an explicit U.S.-Japan alliance within these multilateral settings can undermine Japan's effectiveness. Japanese influence in the ARF and APEC depends in part on other Asian nations' desire to establish an "Asian" identity. In the UN, Japanese adherence to U.S. diplomacy weakens the argument that Japan has a unique role to play on the Security Council. How, then, to bring the U.S.-Japan alliance into multilateralism? Just as Japan's multilateral diplomacy is most effective when Japan can "lead from behind," the U.S.-Japan alliance will be most effective in multilateral settings when there is "coordination from behind." In other words, the United States and Japan must have sufficient high-level coordination of goals and strategy that Japan can comfortably take an independent lead in these forums without either confronting the United States or appearing to be Washington's willing envoy.

And while U.S. and Japanese goals will not coincide in all cases, it is in U.S. interests to encourage Japan to play a larger role in multilateral forums. In the UN, Japanese financial support is critical, particularly as pressure mounts in the Congress to reduce U.S. dues. Japan's political responsibility should increase to match its financial responsibilities, for it would be a significant loss to U.S. interests if the Japanese public turned away from the UN in frustration. At the same time, the United States should make it clear to Japan that leadership cannot be bought. Japan must also be willing to share greater risk, and this means, in particular, relaxing the restrictions on JSDF peacekeeping so that Japanese participation in peacekeeping moves from the symbolic to the substantive.

In APEC, Japan and the United States will continue to have areas of both conflict and cooperation. However, a heavy-handed U.S. approach to trade liberalization in APEC undermines the degree to which that forum can be a tool of U.S. diplomacy for advancing global trade liberalization and deterring the emergence of protectionism in Europe. In the future, U.S. policy toward APEC will require a careful balancing of cooperation and pressure. That balance will be more difficult to maintain (and U.S. isolation more difficult to avoid) if U.S. policymakers use APEC primarily as an arena for bilateral trade battles with Japan.

In the ARF, the challenge will be maintaining any sustained U.S. attention at all. The security forum has become so cumbersome and formulaic that senior U.S. officials can be lured to attend only because of the opportunity to conduct bilateral sessions and perhaps to participate in the annual dinners, which feature skits by foreign ministers singing and performing for their colleagues. Nevertheless, the ARF has become one litmus test in the region for U.S. engagement and therefore should be taken seriously. It is worth a greater investment in time to craft a coordinated effort with Japan and other allies to move beyond talk and implement concrete confidence-building measures. The United States should also give more diplomatic support to Japanese efforts to establish a Northeast Asia forum. While the prospects are dim at present and

Japan's efforts are largely rhetorical, it is better to begin planning with our major allies early for what inevitably will become reality in Northeast Asia.

The Importance of Japanese Idealism

The United States should focus on Japanese multilateral diplomacy for all these reasons and for one more: Japan's increasingly narrow definition of national interest in the formation of foreign policy. The sentimental and idealistic edge is coming off of Japan's multilateral diplomacy. Japan is using multilateral forums as an arena for power politics with China and is taking more assertive steps in these forums to constrain a perceived U.S. shift to unilateralism. Moreover, the Japanese Diet and press are demanding greater accountability, influence, and prestige in exchange for Japan's financial contributions. The United States can no longer take for granted Japanese passivity in multilateral diplomacy or close Japanese adherence to U.S. strategy. U.S. and Japanese objectives need not diverge for Japan's new assertiveness to undermine U.S. diplomacy. Fortunately, there is a general convergence of U.S. and Japanese objectives for the UN, APEC, and the ARF, and that provides the context for more effective power-sharing with Japan in these organizations and forums.

CHAPTER EIGHT

Japan and the International Financial System

Lessons from the Asian Crisis

Introduction

We turn finally to those multilateral institutions where Japanese economic success clearly has brought leadership—the international financial institutions established by the allied powers at Bretton Woods. The diplomatic strategy established by Yoshida and other early postwar Japanese leaders required not only alliance with the United States, but also full entry into these institutions. With U.S. support, Japan borrowed more than $862 million from the World Bank between 1953 and 1968 and joined the International Monetary Fund (IMF) in 1956 with a 2.7 percent voting share (approximately one-tenth of the 27.2 percent share of the United States at that time).[1] As it grew in economic power, Japan gave generously in return. In the 1980s Japan recycled tens of billions of dollars from its chronic current account surpluses through the international financial institutions—a flood of spending that eventually elevated Japan almost to the top leadership positions in these institutions. By 1984 Japan was already the second largest contributor to the World Bank after the United States, and in 1990 Japan joined Germany to share the number-two spot at the IMF (with a voting share of 6.1 percent compared to 19.62 percent for the United States).[2]

Japan's rapid rise in the international financial institutions was so stunning toward the end of the 1980s that many observers looked for a Japanese ideological blitz to follow Tokyo's financial offensive. A 1988 cover story in *Euromoney*, titled "Japan Takes over the IMF," predicted that a Japanese official would replace IMF managing director Michael Camdessus when his term expired in 1992. (Camdessus was reappointed.)[3] In the same issue, World Bank vice president Mooen Qureshi argued that Japan would become "the most important influence in financing Third World Development over the next decade"—a reference not only to Japan's emergence as the leading donor of foreign aid in 1989, but also to Japan's potential for shaping future ideas about development.[4] Japanese MOF officials vowed that given such responsibilities, they would indeed contribute money *and* ideas to the international financial institutions. In Japanese journals and policy papers the buzz word "intellectual contribution" (*chiteki kôken*) became fashionable, and Japanese officials in the various multilateral institutions in Washington went to work trying to turn their financial power into concrete intellectual influence.

These attitudes took concrete form in 1988 when Finance Minister Miyazawa Kiichi proposed a radical new scheme for the IMF to resolve the Latin American debt crisis and in 1990 when Japan sponsored a major project in the World Bank to rethink development patterns in the Third World based on Japan's own economic model. In both cases, Japan offered money to back its ideas, and while neither of these "intellectual contributions" was put into practice, they did mark Japan as a possible challenger to U.S. intellectual leadership of the Bretton Woods system.

The obvious place for Japan to establish its leadership in international finance was not in Latin America, of course, but in Asia. And when the Thai baht collapsed in the summer of 1997 and financial contagion began to spread, the region turned to Japan to put its ideas for international finance and development into practice. The result was a broad Japanese proposal for an Asian Monetary Fund that would combine $50 billion of Japanese money with $50 billion from other Asian nations to provide a quick response to future currency crises in the region. The threat to U.S. and IMF leadership of this "Asians-only" institution was unmistakable, and after a sharp ideological confrontation, the United States and the Europeans, with help from the Chinese, successfully crushed this perceived insurrection against the Bretton Woods system. Chastened, but not resigned to complete defeat, MOF replaced the AMF proposal with a new plan—the Miyazawa Initiative—to provide emergency funds to the region in concert with the IMF instead of in competition. All told, between 1997 and 1999 Japan claimed to have committed a staggering $80 billion to restoring stability to the affected Asian economies. Meanwhile, Washington and Tokyo continued their ideological skirmishing as a new debate emerged about reshaping the international financial architecture in the wake of the crisis that had started with the collapse of the Thai economy.

The U.S.-Japan collision over the Asian Monetary Fund proposal reflected Tokyo's *overestimation* of its own influence in the international financial order and Washington's *underestimation* of the need to share leadership of the international economy with Japan. The Japanese side assumed that its proven ability to recycle billions of dollars could be translated into leadership in the international financial system with the proper additive of an "intellectual contribution." However, a third ingredient was necessary as well: an open and deregulated Japanese economy. As it was, the combination of Japanese economic malaise and slow liberalization undercut Tokyo's influence in the crisis. First, Japanese policy proposals for the international financial architecture were discredited by the failure of Japanese policies for the domestic financial system. Second, the positive effect of Japanese financial assistance to Asia was largely offset by the inability of Japan's economy to pull imports from the region. Finally, the high transaction costs in Tokyo's heavily regulated financial markets meant that the yen had weak standing as a reserve currency even for countries in the region, giving the almighty dollar and therefore the U.S. Treasury Department continued leadership in the crisis.

U.S. officials, on the other hand, probably overextrapolated from Japan's inability to escape from domestic economic malaise that had seized the country after the collapse of the "bubble economy" in 1991. Early Japanese warnings about the potential scope of the Thai crisis in 1997 did not resonate with a U.S. Treasury Department already deeply skeptical about the Japanese government's ability to handle its own banking crisis. Moreover, personal rivalries and ongoing ideological debates between senior Japanese and U.S. officials blinded the U.S. side to legitimate concerns being expressed by Tokyo about shortcomings in the IMF and the international financial system. Eventually the U.S. side moved in partnership with Japan and the other G-7 countries to shore up the international financial system, but U.S. prestige in East Asia would have suffered far less, and recovery would have come much sooner, if coordinated action had been possible from the beginning.

The crisis that shook the international financial system in 1997–98 should have served as a wake-up call for U.S. and Japanese leaders. It highlighted the limits of Japanese financial power, forcing a new realism in Japan's definition of its role in international financial institutions. At the same time, it demonstrated the price that the United

States pays for not working out a consistent way to share intellectual leadership with the world's second largest economy in the maintenance of the Bretton Woods system. As the world's economic experts debate the future of the international financial architecture, these are lessons well worth reviewing.

This chapter tells the story of Japan's rise in the international financial institutions and its efforts to turn money and ideas into real power in response to the Asian crisis, concluding with lessons for the U.S.-Japan relationship.

The Quest for Leadership-sharing in the International Financial System

Japan's Growing Role and America's Lingering Ambivalence

Since the 1970s, the most dramatic change in international finance has been the diffusion of economic power among the advanced industrial states and the growth of the U.S. balance-of-payments deficit. As its relative financial resources have declined, the United States has called on the other advanced industrial states—and particularly Japan—to share the burden of maintaining the liberal international economic order. However, Washington's calls for burden sharing have not been met by an equal enthusiasm for power sharing with Tokyo. As Ogata Sadako has noted with regard to the World Bank, the fundamental dilemma facing the United States has been "its desire to cut financial commitments while maintaining its influence," while the Japanese side has likened its efforts to increase voting shares and influence in the international financial institutions "to the struggle over the revision of the unequal treaties in the Meiji period."[5]

By the early 1980s, however, it was clear that shifting power relationships in the IMF, Asian Development Bank (ADB), and World Bank were inevitable. With the change to floating exchange rates in 1973, the oil shocks of 1973 and 1979, and the tripling of Third World debt between 1973 to 1982, the United States could not afford to hold back Japan, which was emerging as a major creditor nation over the same period. Instead, the United States attempted to channel Japanese money into soft loans and special funds that would not be reflected in voting rights at the international financial institutions. At the IMF, for example, Japan was contributing 16 percent of the resources for the General Arrangements to Borrow (GAB) by 1975. (Through the GAB, ten industrial member countries agreed to lend specified amounts of their currencies to the IMF to facilitate drawing money from the fund.) However, Japan's rank at the IMF remained fifth, with a voting share of only 3.9 percent.[6] At the World Bank, Japan's increased contributions were funneled primarily to the International Development Association (IDA), a subsidiary of the International Bank for Reconstruction and Development (IBRD), which is the core multilateral bank in the World Bank Group and carries the real weight in voting shares. At the ADB, which was established in 1966 by the Johnson administration to integrate the Japanese and Southeast Asian economies as a buttress against communism, Japan established coequal status with the United States fairly early. However, Japanese funding of soft loans through the subsidiary Asian Development Fund soon surpassed U.S. levels without any reflected change in voting shares at the ADB itself.[7]

Japanese frustration with its hampered status in the IMF and World Bank was further exacerbated by the Reagan administration's free market ideological attacks on the international financial institutions in this same period. Reacting against the IMF's growing role in Third World development since the 1970s and the World Bank's perceived departure from economic fundamentals, the new administration warned that it would not support any increases in quotas or funding for the international financial institutions. The Japanese view was summed up by Finance Minister Watanabe Michio, who argued at the IMF–World Bank annual meeting in September 1980 that "appropriate adjustments need to be made so that each member's quota share reflects its economic reality."[8] Eventually the Reagan administration's largely doctrinaire position proved untenable, particularly after the 1982 Mexican financial crisis caused a multibillion-dollar drop in U.S. exports. Eager to tap Japanese and European resources to respond to the crisis, Washington reversed its position and agreed to an increase in Japanese voting shares at the IMF and World Bank. In 1984 Japan moved from fifth to second position at the World Bank and from fifth to third at the IMF.[9]

For Tokyo these promotions represented a long-overdue recalibration of Japanese spending power and Japanese leadership in the international financial institutions. However, Tokyo's claims for expanded leadership continued to be hampered by the closed nature of the Japanese economy. When the yen began its rapid appreciation after the 1985 Plaza Accord, Japan received not higher voting shares to reflect the increased buying power of the yen, but instead greater criticism because of the ballooning Japanese current account surpluses. In order to deflect this criticism and begin gradually restructuring the Japanese economy, the influential 1986 Maekawa Report called for Japan to become an importing nation, an open economy, and to recycle its huge surpluses.[10] Increasing imports and opening the economy could take decades, but recycling Tokyo was prepared to do immediately. In April 1987, therefore, the government announced a three-year plan to recycle $20 billion of its capital surplus to developing and debtor countries.[11]

Ironically, Japan's rapid emergence as the world's largest donor of overseas development assistance (ODA) at the end of the 1980s brought even more criticisms. It was admirable that Tokyo was recycling its surplus, the critique went, but Japan brought no vision to the management of the Bretton Woods system. This charge was used repeatedly by Europeans and Americans to resist Japanese efforts to turn burden-sharing into power-sharing. And it was largely true, since Japan's recycling program in the 1980s had begun primarily as a reaction against international criticism of its closed economy rather than as a plan for reshaping the world of finance and development. Nevertheless, many officials in the Ministry of Finance felt that Japan did, in fact, have a unique intellectual contribution to make based on the successful model of Japan's own economic development. Picking up the gauntlet thrown down by the American and European denizens of the IMF and World Bank, Japan made two aggressive bids to convince the world that it was ready for leadership.

The First "Miyazawa Plan"

Japan's first bid at intellectual leadership came in response to the 1988 Latin American debt crisis. After a decade of easy lending from the advanced industrial nations, Latin America had amassed national debts totaling $420 billion by 1988.[12] Eager to make a dramatic demonstration of Japan's capacity for international financial leadership at this critical juncture, Minister of Finance Miyazawa Kiichi told the G-7 finance ministers' gathering in April 1988 that Japan stood ready to take the lead on a plan for using government funds to bail out the borrowers in Latin America. Other participants were surprised, since Third World debt had been high on the agenda at the finance ministers' meeting before the G-7 and Japan had offered no position.[13] Miyazawa's speech was hastily prepared and offered few specifics, but in subsequent months MOF prepared a more detailed plan in which a special facility at the IMF would acquire and securitize the debt, with the securities backed by the debtor nation's foreign exchange reserves. Japan would provide loans to those debtor nations that did not have adequate reserves (most of them, in fact) from its own surplus. It appeared that Tokyo was serious.

For the Reagan and later Bush administrations, this proposal for heavy government intervention was too Japanese by half. Washington was opposed to government funded bailouts for debtor nations, preferring instead to rely on private sector solutions. The U.S. side argued that the Japanese plan to securitize the debt camouflaged the fact that the IMF—and therefore the U.S., Japanese and other governments—would essentially be assuming the risk of the bad loans. As the *Asian Wall Street Journal* put it, "the last thing reformers need within their own political system is the promise of pie in the sky from Japan or the IMF."[14] The Treasury Department wanted Japan to focus its energies on opening the Japanese economy to take more imports from the Third World, not on coming up with new ways to bail out debtors. "[A] true leadership role in the debt strategy entails more than [recycling]," Assistant Treasury Secretary David Mulford told the press on December 5, 1988.[15]

The Japanese proposal also hit on U.S. sensitivities about the continuing devolution of power within the IMF. Under the Ninth General Review (1987 to 1990), the IMF executive board was debating whether to increase the fund's quota and whether Japan could use the increase to acquire a sufficient share to leapfrog past the Europeans and assume the number-two spot behind the United States. Washington opposed the increase, and many in the U.S. government remained skeptical that Japan was truly ready for global leadership, given the continued growth in its current account surplus. In the view of most U.S. officials, the Miyazawa plan did not answer the requirement for an "intellectual contribution" worthy of the number-two in the IMF—a prejudice reinforced by the ideological divisions and the Treasury Department's continued resistance to further power sharing in the fund.

Once again, however, the U.S. side rapidly changed course as the Third World debt crisis spread beyond the existing capacities of the IMF and World Bank to respond. In late February 1989 riots erupted in Caracas, Venezuela, suggesting that financial instability was leading to political instability in the region. In response, the Bush administration's new Treasury secretary, Nicholas Brady, began putting together a debt relief plan that would do precisely what the Reagan administration had resisted—forgive part of the loans.[16] In early March the Treasury Department briefed the Japanese side on the new plan and reached agreement on a variation of the earlier Miyazawa plan in which debts would be securitized and rescheduled, but conditioned on structural reform in the debtor nations. Brady announced the plan at the Bretton Woods Committee Conference on Third World debt on March 10.[17] Treasury officials remarked that Japan had the key role to play in financing the plan, and MOF officials noted with satisfaction that the so-called Brady plan was clearly a converted version of the original Miyazawa plan.[18]

Japan's support for the Brady plan paid off. Although U.S. officials denied there was a quid pro quo deal, Washington supported quota increases and Japan's elevation, together with Germany, to the number-two spot at the IMF.[19] For its part, Japan increased its original 1987 $20 billion recycling pledge to $65 billion over five years, including several billion dollars to Mexico, Venezuela, the Philippines, and other countries covered by the Brady plan. Although the Miyazawa plan faded from memory, senior MOF officials came away flushed with confidence from their most significant victory at the IMF—a victory based on both money *and* ideas.

The Asian Miracle Report at the World Bank

Following close on the heels of the Miyazawa and Brady plans, Japan made a second bid at intellectual leadership in an international financial institution, this time at the World Bank. Where Japan sought to demonstrate broad vision without technical specifics in the case of the Miyazawa plan, the conflict at the World Bank was very much about specific Japanese lending techniques. This technical skirmish expanded into a broader ideological debate fueled by a Japanese-sponsored World Bank report on the Asian economic "miracle." Though Japan could not win a promotion in this battle—Tokyo had held the number-two spot at the bank for several years already—MOF needed a victory to impose its will on an obstinate multinational bureaucracy at the bank that refused to recognize Japan's new status. The debate about economic development philosophies also had implications for the legitimacy of Japan's own economic policies at a time of heightened bilateral trade friction with the United States.

The conflict had its roots in the World Bank's shift toward a focus on structural adjustments in the mid-1980s, a shift that reflected the influence of the Reagan administration's free market ideology and the failings of the bank's lending practices in the 1960s and 1970s. Bank economists began arguing that soft loans through government development banks resulted in distortions of market interest rates that would ultimately undermine restructuring efforts by the IMF and World Bank. However, lending through government institutions that then set concessional rates for the private sector was exactly the technique that Japan Export-Import Bank (JEXIM) and the Overseas Economic Cooperation Fund (OECF) had been using to recycle Japan's capital surpluses to the Third World. Moreover, the Japanese government had learned the "two step" loan technique (so-called because they went from the Japanese government through the institutions of recipient governments) from the World Bank in the first place.[20]

The bank began pressing Japan to accept its new orthodoxy in the spring and summer of 1989, attempting to block a Japanese two-step loan package then under negotiation for the Philippines. The OECF, which dispersed about 20 percent of its loans through cofinancing with the World Bank and IMF (like the majority of JEXIM loans), agreed to take steps to raise the interest rates on the loan, but only if the rate would still be below market levels. Unappeased, the World Bank's vice president for Operations threatened to halt cofinancing altogether, if Japan did not completely drop the two-step loan formula in the future.

The pressure from the World Bank stung at several levels. First, MOF was frustrated with its inability to translate a leadership position at the bank into actual leadership in bank policies. Second, MOF officials resented a bureaucracy in Washington telling Japan how to provide aid to nations in Asia. Third, Japan's frustration was growing with an overall American inattention to development in Asia, symbolized by Washington's unpaid commitments to the ADB's Asian Development Fund. Finally, the bank's new free market orthodoxy was a challenge to Japan's own philosophies of industrial development, which traditionally involved selective interest rate subsidies to stimulate growth. With the United States and Japan in the midst of the Structural Impediments Initiative (in which the two countries negotiated deregulation and restructuring issues to open the Japanese market), this last issue made the World Bank debate a proxy fight on the legitimacy of MOF's own economic policies at home.

The Japanese side responded to the World Bank pressure by broadening the technical debate on two-step loans to a debate over development philosophy itself. In the fall of 1991 MOF ideologues began a comprehensive criticism of the World Bank's focus on structural adjustment, free market economic ideology, and universal rules of conditionality. First, at the annual IMF–World Bank meeting in Bangkok, Japanese officials urged the bank to learn from Asian—and especially Japanese—development experiences. Then in October 1991 the OECF prepared a working paper titled "Issues Relating to the World Bank's Approach to Structural Adjustment: Proposal from a Major Partner," which trumpeted the government's role in promoting industrial growth, including interest rate subsidies.[21] MOFA and MITI were not included in MOF's ideological campaign, and worried about the impact on bilateral trade and security relations of the Finance Department bureaucrats aggressiveness. Even MOF officials overseeing World Bank policy in Tokyo were nervous.[22] Unfazed by internal division, however, MOF hard-liners brought their campaign to the research directorate of the World Bank itself, offering to provide $1.2 million for a study of the lessons of Asian economic development.

When the Japanese-sponsored report was finally completed in 1993, it pleased neither the MOF ideologues (who were consulted but not included in the project team) nor the World Bank's economists. The authors conceded that in certain cases, such as South Korea, export promotion had been effective; but the report emphasized macroeconomic factors, such as Asia's high savings rates and high levels of private sector investment, to undermine the original Japanese arguments about government intervention. The report concluded that the major lesson from Asia was that industrial policy would not be a successful model for the bank to encourage, although government did have an important role to play in development that had been overlooked in the past.[23]

The MOF ideological assault on the World Bank raised the specter of what Funabashi Yōichi at the time called a "new cold war" over competing economic models.[24] However, throughout this period Tokyo never changed its specific policies in the IMF and World Bank or decoupled its OECF and EXIM loans from the cofinancing pattern already in place. Rather than a fundamental challenge to the orthodoxy of the international financial institutions, MOF was attempting to expand its influence for reasons of status and to maintain its own way of doing business. Moreover, there was considerable unease within the Japanese academic community and government about even the appearance of a Japanese rebellion against the Bretton Woods system, which was seen as an indispensable framework for Japanese lending. Finally, the World Bank itself had readjusted from the extreme elements of the free market approach introduced in the 1980s, even before Japan sponsored the Asian Miracle report. As the bank's chief economist, Lawrence Summers, acknowledged in summarizing its 1991 annual report, "we have lost sight of the role of the government's supporting hand in our support for the [market's] invisible hand."[25]

Nevertheless, the development debate at the World Bank was perceived in MOF as a partial victory, since it helped to moderate the structural adjustment philosophy then prevalent in the institution.

Moreover, between the Miyazawa plan and the Asian Miracle report, MOF had established two leitmotifs that would define Japan's intellectual contribution to the Bretton Woods system in the future: the global economy requires greater contingency funds for regional emergencies, and the emphasis of international financial institutions on structural adjustment should not be universally applied to all Asian nations. However, two other lessons from the Miyazawa plan and the Asian Miracle report were largely forgotten in MOF after 1993: first, that Japan's credibility as a leader in the Bretton Woods system hinges on opening of the Japanese economic market; and second, that consensus-building is a more effective form of leadership in the international financial institutions than unilateral pronouncements. The two leitmotifs on development philosophy would rebound to Japan's credit in the Asian currency crisis at the end of the decade, but ultimately, Japan's leadership would be undermined by the two lessons that were forgotten.

The Asian Financial Crisis

In both the Miyazawa plan and the World Bank debate, the Japanese side argued that it had unique insights based on Japanese and Asian development experiences. That argument was put to the test in 1997 when the region's worst currency crisis ever erupted with the collapse of the Thai baht on July 2, followed by currency crashes in the Philippines, Malaysia, and Indonesia, and finally in South Korea on December 3. By 1998 the contagion was global, affecting Brazil, Russia, and other emerging economies. The speed of the regional and global currency meltdowns stunned observers in Tokyo and directly threatened Japan's own fragile banking system. We begin our examination of Japan's response to the crisis by reviewing the U.S. and Japanese interpretations of its root causes and then turn to Japan's proposals for the Asian Monetary Fund and the new "Miyazawa Initiative."

Explaining the Causes of the Crisis

Although conspiracy theories emerged in Tokyo regarding the causes of the 1997 crisis, as they did elsewhere throughout the region, Japanese officials and economists agreed with their mainstream U.S. counterparts on several of the root causes.

First, there were weaknesses in the financial sectors of the stricken economies that were both masked and compounded by the easy availability of global credit. Because bank and nonbank credit to the private sector greatly exceeded the growth in the real economy (manufacturing, services, etc.), the easy capital flowed into nonproductive sectors such as real estate (especially in Thailand) and ill-considered ventures by industrial conglomerates (especially in Indonesia and South Korea). The globalization of financial markets in the 1990s that permitted the flow of capital into these economies also made for rapid divestment when credit conditions shifted. By 1997 global liquidity had reached unprecedented levels. In 1970, only 10 percent of international transactions were in capital flows. By the mid-1990s, 90 percent of international transactions not directly related to trade were capital flows.[26] The South Korean and Southeast Asian economies expose themselves to even greater volatility in this fluid global capital market by borrowing foreign funds at short maturities in order to lower borrowing costs.[27]

Second, external sector problems in these economies led to precisely the shift in credit conditions that would encourage a massive outflow of capital. Most of these countries ran moderate to large current account deficits in the 1990s. These were benign as long as the foreign borrowing was being used to increase investment in productive capacity, but by 1997 much of the investment was going to speculative ventures. Thailand, South Korea, and Indonesia developed excess capacity that had to be exported. Unfortunately, China's 40 percent devaluation in 1994 and the depreciation of the yen against the dollar by over 25 percent between 1995 and 1996 undercut the export competitiveness of the now desperately overleveraged Asian economies.[28]

Finally, with mounting bankruptcies in Southeast Asia (Thailand's Finance One) and South Korea (Hanbo and Sammi Steel) and disclosures about the extent of private sector short-term borrowing, foreign lenders stopped rolling over short-term loans and companies rushed to exchange local currencies for dollars. Unable to maintain their currency peg to the dollar, these countries were forced to free-float or devalue their currencies, exhaust their reserve holdings, and seek help from the IMF. The contagion then spread because of competitive devaluations throughout the region, including devaluations by nonaffected economies such as Taiwan.[29] With declining asset and currency values, the existing debts become an even greater burden.

These are the broad contours of the roots of the crisis that are beyond controversy. Other explanations are more interpretive, and differences in interpretation led to different prescriptions from the Japanese and U.S. sides as the crisis unfolded.

First, U.S. and IMF analysis tended to focus on the problems of inefficiency and corruption caused in Thailand, South Korea, and Indonesia by the collusive relationship between government and the private sector—the problem of "crony capitalism." While the Japanese government did not deny the existence of such problems, independent Japanese analysis generally ignored this dimension of the problem. For example, MOF's advisory Committee on Foreign Exchange and Other Transactions gave only brief passing mention to the problems of collusion and lack of transparency in its fifty-page report "Lessons from the Asian Currency Crises" in 1998.[30]

Second, Japanese analysis focused on the inefficiencies caused by "perceptions" of foreign institutional investors that were out of touch with economic reality. The Committee on Foreign Exchange and Other Transactions observed that "macroeconomic conditions in these countries did not appear to warrant the currency and financial crises" and that "a contagion effect was generated due to a radical shift in market perceptions."[31] Particularly capricious from the Japanese perspective were hedge funds, which caused huge outflows of capital based on fleeting assessments of the health of the Southeast Asian economies.[32] The focus on perceptions paralleled the Japanese government's argument in 1997–98 that the primary obstacle to Japan's own economic recovery was perceptions rather than structural problems. In fact, it was the perceptions of Japanese banks, and not those of hedge funds, that worsened the situation. As Martin N. Baily, Diana Farrell, and Susan Lund of McKinsey Global Institution argued in an article in *Foreign Affairs* in 2000, hedge funds did not withdraw money from Southeast Asia, but rather "they remained calm throughout the initial crisis, continuing to put money into the country even after the baht's devaluation."[33] It was Japanese and European banks that kept on withdrawing massive amount of money from East Asia, which spread the contagion.[34]

Third, Japanese analysis of the causes of the currency crisis tended to focus on the hazards caused by these countries' heavy reliance on the dollar as a peg in their currency baskets. Thus, the Committee on Foreign Exchange and Other Transactions noted that "the steady appreciation of the dollar had substantially elevated real effective exchange rates in all of these countries and the loss of export competitiveness was a growing concern" without mentioning the impact of the *devaluation* of the yen. Numerous Japanese assessments of the crisis noted the inherent instability of the Asian economies' "overdependence" on the dollar, even as intraregional trade and Japanese investment have grown.[35]

Finally, Japanese analysis tended to shy away from a focus on the degree to which Japan exported its own asset "bubble" to Southeast Asia rather than restructuring at home to increase imports. By one account, between 1994 and 1997 Japanese lending to Asia alone rose from $40 billion to $265 billion, much of it for speculative investment, [36] while imports from Southeast Asia increased only 51.3 percent.[37] The Japanese banks were able to continue this speculative lending primarily because MOF obstructed full transparency and resolution of nonperforming loans at home and because expansionary monetary policy (the decline in the Japanese discount rate from 6 percent in 1991 to 0.5 percent in 1998) encouraged banks to recycle its surplus in the rest of Asia. In addition, whether the blame was laid on the appreciation of the dollar or the depreciation of the yen, the root cause was the same—slow Japanese economic growth.[38] In response, Japanese analysts argued that Japan accounted for only 32 percent of the $754.7 billion total outstanding loan balance in the region in 1997, while the Europeans accounted for 35 percent and that the yen did not move in tandem with other Asian currencies in the months leading up to the crisis.[39]

These differences in interpretation derived from different economic philosophies and from Japanese officials' defensiveness about the condition of their domestic economy. The differences fueled divergent policies between Washington and Tokyo that neither side could afford. In the end, though, there was broad agreement between Tokyo and Washington that a coordinated and common response to the crisis was necessary. At first, however, Japan moved on its own, out of both necessity and ambition.

TIME LINE OF THE CURRENCY CRISES

July 1997	Thailand asks for IMF support.
August 1997	AMF proposal raised.
October 1997	Indonesia asks for IMF support.
November 1997	South Korea asks for IMF support. Agreement on Manila Framework. AMF proposal rejected.
August 1998	Russian currency crisis.
September 1998	Malaysia regulates capital outflow.
October 1998	Miyazawa Initiative announced.
January 1999	Brazilian currency crisis.
June 1999	Köln summit, agreement on regulation of hedge funds.
November 1999	ASEAN ministerial meeting, AMF proposal resurges.

The Crisis Erupts in Thailand

The speculative bubble created by the combination of fluid global capital and reckless faith in the Asian economic miracle burst first in Thailand in the summer of 1997. Thailand had been running current account deficits that were about 8 percent of GDP since 1995, and by early 1997 pressure was mounting to devalue the baht as major Thai financial and real estate firms began declaring bankruptcy. A joint Thai-Singapore intervention temporarily relieved pressure on the baht in mid-May, and as late as June 30 Thai Prime Minister Chavalit Yonchaiyudh was appearing on television confidently promising the nation that the baht would hold at its current value. Two days later, however, the government bowed to the inevitable and acknowledged that the high interest rates necessary to maintain Bangkok's thirteen-year virtual peg to the dollar could not be sustained. Under a "managed float," the baht collapsed 15 percent on July 2 and continued to depreciate throughout the week.

Government officials and banking executives in Tokyo watched the events unfolding in Thailand with apprehension. Japan was owed $37.5 billion of Thailand's debt (out of a total of $70.2 billion). The collapse of the baht meant that Thai companies would face a tougher time servicing their foreign debt. In addition, Japan accounted for 40 percent of total foreign direct investment into Thailand, after Japanese firms had increased their annual levels of investment by 72.5 percent from 1994 to 1995 and by 22.2 percent from 1995 to 1996. With the collapse of the baht, Japanese parts imported for final assembly by Japanese manufacturers in Thailand now became more expensive, hurting the export competitiveness of the Japanese transplants. Meanwhile, domestic demand for Japanese products in Thailand threatened to contract with the Thai economy. As *Mainichi Shimbun* warned shortly after the crisis began, this was a "double punch" for Japanese manufacturers.[40]

Japanese officials also watched events in Thailand knowing that the Thais expected Japan to demonstrate "leadership" in stabilizing the crisis. Thai central bankers and finance officials had been rebuked by both Tokyo and Washington in February when they sought to prop up the baht with bilateral loans outside of the IMF framework. All spring ASEAN officials had also been discussing the need for a separate, non-IMF source of emergency funds in Asia to protect their currencies against speculative attacks.[41] These discussions were aimed in part at Japan, which was the logical source of the funding. MOF, for its part, had pushed at the June Denver G-8 summit for more effecting early warning and monitoring of capital flows and had pledged to assist developing countries to stabilize their financial systems.[42] It was now incumbent on Japan both as an Asian nation and a G-8 member to take proactive measures to respond to the crisis.

Nevertheless, MOF remained cautious about sending the signal that it was ready to bail out any Asian country that overextended itself financially.[43] Initially, MOF attempted to downplay fears about the Thai crisis, declaring that it "could not be compared in scale" to the currency crisis that had hit Mexico in 1994–95.[44] Meanwhile, MOF and Bank of Japan officials told the Thai finance minister in Tokyo on July 11 that they would take steps to fulfill his request for emergency funding.[45] However, these same officials reiterated on July 18 that Japan would only provide assistance if the IMF participated in the bailout. The Japanese government still needed the IMF to provide cover against domestic criticism of Japanese taxpayer money going to foreign debtors, particularly at a time when MOF was under pressure at home to extend emergency loans to the many banks and construction firms then facing insolvency.

As the collapse of the baht pressed the Philippines, Malaysia, and Singapore to allow the depreciation of their currencies (further squeezing the baht in turn) and as Tokyo held off its assistance, Bangkok finally called on the IMF for help on July 28. The terms of the rescue package were negotiated between Thailand and the IMF at a meeting hosted by the Japanese government in Tokyo on August 11. Once again MOF officials took a backseat to the IMF on the negotiations, in spite of a broad recognition that Japan would provide at least half of the total funds necessary extended. MOF officials refrained from demanding specific conditionality of the Thais, preferring instead to let the IMF play "bad cops" to Tokyo's "good cop."[46] By the end of the meeting, the IMF agreed to a $16 billion rescue package that would eventually include the World Bank, the Asian Development Bank, and credits from Japan, China, Australia, Brunei, Hong Kong, Singapore, and Malyasia.[47] Of this, Japan provided $4 billion.[48] Thailand, in turn, pledged to take specific steps to restructure the financial sector and provide greater transparency.

The Asian Monetary Fund Proposal

While MOF took a backseat to the IMF in negotiating the terms of the $16 billion emergency package, it also used the Tokyo meeting to push a new proposal for creation of a special Asian Monetary Fund (AMF) to deal with future crises. The specific terms of the fund were not spelled out by the Japanese side beyond a proposal to establish $100 billion over five years, of which Japan would provide half. U.S. and IMF officials at the meeting were largely caught by surprise, since MOF had only coordinated its proposal with ASEAN nations before the meeting[49]; this fact, together with the ambiguity of the plan, laid the stages for a confrontation that was probably not necessary and that neither Japan nor the United States—let alone the region—could afford.

The motivations behind the AMF proposal were complex, shaped by tactical opportunism, personalities, and conflicting ideas about Japan's proper role in Asia. These motivations help to explain why Japan appeared to be challenging the Bretton Woods system even as it was playing a central supporting role in the IMF's response to the unfolding Asian economic crisis.

First, the unique absence of the United States as a serious player during the crisis must be considered. While the Treasury Department pushed the IMF to provide a loan to Thailand, Washington offered no money of its own. This was a striking contrast to the Mexican bailout in 1995, when the United States provided $20 billion in assistance—but that was precisely why Secretary of the Treasury Rubin decided he could *not* offer funds to Thailand. After the Mexican bailout, an angry congress put restrictions on U.S. emergency funding to the Exchange Stability Fund (ESF). That restriction was close to expiring when the Thai crisis hit. Rubin and Treasury decided that the Thai crisis could be contained without the Clinton administration having to risk further restrictions on ESF by asking congress for an early exemption to provide funds to Bangkok. As Rubin later told the *Wall Street Journal*, "It was important that we have the freedom to use the ESF when it was needed."[50] Without funding to contribute, the United States was largely excluded from meetings in Bangkok in July where the idea of the AMF was first discussed by Japan and ASEAN. Even in Tokyo at the IMF-Bangkok negotiations, U.S. officials were present basically as observers when the AMF proposal was put forward by MOF.[51]

The low U.S. profile during the Thai crisis encouraged the ASEAN governments to push Japan to fill the "leadership gap"—an offer that appealed to many in MOF as well as the broader Japanese elite. As an editorial in *Sankei Shimbun* argued on August 12, 1997, "It is natural for Japan to demonstrate leadership based on Japanese national interests; first in Thailand and then to stabilize the rest of Asia's currencies. The United States may have paid deep attention to the Mexican currency crisis, but it has no interest in stabilizing Thailand's currency."[52]

The editorial ended with a call for Japan to use the Thai bailout to promote internationalization of the yen. In negotiations with the Thais, Japanese officials were stunned by the realization that the baht had been pegged 80 percent to the dollar and only about 5 percent to the yen. Another *Sankei Shimbun* editorial that appeared in late July asked a question on the minds of many in MOF: How could Japan contribute to the stability of the Thai currency when the baht is so heavily pegged to the dollar? For U.S. officials, one answer would have been to open Japanese markets further and stimulate demand for Thai exports, but MOF focused instead on ways to encourage Thailand to reduce its reliance on the dollar. Later MOF officials admitted that the prospects of real internationalization of the yen were not thought through at the time,[53] but there was sense based on both nationalism and the practical lessons of the baht crisis that the hegemony of the dollar in Asia had to be weakened. A large yen–based stabilization fund for Asia might have had that effect.[54]

In addition, the Japanese government shared some of the frustration of ASEAN with the inadequacy of the IMF response in July and August. In spite of the Denver summit pledge to establish global monitoring and to contribute to stabilization of developing economies' financial systems, Japan was the only G–7 country to take action in response to the Thai crisis. Japanese dissatisfaction also focused on the scope of the IMF response. Even though the IMF increased Thailand's quota fivefold to $4 billion in the August agreement, the Thais really needed another $10.5 billion. For officials in both MOF and MOFA, it was clear that a framework for emergency supplemental funding was necessary.[55] As one MOF official explained, this was particularly true because the IMF was not prepared to respond to sudden speculative attacks on a small nation's currency.[56]

Finally, bringing all of these ingredients to boil was the powerful personality of the messenger himself: the new MOF vice minister for International Affairs, Sakakibara Eisuke. As director of the International Finance Bureau, Sakakibara had been given the moniker "Mr. Yen" because his pronouncements on exchange rates could cause markets to suddenly buy or sell yen in anticipation of interest rate changes or government intervention. With a Ph.D. in economics from the University of Michigan and several books extolling the virtues of Japanese-style capitalism, Sakakibara was cut from different cloth than his MOF colleagues. At times he was nationalistic, arguing in a 1990 book, *Beyond Capitalism,* for example, that Japan had developed a superior form of "anthropocentric capitalism."[57] At other times he could be strikingly internationalist, championing deregulation of Tokyo's financial markets under the "Big Bang" and arguing for greater reform across the economy.[58] In both modes, he impressed and alienated numerous colleagues in MOF and abroad. His friendly but intense rivalry with U.S. Undersecretary of the Treasury Lawrence Summers was well known and soon became a factor in the bilateral collision over the AMF proposal.

For Sakakibara, the Thai crisis demonstrated that "the Washington consensus [on Bretton Woods] was over."[59] After his promotion to vice minister in early July, he moved quickly to change the AMF from an informal discussion topic into a formal Japanese proposal. Most officials in MOF agreed that the U.S. and IMF responses to the Thai crisis had been unsatisfactory, but key officials in both MOF and MOFA grew alarmed that Sakakibara's enthusiasm for the AMF might create the impression that Japan was challenging the Bretton Woods system. The MOF directors for international financial institutions and the senior MOF officials seconded to the IMF were put in especially difficult positions and tried unsuccessfully to tone down the proposal, which they viewed as driven by nationalism.[60] Some MOF officials working on the plan for Sakakibara later admitted that they thought it might be shot down by the United States, but energized by Japan's initiative and apparent U.S. complacency—and also by Japan surprise (and, alas, short-lived) spike in GDP growth in 1996 (4.5 percent for the year), they began preparing legislation in early September for Diet approval of the $50 billion Japanese portion of the plan. MOF had no idea how it would handle the critical question of conditionality, which the U.S. side would later come to see as the greatest challenge to the IMF's traditional role.[61] If countries such as Thailand could receive funds from Japan with no conditions, after all, the IMF's leverage to demand restructuring and transparency would be significantly undermined. JEXIM and MOF officials later argued that they never intended separate conditionality from the IMF, but that was never made clear as the plan was being unveiled.[62] Sakakibara later admitted that he had not made up his mind about how to handle conditionality.[63]

MOF proposed to formally present the AMF plan at a string of meetings scheduled in Hong Kong in late September for the G-7 finance ministers, the IMF, and the World Bank. First, however, MOF briefers tried their presentation on a group of Asian central bankers meeting in Shanghai under the Executives' Meeting of East Asia-Pacific Central Banks (EMEAP), an organization that Japan had established several years earlier, and then again at an informal session of Asian finance ministers in Hong Kong on September 12.[64] The Shanghai and Hong Kong briefings contrasted with the complete lack of coordination with U.S. officials and deepened U.S., European, and IMF mistrust of Japanese intentions.[65] After hearing that the Japanese held briefings for Asians only, Summers called Sakakibara at his home in the middle of the night on September 14. "I thought you were my friend," Summers began abruptly, before launching into a two-hour argument about the problems with the Japanese proposal.[66] Summer's intervention notwithstanding, MOF had received enough encouragement from the Asian central bankers and finance ministers to continue pressing ahead. On September 21, Finance Minister Mitsuzuka Hiroshi and Sakakibara outlined their concept for the AMF at the international finance meetings in Hong Kong. While acknowledging that the plan was "not yet concrete," Mitsuzuka and Sakakibara told their counterparts that the AMF would be "compatible" with the IMF, but with a unique focus on the Asian countries' specific needs.[67]

From that moment on, the IMF leadership, and particularly Deputy Director Stanley Fischer, attacked the Japanese proposal as a threat to the authority and effectiveness of the IMF itself.[68] Treasury Secretary Rubin remained officially neutral on the proposal, but his deputies worked the halls in Hong Kong to defeat the idea.[69] China also surprised the Japanese delegation by weighing in heavily against the proposal, both to stop Japanese diplomatic initiative and to insulate the renminbi against any integration of regional foreign exchange policy.[70] Though battered by the U.S., European, and now Chinese criticism of the AMF proposal, Japanese officials—backed by ASEAN—continued lobbying aggressively for it until the Hong Kong meetings ended on September 27.

In the wake of those Hong Kong meetings, MOF officials began to recognize that they had overplayed their hand. Despite statements of support from ASEAN financial authorities, Sakakibara had little domestic support for—or intention to—challenge the existing IMF framework.[71] Trapped in a classic dilemma between East and West, MOF began to backpedal. At press briefings after the Hong Kong sessions, a "senior official" claimed that the new Asian "facility" would be used only in cases where IMF funds were insufficient and only after IMF approval.[72] Later Sakakibara argued that "it was not his thought that Japan will try to seize leadership in Asia" and that the AMF concept would help the U.S. and Europe to open markets in Asia.[73] Privately, MOF officials working for Sakakibara knew that the AMF proposal had no more momentum. They had not worked out the mechanics beyond early draft legislation to provide the funds, and it would be impossible to build internal MOF consensus on how to proceed now that the rest of the G-7 and China were clearly opposed.[74] Already the Budget Bureau of MOF was opposed because the AMF proposal threatened to break the fiscal caps placed on government spending by the 1997 Fiscal Reconstruction Bill.[75] Amazingly, Sakakibara refused to give up, pressing Summers and others to consider the plan until early November. His staff argued that this was necessary to keep pressure on Washington to respond to Japan's initial concerns about the inadequacies of the IMF and, in part, as one of Sakakibara's staff later confessed, to "save face" after the defeat in Hong Kong.[76]

The denouement of the AMF proposal came at a meeting of finance and central bank governors from fourteen Pacific Rim nations in Manila on November 18 and 19. By the end of the meeting, the participants had agreed on a face-saving compromise that incorporated elements of the AMF within an IMF-centered approach. This "Manila Framework" had four basic elements:

1. Implementation of regional surveillance to complement improvements in global surveillance
2. Technical assistance and support for strengthening the financial sectors of related countries
3. Stronger IMF resources to deal with future crises
4. Provision of assistance by member countries of the region to complement the financial support of the IMF and other international financial institutions.

The Japanese government argued that the Manila Framework was "in line with the AMF concept."[77] However, any doubt about the true state of affairs was erased the following week at the APEC summit in Vancouver, in which the assembled leaders of the Pacific Rim nations agreed that the IMF would continue to play the *central* role in managing international financial crises.[78] After the Manila Framework, the IMF created a new facility for providing short-term financial support, named the Supplemental Reserve Facility (SRF), which was later mobilized to rescue the South Korean economy. The SRF addressed many of MOF's original concerns, but the potential for Japanese leadership and the "Asianism" of the AMF proposal were now erased. Economist Itō Takatoshi captured the sentiment of many when he wrote in *Gaikō Forum* that with the failure of the AMF, Japan had suffered a "diplomatic defeat from which it must somehow recover."[79] At the same time, MOF officials recognized that the crisis was becoming larger than

Japan's capacity for independent action. As a senior editorial writer noted in *Sankei Shimbun* (which had championed the AMF), the proposal had failed because of: U.S. dollar hegemony in Asia, China's unexpected opposition, and the mistaken assumption that Japanese money could stop capital flight from stricken Asian countries without the psychological backup of the IMF.[80]

The Contagion Spreads

In any case, by the time of the Bangkok APEC meeting at the end of November, neither the U.S. Treasury Department or the Ministry of Finance had the luxury of pursuing an ideological debate over the IMF system any longer. Indonesian economic stability was coming apart; the South Koreans had abandoned the defense of the won; the U.S. stock market had plummeted; and major Japanese financial institutions were declaring bankruptcy. The assumptions behind the original AMF proposal—that the crisis was contained largely to Thailand and that Japan had the economic power to take unilateral regional leadership—quickly faded in the face of a potential global financial meltdown.

The speed of the Indonesia economic disaster was particularly shocking—to both MOF and U.S. officials. Japanese officials started out fairly confident that Indonesia would escape any contagion from the collapse of the baht. In the summer of 1997, Japan had $23.2 billion in loans outstanding to Indonesia (39 percent of total foreign debt), but most investors thought, like Marubeni Trading Corporation vice president Taida Hideya, that "the fundamentals were not as bad as Thailand"—a view that in hindsight "was far too optimistic."[81] The affect of the baht collapse on Indonesia was almost immediate. The Indonesians widened the band for trading the rupiah on July 11 and on August 14 allowed the currency to float freely, which led to rapid depreciation. This in turn raised questions about the ability of Indonesia to honor its outstanding foreign debt, which then led to new crises of confidence in the rupiah and a vicious cycle of currency depreciation. By October 31 Jakarta was desperate enough to agree to IMF terms for a $23 billion economic adjustment program, this time with the United States participating. International investors soon lost confidence in this program, however, because President Suharto refused to disentangle the government from heavily indebted family-held companies. On January 15, 1998, Suharto signed a new agreement with the IMF, this time pledging to dismantle the monopolies and family-owned businesses that had marked his thirty-two years of rule. One week later the rupiah plunged again, as if the IMF had never stepped in. Panicked, Jakarta announced a freeze on debt payments and then in early February proposed a currency board that would peg the rupiah to the dollar.[82]

Jakarta's new hard line put Japan in an extremely difficult position. The large exposure of Japan's already shaky financial institutions and trading companies in Indonesia made Tokyo reluctant to write off bad loans to the country, as U.S. and European firms were doing, or to cut off economic assistance, as the IMF was threatening. On the other hand, if Tokyo kept rolling over its nonperforming loans to Indonesia or provided emergency funds independent of the IMF, it risked Washington's wrath and the failure to establish a long-term solution to the crisis. Moreover, the IMF's strict demands for austerity in Indonesia hardened the philosophical choice Tokyo would have to make between its perceived role as Asia's champion versus global leader in the IMF. MOF officials hedged. Sakakibara refused to comment on the Indonesian currency board idea, even after U.S. special envoy and former ambassador to Japan Walter Mondale blasted the idea in Jakarta on March 3. In the meantime, Tokyo attempted to negotiate a plan to cut Indonesia's private foreign debt by more than 30 percent through a combination of debt forgiveness and securitization.[83] In the end, though, MOF officials sided with the IMF, and Prime Minister Hashimoto traveled to Jakarta in mid-March to explain to Suharto exactly where Japan stood. On April 8 Indonesia reached a new agreement with the IMF, this time with IMF officials monitoring progress before dispersing funds. The IMF orthodoxy prevailed, but by May social unrest was spreading throughout the country, sparked in large part by the price increases for heating fuel, electricity, and transportation—the result of conditionality imposed with the $40 billion IMF package.[84]

In South Korea problems stemming from the overexposure of banks and chaebols had been steadily mounting all year. The failure of the Hanbo Group in January 1997 and a string of other bankruptcies climaxing with the collapse of the Kia Group in July signaled that Seoul was not immune to the crisis in spite of its advanced industrial status, recently minted by membership in the OECD. By the fall, foreign investors were rapidly losing confidence in the South Korean economy, and despite valiant efforts to intervene in foreign exchange markets in defense of the won, South Korea's central bank exhausted its foreign reserve holdings and was forced to allow the won to drop on November 17. This time the United States, Japan, and the IMF acted quickly and in concert. On December 3 South Korea signed a letter of intent with the IMF for $57 billion in aid, agreeing to restructuring of the corporate sector and enhanced transparency in financial markets. After the Korea Development Bank was forced to abruptly withdraw a $10 billion bond offering because rating services lowered Korea's sovereign debt to "junk bond" status in late December, the United States and Japan provided $10 billion in accelerated funding to stabilize the won. The Clinton administration also orchestrated an agreement by major U.S., European, and Japanese banks to roll over about $15 billion in short-term liabilities.[85] Kim Dae Jung, elected president in mid-December, eventually restored investor confidence in Korea with his vigorous efforts to persuade the South Korean people of the need to reform the economy. In contrast to Indonesia, South Korea turned the corner and began the road to recovery. Japanese interests, represented by one-third of bank claims on South Korean debt, converged with U.S. interests, represented by 37,000 U.S. troops stationed in the South.

Japan Stagnates and U.S. Pressure Grows

Underlying the Japanese response to Indonesia and South Korea throughout this period was the deteriorating situation of Japanese financial institutions at home, coupled with the first signs that the Asian contagion was affecting the U.S. economy. On October 27, 1997 the Dow Jones industrial average posted its second largest loss ever, falling 7.18 percent—enough to prompt stock exchange officials to suspend trading. On February 19, 1998, monthly trade statistics showed the U.S. trade deficit soaring 24 percent to $10.8 billion—a huge increase over government economists' expectations. Meanwhile, Japanese confidence eroded with the failure of the first major bank, the Hokkaidô Takushoku Bank, on November 17, and Yamaichi Securities Co. Ltd., the fourth largest in Japan, on November 24. Tokyo was also surprised by figures suggesting that the economy would be declining for the year (eventually 1997 saw −0.1 percent growth). Declining confidence in the Japanese economy led to selling of the yen, which declined to a sixty-eight month low of 134 to the dollar in January—further jeopardizing recovery in the rest of Asia. On February 6 the Economic Planning Agency acknowledged in Tokyo that the Japanese economy had become "stagnant."[86]

Frustrated with apparent Japanese inaction to stimulate the economy and alarmed at the growing impact of the Asian financial crisis on the U.S. trade deficit and financial markets, U.S. officials turned up the heat on Japan. Pronouncements by the LDP that measures would be taken to stimulate the economy without tax cuts or fiscal spending in early

February failed to convince skeptical U.S. officials. In congressional hearings Undersecretary Summers chastised Japan for its "virtual policy," and Secretary Rubin argued that the objective of growth led by domestic demand in Japan had "not been met."[87] The next week at the London meeting of G-7 finance ministers and central bankers, U.S. officials encouraged their European counterparts to press Japan to stimulate domestic demand.[88] This was followed closely by Federal Reserve Board chairman Alan Greenspan's February 25 statement before the House Banking Committee that "the Japanese economy seems to be shrinking."[89]

On the defensive, officials in Tokyo announced an unprecedented 16 trillion yen ($124.22 billion) stimulus package on April 24, which Treasury Secretary Rubin called "encouraging." The LDP also began deliberation on a "Total Plan" for restoring health to the banking sector, which centered on proposals from U.S. experts for "bridge banks" to manage nonperforming loans. As Toshikawa Toshio lamented in the business journal *Tōyō Keizai*, "it was America that took the lead in Japan's policies."[90] Despite the government's stimulus package, confidence in Japanese management of the economy continued to ebb, and the yen depreciated further, forcing an unusual joint U.S.-Japan bilateral intervention in currency markets on June 18 after the yen hit its lowest level in eight years. In exchange for the joint intervention, Treasury insisted that MOF agree to fix its banking system. Publicly badgered by Washington and seemingly impotent to arrest the slide of the Japanese economy without U.S. help, Prime Minister Hashimoto's popularity plummeted. After the stunning defeat of the LDP in Upper House elections in July, he resigned to be replaced two weeks later by Obuchi Keizō.

One year after the Asian crisis began with the collapse of the Thai baht, the situation in Asia finally began to stabilize. Most of the affected currencies in the region reached a new equilibrium at about 60 to 70 percent of their value from the year before. The Clinton administration backed off its pressure on Japan, in part because Japan had taken action, but also because of concerns that further *gaiatsu* would be counterproductive to political relations and market perceptions and because the world's attention was turning to financial turmoil in Russia and Brazil. Eager to restore international confidence in Japanese financial policy, Prime Minister Obuchi prevailed on an aging Miyazawa Kiichi to assume the post of finance minister. After the defeat of the AMF proposal, Tokyo turning again to the first champion of Japanese "intellectual contribution."

The New "Miyazawa Initiative"

As the Obuchi cabinet's new finance minister, Miyazawa's "intellectual contribution" was a newly repackaged version of the original AMF plan—only this time one clearly aimed to supplement, rather than challenge, the IMF. The "Miyazawa Initiative" came in a completely different environment from that surrounding the AMF proposal the year before. First, by the fall of 1998 the United States was facing the prospect of broader global contagion, which meant that Japanese supplemental funding for Asia was critical. Just as Japan could not manage the Asian crisis without global help from the IMF, the United States could not handle a global crisis without extra help in Asia from Japan. In addition, the Miyazawa Initiative was clearly intended to supplement IMF packages with no hint of a divergence on the critical issue of conditionality. Finally, international and domestic criticism of the IMF's performance was causing the Clinton administration to take a more flexible approach to the responding to the crisis, just as occurred in the Latin American debt crisis of the late 1980s.

The Miyazawa Initiative was announced shortly before the annual general meeting of the IMF and World Bank in October 1998. Once again, the Asian finance ministers and central bankers got a sneak preview in Tokyo before the official announcement, but this time Rubin was personally briefed by Miyazawa as well.[91] MOF had finally learned the political hazards of pushing for "Asian-only" financial policies. The response from both the Asian financial authorities and the U.S. Treasury secretary was positive.

Under the initiative, Japan pledged to provide $30 billion to countries affected by the crisis in Asia. One-half ($15 billion) would come in the form of special account lending for short-term foreign currency reserve needs and the other $15 billion in the form of medium- to long-term loans, primarily from JEXIM, for recovery of the real economy. The JEXIM loans would go through cofinancing with the ADB and World Bank in the form of structural adjustment program loans to the financial sector, two-step loans through the governmental financial institutions, and financial assistance for infrastructure development. Direct ODA loans would be provided by OECF for strengthening of the social safety net. The recipient countries included Indonesia, Malaysia, Thailand, South Korea, the Philippines, and, later, Vietnam.[92]

While Japan received praise even from the IMF's Fischer for the Miyazawa Initiative, one definite driver behind the scheme was the now-desperate situation of Japanese banks. As one MOF official explained, the Miyazawa Initiative was "one part of the overall measures to resolve the financial turmoil in Japan, whereas the AMF had been motivated more by idealism."[93] Japanese banks exposed in Southeast Asia had become as anxious as their U.S. and European counterparts to write off nonperforming loans, but the Japanese bankers had their loans tied up in long-term FDI projects that also involved Japanese trading, construction, and auto companies that had large exposure in the stagnant Japanese economy.[94] The JEXIM loans maintained financing for viable projects in Southeast Asian projects in the "gray zone"—projects driven toward bankruptcy because of the crisis, but still commercially viable in the long run. From MOF and MITI's perspective, this demonstrated Japan's long-term commitment to retaining stable investment in the region while also helping to insulate Japanese firms against nonperforming loans they could not afford. Moreover, as JEXIM officials were quick to point out, the loans were completely untied to procurement from Japanese firms.[95] This was not the case, however, with the Emergency Economic Package put together by the cabinet on November 16.[96] Most of the package aimed at further stimulating the domestic Japanese economy, but it also included 1 trillion yen in tied aid for infrastructure development projects in Asian countries.[97]

The broad praise thrown at the Miyazawa Initiative also could not mask the fact that Japan was not taking other necessary steps to resolve the Asian financial crisis. For example, the government could have arranged for loan repayments from Asian countries to be stretched out, but chose not to do so in order to keep demand from infrastructure projects involving Japanese firms alive. Moreover, Japan could have joined the other APEC nations in accelerated liberalization of tariffs on fish and wood products, but did not (the subject of the previous chapter). The initiative also came under fire for the cumbersome and slow interagency process necessary for its implementation.[98] Finally, Japan's decision to include Malaysia in the initiative raised eyebrows in Washington, since Mahathir had imposed capital controls and other policy moves in defiance of the IMF. Tokyo defended its first yen credits to Malaysia since 1994 by arguing that economic collapse there would hurt the rest of the region and that someone had to support the country even though Mahathir had opted out of the IMF solution to the crisis.[99] Privately, many in Tokyo relished the chance to reward the IMF's greatest critic in the region.

Despite these blemishes, the Miyazawa Initiative became a central part of the solution to the Asian economic problem, instead of a potential problem comparable to the AMF. Moreover, the Obuchi government took great strides to reassure international investors and the region that Japan and the United States were working in concert. Most notable was the joint announcement of the Asian Growth and Recovery Initiative (AGRI) at the APEC summit in November 1998. The AGRI folded the Miyazawa Initiative funds into a joint effort with the United States, the World Bank, and the ADB to provide a $10 billion Asian debt restructuring and refinancing program.[100] In December Obuchi also promised another $3 billion credit account at the ADB for bonds issued by Asian governments and an additional $5 billion loan facility for infrastructure development.[101] All told, the Foreign Ministry claimed by early 1999 to have committed $80 billion to help Asia recover from the crisis.

By 1999 all of the affected Asian economies other than Indonesia began to show signs of recovery and growth again. Soon the initial funds promised under the Miyazawa Initiative also began to run out. While the need for emergency stabilization funds had passed, however, private bank lending from Japan to the region had also declined 39.6 percent in the two years since the crisis erupted in Thailand,[102] and Tokyo felt strong pressure to pick up the slack. This was necessary first and foremost to prevent nonperforming and underperforming loans in the region from further decimating the already weak books of Japanese financial institutions, but Tokyo also wanted to build on the diplomatic success of the Miyazawa Initiative in the region. In Southeast Asia, in particular, Japan's previous largesse had won points for Tokyo and at the 1998 APEC summit, as we saw in the last chapter, this helped Japanese officials to stave off U.S. pressure for accelerated liberalization of the Japanese agricultural market. Finally, Tokyo saw in a continuation of the first Miyazawa Initiative an opportunity to further encourage the use of the yen as an international transaction currency in the region.

At the May 15–16 APEC finance ministers Forum, therefore, Miyazawa pledged to provide yet another 2 trillion yen (U.S. $16.7 billion), this time in the form of guarantees for long-term bonds issued by East Asian governments for direct borrowing from Japan. The package combined a $3 billion Asian Currency Crisis Support Facility arranged between Japan and the ADB in March and more than $13 billion in new guarantees.[103] As MOF explained, this "second stage" of the Miyazawa Initiative had a longer-term aim to strengthen Asian financial institutions—one of the original purposes of the AMF: "Having passed through the initial stage of the currency crisis and the next stage of preventing further stagnation of the economy, the Asian economies are now entering a new stage of cooperation in the construction of a more stable and robust economic system so they can recover and maintain vigorous economic development."[104]

Asia's enthusiasm for Japanese money should not have been surprising, and some MOF officials cautioned that the Japanese government was being drawn into easy lending that no longer had anything to do with helping these countries recover from the crisis.[105] Still, the siren of Asian praise was difficult to resist. At the ASEAN Plus Three summit in Manila in November 1999 several Southeast Asian leaders reiterated their support for the AMF concept, and even China softened its opposition to the plan. Japan responded by introducing a symbolic debt-swapping agreement with the ASEAN Plus Three.[106] Subsequently, on May 6, 2000, the ASEAN Plus Three finance ministers agreed on the Chiang Mai Initiative to expand the ASEAN swap arrangement and establish a network of bilateral swap and repurchase agreement facilities among the ASEAN Plus Three countries.[107] In Tokyo the same month the parliamentary vice minister for Finance told the Diet Lower House Finance Committee that he "wanted to study the AMF proposal one more time,"[108] while MOF's advisory Committee on Foreign Exchange and Other Transactions debated the return of an AMF-style institution in its subcommittee on Asia's Economic and Financial Recovery.[109] For the most part, MOF officials remained cautious, telling *Asahi Shimbun* that given the state of Japan's own economic recovery and the lessons learned about U.S. resistance to the idea, "this was not the environment or timing to bring out another AMF proposal."[110] Nevertheless, the sentiment remained strong in Tokyo that the Miyazawa Initiative had given further legitimacy to Japan's claims at greater leadership in the international financial system. Instead of pressing all-out for an Asian fund, therefore, MOF was already working to change the "Washington consensus" from inside the IMF itself.

The Future of the International Financial Architecture

Japan could take its case to the IMF because the entire Bretton Woods system had come under criticism in the wake of the Asian crisis. This was clear in the way the White House and Treasury, surprised by the sudden global spread of the initial Thai crisis and the mounting political chaos caused in Indonesia by the IMF's conditionality, began looking for ways to signal greater flexibility on the future of the international financial architecture. In a carefully crafted speech before the Council on Foreign Relations on September 14, 1998, the president himself made a broad but vague appeal for reform of the international financial system:

> We must adapt the IMF so that it can more effectively confront the new types of financial crises, minimizing their frequency, severity and human cost. We need to consider ways to extend emergency financing when countries are battling crises of confidence due to world financial distress as distinct from their own errors in policy. We must find ways to tap the energy of global markets without sentencing the world to a cycle of continued extreme crises.[111]

Clinton pointed to the recovery of the Japanese economy as the key to economic growth and stability in East Asia, but his speech came so close to a mea culpa on the role of the IMF in the crisis that Japanese officials felt room to carry the debate further.[112]

The outline of Japan's remedy for the international financial architecture came three weeks later in a speech given in Miyazawa's name by the bright young parliamentary vice minister of Finance, Tanigaki Sadakazu, at the fall meeting of the World Bank in Washington. The speech outlined the new Miyazawa Initiative and then launched into a blunt assessment of the failings of the international financial institutions themselves. In contrast to Clinton's speech at the Council on Foreign Relations, Tanigaki sidestepped the issue of Japan's responsibility for reestablishing growth and acknowledged that a focus on "market mechanisms" is still "essentially valid," but he also went into far more detail about what had to be changed at the IMF and the World Bank.[113]

On the IMF, the Miyazawa speech called for:

- Liberalization of direct investment and long-term capital flows *before* liberalization of short-term-capital flows
- Monitoring of international movements of capital, particularly hedge funds, by debtors *and* creditors
- Recognition that when crises are caused by changes in confidence (Japan's mainstream view of the situation in Indonesia), the IMF should not automatically prescribe its usual combination of fiscal balance improvements with tightening of monetary policy
- Identification of appropriate exchange rate policies so that countries seeking IMF help do not have to shift suddenly from pegged to freely floating exchange rates
- Study of possible capital controls that would not erode investor confidence

- Consideration of the impact of diverse market economies on IMF prescriptions for liberalization and structural reform
- Policies to encourage private creditors to maintain a long-term commitment to the borrowing country

On the World Bank, the Miyazawa speech called for provision of:

- Prompt funds to stabilize markets in countries whose currency is under attack
- Funding for basic social needs when countries are facing currency crises

Most of the proposals in the speech pointed with fairness and accuracy to the shortcomings of the IMF approach to the Asian currency crisis and the need for a new approach. However, three dimensions of the speech contradicted mainstream thinking in the IMF and emerged as points of intellectual contention with the United States as the debate over the future of the international financial architecture unfolded.

Contentious Points in Japan's Intellectual Contribution

The first dimension of the Miyazawa speech that might prove heretical in future discussions of the international financial architecture was the proposal to study capital controls. The speech acknowledged that capital controls could hamper direct investment or might prove inefficient, but called for study of a middle road to dampen the effects of short-term capital movements nonetheless. Again, MOF is short on specific proposals, though the Committee on Foreign Exchange and Other Transactions recommended consideration of a policy in which central banks require a portion of inflowing capital to be deposited for a pre-scribed period of time in order to prevent sudden capital flight (the Chilean model).[114] It is not at all clear that this could be done without hampering FDI and needed liquidity, and the Japanese side has not aggressively pursued the proposal.

The second dimension of the Miyazawa speech that might provide grist for future intellectual debates with the United States and the IMF was the call for strengthening separate Asian institutional capabilities to deal with future crises. The Committee on Foreign Exchange and Other Transactions recommended that the first step should be elevating the surveillance cooperation established by the Manila Framework in November 1997 from the level of deputy finance ministers and bank governors to the principals from each institution: "Because Tokyo is home to the offices of the IMF (the only one in Asia), the World Bank, and the ADB, as well as the ADB Institute, Tokyo provides a ready framework for possibly pursuing interorganizational coordination."[115] Greater surveillance would also be a major theme for U.S. and IMF officials in debates over the future international financial architecture, but to the extent that overzealous MOF or MOFA officials attempt to create a separate Asian identity and institution—even within the IMF—the friction that surrounded the AMF debate could reemerge.

The third contentious issue was Miyazawa's call for a study on exchange rate regimes. MOF officials generally describe their aim as the establishment of "policy targets" rather than a return to something like fixed exchange rates. MOF first tried to propose the idea at the Bretton Woods fiftieth anniversary meeting in 1994, but was rebuffed by other G-7 participants.[116] More recent attempts to convince the G-7 finance ministers meeting in London in February 1998 went no better. U.S. policymakers remain opposed to any government role in determining exchange rates. The Treasury Department even resisted Japan's calls for joint intervention to defend the yen in June 1998 until the Japanese currency's decline threatened to knock the Chinese renminbi off its fixed rate on the eve of Clinton's visit to China. Future regimes for joint intervention to shape foreign exchange markets are clearly not in the Treasury Department's planning after the Asian crisis, though Japanese observers hold out hope that the arrival of the euro will give the idea fresh currency (so to speak).[117]

Internationalization of the Yen

Nevertheless, the focus on exchange rate regimes in the Miyazawa speech reflected the conviction among most Japanese observers that the Asian economies would have been spared the currency crises if they had pegged their currencies more heavily to the yen.[118] It also reflected the Japanese government's continuing frustration with the volatility of the yen, which hurts Japanese firms particularly hard because 20 percent of Japanese assets are externally held (compared with 15 percent for the United States).[119] Internationalization of the yen became a national cause cèlébre for Japanese elites after the financial crisis. The blue-ribbon advisory Committee on Foreign Exchange and Other Transactions made the promotion of greater use of the yen in Asian currency baskets a central part of its postcrisis recommendations to the government, repeating a theme the committee first introduced in 1984.[120] The

Liberal Democratic Party also recommended promoting the internationalization of the yen as a measure to stabilize the intraregional exchange rates of Southeast Asian currencies.[121] Miyazawa elaborated on the same theme again at the ASEM meeting in Frankurt in January, where he proposed that Asian countries link their currencies to new baskets that also included the euro.[122]

The most obvious way to encourage the use of the yen in Asian currency baskets would be to make it worthwhile to hold yen over the long term. This would require liberalizing the Tokyo stock market, stimulating the domestic economy, and encouraging general deregulation so that the transaction costs of holding yen are reduced and the currency can be invested in Japanese assets. However, this internationalization of the yen carries both advantages and disadvantages. On the positive side, it would stabilize Asian currencies and Japan's economic relationship with the region and make it easier for Japan to run current account deficits in the future as the society ages (a lesson learned from the United States in the 1980s). It would also give Japan a tool to share more management of the international economy. And it would protect Japanese exports more against exchange rate risk in Asian trade.[123]

On the other hand, liberalization of financial markets and internationalization of the yen would weaken the MOF's and the Bank of Japan's control of monetary supply and other economic policy tools. As a result, MOF remains internally divided over the real value of an aggressive pursuit of yen internationalization.[124] For his part, Sakakibara steered a middle ground, holding out yen internationalization as a "process" rather than a "goal."[125] Political pressure for internationalization remains high, however, as evidenced by the final report of the Committee on Foreign Exchange and Other Transactions in April 1999, which argued that yen internationalization must be advanced, in the wake of the Asian financial crisis, the debut of the euro, and the implementation of the "Big Bang" liberalization in Tokyo financial markets.[126]

Tokyo's growing enthusiasm for yen internationalization notwithstanding, fundamental questions remain about Japan's ability to take the domestic restructuring steps that would be necessary to make the yen a more attractive currency to hold and use in international transactions. For example, in spite of the MOF advisory committee's confidence that the April 1, 1998, "Big Bang" liberalization of Tokyo financial markets will increase the attractiveness of the yen, the economic crisis has actually led the Japanese government to play a larger role in providing financing, not a lesser role. Government control of the bankrupt

Long-term Credit Bank, expanded credit guarantees, and a more active role for public sector financial institutions all caused the government to be the source of half of lending in Japan in 1999.[127] In addition, Japanese expectations that the euro's debut might weaken dollar hegemony to the advantage of the yen—as Obuchi himself suggested in a speech in January 1999 in Europe—have proven wrong. If anything, some Japanese economists are concluding, the euro's debut has diminished the yen's stature rather than the dollar's.[128] The bottom line is that without confidence in a nation's long-term political and economic stability, that country's currency will not establish a larger share of global transactions. Given these obstacles, it is difficult to see how the $15 billion in yen offered for emergency stabilization under the Miyazawa Initiative could make more than a marginal impact on the currency reserves of the Asian economies.[129]

Toward a Convergence on the International Financial System

In spite of some of the more contentious Japanese proposals for changes in the international financial architecture and the unrealistic expectations about the power of the yen as an international currency, the Miyazawa and Clinton speeches in 1998 actually started a dialectic that led to more convergence in U.S., Japanese, and European views than divergence. For one thing, realistic examination of Japan's proposals revealed that all required either cooperation from the United States or significant restructuring in Japan. Tokyo's ideas for exchange rate regimes, for example, would only work if the other G-7 countries are willing to cooperate. Internationalization of the yen works only if Japan implements the kinds of market liberalization and transparency the IMF called for in South Korea, and even then it may not occur. And Tokyo acknowledges that institutionalization of an Asian financial system cannot be anything more than a complement to the Bretton Woods system.

Moreover, the United States and the IMF leadership have also converged on Japan's position to a significant extent, acknowledging some of the faults in the international financial institutions that Miyazawa pointed to in his speech in October 1998. Outgoing IMF managing director Michel Camdessus admitted in a speech before the Council on Foreign Relations on June 4, 1999, that the IMF needed to shift "from curative medicine to preventative medicine" and announced two new facilities to do just that.[130] In ongoing discussions of the international financial architecture at the G-7 finance ministers meeting in Cologne that same month, Japanese officials in turn conceded the importance of liberalizing financial markets and maintaining firm IMF conditionality, while U.S. officials began to acknowledge that in certain circumstances, basket pegs or capital controls might make sense (but only when there is fiscal discipline, transparency, and an emergency situation—in other words, not in the way Mahathir did it).[131]

The debate heated up again somewhat in the December 16 inaugural meeting of the newly formed Group of 20 Countries to discuss changes in the international financial system. Treasury Secretary Summers argued at the meeting that the IMF cannot become "a source of low-cost financing for countries with ready access to private capital"—the role that the new stages of the Miyazawa Initiative appeared to be filling. MOF officials countered that the IMF must do more activities like the Miyazawa Initiative and argued for the IMF to play a role in long-term lending to assist balance-of-payments adjustments and structural reforms in emerging economies.[132] Japan also pressed publicly for its candidate to replace Camdessus, the controversial "Mr. Yen," Sakakibara Eisuke.

Behind the speeches, however, MOF officials were more candid and realistic about their positions. Sakakibara, they admitted, had no chance, but they wanted to break the European monopoly on leadership of the IMF and create an opportunity for future Japanese leadership. On proposals for a more proactive role for the IMF in lending to the Third World, MOF officials were equally realistic. In contrast to Cologne and G-7 meetings, where Japan had to work quietly with counterparts to achieve action, the G-20 gave more opportunities for posturing. It was no surprise that a consensus proved elusive in a setting with so many more participants. As one MOF official put it just before the G-20 meeting, "we do not really expect our view to come true, but we will continue pressing in hope of establishing a third way in the future."[133] A more consensus-based and modest document staking out the new middle ground on reform of the international financial institutions was produced at the G-7 finance ministers' meeting in Fukuoka in July 2000. The G-7 report trumpeted several steps taken along the lines pushed by Japan—including: establishment of a Financial Stability Forum to monitor capital flows and highly leveraged institutions; the establishment of the G-20 to give borrowers more of a voice in management of the international financial architecture; and mechanisms to strengthen private sector involvement.[134]

Lessons for Japanese Diplomacy and U.S.-Japan Relations

Clear patterns emerge in U.S.-Japan interaction in the diplomacy of international finance from the first Miyazawa plan to the new Miyazawa Initiative. Japan, eager to play a larger leadership role in the international financial institutions commensurate with its financial contribution, throws out a major proposal, backed by promises of billions of dollars of Japanese financing, but vague in the details. The Japanese plan is short on details because there is still insufficient support or consensus, even among MOF's international finance bureaucracy and its counterparts in the Budget and Tax bureaus. The specifics are vague also because the Japanese side is not prepared to have the plan defeated in detail by Treasury or the money hijacked within an American initiative. The goal of demonstrating a unique "intellectual contribution" and Japanese soft power, in short, is only complicated by extensive preconsultations and coordination with Washington.

The United States opposes the Japanese initiative for some good reasons. The plan lacks clarity, its combination of vagueness and boldness gives the impression of a Japanese assault on U.S. hegemony in the international financial system. It risks a moral hazard, since the Japanese are far too eager to give away money without the proper IMF conditions for restructuring and transparency. Japan's plan also appears designed in part to divert attention from ongoing U.S.-Japan economic problems—often problems that, if solved, would do more to resolve the ongoing financial crisis than the promise of Japanese money. In 1998 during the Latin American crisis, for example, the problem was Japan's massive current account surplus and closed market; in 1992 during World Bank debate, the problem was Japanese nontariff barriers being contested in the U.S.-Japan Structural Impediments Initiative; in 1997 during the AMF proposal, the problem was Japan's massive banking debt and macroeconomic malaise. U.S. officials therefore shoot down the Japanese plan, often in public forums, since that is where Tokyo chooses to make its own pronouncement. But as the crisis deepens, Washington is forced to stray from its strict free market dogma because the Europeans start also grumbling and because Japanese money is needed. The United States folds Japan's original proposal—and, more important, the money—into an American-led scheme, either the Brady plan or AGRI.

There are some clear lessons that each side should take away from these episodes. Japan should recognize that its initial posturing, while intellectually satisfying, only defeats the goal it is trying to accomplish because the posturing is out of sync with the real political and economic leverage at Tokyo's disposal. First, in an era of global capital liquidity, Japan is too insignificant on its own to establish and sustain a separate regional institution like the AMF without IMF help. Even the $100 billion Japan proposed for the AMF would not have been enough to deter huge capital movements without concerted actions of the IMF to restore international investor confidence. Second, Japan's arguments for "proactive and preventive" government-supported financing create a moral hazard that even MOF officials recognize is dangerous. Third, the largesse of $80 billion committed in response to the currency crisis notwithstanding, real Japanese leadership does depend on actions to revitalize the economy and absorb imports. Finally, MOF officials are on slippery ground—their arguments against the IMF orthodoxy are increasingly out of step with restructuring that globalism is forcing on the Japanese economy beneath their feet. Meanwhile, the Japanese government's continued shepherding of financial institutions at home weakens any prospect that the internationalization of the yen will give Tokyo greater influence in managing the international financial system.

The United States should also recognize that in spite of its "victories" over Japan in the international financial architecture debate, there is a cost. First, U.S. credibility in East Asia was lost as Washington downplayed the Thai baht crisis and later spent its diplomatic energies crushing the AMF proposal—in the view of many Asians, fiddling while Rome burned. This later accrued to Japan's benefit in the U.S.-Japan confrontation over agricultural liberalization at the 1998 APEC meeting and in the ASEAN Plus Three sessions that began after the AMF defeat. Second, while the AMF as packaged came as an unwelcome challenge to the IMF, it also had elements that the United States and the fund should have applied in the summer of 1997 to stem the growing contagion—particularly, a $50 billion Japanese contribution. Leading U.S. economists, such as Fred Bergsten of the International Institute for Economics, saw the potential to stabilize the region's financial system by building on the Japanese proposal,[135] but the Clinton administration saw the proposal as a challenge that had to be killed. This same pattern occurred a decade earlier in the case of the first Miyazawa plan, of course. Third, the U.S. response to the AMF did significant damage to the overall U.S.-Japan alliance relationship.[136] Even the AGRI, which was supposed to highlight U.S.-Japan cooperation a year after the crisis broke, was attacked in the Japanese press as another example of the United States "hijacking" Japanese leadership and money.[137]

Finally, U.S. officials should have recognized that the AMF proposal was not a national challenge to the United States, but rather an incomplete proposal formed in only one part of MOF that caused considerable opposition and concern elsewhere in the government. By attacking the AMF instead of harnessing it, the administration turned the issue into a win-lose battle over national economic ideologies that are themselves largely constructed by the ideologues on each side. Instead, the United States and the IMF should have played to the pragmatists in MOF and the rest of the government by insisting on early coordination with the IMF, but premised on the condition that Japan would assume leadership and responsibility for the final product. The contentious areas of Japanese divergence from the IMF would not have stood up to the scrutiny of close coordination with the IMF and the U.S. government (since there was such internal disagreement in MOF already), and the promise of Japanese leadership-sharing would have won not only Japanese funding to deal immediately with the crisis, but also goodwill for the alliance. In short, there is an advantage to both shaping Japanese initiatives like the AMF early on and also giving Tokyo a certain amount of room to demonstrate its "independent diplomacy" and "intellectual leadership."

Coordination at this level can be tough, of course. Officials managing the international financial system also must keep the pressure on Japan to make internal changes necessary for the health of the entire system. It is difficult to take off the adversarial hat and put on the coordination hat. International financial diplomacy is also a fluid multiplayer game, where Europe and Japan or the developing world and Japan sometimes have more common cause than the United States and Japan. Moreover, despite the closed and clubby nature of international finance officials and central bankers meetings, there are relatively few mechanisms for rapid policy coordination, and what mechanisms there are remain highly dependent on the personalities of key individuals. Nevertheless, the lessons of the Asian financial crisis demonstrate that the international financial system needs close U.S.-Japan coordination and might even benefit from the kind of institutionalized crisis planning that the U.S. and Japanese defense establishments are developing.

Returning, finally, to the themes of realism and national identity, it is clear that some of the patterns evident in Japan's diplomatic relationship with China or the Koreas are also occurring in Japanese international financial diplomacy. MOF learned to some extent from the crisis its own limited power vis-à-vis the United States. As Sakakibara himself noted afterward, "we were taught a valuable lesson on the influence the

United States wields in Asia."[138] Chinese opposition to Japan's initiative was also revealing for these officials. As influential observers such as Itô Takatoshi noted in *Gaikō Forum* in 1999, this new power game means Japan must also do what other countries do and argue its position in international economic diplomacy based on a clear understanding and explanation of national interest.[139] This same emphasis on national interest also explains the ebbing tide of idealism in Japanese economic assistance as the crisis unfolded. The emphasis on explicit rewards for Japanese firms in Japan's assistance was clear in the return of tied loans in the new Miyazawa Initiative. MITI pressed particularly hard for more tied aid in the Miyazawa Initiative, and this emphasis on national economic benefit in ODA will likely increase in the future as available resources decline. Meanwhile, MOFA gave new emphasis to the use of assistance for environmental protection, security, and political objectives in a 1998 advisory report on ODA reforms.[140] The effects of fiscal tightening and concerns about maintaining Japanese diplomatic "weight" were apparent throughout the crisis.

The bottom line is that no new "Cold War" over competing economic systems has emerged in the post–Cold War era, as some predicted at the beginning of the 1990s. Moreover, Alan Greenspan was probably correct in his April 1998 statement that the Asian crisis raised awareness of the superiority of the Western—and especially U.S.—mode of capitalism.[141] At the same time, however, most of the Asia nations came away from the crisis frustrated with the combination of American hegemony and complacency, and generally pleased with Japan's financial contribution to a resolution of the crisis. That perception gap between East and West sows the seeds for further intellectual friction between Tokyo and Washington, even as Japan's economy moves closer to the global standards pointed out by Greenspan. With proper strategic coordination, however, the international financial system could become a key arena for enhanced U.S.-Japan leadership-sharing.

CHAPTER NINE

Conclusion

Learning from the Loose Changes of the Present

What a decade it might have been. In 1990 Japan's economy was still humming along. The nation's industries led the United States in half a dozen critical military-related technologies, and economists speculated that Japan's GDP could surpass that of the United States sometime early in the next century. Diplomatically, the end of the Cold War had opened up new opportunities for normalization with North Korea and a special new relationship with Beijing. Economic integration in East Asia based on Japanese investment was expanding, and exciting new concepts for cooperative multilateral forums were gaining support across the region.

Had those trends continued, Japan might have emerged as a new kind of superpower, its alliance with the United States only one minor pillar of a security strategy based on economic leverage in the region. Indeed, the alliance might have weakened considerably as the Japanese economic model gained more adherents in the region and ideological clashes grew with Washington. Tokyo's closer relations with Beijing and stronger regional institutions would have buttressed Japanese regional leadership and perhaps allowed a smoother resolution of the unfinished business from World War II.

As it turned out, of course, the first decade of the post–Cold War era proved deeply frustrating for Japan. The Gulf War was a diplomatic disaster and a national humiliation. The collapse of the bubble economy undercut the message of egalitarian growth that the Japanese economic model seemed to convey to its people and the region and caused deep uncertainty about the future. By the middle of the decade collisions with Beijing over nuclear testing, defense guidelines, Taiwan, territorial disputes, and—above all—history shook Japanese confidence about strategic convergence within the region. North Korean nuclear weapons and missile development further eroded Japanese complacency about regional threats to national security. Strategic dependence on the United States only increased, yet Washington's attention to Japan waned. Other tools—APEC, the ARF, a UN Security Council seat—all proved disappointing or elusive. And by 2000 it was clear that despite a series of massive stimulus packages and the resulting 130 percent of GDP in debt, the economy had still grown at an average of little more than zero percent since the collapse of the bubble. For Japan, it was the lost decade.

Lost, but not without consequences, for Japan's foreign policy was tugged reluctantly toward a new realism with each new challenge. As was noted in chapter 1, this was realism in several meanings of the word. In the terms of contemporary international relations theory, Japan grew more acutely sensitive to power balances in the region, particularly vis-à-vis China. In terms of the intellectual contest between realism and idealism, the sentimental, hopeful, and complacent aspects of Japan's previous worldview lost ground to a somewhat more Hobbesian and self-interested perspective. And where Japan's approach to international affairs had been driven by self-interest in the past—that is, in its focus on economic tools and economic benefit—the challenges of the post–Cold War environment forced a new realism about the saliency of those tools and the need for a more assertive diplomatic agenda to compensate for relative decline in economic power. Still reactive, Japan's changing circumstances made it markedly less passive in international affairs. As one official in the Japanese government smartly summarized this shift, "we [in Japan] have developed much more consciousness about the integrity and dignity of the nation-state."[1]

But as we have seen, the shift has been evolutionary rather than revolutionary. Important elements of continuity are clear in Japan's foreign policy priorities in the 1990s. Alliance with the United States remains the main pillar of Japan's approach to the world. Economic tools, despite declining resources, are still the first choice for Japanese policymakers. The strong undertow of pacifism has prevented a more hostile attitude toward North Korea and China from changing the basic parameters of Japanese defense policy or defense spending. And no political leader has attempted to build a base of support for an alternate strategic vision to the Yoshida Doctrine.

In part, these areas of continuity can be explained by the stubborn resistance of Japanese norms and institutions to external changes. But it is also worth noting that Japan's norms and institutions were themselves shaken by a decade of economic malaise, growing insecurity about China and North Korea, and diminishing attention from the United States. The LDP regained power and held on through a series of coalition arrangements and stimulus packages that only postponed further dealignment and eventual realignment of the Japanese political scene. Meanwhile, profound generational changes on issues of security, the Constitution, history, and China gnawed at many taboos, creating a new consensus that is at the same time more insecure about external security and power relations and more ambitious about Japan's international identity.

Moreover, none of the shocks described in these pages could be called a real "crisis"—at least not of the sort that Japan would face in the event of war in the Taiwan Straits or a calamitous rise in bankruptcies and unemployment at home. In many respects, Japan's situation is still quite comfortable, both in terms of the relative lack of displacement from economic restructuring and the decreased number of opponents actually aiming weapons at Japan since the demise of the Soviet Union. One could therefore extrapolate from "the small changes of the present" both what trends are likely to continue and what might happen if things became decidedly *less* comfortable in the future.

Likely Trends

We should begin with those trends that do not depend on sudden shocks or discontinuities in the international system.

First, Japan will almost certainly face even more serious decline in the economic resources available for foreign policy. With debt at 130 percent of GDP, close to $1 trillion in nonperforming or underperforming loans, a pension system that is close to bankruptcy, and municipal and prefectural governments all in debt, Japan already faces a considerable demand on revenue. Considering the amount of restructuring that is still likely in uncompetitive sectors that have only survived on massive public works budgets recently, there will be a greater strain on budgets in the years to come. And above all, the aging of the population (Japan's population will peak and begin to decline by 2008 at the latest) will force the Japanese government to dramatically shift revenue from income taxes to consumption taxes. (The consumption tax is 5 percent in 2000, and will almost certainly have to increase in the future.) Japan is currently the world's largest creditor nation, but these demands could conceivably erase that position within the first decade of the new century.

We have already seen that the sense of economic stagnation in Japan has put pressure on Japanese ODA spending, UN dues, and host-nation support for U.S. military forces in Japan. It is likely this pressure will increase. The grand scale of loans and grants represented by the Miyazawa Initiative, for example, will be more difficult to justify in the future. With fading support for UN dues and ODA, the government will increasingly be forced to scrutinize its contributions for direct benefit to national interest. "No more taxation without representation" will become a common refrain. On the other hand, this could fuel a healthier debate in Japan about broad leadership and responsibility sharing in the international community. In many respects, Japan's massive ODA spending has been an excuse for non-action—hence the derisive term "checkbook diplomacy" to describe Tokyo's penchant for buying its way out of significant risk sharing in international crises like the Gulf War or East Timor. With less to spend, Japan will be forced—and, as we have seen, is already being forced—to develop more effective diplomatic practices and strategies in other areas.

Second, it is likely that the Japanese political elite will continue moving incrementally, but with ever more acceleration, toward acceptance of a more "normal" national security policy. This trend is fueled by the economic problems Japan faces, by the growing sense of vulnerability to China and North Korea, and by generational change. The fact that 90 percent of politicians under the age of fifty support constitutional revision, as we noted in chapter 2, suggests the irreversibility of Japan's shift in this direction. While the trappings of a national security state increase, however, it is not certain that this will translate into Japan playing a larger "security role" in international society. Given uncertainties about the economy and continuing political realignment, for example, the Japanese political leadership may eschew risk in faraway crises that do not have direct bearing on "national interest"—elements of Takemura's "small but shining Japan." Nevertheless, the taboos that prevent a more normal security policy will gradually be streamlined and the Diet will likely pass legislation in the years ahead that expands participation in peacekeeping, strengthens crisis management, and centralizes security decision making. Eventually the Diet will probably also revise the Constitution, with incremental changes to recognize the right of collective defense. Again, these are healthy trends, since the process will be democratic, transparent, and closely scrutinized by Japan's neighbors and ally.

Third, Japan's economic dependence on the region will continue to deepen, but so too will uncertainty about the safety of the neighborhood. With a declining working-age population at home, Japan will need more immigrants. With growth rates higher in Southeast Asia and China than at home, Japan will continue to turn to the region as a market and not just an offshore manufacturing base. And cognizant of a new rivalry with China, Japan will press Southeast Asia, Russia, and even Central Asia to broaden cooperation beyond economic areas to include a more explicit security and political agenda. Both Southeast Asian nations and Central Asia may be reluctant to play that game. The internal regional game will likely be complemented by greater efforts to bring external players into Asia as a partner for Tokyo. Japan-India strategic cooperation is only just beginning in fits and starts. Its future will depend on resolution of the nuclear problem and the pressure for cooperation caused by Chinese actions. A Japan–European Union axis in international economic organizations has emerged to some extent, but primarily on an ad hoc basis. Security cooperation between Japan and Europe may prove more difficult, as evidenced by the hollowness of the ASEM dialogue on security. Nevertheless, it exists as a future card for Japanese diplomacy.

Meanwhile, the uncertainty about China's future direction will plague Japan for some time. Without a transition to democracy, Beijing's own outlook on Japan's role in Asia will likely remain zero sum. And the transition to democracy in China, if and when it occurs, could be an even messier process, ripe with demagoguery and nationalism. As we have seen, the two countries share economic interests, but in terms of national identity they are increasingly at odds. The Japanese and Chinese visions of their respective national roles in Asia and the steps they must each take to move beyond the constraints of the past are simply more powerful than the countervailing images of an Asian-Pacific community of nations. Japan-China relations need not necessarily sour in the future, but a return to the confidence about bilateral cooperation that characterized the early 1990s is unlikely for some time.

Fourth, Japan will continue to rely heavily on the U.S.-Japan security relationship, precisely because of this uncertainty about China and North Korea and because of continuing dependence on sea lanes as far as the Gulf. Tokyo can be counted on to continue implementing those steps, such as the defense guidelines, that are necessary to keep Washington engaged as a military partner. At the same time, domestic political pressure will continue to mount for greater Japanese ownership of the alliance. Tokyo will insist on a level of consultations on security issues comparable with NATO, for example, as well as more say in U.S. decisions on force structure in Japan. Mismanagement of these expectations could accelerate calls for reduced U.S. military presence in Japan.

Fifth, as we have seen, Japan expects a clearer recognition of its status as a diplomatic player in Asia and in international organizations. In retrospect, proposals like the Asian Monetary Fund are seen by Tokyo as poorly executed, but the principle that Japan should introduce its own strategic vision in the IMF, the UN, and international arms control is now set. This bid for a larger presence in international diplomacy has only increased with economic uncertainties. This is not to say that Japan necessarily must emphasize its "independent" diplomacy in terms of distance from the United States, but the move in that direction will be directly related to how seriously Washington takes Tokyo's proposals for a shared leadership role in early stages of episodes like the 1990 Cambodian peace talks or the 1997 Asian financial crisis. If Tokyo is shunned, it will push for an independent role. This will be more likely in peripheral geographic areas such as Burma, or in policy proposals that have some support in the United States, such as a no-first-use doctrine on U.S. nuclear weapons. With U.S. suppression of Japanese diplomatic aspirations, however, the divergence could spread to core issues like policy toward Iran or nonproliferation.

Finally, complicating all of these trends will be the continuing process of political realignment in Japan. The first stage of that process—the collapse of the old Socialist Left—is almost complete (with the Communist Party the surviving beneficiary). However, the reconsolidation of the conservatives is still quite open-ended and fluid. The overlap in policy views among the LDP, the DPJ, and the Liberal Party has made any number of combinations possible—either in coalitions or the formation of new parties. It is therefore counterproductive in many respects for aspiring political leaders in Japan at this stage to articulate foreign or security policy strategies that are too clear—and therefore too divisive. Moreover, the emerging generation of political leadership in Japan (those in their sixties) are products of the LDP of the 1970s and 1980s in which promotion depended on risk-aversion and gradual accumulation of interest group and internal faction support. With the declining cohesion of these interest groups and the growing influence of special interests, the ability of these new leaders to control foreign policy, let alone articulate a foreign policy strategy, will be limited. It is possible that the next tier of political leaders, those now in their forties and fifties, will introduce a new style of national leadership that draws its influence from a national mandate, but that may not occur soon. New shocks to the system would change this situation and accelerate political realignment—so might internal decisions over constitutional revision—but for some time the growing consciousness among the Japanese of the dignity and integrity of the nation–state may not be matched with equally effective leadership.

Variables

The trends just listed will unfold incrementally, absent major shocks. But several endogenous and exogenous shocks to Japan are possible in the years ahead, and any of these could lead to more pronounced discontinuous change in the nation's foreign and security policies.

First, there is the Japanese economy. The spectrum of possibilities can be somewhat artificially divided into three scenarios to demonstrate what might occur. In the optimistic scenario, Japanese political and economic leaders may accelerate the shift in regulatory and fiscal policy away from the old economy and toward the more competitive information technology sectors. This short-term pain could position Japan to grow at 1 to 2 percent per year before the aging of the population closes the window toward the end of the first decade of the new century. (Coming out of a recession, initially growth could even hit 3 or 4 percent.) This would require a long-term view that is not easy for a parliamentary political system, in which the Diet can be dissolved before the shift from pain to gain occurs. However, it may occur because of the impact that international financial markets are already beginning to have on the real economy through increased FDI. The scenario depends on a growth explosion in the information technology sector, a healthy international economy, sustained foreign investment, and careful fiscal policy. That creates a lot of ifs. At the same time, Japan's main resources—an industrious and well-organized society that has always responded to challenges—should not be discounted. In this scenario economic resources would continue to decline in relative importance as described, but Japan would be positioned to play a more confident and effective role in international organizations and in Asia based on a combination of continued economic contributions and expanded political assertiveness.

At the other extreme, the Japanese economy could contract rapidly following the wrong combination of external stagnation, failing domestic financial institutions, and ineffective stimulus packages (undermined by rising long-term interest rates and exhaustion of public works, or ill-timed consumption tax increases). This pessimistic scenario for the economy would probably lead to a vicious cycle in which Japan's financial contributions to international organizations, ODA, and U.S. forces would be dramatically cut, prompting mounting criticism of

Japan, which in turn would combine with displacement and confusion at home to fuel resentment and nationalism reminiscent of the 1930s. Unlike the 1930s, Japan would not turn militaristic, but there would be significantly more isolationism and inward focus.

Finally, there is the middle scenario, in which Japan muddles through without a dramatic collapse or proactive restructuring. Like a frog that cannot feel itself being boiled alive as the heat increases, Japanese politicians may find the situation just comfortable enough to avoid hard choices, condemning the nation to continued GDP growth rates at 0 to 1 percent for decades, but possibly without a painful hard landing. This scenario would obviously accelerate the trends in decreased spending on foreign policy. It would also increase the desperation in Japan's bid for an active diplomatic role while significantly undermining Japanese national power and credibility. In some ways, it is the worst scenario since the meltdown scenario at least contains the possibility of a phoenix-like return of the Japanese economy based on the total collapse of the old order.

In short, a relative decrease in Japanese economic tools may force a healthy debate on a larger diplomatic and security role, but a sudden collapse of resources would lead to a far less healthy debate about Japan's role in the world and could lead to problematic new directions.

China's future political development is also intertwined with Japan's, and there is no doubt that either instability in China or a Chinese decision to use force—most likely against Taiwan—could lead to a sudden and discontinuous change in Japan's foreign policy priorities. As was noted in chapter 3, it is an open question how Japan would immediately respond to a Chinese attack on Taiwan, but it is clear that Chinese aggression has an impact on Japanese foreign and security policy, Japan's culture of pacifism notwithstanding. Much would depend on the nature of the attack, the provocation or reason, and the manner in which the United States called on Japan for support. Japan might attempt to forestall the U.S. use of force in responding to the attack in the short term, pushing more than any party for a negotiated settlement, but the longer-term impact on Japanese security thinking would be profound. If the United States activated the Defense Guidelines and Tokyo agreed, Japan would be taking an irreversible step toward military confrontation with China and toward a complete military partnership with the United States. If Japan refused support, U.S. confidence in the alliance would be terminally weakened and Japan would be forced to hedge against a reduced U.S. commitment to Japan's defense in the future. If, on the other hand, the United States failed to respond to the

Chinese use of force, that would terminally undermine Japanese confidence in the U.S. defense commitment, also increasing Japanese hedging and unilateral military capabilities. In short, a Chinese use of force would dramatically increase Japanese security realism and reduce the constraints on unilateral military power no matter what the immediate response or outcome.

The Korean Peninsula is the other major external variable in the region that could lead to significant new departures in Japanese foreign policy. Aggression from North Korea raises the same likelihood of untying the constraints on military power presented by a Taiwan Straits scenario—only in the case of Korea it is far more likely that Japan would provide political and military (rear area) support to the United States. Unification of the peninsula is more complicated, since that would likely lead to major restructuring of U.S. military presence in the region and a search for new security mechanisms in Northeast Asia. After Japan's growing involvement with the security agenda on the peninsula in the second half of the 1990s, there should be no question that Tokyo will seek a central role in determining the final disposition of a unified Korea. Moreover, there is room for optimism that the growing security and political coordination between Seoul and Tokyo in this same period lays the groundwork for cooperation in the unification process. Of course, Japan-ROK ties do not exist in a vacuum, as we saw, and cooperation between Tokyo and Seoul will vary depending on the degree to which Korea finds itself caught in a Sino-Japanese power game.

The United States as a Variable

Finally, there is the variable that is most important, and over which the United States should have the greatest control: the U.S. security commitment to Japan. Sudden U.S. economic contraction, U.S.-Japan rivalry, or U.S. withdrawal from Asia would obviously have a calamitous impact on Japan's strategic situation and lead to wholesale change in Japanese foreign policy. In general, however, the U.S. pillar in Japan's foreign policy framework provides continuity and stability because the United States and Japan share an overlapping set of strategic objectives. Indeed, there has probably been more convergence of strategic objectives than divergence since the end of the Cold War. These common strategic objectives include:

- Maintaining U.S. forward presence and the U.S.-Japan alliance
- Balancing and integrating China

- Deterring and engaging North Korea
- Incorporating a more stable and democratic Russia into the Asia-Pacific region
- Maintaining freedom of sea lines of communication and access to natural resources
- Enhancing stability and political cohesion within ASEAN
- Preventing the spread of weapons of mass destruction
- Supporting open regional and global economic integration

Where we have found areas of divergence in U.S. and Japanese foreign policy in this study, they have primarily been tactical. In cases such as Burma or the Asian Monetary Fund proposal, for example, Japan's independent foreign policy was marginal to the U.S. core interests, supported by significant constituencies in Washington, or eventually incorporated in U.S. policy. In other areas we have found that Japan has forged coalitions to constrain the United States. Japan has proven effective at enlisting Asian help to defend itself against U.S. pressure on liberalization in APEC and enlisting European help to press the U.S. on antidumping in the WTO. And since the Senate's rejection of the Comprehensive Test Ban Treaty Japan has gravitated toward like-minded U.S. allies, such as Australia and Canada, in pressing Washington for a more proactive nuclear disarmament stance in the NPT process. However, these areas are as much a response to perceived U.S. unilateralism as they are hegemonic challenges to the United States. Moreover, as we have seen, Japan's alternatives to the U.S.-Japan alliance—whether in the UN Security Council or in building lasting regional institutions—are proving less formidable than once expected. This is true both because of domestic Japanese obstacles and because of rivalry on an international scale. On the whole, Japan has been supportive of U.S. leadership in international institutions and regional diplomacy.

Because U.S. strategic interests remain convergent with Japan's and because Japan's alternatives are so limited, one might be tempted to assume that diplomatic coordination between Washington and Tokyo is of less consequence today than it was during the Cold War. In certain respects that coordination has fallen well below Cold War levels as alliance management has declined in priority for U.S. political leadership. But this complacency is misguided. Japanese aspirations for a more normal role in international society and a more balanced relationship with the United States mean that the lack of U.S support for Japan's diplomatic profile will spawn further Japanese unilateralism in foreign policy, even though it may not be in longer-term Japanese interests. Moreover, heightened Japanese *attention* to security threats and power balances in the region means that U.S. *inattention* to these same areas (North Korean missiles, Chinese expansion in the Senkakus, etc.) will lead to more hedging and security unilateralism by Japan than in the past.

Assertive, proactive, and even independent Japanese foreign policy can serve U.S. interests, if there is close coordination and a recognition of shared objectives. But if Japanese foreign policy choices are motivated by resentment of the United States (fear of entrapment) or hedging against U.S. inattention to Japanese security interests (fear of abandonment), then it will ultimately undermine U.S. global leadership. Japan may not be able to develop effective unilateral hedges against the United States or sustainable coalitions with Europe and Asia to constrain the United States, but if Washington is spending all of its time trying to corral allies like Japan, U.S. foreign policy will be that much less effective and credible.

The good news is that the U.S.-Japan alliance starts out with common strategic objectives. The question is whether the United States will begin coordinating its foreign policy with Japan in a way that keeps us focused on those objectives.

Coordinating Foreign Policy in U.S.-Japan Relations

Obstacles to Bilateral Coordination

As we have seen, there are both structural and attitudinal obstacles to coordination of U.S. and Japanese foreign policy. Any effort to build a more effective partnership in international affairs will have to take account of these obstacles.

- *The impact of economic friction.* In the 1980s, trade friction created adversarial positions between the United States and Japan that constantly threatened to undermine security and political cooperation. That friction was exacerbated by the U.S. sense of economic decline relative to Japan. In recent years the roles have been reversed and Japan appears less "threatening" to the United States. However, economic friction continues on the macroeconomic side, in some ways creating an even more corrosive environment than it did in the 1980s. This time the United States presses Japan for domestic demand-led growth in order to prevent an explosion in the bilateral current account deficit and to avoid a hard landing in the Japanese economy that will harm the United States. Japanese officials, in contrast, are losing confidence in domestic stimulus and fear the long-term effect of budget deficits on national solvency. Many Japanese officials would like to grow out of the current malaise on the back of a weaker yen, which puts more pressure on the United States to accept imports, of course. U.S. exasperation with Japan's inability to fix its economic problems causes senior officials in Washington to dismiss Tokyo as hopeless, and Japanese resentment of American hubris inspires visions of a more independent world role. This vicious cycle clearly caused a breakdown of bilateral coordination in the Asian financial crisis and has had an overall negative impact on most of the cases studied in this volume. And it is not likely to improve any time soon.

- *Same bed, different dreams.* There is a saying in Japan that two people can be in the "same bed, with different dreams." The United States and Japan share common strategic objectives, but national aspirations are different with regard to the bilateral relationship. The United States remains essentially a status quo power and expects a Japan that is compliant and willing to fund U.S. forces and U.S. foreign policy. Japan is also a status quo power in the sense that it does not oppose U.S. benign hegemony, but the Japanese elite clearly is not satisfied with the status quo in U.S.-Japan bilateral relations. Tokyo, as we have seen, expects more consultation, authority, and leadership sharing—in short, no taxation without representation. Granting such a role to Japan does not come naturally to most U.S. policymakers. The United States reluctantly has ceded leadership to Japan in the IMF and World Bank because of the need for Japanese money. It is not clear whether U.S. policymakers will be willing to share leadership as Japan contributes relatively less money and focuses more on intellectual contributions. This problem is obviously made worse by U.S. officials' poor opinion of domestic Japanese economic policymaking and the distraction with "rising" powers such as China.

- *Japanese politics.* The Japanese political system also complicates bilateral coordination of foreign policy. The generation of Japanese politicians currently in their thirties and early forties tend to speak English and are more confident in their ability to play a role on the international stage. But they must wait their turn. For now, the senior leadership in Japan tends to be less international and more parochial. In addition, cabinet members and parliamentary vice ministers are frequently shuffled out of their jobs before gaining any substantive expertise. And given the fluidity and uncertainty of coalition politics in Tokyo, Japanese cabinet ministers increasingly interact with the world uncertain of what their nation's longer-term policy on any issue will be or whether they can implement anything promised to the United States. For all these reasons, it is difficult to convince senior U.S. officials to invest time in personal relationships with their Japanese counterparts. Yet with set-piece meetings in which both sides read from their prepared texts, it is impossible to establish the kind of working relationship necessary for bilateral management of complex foreign policy challenges.

- *Bureaucratic divisions.* Pluralization of foreign policymaking in both countries complicates things, as media grows more intrusive, U.S. politics becomes more partisan, and NGOs grow more active on both sides. Even within the government, there are more actors competing with the State Department and Ministry of Foreign Affairs for ownership of the U.S.-Japan relationship. It is crucial that State and MOFA have close working relationships, but those two agencies alone cannot control the broadening agenda of the two countries.

- *Japan's squeaky wheel diplomacy.* The American saying that "the squeaky wheel gets the grease" has an opposite version in Japan: "The nail that sticks up gets hammered down." In the past Japan pursued a foreign policy that avoided becoming that nail that gets hammered down, but recently Japan's diplomacy has turned in desperation to the squeaky wheel. The pattern goes like this: A crisis hits in which the United States either moves unilaterally or does not seem to address Japanese security or economic concerns. Japan in desperation announces its own unilateral measures that implicitly threaten to undermine U.S. policy (whether intended or not). Washington then suddenly elevates consultation with Japan to a new level in response, and stability and coordination are restored. Examples in this study have included:

Asian financial crisis → Japan's AMF proposal → U.S. agrees to AGRI and financial architecture debate in G-7.

Taepo-dong launch → Japan suspends KEDO funds → U.S. establishes trilateral coordination and oversight group (TCOG).

Senate rejection of CTBT → Japan presses for U.S. disarmament at NPT → U.S. establishes new bilateral commission for regular consultation on arms control and nonproliferation.

Chinese incursions in Senkakus → Japan surprises Beijing and Washington by not backing down → U.S. finally acknowledges that the alliance would apply in case of conflict.

The good news about this pattern is that, in the end, it does result in higher levels of coordination between the United States and Japan. The bad news is that the process is highly disruptive to both U.S. and Japanese foreign policy—and it usually begins with U.S. inattention to alliance management with Japan.

- *Japan's unilateralism.* Japan also shares blame for not always coordinating its foreign policy with the United States in advance. MOF did not brief the United States in advance on the AMF, precisely because it expected opposition. MOFA frequently chooses not to prebrief the United States on policy toward China, Burma, or even North Korea because it does not want to be forced to address issues that are priorities for Washington and not Tokyo. MOFA also sometimes keeps its negotiations with these countries private in order to maintain leverage vis-à-vis the United States as Washington conducts its own negotiations with the same countries. Obviously, when Washington consults and briefs Japan, Tokyo will be more likely to do the same. But even with full consultation, the Japanese side will always place some priority on safeguarding its special relationships with Asian nations from entrapment in U.S. foreign policy.

- *Superpower/middle power imbalances.* Finally, even with the best of intentions by policymakers in Washington and Tokyo, U.S.-Japan diplomatic coordination will be complicated by the gap in national means and national wills between the two countries. The United States has a national security structure, power projection and strategic capabilities, and preeminent status in international institutions that Japan will never match, even with constitutional reform or the recognition of collective defense. The United States remains a proactive shaper of the international environment; Japan, a reactive player in the game. Japan's legacy of defeat and postwar occupation only reinforces this gap, not to mention the cultural and even racial biases that have colored U.S.-Japan relations for over a century.

Building a Foreign Policy Alliance

These obstacles should not discourage efforts at closer coordination of U.S. and Japanese foreign policy. If anything, they point to the reasons why such efforts are overdue. Some of the specific steps that the United States can take to realize joint action with Japan and reinforce U.S. foreign policy are suggested in the individual cases studies in this volume.

Drawing from those lessons, the following ten universal principles should guide U.S. coordination with Japan.

1. *Recognize Japan as an independent actor.* It should be clear by now that despite a general convergence of U.S. and Japanese strategic interests, Japan is less likely to assume that what it sees as a security threat will be seen the same way by the United States. And therefore, the United States can no longer assume that Japan will continue to take its own foreign policy cues from the United States without the kind of full consultation and coordination that characterize our relationship with European allies.

2. *Support an active Japanese foreign policy identity.* U.S. officials need to appreciate that there are two aspiring powers in Asia, not just China but also Japan. Where possible, U.S. foreign policy should support and encourage Japanese diplomatic initiatives. The United States should make it clear to Beijing the U.S. policy places a priority on a larger Japanese role in the region and that this will ultimately contribute to better Sino-Japanese relations and regional stability.

3. *Form common strategies early.* Japanese diplomatic leadership will resonate with U.S. foreign policy objectives if the United States articulates a clear strategy to Japan well before crises strike and helps Tokyo form a role within the broad parameters of that strategy. If the U.S. side makes such investments, Japanese officials should be expected to do the same. Consultation must be a two-way street.

4. *Raise the bar of expectations.* The United States should make it clear to Japan that increased leadership requires increased risk. U.S. policy should encourage Japan to back up its diplomacy with the dispatch not only of money but also of peacekeepers and civilian personnel. Where Japan has unique relationships—in Burma, for example—the United States can allow a different diplomatic approach from Tokyo, but should expect Japan to quietly press on issues such as human rights as well.

5. *Avoid hitting down the nail that sticks up.* Open confrontation on Japanese proposals such as the AMF is self-defeating except as a last resort. The United States can win these confrontations, but *gaiatsu* only breeds resentment and complicates coordination. It is far better to work such issues inside the Japanese system so that they can be shaped to support U.S. objectives.

6. *Invest in personal relationships.* Senior U.S. officials must be willing to invest in longer-term relationships with their Japanese counterparts.

Toward the end of the Clinton administration, there was a mismatch that was not sustainable as deputy assistant secretaries on the U.S. side became the principal interlocutors for Japanese officials of far senior rank. The Japanese side must have senior officials available on the U.S. side for informal and unexpected consultations and coordination.

7. *Elevate formal consultations.* Given the fluidity of Japanese politics and the expectations of greater representation for Japan, it is not enough to rely on these behind-the-scenes personal relationships alone. Formal mechanisms for consultation will also have to be expanded. Useful examples include the U.S.-Japan-ROK trilateral coordination and oversight group, instituted in 1999, and the U.S.-Japan commission on nonproliferation and arms control, instituted in March 2000. These forums keep U.S. officials focused on coordination with Japan (and Japanese officials on the United States); they parallel similar mechanisms with European allies; and they demonstrate the priority the United States places on partnership with Japan.

8. *Listen to Japan.* Obviously personal relationships and formal commissions will breed more resentment if the U.S. side uses them only to lecture Japanese officials. Japan has insights, particularly on Asian issues, that are valuable and important and should be reflected in U.S. policy.

9. *Beware of brokering.* The United States should tread carefully on disputed issues of history or territory. Even the best-intended efforts to broker the Northern Territories dispute, the Senkaku dispute, or Sino-Japanese history problems will run counter to the Japanese sense of maturity and independence.

10. *Encourage interagency cooperation.* U.S. policymakers face a conundrum. They must have close relations with MOFA to manage the alliance, but increasingly bilateral issues are beyond MOFA's control. And going to other agencies directly only weakens MOFA. The parallel problem exists for Treasury and MOF. The solution is to encourage bilateral interagency consultations, perhaps at the undersecretary level, and to set a clear direction in summit meetings between the president and prime minister. The alliance, in short, must be built from the top down.

Nitobe Inazō, the great Japanese diplomat and scholar of the prewar years, once wrote that Japan's internationalism must begin at home. The changes in Japanese thinking about the world are healthy and offer important opportunities to strengthen the U.S.-Japan relationship. As Nitobe put it, the international man must first look down to see where his own feet are planted before raising his head to see where his nation must go. The United States should welcome a Japan that focuses more on its core national interests. And as Japan raises its head, it should always see its ally, the United States, standing ready to help.

Notes

Introduction

1. Karel G. van Wolfren, "The Japan Problem," *Foreign Affairs,* Vol. 65, No. 2 (Winter 1986/87), p. 289.
2. J. A. A. Stockwin et al., *Dynamic and Immobilist Politics in Japan* (Honolulu: University of Hawaii Press, 1988).
3. Kent E. Calder, "Japanese Foreign Economic Policy Formation: Explaining the Reactive State," *World Politics* Vol. 40, No. 4 (July 1988), pp 517–41.
4. Other explanations of the pervading dysfunction of Japanese foreign policy include: Michael Blaker, "Evaluating Japan's Diplomatic Performance," in Gerald L. Curtis, ed., *Japan's Foreign Policy After the Cold War: Coping with Change* (New York: M.E. Sharpe, 1993), pp. 1–42; and Edward J. Lincoln, *Japan's New Global Role* (Washington, DC: Brookings Institution, 1992).
5. Susan J. Pharr, "Japan's Defensive Foreign Policy and the Politics of Burden Sharing," in Gerald L. Curtis, ed., *Japan's Foreign Policy after the Cold War: Coping with Change* (New York: M.E. Sharpe, 1993), p. 235.
6. Eric Heginbotham and Richard J. Samuels, "Mercantile Realism and Japanese Foreign Policy," *International Security,* Vol. 22, No 4 (Spring 1998), p. 182. Samuels also expands on this theme in *Rich Nation/ Strong Army: National Security and the Technological Transformation of Japan* (Ithaca, NY: Cornell University Press, 1994).
7. Peter J. Katzenstein and Takashi Shiraishi, *Network Power: Japan and Asia* (Ithaca, NY: Cornell University Press, 1997), p. 34. On the concept of Japanese foreign direct investment in Asia as a manifestation of Japanese power and influence, see also, Kōzō Yamamura and Walter Hatch, *A Looming Entry Barrier: Japan's Production Networks in Asia,* National Bureau of Asian Research Analysis, Vol. 8, No. 1, 1998; and David Arase, *Buying Power: The Political Economy of Japanese Foreign Aid* (New York: Lynne Rienner, 1995); Walter Hatch and Kōzō Yamamura, *Asia in Japan's Embrace: Building a Regional Production Alliance* (Cambridge: Cambridge University Press, 1996); and Dennis J. Encarnation, *Rivals Beyond Trade: America versus Japan in Global Competition* (Ithica, NY: Cornell University Press, 1995). For the counterargument that Japanese investment in Southeast Asia was forced by macroeconomic factors rather than deliberate foreign or economic policy strategy, see Charles Chang, David Fernandez, and James Reidel, "U.S.-Japanese Economic Relations and the Southeast Asia Connection: A Boring Analysis," in Chihiro Hosoya and Tomohito Shinoda, *Redefining the*

Partnership: The United States and Japan in East Asia (Lanham, MD: University Press of America, 1998), pp. 83–102.

8. Steven Vogel, "The Power behind "Spin On's": The Military Implications of Japan's Commercial Technology," in Wayne Sandholtz, Michael Borrus, et al., *The Highest Stakes: The Economic Foundations of the Next Security System,* (New York: Oxford University Press, 1992), p.76. Those who argue that Japanese economic power leads to a different definition of national security come from several different theoretical traditions. Some, like Richard Samuels and Eric Higenbotham, argue that the neorealist focus on states' responses to the distribution of power works for Japan, if one also considers technoeconomic security in conjunction with traditional measures of national power and statecraft; see Heginbotham and Samuels, op. cit. 6, pp. 171–203. Others, like Glenn Hook, Mike Mochizuki, and Michael O'Hanlon, argue in the neoliberal tradition that the growth of economic interdependence in Northeast Asia will render Japan's economic foreign policy tools more effective, allowing Tokyo to move beyond its troubled debate over military roles. See Glenn D. Hook, *Militarization and Demilitarization in Contemporary Japan* (London: Routledge, 1996), and Mike Mochizuki and Michael O'Hanlon, "A Liberal Vision for the U.S.-Japanese Alliance," *Survival,* Vol. 40, No. 2 (Summer 1998). A third tradition is represented by Peter Katzenstein and Takashi Shiraishi, who reject the neorealist and neoliberal approaches in favor of a constructivist approach. In contrast to the positivist model of social science, which measures material factors (whether military or economic), constructivism focuses on ideational factors (ideas of national purpose, historical experiences, inherited cultural norms, etc.). See, for example, Katzenstein and Shiraishi, op. cit., 7. See also Thomas Berger, "Set for Stability? An American Perspective on the Prospects for Conflict and Cooperation in East Asia," paper for the Graduate Institute of Peace Studies, Kyung Hee University, Seoul, September 24–26, 1998.

9. See, for example, Herman Kahn, *Japan: The Emerging Superstate* (Englewood Cliffs, NJ: Prentice-Hall, 1970). Kenneth Waltz argued in 1981 that even a nuclear armed Japan would be more "normal" and stable than the current ambiguous arrangement. See Kenneth Waltz, "The Spread of Nuclear Weapons May Be Better," *Adelphi Paper* No. 171 (London: IISS, Autumn 1981). More recent structural realist arguments that Japanese economic power will lead to the pursuit of military power include: George Friedman and Meredith LeBard, *The Coming War with Japan* (New York: St. Martin's, 1991); and Christopher Layne, "The Unipolar Illusion," *International Security,* Vol. 17, No. 4 (Spring 1993), pp. 5–51.

10. Rajan Menon, "The Once and Future Superpower: At Some Point Japan Is Likely to Build a Military Machine that Matches Its Economic Might," *Bulletin of the Atomic Scientist,* Vol. 52, No. 1 (January/February 1997), p. 34. Menon argues from the neorealist perspective, which sees changes in the balance of power in Northeast Asia as the principle driver for change in Japanese security and foreign policy. Aaron Friedberg described those changes in 1993 as creating conditions "ripe for rivalry" in the region; see Aaron Friedberg, "Ripe for Rivalry: Prospects for Peace in a Multipolar Asia," in Michael E. Brown, Sean M. Lynn-Jones, and Steve E. Miller, eds., *East Asian Security* (Cambridge, MA: MIT Press, 1995).

11. Carol Gluck, "Patterns of Change; A 'Grand Unified Theory' of Japanese History," *Bulletin of the American Academy of Arts and Sciences,* Vol. 48 (March 1995), p. 38.

12. As international relations theory has moved in the direction of monocausal explanations for state behavior, regional experts have been caught in a bind. Material determinants alone simply cannot explain Japanese state behavior adequately. Constructivists like Peter Katzenstein and Thomas U. Berger have done an enormous service by providing a theoretical and methodological framework for examining norms and institutions as determinants of foreign and security policy in Japan and Germany. But there is also a problem with examining these factors in isolation from the material factors that neorealists recognize as paramount—even with Japan. Something of a synthesis has emerged in what Gideon Rose calls "neoclassical realism." Critics charge that the neoclassical realists' allowance for variation in state preferences is not true "realism." If studies like this are to remain relevant to policy, however, there must be both an allowance for—and explanations of—such variation. On the critique of monocausal mania, see Stephen M. Walt, "Rigor or Rigor Mortis? Rational Choice and Security Studies," *International Security,* Vol. 23, No. 4 (Spring 1999), pp. 5–48. On norms and institutions, see Peter J. Katzenstein, ed., *The Culture of National Security: Norms, Identity and World Politics* (New York. Columbia University Press, 1996). On neoclassical realism, see Gideon Rose, "Neoclassical Realism and Theories of Foreign Policy," *World Politics,* Vol. 51, No. 1 (October 1998), pp. 144–172. For a critique, see Jeffrey W. Legro and Andrew Moravcsik, "Is Anybody Still a Realist?" *International Security,* Vol. 24, No. 2 (Fall 1999), pp. 5–55.

13. Examples are discussed later but include the unilateral imposition of sanctions on North Korea in the wake of the Taepodong missile launch; the decision to develop indigenous reconnaissance satellites in the same period; and the deployment of fighter squadrons and destroyers near the Senkaku Islands in response to penetrations by Chinese naval survey vessels in 1997 and 1998.

Chapter 1

1. John Dower, *Empire and Aftermath: Yoshida Shigeru and the Japanese Experience, 1878–1945* (Cambridge, MA: Harvard East Asian Monographs, 1979), p. 369.

2. Kenneth B. Pyle, *The Japanese Question: Power and Purpose in A New Era: 2nd ed.* (Washington, D.C.: AEI, 1996), p. 59.

3. Ibid., p. 26.

4. Ozawa Ichirō, *Nihon Kaizou Keikaku* (Blueprint for a New Japan) (Tokyo: Kōdansha, 1993), p. 109.

5. Japan Ministry of Foreign Affairs, *Waga Gaikou no Kinkyou* (Our Recent Diplomacy, Diplomatic Blue Book) (Tokyo: Ministry of Foreign Affairs, September 1957), pp. 7–8.

6. Economists at the Nomura Research Institute made this argument to the author in late 1988.

7. Department of Defense (U.S.), *Critical Technologies Plan,* March 15, 1990.

8. For an influential Ministry of International Trade and Industry (MITI)–sponsored commission report that captured exactly this zeitgeist, see *Tsushou Sangyou Shou Daijin Kanbou* (Minister's Office of the Ministry of International Trade and Industry), *Nihon no Sentaku* (Japan's Choices), June 1988.

9. The Nikkei index plummeted three times: first, it fell by 10,666 yen between January 4 and April 5, 1990; second fall is as described above; and third, it fell by 12,837 yen between March 18, 1991, and August 18, 1992. See Takao Yoshikazu, *Heisei Kinyū Kyoukou* (Financial Panic in Heisei Era) (Tokyo: Chûkou Shinsho, 1994), chapter 1.

10. The author covered Ozawa for the local *Iwate Nippou* newspaper in 1986.

11. Jiyû Minshutou (Liberal Democratic Party), "*Kokusaishakai ni okeru Nihon no Yakuwari: Anzenhoshou Mondai ni Kansuru Teigen*" (Japan's Role in the International Society: Proposals on Security Issues), April 11, 1997.

12. Ozawa Ichirō, op. cit., n. 4.

13. Takemura Masayoshi, *Chiisakutomo Kirari to Hikaru Kuni Nihon* (Japan: A Small But Shining Nation) (Tokyo: Kōbunsha, 1994).

14. Mike Mochizuki has described the competing visions of Japan's world role as "great power internationalism" versus "civilian internationalism." See Mike Mochizuki, *Japan: Domestic Change and Foreign Policy,* RAND Report, No. MR–616–OSD (Santa Monica, CA: RAND, 1995).

15. The Prime Minister's Office, "*Gaikou ni kansuru Yoron Chousa*" (Public Opinion Polls about Foreign Policy), January 24, 2000 (http://www.sorifu.go.jp/survey/Gaikōu/images/zu31.gif).

16. Kawachi Takashi, "A New Backlash against American Influence," *Japan Echo,* Vol. 25, No. 2 (April 1998), p. 44.

17. See, for example, Nishibe Susumu, "*Chie no Jidai: Amerikateki Shugi ni Nomareru Mae ni, Nihon teki Bitoku wo Kyouka Seyo*" (The Era for Wisdom: Before Being Swallowed by Americanism, Strengthen Japanese Virtues), in *Nihon no Ronten 2000* (Major Issues of Japan in 2000) (Tokyo: Bungei Shunjū, 2000), pp. 84–87. This theme has not been isolated. The political journal *Ronza* published a special edition for March 2000 titled "Can Japan Overcome Americanism" featuring articles by mainstream economists and politicians. Even those in favor of reform and deregulation addressed the problem of identity and purpose in a time of U.S. unipolarity.

18. Saeki Keishi, "*Han Gurōbaruka no Nami ga Toukarazu, America no Saihaken wo Houkai Saseru*" (The Anti-Globalism Wave Will Destroy America's Hegemony in the Not-So-Distant Future), in *Nihon no Ronten 2000,* Ibid., p. 73.

19. Ina Hisayoshi argues against this trend in "Fear of U.S.-China Ties Rests on Flawed Premises," *Nikkei Weekly,* December 18, 1996.

20. Honda Masaru, "*Taibei Tsuizui Tou Ugoki, Nichibei Anpo Chouin kara 40-nen*" (Recent Trends to Question Japan's Dependence on U.S., 40 Years Since the Signing of U.S.-Japan Security Treaty), *Asahi Shimbun,* January 19, 2000.

21. "*Nichibei Anpo Jouyaku Chouin kara 40 nen: Shutaisei Towareru Jidai ni*" (Japan's Autonomy Questioned on the 40th Anniversary of the U.S.-Japan Alliance), *Asahi Shimbun,* January 19, 2000.

22. *Purojekuto 2010 "Jouji Chūryū Naki Anpo," Bunkakai Katsudou no Kiroku* (Records of the Project 2010 "No Base Alliance" Analysis Group) (Tokyo:

Project 2010 Jimukyoku, February 1997-January 1998). See also Terashima Jit-surō, *Kokka no Ronri to Kigyou no Ronri* (The Logic of the State and the Logic of the Firm) (Tokyo: Chûou Kouron, 1998).

23. Public opinion poll by *Asahi Shimbun,* cited in Hosokawa Morihiro, "Are U.S. Troops in Japan Needed?" *Foreign Affairs* Vol. 77, No. 4 (July/August 1998), pp. 2–5.

24. "*Nichibei Kyoudou Yoron Chousa*" (Japan-U.S. Joint Survey of Public Opinions), *Yomiuri Shimbun,* December 19, 1999.

25. Research Commission on Security of the Policy Research Council, Liberal Democratic Party of Japan, "Joint Declaration and Future National Security: Implementing Review of Guidelines for Japan-U.S. Defense Cooperation," April 18, 1997, p. 2.

26. For example, see, "*Kinpaku Shumirēshon, Dainiji Chousen Sensou Boppatsusu*" (Emergency Simulation: The Second Korean War Breaks Out), *Bungei Shunjū,* April 1, 1999, pp. 106–130. "Hatoyama Argues Japan Could Strike First If Attack Is Imminent; Kan Disagrees," *Japan Digest,* March 2, 1999. Kajiyama Seiroku, "*Sokoku Boueiron*" (On Defense of My Mother Country, Japan), *Bungei Shunjū,* June 1999, pp. 170–171.

27. Japan Defense Agency, *Defense of Japan,* 1999.

28. *Sourifu* (Prime Minister's Office), "*Jietai-Bouei Mondai ni Kansuru Yoron Chousa*" (Polling on the JSDF and Defense Problems), available at the Prime Minister's Office web site (http://www.sorifu.jp).

29. This was a major theme in Michael J. Green, *Arming Japan* (New York: Columbia University Press, 1995).

30. Iokibe Makoto, "*Sofuto Powā Rikkoku he no Michi: Aete Anpo Rongi no Ryoukyoku wo Haisu*" (The Road to Softpower National Revival: Dispense with Both Extremes of the Security Debate), *Ronza,* July 2000, pp. 94–114.

31. Tawara Soichirō, "*Amerika ni Iyaounaku Jiritsu wo Semarareta Nihon: Tsugi Naru Mondai wa Kempou Kaisei*" (Japan's Autonomy Unambiguously Pressed by the United States: The Next Theme Must Be Constitutional Revision) in *Nihon no Ronten 2000,* op. cit., n. 17, p. 176.

32. Kawachi Tomoaki, "How the Japanese View Their Pacifist Constitution," *Japan Echo,* Vol. 3 (August 1997), p. 47.

33. *Kempo Yomiuri Teigen* (The Yomiuri Constitutional Proposal), July 10, 1998 (http://www.yomiuri.co.jp).

34. Ishibashi Kazuya, "*Ima Koso Hirakareta Kempou Rongi wo*" (It's Time to Start a Constitutional Debate), *Gekkan Jiyū,* October 1997.

35. "*Kempo Kaisei 60% ga Sansei: Kokkai Giin Honsha Ankēto*" (60% of Diet Members Favor Constitutional Revision According to Our Poll), *Yomiuri Shimbun,* March 21, 1997.

36. Yōichi Funabashi, *Asia-Pacific Fusion: Japan's Role in APEC* (Washington, DC: Institute for International Economics, 1995), p. 223.

37. Ogura Kazuo, "*Azia no Fukken no Tameni,*" *Chūou Kouron,* July 1993; translated as "A Call for a New Concept of Asia," *Japan Echo,* Vol. 20, No. 3 (Autumn 1993), pp. 37–44.

38. Yōichi Funabashi, "The Asianization of Asia," *Foreign Affairs,* Vol. 72, No. 6 (November/December 1993).

39. Noda Nobuo, "*Kiken na Ajia Shugi no Taitou,*" *This Is Yomiuri,* January 1995, pp. 154–169; translated as "The Dangerous Rise of Asianism," *Japan Echo,* Vol. 22, No. 1 (Spring 1995), pp. 6–11.

40. Liberal Democratic Party Research Commission on Foreign Affairs, *Foreign Policy of the Liberal Democratic Part—Part I: Japan's Asia-Pacific Strategy: The Challenges of Transformation* (Tokyo: Liberal Democratic Party, undated, released in English in May 1997), p. 23.

41. Itō Ken'ichi, Nishio Kanji, Kitaoka Shin'ichi, *Japan's Identity: Neither the West nor the East* (Tokyo: The Japan Forum on International Relations, Inc., February 1999), p. 1. Exerted from the Japanese version, *Nihon no Aidenthithi-: Seiyou Demo Nai, Touyou Demo Nai* (Tokyo: Foresto Shuppan, 1999).

42. Ibid., p. 36.

43. Kojima Akira, Yamakage Susumu, Watanabe Taizō, "*Shounenba ni Kita Ajia no Kiseki*" (Asian Miracle at the Crossroad), *Gaikō Forum,* No. 112, November 1997, p. 26.

44. Yōichi Funabashi, "Tokyo's Depression Diplomacy," *Foreign Affairs,* Vol. 77, No. 6 (November/December, 1998), p. 27.

45. Kikkawa Mototada, *Manei Haisen* (Loss of the Money War) (Tokyo: Bungei Shunjū, 1998), p. 171; and "*Imakoso Doru Shihai kara Hanare, En wo Kijiku to Suru Ajia Keizaiken wo Kochiku Suru beki Toki*" (Now Is the Time to Break from Dollar Hegemony and Form an Asian Economic Bloc Pivoting on the Yen), in *Nihon no Ronten 2000,* op. cit., n. 17, p. 80.

46. Woodrow Wilson Center Japan expert Alexei Kral found, for example, that the Japanese junior high school history and world affairs texts refer directly to "murder" of as many as "200,000 people" in Nanjing. See Alexei T. Kral, "Cultural Nationalism in Japanese Textbooks," Woodrow Wilson Center, July 2000.

47. Funabashi, op. cit., n. 36, p. 240.

48. William Lee Howell, "The Inheritance of War: Japan's Domestic Politics and International Ambitions," in Gerrit W. Gong, ed., *Remembering and Forgetting: The Legacy of War and Peace in East Asia* (Washington, DC: The Center for Strategic and International Studies, 1996), p. 90.

49. Noda, op. cit., n. 39.

50. *Sourifu Kouhoushitsu han* (Public Relations Division of the Prime Minister's Office), *Gekkan Yoron Chousa* (Monthly Public Opinion Polls) (May 1998), p. 13. This figure combines those in favor and those who "if they had to say which way" were in favor.

51. Akiko Fukushima, *Japanese Foreign Policy: The Emerging Logic of Multilateralism* (New York: Macmillan, 1998), p. 182.

52. Fukushima Kiyohiko, *Corporate Governance: An Aspect of Asia's Currency Crisis and Its Implications,* Nomura Research Institute Report, June 1998, p. 11.

53. Ishihara Shintarō, "*Shin Ajia Jouiron*" (New Anti-foreign Sentiment in Asia), *Bungei Shunjū,* August 1998, pp. 110–124.

54. Nakamura Yōichi, *Zero Seichou Nihon Keizai: 2025-nen no Keizai Kouzou wo Yomu* (A Japanese Economy with Zero Growth: Reading the Economic Structure in 2025) (Tokyo: Nihon Keizai Shimbunsha, 1998).

55. Ibid. p. 15.

56. Terashima, op. cit., n. 22, p. 51.

57. Ōmae Ken'ichi, ed., *Nihon Saiken heno Shinario* (Scenarios for Japan's Restoration) (Tokyo, Japan: Daiamond, 1998). For similar arguments, though somewhat less "globalist" than Ōmae, see Takenaka Heizo, "*Kiseikanwa Isoganakereba Nihon Keizai no Haadorandingu wa Sakerarenai*" (Without Speeding Up Deregulation, Japan's Economy Cannot Avoid a Hard Landing), excerpted in *Bungei Shunjû 1997 Nihon no Ronten* (Japan's Debate in 1997) (Tokyo: Bungei Shunjū, 1996), p. 214; Imai Ken'ichi, "*Nihon Sangyou no Katachi to Kata,*" *Jitsugyou no Nihon,* August 1997, pp. 10–15, translated as "Rethinking the Japanese-Style System," *Japan Echo,* Vol. 24, No. 4 (October 1997), pp. 39–43; and Takeuchi Yasuo, "*Kaisha Houkenshugi no Owari,*" *This Is Yomiuri,* July 1997, pp. 38–49, translated as "End of the Line for Japan's Corporate Feudalism," *Japan Echo,* Ibid., pp. 35–38.

58. Cited in Fukushima Kiyohito, *Corporate Governance: An Aspect of Asia's Currency* ...mura Research Institute Report, June 1998, p. 9

59. ... of Economic Organizations), *Reviving the Japanese* ...mic Society in the Twenty First Century: Proposal for ... October 12, 1998, p. 1.

60. ...Recovery in Asia, July 12, 1998, p. 2.

61. ...ādo ni Hanpatsu suru yori, Nihon wa Ima Beikoku ...that Reacting against Global Standards, Japan ...United States), excerpted in *Bungei Shunjū Nihon* ...e in 1999) (Tokyo: Bungei Shunjû, 1998), pp. ...

62. Ozawa Ichirō, op. cit., n. 4.

63. Kajiyama Seiroku (interview by Tawara Soichirō), "*Kono Kuni wa Dokohe Mukauka? Souri no Ketsudan ha Itsu no Koto ka?*" (Where Is This Country Heading? When Will the Prime Minister Make a Decision?), *Chūou Kouron,* November 1998, pp. 44–56. In an interview with the author, Kajiyama argued that uncompetitive companies must die so that competitive companies can grow.

64. The Ministry of Foreign Affairs of Japan, *Challenge 2001—Japan's Foreign Policy toward the 21st Century,* January 4, 1999 (http://www.mofa.go.jp/policy/other/challenge21.html).

65. Itō Ken'ichi, Yamaoka Kunihiko, Nakanishi Hiroshi, Kamiya Matake, et al., *Japan's Initiatives towards U.S., China and Russia,* The Japan Forum on International Relations, Inc. Report (Tokyo, April 1999), p. 7 (http://www.jfir.or.jp/e-jf-pr–18/pr18-top.html).

66. Ibid., p. 14.

67. *21 Seiki Nihon no Kouzou Kondankai Saishū Houkokusho, 21 Seiki Nihon no Kouzou: Nihon no Furonthia wa Nihon no Naka ni Aru* (Report of the Commission on Japan's Goals for the 21st Century: Japan's Doctrine for the 21st Century: Japan's Frontier Is within Japan), Tokyo, January 31, 2000.

68. Ibid., summary of the English version, p. 10.

69. Kenneth N. Waltz, *Theory of International Politics* (Reading, MA: Addison-Wesley, 1979).

70. Robert Osgood, *Ideas and Self-Interest in American Foreign Relations* (Chicago: University of Chicago Press, 1953).

71. Kenneth B. Pyle, "Japan: Opportunisum in the Pursuit of Power," in Robert A. Pastor, ed., *A Century's Journey: How the Great Powers Shape the World* (New York: Basic Books, 1999), p. 289.

Chapter 2

1. See Michael Blaker, "Evaluating Japan's Diplomatic Performance," in Gerald L. Curtis, ed., *Japan's Foreign Policy After the Cold War: Coping with Change* (New York: M. E. Sharpe, 1993), pp.1–42; Edward J. Lincoln, *Japan's New Global Role* (Washington, DC: Brookings Institution, 1992); Kent E. Calder, "Japanese Foreign Economic Policy Formation, Explaining the Reactive State," *World Politics,* Summer 1988, pp. 517–541.

2. Chalmers Johnson, *MITI and the Japanese Economic Miracle: The Growth of Industrial Policy, 1925–1975* (Stanford, CA: Stanford University Press, 1982).

3. Ellis S. Krauss, "Japanese Political Economy Today: The Patterned Pluralist Model," in Daniel I. Okimoto and Thomas P. Rohlen, eds., *Inside the Japanese System: Readings on Contemporary Society and Political Economy* (Stanford, CA: Stanford University Press, 1988), pp. 208–210.

4. Richard J. Samuels, *The Business of the Japanese State: Energy Markets in Comparative and Historical Perspective* (Ithaca, Cornell University Press, 1987).

5. "Nikkei Poll Rates Democrats Ahead of LDP for First Time," *Japan Digest,* August 4, 1998.

6. Bureaucracy bashing in the Japanese Diet and media has been mounting. See Gerald Curtis, *The Logic of Japanese Politics: Leaders, Institutions and the Limits of Change* (New York: Columbia University Press, 1999), p. 57; Matsubara Ryūichi, "*Koukyousei wa Minkan nimo Hitsuyouda*" (The Concept of Public Interest Is Required for Every Citizen), *Ronza,* July 1996, translated as "Why Bureaucrats Don't Serve the Public Inters," in *Japan Echo,* Vol. 23, No. 3 (July 1996), pp. 38–43; Sakaiya Taichi, "*Gendai Kanryou Chou Munouron*" (The Myth of the Competent Bureaucrats), *Bungei Shunjū,* October 1997, pp. 94–103.

7. Keizō Takemi, "Dynamism of Domestic Politics and Relationship between China, Japan, and the U.S.," Trilateral Conference on Enhancing the Traditional Relationship between China, Japan, and the United States, October 15–17, 1999, Tokyo.

8. Masaru Tamamoto, *The Making of a Silent Revolution,* SAIS Policy Forum Series, Report No. 8, January 1999.

9. Ōtake Hideo, ed., *Power Shuffles and Policy Processes: Coalition Government in Japan in the 1990's* (Tokyo: Japan Center for International Exchange, 2000), p. 15.

10. T. J. Pempel, "Regime Shift: Japanese Politics in a Changing World Economy," *Journal of Japan Studies,* Vol. 23, No. 2 (1997), p. 335. See also T. J. Pempel, *Regime Shift: Conservative Dynamics of the Japanese Political Economy* (Ithaca, NY: Cornell University Press, 1998), pp. 1–41; and Michael J. Green and Richard L. Samuels, *Recalculating Autonomy: Japan's Choices in the New World Order* (Seattle, WA: Bureau of Asian Research, 1994).

11. Mike Mochizuki introduced the "great power internationalism" and "civilian internationalism" in Japan: *Domestic Change and Foreign Policy* (Santa Monica,

CA: RAND, 1995), p. 47. I first used this X/Y axis to explain the public policy pressures on Japanese politics in Green and Samuels, *Recalculating Autonomy* (Ibid.). A more systematic presentation of this same sort of quadrant was developed by Kabashima Ikuo in 1999 based on detailed polling of Diet members. See Kabashima Ikuo, "An Ideological Survey of Japan's National Legislators," *Japan Echo,* Vol. 26, No. 4, (August 1999), pp. 9–16. Kabashima distinguishes between conservative and progressive views of egalitarianism and conservative versus progressive views on security as the x and y axes. His poll finds that the LDP and DPJ are least cohesive of the political parties with divisions in the Liberal Party that later contributed to a split in the party in March 2000. In 1994 Kabashima used similar coordinates to demonstrate that voters are not yet lured to support the "high politics" of Ozawa as he attempted to realign politics along his vision of a "normal" nation. This time the x axis was liberal-conservative and his y axis reform–*status quo*. He placed the voters just inside the conservative and reform quadrant and all political leaders except the communists in the conservative status quo quadrant. Kabashima's analysis helps to capture why there is no national leader succeeding with an explicit articulation of the substantive changes in Japanese strategic culture. See Kabashima Ikuo, "*Shintou no Toujou to Jimintou Ittou Yūi Taisei no Houkai*" (The Birth of A New Political Parties and a Collapse of the Primacy of the LDP), *Revaiasan,* no. 15, Mokutakusha, 1994, p. 16, cited in Ōtake Hideo, *Nihon Seiji no Tairitsujiku: 93 nen Ikou no Seikai Saihen no Naka de* (The Competition Axis in Japanese Politics: Inside Political Realignment since 1993) (Tokyo: Chūou Kouronsha, 1999), pp. 64–65.

12. "*Kempo Kaisei 60% ga Sansei: Kokkai Giin Honsha Ankēto*" (60% Favor Constitutional Revision in Our Dietmembers' Poll), *Yomiuri Shimbun,* March 21, 1997.

13. Murata Koji expresses the younger generation's pragmatism and impatience over constitutional revision in "*Wakai Seidai no Kaiken Ron*" (The Younger Generation's Case for Constitutional Reform), *Chūou Kouron,* June 2000, pp. 50–65.

14. See, for example, Satō Seisaburō and Matsuzaki Tetsuhisa, *Jimintou Seiken* (LDP Administration) (Tokyo: Chūou Kouronsha, 1986); and Inoguchi Takashi and Iwai Tomonobu, *Zoku Giin no Kenkyū* (A Study on *Zokugiin*) (Tokyo: Nikkei Shimbunsha, 1987).

15. Quansheng Zhao, *Japanese Policymaking: The Politics behind Politics: Informal Mechanisms and the Making of China Policy,* (London: Oxford University Press, 1994), p. 194.

16. Based on a series of interviews with the staff of the foreign affairs and defense committees of the PARC, October 1995 to December 1999.

17. Interview with *Yomiuri Shimbun* reporter, April 25, 2000.

18. Nakajima Kuniko, "*Nihon no Gaikou Seisaku Kettei Katei ni Okeru Jiyūminshutou Seimuchousakai no Yakuwari*" (The Role of the LDP Policy Affairs Research Council in Japan's Foreign Policy Making Process), in Hashimoto Kohei, ed., *Nihon no Gaikou Seisaku Kettei no Youin* (Domestic Determinants of Japanese Foreign Policy) (Tokyo: PHP, 1999), pp. 84–85; LDP Research Commission on Foreign Affairs, *Foreign Policy of the Liberal Democratic Party, Part I: Japan's Asia*

Pacific Strategy: The Challenges of Transformation, Liberal Democratic Party, May 1997.

19. Interview with Takemi Keizō, Parliamentary Vice Minister of Foreign Affairs, November 3, 1998.

20. *Minshutou Gaikou Anzen Hoshou Goudou Bukai* (Democratic Party Joint Committee on Defense and Foreign Policy),"*Gaidorain Kanren Houan heno Taiou nitsuite*" (Regarding Treatment of the Guidelines Related Legislation), September 18, 1998, p. 2.

21. Interviews with members of the Liberal Party, the Democratic Party, and staff members from the LDP National Security Commission, November 1 and December 3–6, 1998.

22. Interview with senior MOFA official, Comprehensive Foreign Policy Bureau, October 31, 1998.

23. "Our Basic Philosophy and Policies: Building a Free and Secure Society," the Democratic Party of Japan, April 27, 1998. See also *Minshutō* (Democratic Party), *Minshutō Anzen Hoshou Kihon Seisaku* (Basic Security Policy of the Democratic Party of Japan), June 1999.

24. The Liberal Democratic Party, *Nihon Saihen heno Shinario: Jiyūminshutou no Kihon Seisaku* (Scenarios for the Revitalization of Japan: the Liberal Party's Basic Policies) (Tokyo: The Liberal Democratic Party, 1998).

25. "*Kihonseisaku Taikou An*" (Draft Basic Policy Outline), Kōmeitō, 1998; and interview with former MOFA official and Kōmeitō Lower House representative Endō Otohiko, November 6, 1998.

26. Kabashima (1999), Op. cit., n. 11, pp. 46 and 61.

27. See, for example, Kaga Kouei, "*Naitou Kyokuchou wa Naze Yameta ka?*" (Why Did Director General Naitō Quit?), *Bungei Shunjū,* March 1994, pp. 160–176.

28. See, for example, Kishi Nobuyoshi, "*Ohkurasho Ochita Zettai Kenryoku*" (The Fall of MOF's Total Power), *Bungei Shunjū,* July 1998, p. 184.

29. On ODA, see Robert M. Orr, *The Emergence of Japan's Foreign Aid Power* (New York: Columbia University Press, 1990). On defense, see Michael J. Green, *Arming Japan: Alliance Politics, Defense Production, and the Post-war Search for Autonomy* (New York: Columbia University Press, 1995).

30. For two sides of this debate, see Robert M. Orr, Jr., op. cit., n. 30; and Edward J. Lincoln, *Japan's New Global Role* (Washington, DC: Brookings Institution, 1992), pp.122–133.

31. Keizai Kōhō Center, *Japan: An International Comparison,* cited in Kent Calder, "The Institutions of Japanese Foreign Policy," in Richard L. Grant, ed., *The Process of Japanese Foreign Policy: Focus on Asia* (London: Royal Institute of International Affairs, 1997), p. 3.

32. Lincoln, Op. cit., n. 30, p. 130.

33. Fujioka Akihisa, *Kanchou Zenkeiretsu Chizu* (Complete Guide to the Bureaucracies' Groupings) (Tokyo: Nikkei Shinbunsha, 1994), p. 44.

34. Interview with MOFA officials, November 2, 1998.

35. In a 1994 poll 51 percent of Diet members said that MOF's influence had increased since the fall of the LDP. See Mochizuki, op. cit., n. 11, p. 19.

36. Kishi, op. cit., n. 28, p. 191; Kōzō Yamamura, "The Japanese Political Economy after the Bubble: Plus ca Change?" *Journal of Japanese Studies,* Vol. 23, No. 2 (1997), p. 311.

37. Interview with officials in the International Bureau, MOF, December 2–4, 1998.

38. See, for example, Tawara Sōichirō interview with Sakakibara Eisuke, "*Ōkurasho Dake ga Warui noka?*" (Is MOF Alone to Blame?), *Chūou Kouron,* March 1998, pp. 78–91.

39. Yamamura Mikiyoshi, "*Kono Neokanryo 47 nin Nihon wo Makaseruka?*" (Can We Leave Japan to These 47 Neo-bureaucrats?), *Bungei Shunju,* July 2000, p. 205.

40. Interview with MITI officials, November 4, 1998.

41. *Kasumigaseki Handobukku: An Insight Into Japan's Bureaucracy* (Tokyo: IPMS Group, 1998), p. 3. Figures taken from the Management and Coordination Agency.

42. Shiela A. Smith, "The Evolution of Military Cooperation in the U.S.-Japan Alliance," in Michael J. Green and Patrick M. Cronin, eds., *The U.S.-Japan Alliance: Past, Present and Future* (New York: Council on Foreign Relations, 1999), pp. 69–93.

43. Public opinion polls by the Prime Minister's Office demonstrate a growing public priority on international security as a dimension of Japan's diplomacy.

44. Interviews with MOF officials, December 2–4, 1998.

45. Jimintou Kokubou Sanbukai (The Three Joint Defense Committees of the LDP), *Boueicho no Kokuboushou he no Ikou ni tsuite* (Regarding the Transition of the JDA to a Defense Ministry), March 8, 2000.

46. Honshio Jirō, *Dokyumento: Keidanren: Zaikaishunojin no Honne* (Documentary Keidanren: The Big Business Leaders' Honne) (Tokyo: Koudansha, 1993), p. 318.

47. Barbara Wanner, "Economic Problems, Political Changes, Challenge Japan's Cozy Business-Government Ties," *Japan Economic Institute Report,* June 9, 2000, p. 11.

48. Calder, Op. cit., n. 31, p. 18.

49. *Keizai Dōyūkai,* (Japan Association of Corporate Executives), *Report of the Study Group on Security Issues,* April 8, 1996. (http://www.Dōyūkai. or.jp/database/teigen/960408e.htm).

50. *Kansai Keizai Dōyūkai* (Kansai Association of Corporate Executives), *Toward Facilitating Straightforward Discussion: Our Honest Viewpoint on Japan's National Security—In Pursuit of Strategic and Independent Decision Making and Responsible Action,* January 1998 (http://www.kDōyūkai.on.arena.ne.jp/teigen-iken/1998Mar/anzen/eibun(anzen).html).

51. For details see the Library of Congress, *Japanese Public Policy: Perspectives and Resources* (Washington, DC: The Japan Documentation Center of the Library of Congress, 1995). JDA also utilizes the National Institute for Defense Studies for second-rack defense diplomacy and places mid-level officials in the Pentagon's Institute for National Security Studies and the National Defense University.

52. Rinn-Sup Shinn, "Japan's Foreign Affairs Establishment," Congressional Research Service, May 16, 1996, p. 23. Akiko Fukushima, National Institute for Research Advancement (NIRA), "The Role of Think Tanks in a Civil Society," a speech for the Middle East Think Tank Conference, "How to Market Ideas: From Education to Advocacy," Cairo, November 3, 1997.

53. For example, see Ikegami Kiyoko, "*GO/NGO no Kyouchou ni Mukete*" (Toward a Cooperation between GO and NGO), in Hashimoto, ed., Op. cit., n. 18, pp. 427–459. Also see "*Gaikoukan dakeno Jidai no Shuen*" (The End of Diplomats' Dominance over Diplomacy), *Gaikō Forum,* March 1999, pp. 12–21.

54. In 1990, the budget of the subsidy system for NGO projects was 300 million yen, while in 1998, it was 1.15 billion yen. See "*Tayoukasuru Nihon Gaikou no Akuta-tachi*" (Diversity of the Actors of Japanese Foreign Policy), *Gaikō Forum,* March 1999, p. 37.

55. In 1989, the budget of Grant Assistance for Grassroots Projects was 300 million yen, which increased to 5,700 million yen in 1998. Ibid.

56. Calder, Op. cit., n. 31, p. 22.

57. See Shinoda Tomohito "*Taigai Seisaku Kettei no Akutā tositeno Ozawa Ichirou*" (Ozawa Ichirō's Role in Formulating Foreign Policy), in Hashimoto, ed., Op. cit., n. 18, pp. 25–69. See also Tase Yasuhiro, "*Naikaku Souri Daijin no Kodoku*" (The Power Short Prime Minister), *Chūou Kouron,* April 1993, pp. 64–73.

58. Shinoda Tomohito, *Leading Japan: The Role of the Prime Minister,* chapter 3 (Westport, Connecticut, London: Praeger, 2000), p. 45.

59. Ibid.

60. See, for example, "*Naikaku Gyousei Kikou Kaikaku Taikou wo Teigen Suru*" (Proposal for Totally Reorganizing the Cabinet and Administration), *This Is Yomiuri,* June 1996, pp. 34–57. Also Barbara Wanner, "Tokyo Confronts Crisis Management Shortcomings in Wake of Hanshin Earthquake Disaster," *JEI Report,* No. 4 A, February 3, 1995; "*Kita Chosen Jousei nado Bunseki Naikaku Jouhou Kaigi ga Hatsukaigo*" (Cabinet Intelligence Council Inaugurated to Analyze Intelligence on Conditions in North Korea and Elsewhere), *Nihon Keizai Shimbun,* January 11, 1999.

61. *Kiki Kanri Purojekuto Chīmu* (Crisis Management Project Team), "*Chūkan Houkoku(an)*" (Draft interim report), *Jiyū Minshutou Seichoukai* (LDP Policy Affairs Research Council), June 3, 1999; *Jimintou Gaimu-Anpo Goudou Bukai* (LDP Foreign Affairs and National Security Joint Committee, "*Gaidorain Kanren Houan heno Taiou nitsuite*" (Regarding the Guidelines Legislation), LDP, September 18, 1999.

62. Yawata Kazuo, "*Shouchou Saihen: Kasumigaseki to Nagatachou ha Ichido Kowashite Tsukurinaoshitahou ga Ii*" (Realigning the Ministries: *Kasumigaseki* and *Nagatachō* Should Break It Once and Try Again), *Economisuto,* January 6, 1998, pp. 37–39; Harano Joji, "The Hashimoto Reform Program," *Japan Echo,* Vol. 24, No. 2 (1997), pp. 30–33.

63. Nakano Kōichi, among others, argues that the administrative reforms will not change the fundamental collusion of bureaucrats and politicians. See "The Politics of Administrative Reform in Japan," *Asian Survey,* Vol. 38, No. 3 (March 1998), p. 307. It is true that the reduction to twelve cabinet ministers has not eliminated the ministries that lost cabinet rank. Still, those institutions that were merged with others—labor, welfare, environment, and science and technology—will now have to share ministers, which will inevitably weaken their independent influence.

64. Ko Murayama argues that the Hashimoto reforms forced the MOF and the other bureaucracies to realize reform is inevitable. See "The Changing Rela-

tionship between Japan's LDP and the Bureaucracy: Hashimoto's Administrative Reform Effort and Its Politics," *Asian Survey,* Vol. 38, No. 10 (October 1998), pp. 968–985. Murayama notes rather more pessimistically that, for the time being, this will only lead to further immobility in Japanese policymaking.

65. Gerald L. Curtis, Op. cit., n. 7, p. 44.

Chapter 3

1. The argument in this chapter draws heavily on Michael J. Green and Benjamin L. Self, "Japan's Changing China Policy: From Commercial Liberalism to Reluctant Realism," *Survival,* Vol. 38, No. 2 (Summer 1996), pp. 35–57; and Michael J. Green "Managing Chinese Power: The View from Japan," in Alastair Iain Johnston and Robert S. Ross, eds., *Engaging China: The Management of an Emerging Power* (London: Routledge, 1999), pp. 207–234.

2. Warren Cohen, "China in Japan-American Relations," in Akira Iriye and Warren Cohen, eds., *The United States and Japan in the Postwar World* (Lexington, KY: University of Kentucky Press, 1989), pp. 36–60.

3. *Asahi Shimbun,* June 5, 1989; evening version, June 13, 1989; and June 21, 1989.

4. During a trip to China as foreign minister in January 1994, Hata held the aid plan to a three year schedule, a cut from the previous five-year plans, and informed his counterparts of Japanese concerns about the Chinese military buildup, urging increases in transparency in Chinese defense policy. See Tomoda Seki, "*Taichū Senryaku: Sairyou no Shinario, Saiaku no Shinario*" (Strategy toward China: The Best Scenario, the Worst Scenario), *Chūou Kouron,* December 1995, pp. 54–62.

5. Christopher Johnstone, "Grant Aid Suspension Heightens Tensions in Japan-China Relations," *Japan Economic Institute Report,* September 15, 1996.

6. Between 1985 and 1997 the percentage of Japanese who said they did not feel friendly relations toward China rose from 18 percent to 51 percent with sharp and sustained increases beginning in 1991, according to polls taken by the Prime Minister's Office in Japan. See *Asahi Shimbun,* February 27, 1997.

7. Liberal Democratic Party Research Commission on Foreign Affairs, *Foreign Policy of the Liberal Democratic Party, Part I: Japan's Asia-Pacific Strategy: The Challenges of Transformation* (Tokyo: LDP, undated translation released in early May 1997), p. 23.

8. The first yen loan package (1978–1983) totaled 330 billion yen. The second yen loan package (1984–1989) totaled 470 billion yen. The third yen loan package (1990–1995) totaled 800 billion yen.

9. "*Taichū Enshakkan Houshiki Minaoshi*" (Reviewing the Yen Loan Process), *Nihon Keizai Shimbun,* January 1, 1995. According to the government's 1991 ODA Charter, Japanese ODA would be distributed based on four principles: (1) to support sustainable development; (2) to prevent the use of aid for military purposes or in support of international conflict; (3) to give full consideration to the recipient's military expenditures and the development, production, import, or export of missiles and weapons of mass destruction; and (4) to give full consideration to the recipient's advancement of democracy, efforts at introducing a market-style economy, and protection of basic human rights and freedom.

10. "Tokyo Issues Standard Protest of Latest Chinese Nuclear Test," *Japan Digest*, May 16, 1998.

11. "*News Asia: Dai–4-ji Taichū Enshakkan/Kakujikken de Takamaru Touketsuron/Towareru Gaikou Senryaku*" (News Asia: The Fourth Yen Loan Package to China/A Growing Call for Freezing after the Nuclear Tests/Foreign Policy Strategy under Question), *Yomiuri Shimbun,* June 11, 1996.

12. "*Kaku Jikken Mondai*" (The Nuclear Test Problem), *Asahi Shimbun,* May 20, 1995.

13. "Kōno Says Chinese Nuclear Test Won't Affect Aid," *Japan Digest,* May 18, 1998.

14. "Tokyo Will Protest Chinese Nuclear Testing by Limiting Aid Grants," *Japan Digest,* May 19, 1995.

15. Masahiko Sasajima, "ODA to China: How Effective Is It?" *Daily Yomiuri,* February 5, 1997.

16. "Persistent Calls Are Heard from the LDP for a Freeze on Aid to China," *Japan Digest,* March 21, 1996.

17. "*Nicchu Minkanjin Kaigi/Sutoreito na Hihan no Oushū*" (Straight Criticism at the Japan-China Peoples' Meeting), *Yomiuri Shimbun,* April 5, 1996.

18. Chalmers Johnson has noted that "between the mid-1950's and the late 1970's, Japan's peculiar attitude toward China permitted the PRC to take political advantage of Japan in their bilateral relations." See "The Patterns of Japanese Relations with China, 1952–1983," *Pacific Affairs,* Fall 1986, p. 403.

19. Yosano Fujita, "*Nicchū Kankei no Kiki wo Maneku Jinteki Nettowāku no Shoumetsu*" (The Destruction of Human Networks Is Beckoning a Sino-Japanese Crisis), *Foresight,* December 1996, pp. 32–35. Fujita catalogues the decay of personal networking even at the Chinese Embassy in Tokyo, which he notes has lost its effective entree into the Diet.

20. "*Chūgoku, Shitataka Kousaijutsu*" (China's Real Tough Friendship with Japan's Political Parties), *Asahi Shimbun,* June 19, 2000.

21. Japan-Taiwan channels consist of dense networks. At a parliamentary level, the Nikka Giin Kondankai (Japan-Taiwan Parliamentary Salon) functions as the largest institutionalized organ with approximately 300 Diet members. Most of the board members of Japan-PRC Parliamentary League are also affiliated with this Japan-Taiwan parliamentary organ. Until the early 1990s, the pro-Taiwan school in Japan was monopolized mainly by the LDP conservative politicians with strong belief in anticommunism or with strong personal preference over Taiwan. Recently, however, this is no longer the case. The DPJ has also become active in developing Japan-Taiwan relationships in order to encourage and support the development of democracy in Taiwan. Additionally there are many Track II channels between Japan and Taiwan, including: Asia Open Forum, where many politicians or businessmen gather to discuss economic or political issues; Tairiku Mondai Kenkyūkai (The Study Group on the Continental Affairs), where most pro-Taiwan scholars in Japan gather and discuss various issues; and the Japan International Forum, which holds regular meetings with Taiwanese policymakers. In addition, an increasing number of next-generation politicians show an anti-PRC sentiment because of the China's adamant use of the history card as well as the unclear

future of China's rising economic and military power. See, for example, "*Nic-chū Kankei Samagawari*" (Changes in Japan–China Relations), *Asahi Shimbun,* August 20, 2000.

22. "*Senkaku Shotou Mondai, Tainichi Hihan Sarani Kageki*" (Criticism of Japan Already Becoming Extreme in Senkaku Islands Problem), *Mainichi Shimbun,* October 2, 1996; "*Takeshima, Senkaku Shotou, Yuzuranu Nicchūkan*" (Japan, China and Korea Not Turning Over the Takeshima, Senkaku Islands), *Mainichi Shimbun,* February 29, 1996; Bruce Gilley, Sebastian Moffett, Julian Baum, and Matt Forney, "Rocks of Contention," *Far Eastern Economic Review,* September 19, 1996, pp. 14–15.

23. Sasajima Masahiko, "Storm over Senkakus: How to Deal with Hot Non-Issue," *The Daily Yomiuri,* October 2, 1996, p. 7.

24. "China Seen Drilling Oil Well Near Senkakus, Gives Japan Another Headache," *Japan Digest,* February 14, 1996.

25. "*Gaimu Kanryou no Nashonarizumu*" (Nationalism of the Foreign Ministry Officials), *Asahi Shimbun AERA Weekly,* May 31, 1999, pp. 17–18.

26. "China, Taiwan, Denounce Japanese Rightists 'Lighthouse' on Senkaku Islands," *Japan Digest,* July 19, 1996.

27. Allen S. Whiting, *China Eyes Japan* (Berkeley, CA: University of California Press, 1989).

28. "LDP Deliberately Inserts Japanese Claims to Islands in Party Platform," *Japan Digest,* October 1, 1996.

29. "Chinese General Calls for Mobilization to Defend 'National Sovereignty,'" *Japan Digest,* September 26, 1996.

30. Larry A. Niksch, "Senkaku (Diaouyu) Island Dispute: The U.S. Legal Relationship and Obligations," *PACNET,* No. 45, Pacific Forum CSIS, November 8, 1996.

31. "*Senkaku Shotou ha Anpo Jouyaku no Tekiyou Taishou, Yuuji niha Bouei Gimu, Beikokubou Jikanho Dairi ga Kenkai*" (US-Japan Security Treaty Covers Senkaku Islands, the US Deputy Assistant Secretary of Defense Expresses a View), *Yomiuri Shimbun,* November 28, 1996.

32. *Heisei 11-nendo Bouei Hakusho* (1999 Defense White Paper), pp. 67–68. See also "*Chūgoku Chousasen ga Ryoukai Shinpan, Senkaku Shotou Shuuhen Kaiiki*" (Chinese Research Vessel Intrude into Japanese Territorial Water Around Senkaku Islands), *Nihon Keizai Shimbun,* September 4, 1996. The next spring and summer a Chinese research vessel was found conducting unilateral exploration of the sea-bed. "*Sinpan Chousasen, Senkaku Fukin ha 'Chūgoku Ryoudo,' Kaiho no Keikoku ni Outou*" (Chinese Research Vessel, Intruding into Japanese Territorial Water, Responded to the Warning of Japan Maritime Security Agency Claiming that the Areas Surrounding Senkaku Islands Are Chinese Territories), *Sankei Shimbun,* April 26, 1997. Also see "*Chūgoku no Chousasen wo mata Kakunin, Kagoshima to Okinawa Kinkai ni 3-seki, Kaijou Hoanchou*" (3 Chinese Research Vessels Were Confirmed Intruding into Japanese Territorial Waters Again, Near the Sea of Kagoshima and Okinawa, Maritime Agency Announced), *Yomiuri Shimbun,* July 31, 1998.

33. Translated from a citation in Tanaka Akihiko, *Anzen Hōshou* (National Security) (Tokyo: Yomiuri Shimbunsha, 1997), p. 227.

34. Article VI of Treaty of Mutual Cooperation and Security Between the United States of America and Japan states: "For the purpose of contributing to the security of Japan and the maintenance of international peace and security in the Far East, the United States of America is granted the use by its land, air and naval forces of facilities and areas in Japan."

35. Where the 1976 National Defense Panel Outline (NDPO) authorized a force structure to defend against "limited small-scale attack," the revised 1995 NDPO cleared the way for preparing to support "the smooth and effective implementation of U.S.-Japan security arrangements" in response to "situations that arise in the areas surrounding Japan." "National Defense Program Outline in and after FY 1996" (tentative unofficial translation), Security Council and Cabinet of Japan, November 28, 1995, p. 6.

36. China's missile test took place March 8–15; military operation training, March 12–20; and sea-air-ground forces joint operation exercise, March 15–25. Taiwan election was held on March 23.

37. Relayed by a Japanese correspondent stationed in Beijing in 1996. Interviewed on December 8, 1998.

38. See, for example, "*Yūji Meguru Hatsugen, Seifu Jimintou Hoshu Saihen Niramu? Chūtai Kinchou,*" (Statement on the Crisis: LDP, Government Preparing for Conservative Realignment? The China-Taiwan Stand-off), *Asahi Shimbun,* March 16, 1996.

39. U.S.-Japan Security Consultative Committee, "Completion of the Review of the Guidelines for U.S.-Japan Defense Cooperation," New York, September 23, 1997, in Michael J. Green and Mike M. Mochizuki, *The U.S.-Japan Security Alliance in the 21st Century,* Study Group Paper, (New York: Council on Foreign Relations, 1998), pp. 55–72.

40. "China Says It Won't Accept Taiwan in U.S.-Japan Alliance," *Reuters,* August 22, 1997.

41. "'*Shūhen Jitai ni Taiwan,*' *Gaimushou Kyokuchou Shin Kenkai . . .*" ("Area Around Japan Includes Taiwan, a New Interpretation from the MOFA Bureau Director), *Mainichi Shimbun,* May 28, 1998.

42. "*Shin Bouei Shishin: Houbeimae no Kou Takumin Shuseki, Nihon Dake wo Yaridama*" (The New Guidelines: Premier Jiang Zeming before His Visit to U.S. Japan Is the Only Scapegoat), *Mainichi Shimbun,* October 20, 1997.

43. "*Chūgoku ga TMD Kakusan ni Dannen/ Nihon Haibi wo Keikai . . .*" (China Objects to TMD Proliferation, Warns against Japanese Deployment), *Yomiuri Shimbun,* December 6, 1995. See also Alistair Iain Johnston, "Prospects for Chinese Nuclear Force Modernization: Limited Deterrence vs. Multilateral Arms Control," *China Quarterly,* Spring 1996, p. 548; Michael J. Green, "TMD and Strategic Relations with China," in Ralph Cossa, ed., *Restructuring the U.S.-Japan Alliance* (Washington, DC: CSIS, 1998); and Banning Garrett and Bonnie Glaser, "Chinese Perspectives on Nuclear Arms Control," *International Security,* Vol. 20, No. 3 (Winter 1995/96), pp. 43–78.

44. Jiang Zemin's scheduled visit to Tokyo in the fall of 1998 caused the Obuchi government to hesitate on making a formal commitment to joint research and development of Navy Theater Wide systems for missile defense, but the North Korean Taepo-dong launch in August of that year cleared the political obsta-

cles and the Japanese cabinet formally approved participation in TMD a month before Jiang arrived in Tokyo. The Chinese were furious at North Korea for presenting an excuse for Japanese participation in TMD, but after the March 1996 missile tests in Taiwan Strait, there was no question that the JDA and MOFA were ready to participate.

45. *Yomiuri Shimbun,* September 6, 1986.

46. *Yomiuri Shimbun,* April 26, 1988.

47. *Mainichi Shimbun,* August 11, 1995.

48. "Chinese Assault on Opposition to War Apology May Finally Have Reached LDP," *Japan Digest,* April 6, 1995, and "Murayama Apologizes for Invasion and Colonization of Asia," *Japan Digest,* August 21, 1995.

49. Japanese officials also expressed dismay at Beijing's 1995 Patriotic Education Campaign, which fomented anti-Japanese nationalism in China.

50. The polling analysis is also by Kojima. See Kojima Tomoyuki, *Gendai Ghūgoku no Seiji* (The Politics of Modern China) (Tokyo: Keio University Press, 1999), pp. 385–386.

51. Japan Ministry of Foreign Affairs, *1999 Heisei 11 nendoban (Dai 42-gou) Gaikou Seisho* (1999 Diplomatic Blue Book, Vol. 42), p. 33.

52. "Was Jiang Zemin Deliberately Rude to Emperor? Some Japanese Think So," *Japan Digest,* December 4, 1998. See also *Yomiuri Shimbun, Nikkei Shimbun,* November 27, 1998.

53. "*Shunou Kaidan, Nihongawa no Happyou yori Hageshii Hatsugen ga Hanmei*" (In the Summit Meeting a Tougher Statement than Revealed by the Official Announcement), *Yomiuri Shimbun,* November 28, 1998. Also, interviews with MOFA officials, December 4, 1998.

54. Interview at *Nicchū Keizai Kyoukai* (Japan-China Economic Association), December 7, 1998.

55. Japan-China Joint Declaration on Building a Partnership of Friendship and Cooperation for Peace and Development (Provisional Translation), November 26, 1998.

56. See, for example, Kojima Tomoyuki, "*Kou Takumin Shuseki no Hounichi ha Seikousuru*" (Premier Ziang Zemin's Visit to Japan Will Succeed), *Sankei Shimbun,* November 25, 1998.

57. Interview on December 7, 1998. I was in Japan for the annual meeting of the Asia Political Economy Association (Ajia Seiji Keizai Kyoukai) and could not find one China scholar who was not distressed by the visit.

58. Cited in Christopher B. Johnstone, "Japan's China Policy: Implications for U.S.-Japan Relations," *Asian Survey,* Vol. 38, No. 11 (November 1998), p. 1072.

59. JETRO, "Sino-Japanese Trade Hits All-Time High," February 2, 2000 (http://www.jetro.go.jp/it/e/press/2000/feb2.html). In yen terms, Japan's trade with the PRC totaled 7,532 billion yen in 1999. The Japan's trade data is available at the web site of the Japan Ministry of Finance, *Value of Exports and Imports by Area (Country): 1999 (Fixed Annual) (Calendar Year),* February 2000 (http://www.mof.go.jp/english/trade-st/199928ce.htm#KUNI). The annual foreign exchange rate between U.S. dollar and Japanese yen is available at Federal Reserve Statistical Release, *Foreign Exchange Rate (Annual),* January 3, 2000 (http://www.bog.frb.fed.us/releases/G5A/current).

60. Johnstone, op. cit., n. 58.

61. Japan's outward investment to the People's Republic totaled 136.3 billion yen in fiscal year 1998 (April 1998–March 1999), (Japan Ministry of Finance, *Foreign Direct Investment Statistics: Outward Direct Investment (Country & Region)*, 2000 (http://www.mof.go.jp/english/e1c008.htm). The average foreign exchange rate during the same period was 128.02 yen/U.S. dollar (calculated from the central rates of the Tokyo Inter-Bank Rates, Bank of Japan (http://www.boj.or.jp/en/dlong_f.htm). Thus, in U.S. dollar terms, Japan's outward investment to the People's Republic was $1.06 billion in fiscal year 1998.

62. Liberal Democratic Party, op. cit., n. 7, p. 23.

63. Masayoshi Kanabayashi, "Japan May Cut Aid as China Boosts Arms Outlay," *Wall Street Journal,* July 27, 2000.

64. "*Tokubetsu Enshakkan Gyakufū Tsuyomaru*" (Winds against the Yen Loans Strengthen), *Asahi Shimbun,* August 10, 2000. *Sankei Shimbun* Beijing bureau chief Komori Yoshihisa gave voice to the LDP's frustration in a series of articles from China, noting, "the Japanese aid policy to China completely contradicts the Japanese government's ODA Charter" because of "China's expansion of defense spending and development of weapons of mass destruction. See Komori Yoshihisa, "*Machigaidarake no Chūgoku Enjo*" (Too Mistakes of Aid to China) *Chūou Kouron,* March 2000, p. 109.

65. Source: *Chūgoku, Nicchū no Shuyou Keizai Shihyou* (China, Japan–China Major Economic Figures), Japan–China Economic Association Research Department, 1998.

66. From the Ministry of Finance International Financial Almanac 1999, cited in Tanaka Naoki, *The Outlook of Japan-Chinese Economic Relations in the 21st Century,* Keidanren, October 1999.

67. *Touyou Keizai Geppou (Tōyō Keizai* Statistical Monthly), "*Seizouyou no Ajiashifuto ga Kyuukasoku*"(Manufacturing Industry's Shift to Asia Increases Rapidly), May 1996, pp. 19–23, cited in Christopher Johnstone, "A Level Playing Field? U.S. and Japanese Competition in the Chinese Market," *Japan Economic Institute Report,* August 30, 1996. Also interviews with Japan–China Economic Association, December 8, 1998.

68. Tanaka, op. cit., n. 33, p. 2.

69. Interview with Japan–China Economic Association, December 7, 1998.

70. "*Mushou Enjo Shūketsu wo Ri Ho ga Hihan*"(Li Peng Criticizes Suspension of Grant Aid), *Nihon Keizai Shimbun,* September 20, 1995.

71. "*Chūgoku, Ri Ho Shushou, Zaikai Houchudan tono Kaidan ni Oujiru—Senkaku Nicchuu Bijinesu ni Eikyomo*"(China's Li Peng Meets with Business Group—Argues Senkakus Will Impact Japan–China Business), *Nihon Keizai Shimbun,* September 20, 1996.

72. "*Beijing de Jūgatsu ni Shimpojium, Nicchū Keizai Iinkai ga 25 Shūnen Jigyou*" (A Symposium in Beijing in October, Japan–China Economic Association's Project on the Twenty-fifth anniversary*), Nihon Keizai Shimbun,* July 10, 1997.

73. The Chinese government's decisions to replace Toshiba with Siemens of Germany on the 18 million gigawat Sansha Dam project and to hold a Japanese consortium at bay on the Beijing–Shanghai bullet train project are two examples frequently cited by Japanese businessmen.

74. Interviews with Japan–China Economic Association, December 8, 1998.

75. Fujisawa Kazuo, *Keidanren Chūgoku Iinkai Chousadan Danchou Shoken* (Report of the Delegation Head from the Keidanren China Committee), No. 1, February 15, 1994, p. 5, and No. 2 (1995), p. 3.

76. Imai Ryūkichi, "Japan's Nuclear Policy: Retrospect and the Immediate Past, Perspectives on the Twenty-first Century," *IIPS Paper* 196E (Tokyo), November 1996, pp. 21–23.

77. Japanese press reports indicate a Chinese intention to construct a large-scale reprocessing plant in Lanzhou. See *Nihon Keizai Shimbun,* March 12, 1995. See also Isaka Satoshi, "Energy Experts Promote Asian Nuclear Network," *Japan Economic Journal,* April 25, 1997.

78. Peter Evans, "Japan's Green Aid," *The China Business Review,* July–August 1994, p. 39.

79. Peter Evans, "Official Japanese Energy and Environmental Assistance Programs to the People's Republic of China," paper prepared for the U.S. Department of Energy, November 1996.

80. Kanayama Hisahiro, "The Future Impact of Energy Problems in China," *Asia-Pacific Review,* Vol. 2, No. 1 (Spring 1995), p. 230.

81. Nihon Keizai Shimbun, op. cit., n. 71. Also interviews with Japan–China Economic Association, December 8, 1998.

82. Industrial Structure Council, *1997 Report on the WTO Consistency of Trade Policies by Major Trading Partners* (Tokyo: Ministry of International Trade and Industry, 1997), p. 300.

83. Ibid., p. 300.

84. Japan Forum on International Relations, *The Policy Recommendations: The Future of China in the Context of Asian Security,* Tokyo, January 25, 1995, p. 14.

85. Liberal Democratic Party, op. cit., n. 7, p. 22.

86. Ina Hisayoshi, "Japan's Leaders Lack Depth, Objectivity in Their Thinking on China Question," *Japan Economic Journal,* August 26, 1996.

87. *Tokyo Shimbun,* July 14, 1997.

88. Johnstone, op. cit., n. 58.

89. "Anpo wo Kataru to Iukoto" (Speaking of Dialogue on Security), Asahi Shimbun, April 1997; Liberal Democratic Party, op. cit., n. 7.

90. "Qian Ratchets up Complaint on Guidelines, Rejects 'Official' Three-Way Talks," *Japan Digest,* September 30, 1997. Also interviews with MOFA officials, December 4, 1998.

91. Interview with senior MOF officials, Tokyo, December 3, 1998. These same officials noted that the Chinese leadership appeared apprehensive about yen hegemony in the region and were determined to maintain future currency reserves that kept the yen behind the dollar and the Euro (40 percent Dollar, 40 percent Euro, and 20 percent yen, according to People's Bank–MOF discussions).

92. "Hashimoto to Propose Four-Way Security Summit with U.S., China, Russia," *Japan Digest,* April 17, 1998. Interview with senior MOFA officials, April 26, 1998.

93. "China Rejected Hashimoto Request for Perm 5+2 Session on N-Tests," *Japan Digest,* June 8, 1998; and *Nihon Keizai Shimbun,* June 7, 1998.

94. "Clinton, Jiang Urge Japan to Act on Economy: Tokyo Feels Pressure, Isolation," *Japan Digest,* June 29, 1998.
95. The Liberal Democratic Party, op. cit., n. 7, p. 23.
96. This catch phrase was suggested to the author by a senior JDA official in 1996.

Chapter 4

1. Oknim Chung, "The Origins and Evolution of the Japanese-American Alliance: A Korean Perspective," Stanford Asia/Pacific Research Center Discussion Paper, September 1998, p. 14.
2. B. C. Koh notes that this phrase is frequently used in both Japanese (*Chikakute Toui Kuni*) and Korean (*Kakkapkodo mo Nara*) to describe the relationship. See B. C. Koh, "Japan and Korea," in Bae Ho Hahn and Chae-Jin Lee, eds., *The Korean Peninsula and the Major Powers* (Seoul: Sejong Institute, 1998), p. 33.
3. Martin Weinstein, *Japan's Postwar Defense Policy, 1947–1968* (New York: Columbia University Press, 1971), pp. 50–55.
4. Kōji Murata, "The Origins and the Evolution of the U.S.-ROK Alliance from a Japanese Perspective," paper presented to the Conference on America's Alliances with Japan and Korea in a Changing Northeast Asia, Stanford University Asia-Pacific Research Center, August 21–23, 1998. See also Murata Kōji, *Daitouryou no Zasetsu* (A Setback of the President) (Tokyo: Yūhikaku, 1998).
5. One former JDA official confessed in an open conference in Washington in 1997 that much of his career after 1968 was spent "burying the Sato-Nixon communiqué as deep as possible." Remarks by Hoshuyama Noboru at the Nixon Shocks and U.S.-Japan Relations, 1969–1976, a conference of the National Security Archives and the Woodrow Wilson Center, Washington, D.C., March 12, 1997 (http://www.gwu.edu/~nsarchiv/japan/shocks.htm).
6. Murata, op. cit., n. 4, p. 12.
7. Chae-Jin Lee and Hideo Sato, *U.S. Policy toward Japan and Korea* (New York: Praeger, 1982), p. 28.
8. Chong-Sik Lee, *Japan and Korea: The Political Dimension* (Palo Alto, CA: Hoover Press, 1985), p. 28. The Japanese negotiator, Kuboto Kanōchirō, made other claims that enraged the South Korean side. The Kishi government and the LDP supported him, however, and let the negotiations collapse without any retraction.
9. Chung, op. cit., n. 1, p 15. See also Anh Byung-Joo, "Japanese Policy toward Korea," in Gerald Curtis, ed., *Japan's Foreign Policy after the Cold War: Coping with Change* (New York: M. E. Sharpe, 1993), p. 264.
10. Lee, op. cit., n. 8, p. 56.
11. Japan Defense Agency, *The Defense of Japan, 1982,* p. 91.
12. Lee, op. cit., n. 8, pp. 129–139.
13. *Yomiuri Shimbun,* June 11, 1985.
14. Victor D. Cha, *Alignment Despite Antagonism* (Stanford, CA: Stanford University Press, 1999), pp. 209–210, p. 443.
15. Okonogi Masao, "*Masatsu to Kyouchou no Nikkan Kankei*" (Japan-ROK Relations: Friction and Cooperation), *Gaikō Forum,* November 1995, pp. 12–20.
16. Lee, *Op. Cit.,* 8, p. 67.

17. Sato Katsumi, *Kita Chosen "Han" no Kaku Senryaku* (The North Korea's "Revenge" Nuclear Strategy) (Tokyo: Kōbunsha, 1993), p. 68. This figure is also used by Japan's Agency for Public Security (Kōanchō), see Nicholas Eberstadt, "Financial Transfers from Japan to North Korea," *Asian Survey,* Vol. 46, No. 5 (May 1996), p. 523.

18. The value of Japan–North Korea trade on a customs clearance basis was: 1990/$472.6 million, 1991/$507.7 million, 1992/$481.6 million, 1993/$472.1 million, 1994/ $493.5 million, 1995/$594.6 million, 1996/516.9 million, 1997/$481.1 million. In 1997 41.6 percent of Japanese imports from North Korea consisted of fish and vegetable products, while 31.6 percent consisted of textile goods. See *Tsūshou Sangyoushou* (ed.*), 1998 Tsūshou Hakusho* (White Paper on Trade and Industry) (Tokyo: Ōkurashou Insatsu kyoku, 1998), pp. 319–320.

19. Projections for Japanese reparations run to $5 billion, though the Japanese government has never discussed a specific figure. Interview with MOFA official, Tokyo, June 21, 1999.

20. Koh, Op. Cit., 2, p. 57.

21. Don Oberdorfer, *The Two Koreas: A Contemporary History* (Reading, MA: Addison-Wesley, 1997), p. 221.

22. *"Nicchou Honkoushou Sutāto"* (Japan-DPRK Official Negotiations Start), *Nihon Keizai Shimbun,* January 30, 1991.

23. Ibid. See also, Koh, op. cit., n. 2, p. 58.

24. *"Kin Nissei Shuseki Kaiken/Nicchou Koushou Suishin Kakushin"* (Interview with Premier Kim Il Sung: Conviction in Further Advancement in Japan-DPRK Normalization Talks), *Kyōdō Tsūshin,* June 3, 1991.

25. *"Kankoku Gaimujikan ga Yousei/Nicchou Koushou wa Shinchou ni"* (ROK Vice Minister of Foreign Affairs Asks for Cautious Approach in Japan-DPRK Normalization Talks), *Nihon Keizai Shimbun,* December 18, 1991. See also *Nihon Keizai Shimbun,* January 10, 1991, for President Roh's comments.

26. Koh Odagawa, *"Nicchou Koushou no Ayumi wo Tadoru"* (Looking Back the History of Japan-North Korea Talks), in *Kitachousen Sono Jitsuzou to Kiseki* (North Korea: Its Real Image and History), (Tokyo: Koubunken, 1998), p. 268.

27. See *Nihon Keizai Shimbun, Asahi Shimbun, Yomiuri Shimbun,* for November 5, 1992. See also Koh, op. cit., n. 2, p. 59.

28. American Enterprise Institute Analyst Nicholas Eberstadt estimates that Chōsen Sōren remittances never surpassed $100 million after the collapse of the bubble in 1991. Quoted in Oberdorfer, op. cit., n. 21, p 453.

29. *"Nicchou Koushou ni Eikyousezu"* (No Influence on Japan-DPRK Normalization Talks from Missile Launch), *Nihon Keizai Shimbun,* June 13, 1993.

30. Leon V. Sigal, *Disarming Strangers: Nuclear Diplomacy with North Korea* (Princeton, NJ: Princeton University Press, 1998), p. 90.

31. For authoritative accounts of the crisis, see Oberdorfer, op. cit., n. 21, pp. 305–226; and Sigal, ibid., pp. 129–204.

32. See *"Beigun Kouhou Shien wo Gokuhi Kenkyu, 93nen, Chousen Hantou Kiki de Boueichou"* (JDA Secretly Studied on Rear Area Support for U.S. Forces During the Crisis on the Korean Peninsula in 1993), *Tokyo Shimbun,* February 15, 1999; *"94nen Chousen Kinchouji no Beigun, Tainichi Youbou"* (U.S. Forces Request

on Japan During the Korean Peninsula Crisis in 1994), *Asahi Shimbun,* March 3, 1999; *"Kukou, Kouwan no Teikyou Kentou, 94nen no Kinpakuji ni Boueichou"* (JDA Examined Options to Allow U.S. Forces to Use Airports and Seaports in Japan During the Crisis on the Korean Peninsula), *Asahi Shimbun,* March 23, 1999; *"94nen Chousen HantouKiki, Beikan Shien he Yuji Keikaku"* (Contingency Plan to Support U.S. and South Korea During the Crisis on the Korean Peninsula in 1994), *Asahi Shimbun,* April 15, 1999.

33. Based on discussions with former Prime Ministers Hata and Hashimoto and with LDP and MOFA officials. For accounts of the crisis in Japanese, see: Okonogi Masao, ed. *Kitachousen Handobukku* (Handbook on North Korea) (Tokyo: Kōdansha, 1997); Izumi Hajime, *"Beichou Kankei no Kiseki to Kongo no Yukue,"* (History and Future of the U.S.-DPRK Relations) in *Kitachousen Sono Jitsuzou to Kiseki,* ibid., 26, pp. 189–214; Takesada Sadashi, *Boueichou Kyoukan no Kitachousen Shinsou Bunseki* (A Deep Analysis of North Korean Issues by a JDA Scholar) (Tokyo: KK Bestsellers, 1998); and *Boei Nenkan* (Annual Report on Japan's Defense) (Bouei Nenkan Hakkoukai, annually from 1994 to 2000).

34. For details see Richard P. Cronin and Zachary S. Davis, "The U.S.-North Korea Nuclear Accord of October 1994: Background, Status and Requirements of U.S. Nonproliferation Law," CRS Report for Congress (Washington, DC: Congressional Research Service, April 11, 1997).

35. Umetsu Itaru, *"Chousen Hantou Enerugī Kaihatsu Kikou no Katsudou to Kongo no Mondai"* (KEDO's Activities and Future Issues), *Kokusai Mondai,* No. 433 (March 1996), p. 26.

36. *"Jiminto, Niccho Kaizen Fukumaru"* (LDP, Improvement of Japan-DPRK Ties Deepening), *Yomiuri Shimbun,* January 13, 1997.

37. *"Nicchou Kokkou Seijouka Koushou, Getsunai ni Saikai, Yonsha Kyougi Shinten Uke Seifu ga Houshin"* (Government Decides to Reopen Normalization Talks with DPRK within the Month Based on Four Party Talks Progress), *Yomiuri Shimbun,* January 6, 1998.

38. Ibid. In March 1997 the Japanese families organized into the National Association for the Rescue of Japanese Kidnapped by North Korea and were actively lobbying the LDP and appealing to a sympathetic media. The group placed full-page adds in the *New York Times,* including one on April 2, 1998. In 1994 a North Korean agent defected with detailed information on the North's kidnapping strategy. For the details of the abduction operations of Japanese citizens by the *Yodogō* hijackers, see Takazawa Kōji, *Shukumei* (Their Fate) (Tokyo: Shinchou Shuppansha, 1998).

39. Barbara Wanner, "Japanese North Korean Politicians Agree that Peace Talks Should Resume," *JEI Report,* No. 44B, November 21, 1998, p. 8.

40. See, for example, *"Hawai Shetei no Shin Dandoudan Kitachousen Kaihatsu, 15-nen Inai Kansei, CIA Koukan Shougen"* (A CIA High Official Testified That North Korea Will Develop a New Ballistic Missile That Could Reach Hawaii in 15 Years), *Yomiuri Shimbun,* February 8, 1997.

41. Although Tokyo declared the suspension of the talks, the negotiations had already been suspended, technically, by the DPRK unilaterally since June 1998.

42. Yvonne Chang, "Angry Japan Sets Measures Against North Korea," Reuters, Tokyo, September 1, 1998.

43. Ibid.
44. "Japan Wants Fund to N. Korea Cut," Associated Press, Tokyo, September 8, 1998.
45. Interview with Kajiyama Seiroku, the LDP, November 2, 1998.
46. "*Kikendo ga Takamattekita Chousen Kiki no Honshitsu*" (How the North Korea Crisis Increased the Danger), *Foresight,* December 1998, p.37.
47. Jane A. Morse, "U.S.-N.Korea Plan to Resume Talks Thursday," Reuters, Washington, September 2, 1998.
48. Interview with MOFA officials, September 25, 1998.
49. Telephone interview with KEDO official, January 12, 1998.
50. The September 5 U.S.-DPRK agreement shown to the Japanese government stated that the United States would "accelerate" LWR construction. The public September 9, 1998 U.S. Press Statement stated that "accelerated construction of the LWR project should begin by November 1998." See, East Asia Pacific Affairs Bureau, Korea Desk, Department of State "U.S. Press Statement," September 9, 1998. On September 10 State Department spokesman James P. Rubin, Spokesman, said: " . . . The U.S. will fully respect the positions of the R.O.K. and Japan and consult closely with them regarding the LWR project implementation, as addressed in the U.S. press statement resulting from the New York talks. As we pursue our negotiations with North Korea on these difficult issues, we will continue to consult closely with Congress and our allies, the R.O.K. and Japan. There should be no doubt about our firm commitment to our bilateral security arrangements with the R.O.K. and Japan." But this statement came after Japanese officials were incensed that the administration had promised to accelerate construction of the LWR in the original September 5 agreement.
51. "KEDO Executive Board Agrees on Cost-Sharing for Light Water Reactor Project," KEDO press release, November 10, 1998.
52. MOFA officials in early September had attempted to condition Japan's KEDO funding to progress in the U.S.-DPRK missile talks and received some reassurances from Washington that this would be done "Japan May Give Nuclear Plant Funds," Dow Jones Newswires, Tokyo, September 9, 1998.
53. Kazuyuki Matsuura, "Government Seeks Censure of North Korea by United Nations," *Daily Yomiuri,* September 4, 1998, and Sau Chan, "UN Urges Against North Korean Launches," Associated Press, September 15, 1998.
54. "*Chousen Hantou Heiwa Yonsha Kyougi, Bunkakai Sanka mo, Yanai Jimujikan*" (Vice Minister Yanai Expresses Interest in Participating in the Four Party Talks Subcommittee), *Yomiuri Shimbun,* October 27, 1998.
55. U.S. Department of State, "Joint U.S.-Japan Statement: Security Consultative Committee," New York, September 20, 1998.
56. "Cabinet Approves Spy Satellite Plan," *Japan Digest,* November 8, 1998. In fact, the lag in intelligence sharing was within the Japanese system, rather than between the two governments. Nevertheless, the satellite program quickly won the support of all parties other than the Communists.
57. "Japanese Navy Fires on Suspected North Korean Ships During Japan Sea Chase," *Japan Digest,* March 24, 1999.
58. "North Korea Is Said to Be Building 'Missile Silos,'" *Japan Digest,* January 8, 1998.

59. Japan–Republic of Korea Joint Declaration, "A New Japan–Republic of Korea Partnership toward the Twenty-first Century" (Provisional Japanese government translation), October 8, 1998.

60. Victor Cha, "Rooting the Pragmatic in Japan-ROK Security Relations," *Comparative Connections: An E-Journal on East Asian Bilateral Relations,* Pacific Forum Center for Strategic and International Studies, July 1999, p. 2, www.csis.org/pacfor.

61. "A Letter to President William J. Clinton," written by an Independent Task Force on managing Change on the Korean Peninsula sponsored by the Council on Foreign Relations, Project Director Michael J. Green, October 7, 1998.

62. U.S. Department of State, *Review of United States Policy Toward North Korea: Findings and Recommendations/ Unclassified Report by Dr. William J. Perry, U.S. North Korea Policy Coordinator and Special Advisor to the President and the Secretary of State,* Washington, DC, October 12, 1999 (http://www.state.gov/www/regions/eap/991012_northkorea_rpt.html).

63. Ibid.

64. Specifically, Obuchi stated: "regarding North Korea, I intend to continue to coordinate closely with the United States and the Republic of Korea in order to resolve the international concerns about last year's missile launch, and the suspected secret nuclear facilities, and to resolve the various issues outstanding in Japan's relations with North Korea. Provided that North Korea indicates that it is ready to take a constructive approach, Japan is ready to achieve improvements in its dialogues and exchanges with North Korea" (http://www.mofa.go.jp/announce/announce/1999/1/119–2.html).

65. For example, see "*Nonakashi Shudou Nyuunan Rosen,*" *Yomiuri Shimbun,* November 27, 1999.

66. "Japan, N. Korea Seen Resuming Talks after 7-year Gap," Reuters, Tokyo, March 21, 2000.

67. "*Nicchou Kaizen Yatto Ashiba: Seijouka Koushou Muzukashisa Masu Men mo*" (Japan and North Korea Finally Got A Foothold: Difficulties May Mount with Japan-DPRK Normalization Talks), *Asahi Shimbun,* July 27, 2000.

68. Interview with Professor Izumi Hajime, September 10, 1999.

69. See Koh, op. cit., 2, pp. 41–44.

70. "*Takeshima no Ryouyuuken Mondai: Nikkan no Haremono ni Hinokona*" (The Takeshima Territorial Rights Problem: Spark of Japan-ROK Division), *Asahi Shimbun AERA Weekly,* February 26, 1996.

71. "*Kim De Jun Daitouryou Hounichimae ni Togenuki Nikkan Gyogyou Kyoutei Kihon Goui*" (Basic Agreement on a Fisheries Pact, Major Thorn Removed before President Kim Dae Jung's Japan Trip), *Asahi Shimbun,* September 25, 1998.

72. "Japanese, South Korean Boats Play Tag at Sea as Fisheries Dispute Escalates," *Japan Digest,* February 5, 1998.

73. *Asahi Shimbun,* January 30, 1998; *Chosun Ilbo,* January 2, 1998, and January 13, 1998; and interviews with MOFA press club journalists, December 3 and January 8, 1998.

74. "Kim Dae Jung Inaugural Gives Tokyo Both Hopes and Worries," *Japan Digest,* February 26, 1998.

75. *Asahi Shimbun, Nihon Keizai Shimbun,* June 28, 1998.

76. *"Nikkan Shingyogyou Kyoutei Kecchaku"* (Resolution of the New Japan–ROK Fisheries Agreement*)*, *Sankei Shimbun,* September 25, 1998.

77. Ibid.

78. *Chosun Ilbo,Yomiuri Shimbun,* September 25, 1998.

79. "GNP Deters ROK–Japan Fisheries Accord," *Korea Times,* December 15, 1998. The treaty was eventually ratified by both government's in 1999.

80. *"Nakagawa Nousuishou no Ianfu Hatsugen"* (Agriculture, Forestry, and Fisheries Minister Nakagawa's Comment on Comfort Women Issues), *Sankei Shimbun,* August 5, 1998.

81. *"Nikkan Gyogyou Koushou ni Eikyou mo, KankokuYoron Hanpatsu no Osore, Nakagawa Nousuishou Ianfu Hatsugen"* (Agriculture and Fisheries Minister Nakagawa's Comfort Women Statement, Fear of a Reaction in South Korean Public Opinion, Could Influence Japan–Korea Fisheries Talks), *Asahi Shimbun,* August 1, 1998.

82. Yoshimi Yoshiaki, "State Crime Should Be Compensated by the State," *Asahi Shimbun,* August 22, 1995.

83. *Yomiuiri Shimbun,* August 4, 1998.

84. Koh, op. cit., n. 2, pp. 40–41.

85. "Seoul to Compensate Comfort Girls Itself, Demanding No Compensation," *Japan Digest,* April 22, 1998.

86. Koh, op. cit., n. 2, p. 38; and Lee, op. cit. n. 8, p. 132.

87. *"Nikkan Shunou Kaidan deno 'Shazai' ni Iron Aitsugu, Jimintou nado Ichibu Giin"* (Debate Continues among Some Diet Members in the LDP and Elsewhere about the "Apology" during the Japan–ROK Summit), *Asahi Shimbun,* October 7, 1998.

88. "Japan–Republic of Korea Joint Declaration: A New Japan Republic of Korea Partnership toward the Twenty-first Century" (Provisional translation by the Japanese government), October 8, 1998.

89. Sasae Kenōchirō, *"20 Seiki no Kako kara 21 Seiki no Mirai he"* (From the Twentieth Century Past to the Twenty-First Century Future), *Gaikō Forum,* No. 124 (December 1998), p. 72.

90. *"Nikkan Kankei, Nihonjin no 8 Wari Kako Seisan wo, Yoron Chousa"* (Opinion Poll Shows over 80% of Japanese See Closure on Past in Japan–ROK Relations), *Sankei Shimbun,* October 21, 1998.

91. *"Kankoku no Nihon Taishuu Bunka Kaihou"* (Korea Opens to Popular Culture from Japan), *Asahi Shimbun,* October 20, 1998; *"Kankoku Seifu Hyoumei 'Tennou' no Koshou, Koushiki ni Shiyou"* (Korean Government Officially Uses "Emperor" in Statement), *Nihon Keizai Shimbun,* September 11, 1998.

92. *Sankei Shimbun,* ibid.

93. Comments to author, January 14, 2000.

94. Japan–ROK trade has grown steadily since 1980. The volume has doubled for Japan's exports to South Korea, bringing Japan's 1996 trade surplus with the South to 1.5 trillion yen (US $ 11.7 billion with Y125=$1.00). Most of this trade has been in steel, iron, and other intermediate manufacturing inputs. Trade in autos, semiconductors, and other protected areas of South Korea's market has been predictably low. In some ways, Korea's dependence on Japan for exports has decreased in relative terms, as the rest of Asia's economies have

absorbed the ROK's exports—at least until the economic crisis hit in 1997. Foreign direct investment (FDI) between Japan and Korea is also lower than each country's FDI with other booming Asian economies, but Japan's FDI in South Korea was still $6 billion in 1995. Douglas Oustrom, "Complementarity and Competition: Korean-Japanese Trade Relations," in *Korea's Trade Relations* (Washington, DC: The Korea Economic Institute of America, 1998), pp. 100–105; and Japan Ministry of Finance Homepage, February 1998 (http://www.miti.go.jp/index-e.html).

95. Martin Feldstein, "Japan's Folly Drags Asia Down," *Wall Street Journal,* November 25, 1997; and Edward Lincoln, "Maybe It's the Teacher's Fault," *U.S. News & World Report,* December 15, 1997; *Hangyerae Sinmoon* editorial, January 10, 1998; *Moonhwa Ilbo* editorial, February 20, 1998.

96. Ahn Byung-Joo, *Korea Focus,* Vol. 6, No. 3 (January–February 1998). "Korea and the World," excerpted from *Munghwa Daily.*

97. Teruaki Ueno, "Japan Makes Historic Apology to South Korea," *Yahoo! News,* October 8, 1998.

98. *Chosun Ilbo,* October 29, 1998.

99. Ministry of Foreign Affairs and Ministry of International Trade and Industry (Japan) and Ministry of Foreign Affairs and Trade and Ministry of Commerce, Economics, and Industry (ROK), "Japan/Korea Economic Agenda 21: For the Strengthening of Japanese/Korean Partnership toward the 21st Century," March 21, 1999. See also JETRO-Korea Institute for Economic Policy, "Towards Closer Japan-Korea Economic Relations: Proposal for Formulating a 21st Century Partnership" (Joint Communiqué), May 23, 2000.

100. Mark Castellano, "Post Crisis Japan-South Korea Economic Relations: The Ups and Downs of Trade and Foreign Investment," *Japan Economic Institute Report,* No. 13 A, April 2, 1999.

101. Victor Cha, *Alignment Despite Antagonism: The United States-Korea-Japan Security Triangle* (Stanford, CA: Stanford University Press, 1999), p. 204.

102. *Yomiuri Shimbun,* May 24, 1995.

103. Tadashi Kimiya, Ibid., 95, *"Hokutou Ajia no Chitsujo Keisei Nikkan no Sekimu"* (Building a Northeast Asian Order: The Responsibilities of Japan and ROK), *Gaikō Forum,* No. 119 (June 1998), p. 48.

104. One useful example is the "Korea-Japan" Shuttle, a regular Track II dialogue conducted by CSIS Pacific Forum, Okazaki Institute, and Yoido Society.

Chapter 5

1. Charles Glover, "Dreams of the Eurasian Heartland," *Foreign Affairs,* Vol. 78, No. 2 (March/April 1999), pp. 9–13.

2. Ministry of Foreign Affairs, *Diplomatic Bluebook, 1998: Japan's Diplomacy toward the 21st Century: New Developments and New Challenges Facing the International Community,* p. 10.

3. *"Hoppou Ryoudo wo Meguru Ugoki"* (Developments on the Northern Territories), *Sankei Shimbun,* February 8, 1999.

4. Donald Keene, *The Japanese Discovery of Europe, 1720–1830* (Stanford, CA: Stanford University Press, 1952), quoted in Joseph Ferguson, "Nordpolitik:

Japan's New Russia Policy," *Journal of Public and International Affairs 1998,* the Association of Professional Schools of International Affairs, Woodrow Wilson School of Public and International Affairs, Princeton University, pp. 24–46 (http://www.wws.princeton.edu/~jpia/2.html). Ferguson's article was one of the first English-language assessments of the new Japanese approach to Russia.

5. The Soviets had given Tokyo an indication that they would not extend the pact when it expired in 1945, but Japanese diplomats nevertheless held out hope that Moscow would remain neutral and possibly broker peace talks with the allied powers. See Takakazu Kase, *The Road to the Missouri* (New Haven, CT: Yale University Press), 1950, p. 222.

6. Hasegawa Tsuyoshi, *The Northern Territories Dispute and Russo-Japanese Relations: Volume 1, Between War and Peace, 1679–1985* (Berkeley: University of California, 1998), p. 115.

7. Ferguson, op. cit., n. 4, pp. 26–27; *Asahi Shimbun,* November 4, 1998; Harry Gelman, *Russo-Japanese Relations and the Future of the U.S.-Japan Alliance* (Santa Monica, CA: RAND, 1993).

8. *Asahi Shimbun,* November 4, 1998.

9. Interview with MITI official from the Petroleum Division, Agency for Natural Resources and Energy (ANRE), March 30, 1994. See also Ferguson, op. cit., n. 4, p. 28.

10. In 1981 the Japanese government established Northern Territories Day and began sponsoring annual national demonstrations for the return of the islands. Large banners declaring "Return the Northern Territories" hung from the LDP Party Headquarters in Tokyo and in local government buildings throughout the north of Japan throughout the 1980s and early 1990s.

11. Japan subsequently decided to provide food and medical goods of 6.5 billion yen in January 1992, as humanitarian grant aid. In September 1992 Japan exchanged a note with Russia for a $100 million Export-Import Bank loan. In October 1992, at the Tokyo Conference on Assistance to the Newly Independent States, Foreign Minister Watanabe announced emergency humanitarian aid of $100 million. See Japan Ministry of Foreign Affairs, *Diplomatic Blue Book, 1992,* pp. 284–285.

12. Mori Shin,ichirō, "*Nihi Ro Shunou 'Kawana Kaidan' no Butaiura*" (Behind the Stage at the Japan-Russia Summit at Kawana), *Sekai,* June 1998, p. 128.

13. Chikahito Harada, *Russia in Northeast Asia,* Adelphi Paper 310 (London: IISS, 1997), p. 50.

14. *Sankei Shimbun,* February 8, 1999.

15. Japan promised $200 million for Export-Import bank loans for energy-related trade; $1.8 billion for MITI trade insurance for oil and gas; $700 million for GAZPROM gas pipeline development; $700 million in trade insurance for oil field rehabilitation; $100 million for denuclearization projects; and $100 million for nuclear safety training. Japan Ministry of Foreign Affairs, "*NIS Shien no Kuronorojii*" (Chronology for Aid to the Newly Independent States), May 10, 1994.

16. Oksana Lomazova, "Russia-Japan Oil Market," unpublished research study, November 16, 1997, pp. 1–3; "Sakhalin's Summer 'Shelf' Season," *Russian Far East Update,* September 1997, p. 7.

17. Watanabe Koji, "Engaging Russia: A Japanese Perspective," in Watanabe Koji, ed., *Engaging Russia in the Asia Pacific* (Tokyo: Japan Center for International Exchange, 1999), p. 71. For further detailed description of the Yeltsin visit, see Kimie Hara, Japanese-Soviet/Russian Relations since 1945 (London: Routledge, 1998), pp. 192–211.

18. For details, see Tsuyoshi Hasegawa, *The Northern Territories Dispute and Russo-Japanese Relations: Volume 2, Neither War Nor Peace, 1985–1998* (Berkeley: University of California at Berkeley, 1998).

19. Hasegawa Tsuyoshi, "Why Did Russia and Japan Fail to Achieve Rapprochement," in Gilbert Rozman ed., *Japan and Russia: The Tortuous Path to Normalization, 1949–1999* (New York: St. Martin's Press, 2000), pp. 273–312. See also Fujimura Mikio, "*Hoppou Ryoudo Mondai de Nihon Shiji kara Koutaisuru Beikoku*" (U.S. Pulls Back Support on Northern Territories Problem), *Foresight,* July 1997.

20. Nishimura Yōichi, "*Eurasia Gaikou no Butai Ura*" (Behind the Scenes of Eurasia Diplomacy), *Sekai,* March 1998, p. 143.

21. For example, see *Anzen Hoshou Mondai Kenkyūkai* (Council on National Security Affairs), *Kawaru Nichi Ro Kankei* (The Changing Japan-Russia Relations) (Tokyo: Bungei Shinsho, 1999); or Suetsugu Ichirō, "'*Nichi Ro Heiwa Jouyaku' no Souki Teiketsu wo*" (An Early Conclusion of Japan-Russia Peace Treaty Needed), *Gekkan Jiyū,* September 1999, pp. 48–51.

22. See for example, Hakamada Shigeki, "Japanese-Russian Relations in 1997–1999: The Struggle against Illusions," in Rozman, ed., op. cit., n. 19, pp. 229–251.

23. "Hashimoto Objects to Inclusion of Russia in G-7 Economic Forum," *Japan Digest,* March 24, 1997.

24. Hasegawa, op. cit., n. 18., p. 553.

25. Funabashi Yōichi, "*Shushou, Hashimoto Gaikou wo Kakaru*" (Former Prime Minister Hashimoto Talks about His Diplomacy), *Asahi Shimbun,* July 30, 1998.

26. "Usui, Grachev Sign CBM Pact in Moscow," *Japan Digest,* May 14, 1996.

27. "Destroyer Visit to Vladivostok Will be First by Japanese Warship since 1925," *Japan Digest,* July 15, 1996.

28. "*Tai Ro Kankei no Reikyaku wa Sakeyo!*" (Let's Avoid Cold Relations with Russia), *Sankei Shimbun,* November 12, 1996. Cited in Ferguson, op. cit., n. 4, p. 28.

29. "Ikeda, Prmakov, Agree to Resume Peace Talks, Meet in November," *Japan Digest,* July 23, 1996.

30. Nishimura, op. cit., n. 20, p. 141.

31. "Japan Drops Its Objections to Letting Russia into a G-7-and-a-Half," *Japan Digest,* May 19, 1997.

32. "*Nichiro 'Kawana Kaidan': Roshia ni Sekkyoku Shisei, Bouei Kouryuu Nicchū yori Shinten*" (Russo-Japan Kawana Meeting Shows Assertive Posture, Defense Cooperation Proceeds Further than with Chinese), *Tokyo Shimbun,* April 21, 1998.

33. "Clinton Suggests Three-Way Summit to Improve Tokyo-Moscow Relations," *Japan Digest,* June 23, 1997.

34. Sakurai Kaoru, "*Hashimoto 'Tai Ro Gaikou ni Hisomu Shikaku*" (The Blind Spot in Hashimoto's Russia Diplomacy), *Foresight,* November 1997, pp. 106–107.

35. Interview with Tamba Minoru, "*Kurasunoyarusuku Kaidan kara Eritsin Daitouryou Hounichi he*" (From Krasnoyarsk to Yeltsin's Japan Visit), *Gaikō Forum,* April 1998, p. 13.

36. Japan Ministry of Foreign Affairs, *Diplomatic Bluebook, 1998,* p. 22.

37. "Japan: Q&A Session in Hashimoto News Conference," FBIS-EAS-98–001, January 1, 1998; "Obuchi, Wrapping Up Warm Visit, Pledges $1.5 Billion Aid Loan to Russia," *Japan Digest,* February 24, 1998.

38. "Ailing Yeltsin to See Obuchi Just One Day, Give Cloudy Answer on Territories," *Japan Digest,* November 4, 1998. Also see Hakamada Shigeki, "Japanese-Russian Relations in 1997–1999," in Rozman, ed., op. cit., n. 19, p. 244.

39. *Tokyo Shimbun,* April 21, 1998.

40. "*Nichiro 'Kawana Kaidan' Roshia ni Sekkyoku Shisei*" (Russia's Forward Stance in the Kawana Japan-Russia Summit), *Tokyo Shimbun,* May 21, 1998.

41. The geostrategic motivation behind Japan's new Russia policy was not lost on Russian Foreign Minister, Yevgeny Primakov, who noted publicly in 1997 that "both countries share a concern about China." Russian Defense Chief Grachev Pavel was even less subtle when he noted that if Japan was concerned about Russian sales of SU–27s to China, Japan could always buy those planes directly from Russia for a higher price and solve the problem. The JDA opted to buy a handful of the jets instead, tearing apart the combat aviation suite to pick up hints for Japan's indigenous aircraft development programs.

42. "*Rosiaki Shijou, Hi-koukai*" (The Japan Self Air Defense Force Pilots Conducting Test Ride on Russian Fighting Aircraft Secretly), *Asahi Shimbun,* March 30, 1998.

43. *Boueichou* (Japan Defense Agency), ed., *Heisei 11-nenban Bouei Hakusho* (1999 Defense White Paper), pp. 178–181.

44. See Watanabe, op. cit., n. 17, p. 69.

45. Sakurai Kaoru, "*Nichiro Heiwa Jouyaku Sakiokuri Nerai 'Kyoudou Keizai Katsu dou' to iu Otoshidokoro*" (Russia's Ultimate Aim from Pushing Off the Peace Treaty Is "Joint Economic Development"), *Foresight,* March 1998, pp. 42–43; Hakamada Shigeo, "*Roshia no Seihen to Eritsin Rainichi*" (Political Change in Russia and Yeltsin's Japan Visit), *Chūou Kouron,* May 1998, pp. 224–230; Barbara Wanner, "Japanese, Russian Officials at Odds over Kosovo, Territorial Dispute," *Japan Economic Report,* No. 14 B, April 9, 1999, p. 4.

46. "Russians Admire Japan But Feeling Is Unreciprocated, Asahi-Tass Poll Finds," *Japan Digest,* November 11, 1998.

47. "*Heiwa Jouyaku Teiketsu 2000-nen ha Bimyou, Panofu Chūnichi Rosia Taishi ga Kouen*" (Russian Ambassador to Japan Panov Spoke That the Conclusion of the Peace Treaty by 2000 May Be Difficult), *Asahi Shimbun,* May 26, 1998.

48. Bates Gill, "China's Newest Warships," *Far Eastern Economic Review,* January 27, 2000, p. 30.

49. "*Chū Ro TMD Taiou Kyougi*" (China and Russia Consult on Responses to TMD), *Tokyo Shimbun,* March 12, 1999.

50. "Japan Russia Talks: Concluding a New Pact that Will Not Cover the Territorial Issue," *Mainichi Shimbun,* August 4, 2000.

51. Gilbert Rozman, "Japan and Russia: Great Power Ambitions and Domestic Capacities," in Rozman, op. cit., n. 19, p. 357.

52. *Gaikō Forum,* op. cit., n. 35.

53. Zaidan Houjin Sangyou Kenkyūjo to Sekai Heiwa Kenkyūjo (The Industry Research Institute and the International Institute for Peace), "*Enerugī Anzen Hoshou Mondai ni kansuru Chousakai: Enerugî Anzen Hoshou to Kankyou mondai*" (The Energy Security Commission Report on Energy Security and Environmental Problems), Tokyo, April 1993.

54. Interview with a senior MITI official at the Agency for Natural Resources and Energy (ANRE), Tokyo, March 30, 1994.

55. "*Deita wa Kakaru Nichi Ro Boueki Soren Kaitaigo ni Hangen*" (The Data Speaks: Russo-Japanese Trade Fallen to Half Level of the Soviet Era), *Tokyo Shimbun,* May 26, 1998.

56. Nichi Ro Keizei Iinkai (Japan-Russia Economic Council*), Nichi Ro Keizai Kouryuu Sokushinjou no Shougai to Teigen* (Proposals and Obstacles Concerning the Promotion of Japan-Russian Economic Exchange), *Keidanren,* July 1994.

57. "*Ou-Bei-Kankoku Kigyou ni Kurabe Roshia Shinshutsu Nibui Nihon, Jetoro Chouysa*" (Compared with EU, U.S., and Korea, Japan's Investment in Russia Is Weak: JETRO Survey), *Yomiuri Shimbun,* October 30, 1997.

58. "*Tai-Ro Toushi Kakudai Kitai*" (Hopes for More Investment in Russia), *Asahi Shimbun,* July 15, 1998.

59. Harada, *Russia and North-east Asia,* op. cit., n. 13, p. 23.

60. Oksana Lomazov, "Russia-Japan Oil Market," paper prepared for the Trilateral Forum on North Pacific Security, Tokyo December 9–11, 1998; "Japan to Join Russia in Gas Exploration," *Asahi Shimbun,* October 16, 1997; "Sakhalin's Summer 'Shelf' Season," op. cit., n. 16; "Japanese Forming Consortium to Study Irkutsk-Beijing Gas Pipeline," *Japan Digest,* October 20, 1997. See also Sugano Tetsuo, "Russia's Economy and the Development of the Far East," in Watanabe, ed., op. cit., n. 17, p. 83.

61. "*Juyou Hikuku Saharin Oki no Nichi Ro Kyoudou Tennen Gasu Kaihatsu*" (Demand Is Shrinking for Japan-Russia Joint Gas Development in Seas around Sakhalin), *Asahi Shimbun,* March 7, 1999.

62. Lomazova, op. cit., n. 16, p. 5.

63. See MOFA, "*NIS Shien no Kuronorojī*" (Chronology for Aid to the Newly Independent States), May 10, 1994; Kiyoshi Sakurai, "Oceans around Japan Full of Nuclear Waste," *Tokyo Business Today,* April 1994, pp. 36–38.

64. Ryūkichi Imai and Seizaburō Satō, eds., *Dismantlement of Nuclear Weapons: From Balance of Terror to Peace Dividend* (Tokyo: Denryoku Shimbo, 1993).

65. "Japanese and Russian Groups Will Develop Fuel from Russian Weapons Plutonium," *Japan Digest,* May 19, 1999.

66. "Despite Rising Anti-Nuclear Sentiment, Tokyo Funds Russian MOX Project," *Japan Digest,* February 29, 2000.

67. *Keizai Dōyūkai niokeru Hashimoto Souri Daijin Enzetsu* (Prime Minister Hashimoto Ryutaro's speech at the Keizai Dōyūkai, the Japan Association of Corporate Executives), "*Kongo no Wagakoku Gaikou no Arikata—Tai Ro Gaikou wo Chūsin ni*" (The Future Course of Japanese Foreign Policy—A Focus on Japan's Russia Foreign Policy), Tokyo, Japan, July 24, 1999, cited in Japan Ministry of Foreign Affairs, *Gaikou Seisho* 1998 (Diplomatic Blue Book 1998), p. 210.

68. Tanabe Yasuo, "*Kasupi Kai Sekiyu Shigen no Seiji Keizai Gaku*" (The Political Economy of Caspian Sea Oil Resources), *Gaikō Forum,* August 1998, p. 64.

Tanabe was director of the Oil Development Division in the Agency for Natural Resources and Energy before writing this assessment.

69. Marc Castellano, "Japan Eyes Closer Ties with Central Asia: Georgian President Visits Tokyo," *Japan Economic Institute Report,* March 12, 1999, p. 9.

70. "Japan Attempts to Formulate a Silk Road Strategy," *The Cyber Caravan,* Vol. 1, No. 3, February 14, 1999; Tanabe, op. cit., n. 68, pp. 65–68.

71. Castellano, op. cit., n. 69, p. 8.

72. See, for example, Amy Myers Joffe and Robert A. Manning, "The Myth of the Caspian 'Great Game': The Real Geopolitics of Energy," *Survival,* Vol. 40, No. 4 (Winter 1998–1999), pp. 112–131.

73. "*Shuchou/Yuurashia Gaikou/Kokusai Senryaku no Furonthia ni/Kokueki to Tomoni Kunizukuri he Shien wo*" (Eurasia Diplomacy/Supporting Nation Building and National Interests at the Frontier of International Strategy), *Sankei Shimbun,* February 28, 1998.

74. "Japan: Tokyo Formulates Action Plan on Eurasian Diplomacy," *Tokyo Shimbun,* March 7, 1998, Foreign Broadcasting Information Service-EAS-98–069.

75. Wanner, op. cit., n. 45, p. 9.

76. Sheverdnadze's visit elicited the promise of 670 million yen. See Ibid.

77. Hasegawa, op. cit., n. 6, p. 567.

Chapter 6

1. Interview with Foreign Ministry official (Singapore), December 8, 1999.

2. Interview with MOFA official, January 10, 2000. As this official recalled of exchanges with U.S. officials in Washington, "they were not strategic in their thinking about Cambodia and Myanmar"

3. Iokibe Makoto, *Sengo Nihon Gaikoushi* (Japan's Postwar Diplomacy) (Tokyo: Yuhikaku ARMA, 1999), p. 130. Also see Itō Tetsuo, "*Dainiji Sekai Taisen go no Nihon no Baishou Seikyuken Shori*" (Japan's Treatment of Claims for Reparations after World War II), *Gaimushou Chousa Geppou* (Monthly Research Journal of the Japan Ministry of Foreign Affairs), No. 1 (1994), pp. 77–115.

4. This is the amount of net consumption in ODA projects in 1998. See Japan Ministry of Foreign Affairs, ODA White Paper 1998.

5. Japan Ministry of Finance, "Foreign Direct Investment: Outward Direct Investment (Country & Region)," May 27, 1999 (http://www.mof.go.jp/english/e1c008.htm).

6. Japan Ministry of Finance, "Trade Statistics: Value of Exports and Imports 1999," February 17, 2000 (http://www.mof.go.jp/english/trade-st/199928ce.htm).

7. "Current Status: New Miyazawa Initiative as of September 30, 1999," Japan Bank for International Cooperation.

8. JETRO, *1999 Nenban JETRO Toushi Hakusho* (JETRO White Paper of Investment 1999), Nihon Boueki Shinkoukai, 1999, p. 191.

9. Alan Rix, "Managing Japan's Aid: ASEAN," in Bruce M. Koppel and Robert M. Orr, Jr., eds., *Japan's Foreign Aid: Power and Policy in a New Era* (Boulder, CO: Westview Press, 1993), p. 19.

10. Kenneth B. Pyle, *The Japanese Question: Power and Purpose in A New Era, 2nd ed.* (Washington, DC: AEI, 1996), p. 132.

11. Inada Juichi, "Stick or Carrot? Japanese Aid Policy and Vietnam," in Orr and Koppel, op. cit., n. 9, p. 115.
12. Ronald Bruce St John, "Japan's Moment in Indochina: Washington Initiative . . . Tokyo Success," *Asian Survey,* Vol. 35, No. 7 (July 1995), p. 673.
13. Interview with MOFA official, January 10, 2000.
14. "*Fukuda Dokutorin kara Hashimoto Dokutorin made*" (From the Fukuda Doctrine to the Hashimoto Doctrine), *Gaikō Forum,* No. 112 (November 1997), p. 15.
15. Japan Ministry of Foreign Affairs, "Chairman's Statement The Sixth Meeting of the ASEAN Regional Forum, Singapore," July 26, 1999 (http://www.mofa. go.jp/region/asia-paci/asean/conference/arf/state9907.html).
16. Japan Ministry of Foreign Affairs, "Statement by Foreign Minister Keizō Obuchi on Japan and East Asia: Outlook for the New Millennium," May 4, 1998 (http://www.mofa.go.jp/announce/announce/1998/5/980504.html).
17. Ogura Kazuo, "*Kenshou: Kanbojia Wahei to Nihon Gaikou*" (Peace in Cambodia and Japanese Diplomacy), *Sekai,* November 1999, pp. 129–148. This interview by Ogura Kazuo with Kouno Masaharu, Imagawa Yukio, and Akashi Yasushi, the principle architects of Japan's Cambodia policy after 1990, gives an eyewitness account of the triumphs MOFA saw in its approach. See also Kōno Masaharu, *Wahei Kousaku* (A Cambodian Peace Strategy) (Tokyo: Iwanami Shoten, 1999).
18. Ogura Kazuo, Ibid., p. 140.
19. Richard H. Solomon, "Bringing Peace to Cambodia," in Chester A. Crocker, Fen Osler Hampson, and Pamela Aall, eds., *Herding Cats: Multiparty Mediation in a Complex World* (Washington, DC: United States Institute of Peace Press, November 1999), p. 293.
20. Ibid., p. 303.
21. Ogura Kazuo, op. cit., n. 17, p. 131.
22. Ibid.
23. Takeda Yasuhiro, "Japan's Role in the Cambodian Peace Process: Diplomacy, Manpower, and Finance," *Asian Survey,* Vol. 38, No. 6 (June 1998), p. 557.
24. Kōno Masaharu, "In Search of Proactive Diplomacy: Increasing Japan's Diplomatic Role in the 1990's: Cambodia and the ARF as Case Studies," Draft Working Paper, Brookings Institution, March 8, 1999, p. 57.
25. Takeda, op. cit., n. 23, p. 564.
26. Ibid., p. 567.
27. "Japan, France Will Pay off Most of Cambodia's Debt to IMF," *Japan Digest,* September 30, 1993.
28. Imagawa Yukio, "The Recent Situation in Cambodia," unpublished paper, February 1999, p. 5.
29. "*Bei Gikkai, Tai Kanbojia Atsuryoku Tsuyomeru*" (U.S. Congress Increases Pressure on Cambodia), *Yomiuri Shimbun,* July 18, 1999.
30. "Hashimoto Publicly Rejects U.S. View on Cambodia," *Japan Digest,* July 23, 1997.
31. "Cambodia Breaks Ground on Japan-Funded Mekong Bridge," *Japan Digest,* February 4, 1999.
32. "*Tai Kanbojia Seisaku, Bei no Shin'i Wa?*" (What Is the Real Intention of U.S. Cambodia Policy?), *Sankei Shimbun,* July 10, 1999.

33. Yukio Imagawa, op. cit., n. 28, p. 6.

34. *"Keizai ka Jinken ka, Nayamu Bei"* (Economics or Human Rights? A Distressed USA), *Mainichi Shimbun,* July 23, 1997.

35. *"Seifu, Kanbojia Mushou Enjo Saikai ni Joken"* (Conditions for Resumption of Grant Aid to Cambodia), *Sankei Shimbun,* July 21, 1997.

36. "Japan Will Give Cambodia a 3 Billion Yen Aid Loan, Its First in 31 Years," *Japan Digest,* February 17, 1999.

37. Marc Castellano, "Tokyo Hosts Consultative Group on Cambodia: $470 Million in Aid Pledged," *Japan Economic Institute Report,* March 5, 1999, p. 9.

38. "Cambodia: Where Do We Go from Here," Hearing before the Subcommittee on Asia and the Pacific of the Committee on International Relations, House of Representatives, Second Session, September 28, 1999. Statement by Congressman Dana Rohrabacher, California.

39. "MITI Recruits Marubeni, Juki to Jump Start Cambodian Apparel Industry," *Japan Digest,* May 18, 1999.

40. Interview with MOFA official, January 10, 2000.

41. Steven W. Hook and Guang Zhang, "Japan's Aid Policy Since the Cold War: Rhetoric and Reality," *Asian Survey,* Vol. 38, No. 11 (November 1998), pp.1062–1063.

42. The Ministry of Foreign Affairs of Japan, "Japan's Position Regarding the Situation in Myanmar," March 1997 (http://www.mofa.go.jp/region/asia-paci/maynamar, December 20, 1999).

43. "Cabinet Approves 1 Billion Yen Humanitarian Grant to Help Myanmar Farmers," *Japan Digest,* March 21, 1995.

44. Robert I. Rotberg, ed., *Burma: Prospects for a Democratic Future* (Washington, DC: Brookings Institution, 1998), p. 2.

45. "Press Conference by Prime Minister Hashimoto Ryūtarō on the Occasion of His Visit to the Association of Southeast Asian Nations (ASEAN), Singapore, January 13, 1997 (http://www.mofa.go.jp/region/asia-paci/asean).

46. "Tokyo Supports ASEAN Decision to Admit Burma While U.S. Opposes It," *Japan Digest,* June 2, 1997.

47. Marc Castellano, "Japan to Consider Resumption of Limited Aid to Myanmar," *Japan Economic Report,* No. 47B, December 17, 1999, p. 9.

48. Ministry of Foreign Affairs of Japan, "Japan-Myanmar Relations," September 1999, p. 1 (http://www.mofa.go.jp/region/asia-paci, December 20, 1999).

49. "Tokyo Gives Burma New Aid: Japanese Business Defiantly Supports Junta," *Japan Digest,* June 4, 1997; *"Myanmā, Keidanren, Chousadan wo Okuru"* (Keidanren Sends Survey Mission to Myanmar), *Nihon Keizai Shimbun,* June 27, 1994.

50. Mark Mason, "Foreign Direct Investment in Burma: Trends, Determinants, and Prospects," in Rotberg, ed., op. cit., n. 44, p. 218.

51. *"Myanmā, Tainichi Entai Saimu 800 Oku En Ijouni"* (Myanmar's Outstanding Debt to Japan over 80 Billion Yen), *Nihon Keizai Shimbun,* January 22, 1994.

52. Interview with MOFA official Murayama Ichiro, *The Myanmar Monitor,* Vol. 3, No. 2, February 4, 1999.

53. *"Seifu, Myamā heno ODA wo Saikai"* (Government to Reopen ODA to Myanmar), *Nihon Keizai Shimbun,* March 17, 1995.

54. "*Myanmā,ni Mushou Enjo, Chūgoku, Keizai Kyouryoku no Oboegaki Chouin*" (China Signs Aid MOU with Myanmar, Giving Untied Aid), *Nihon Keizai Shimbun,* March 26, 1999.

55. "China's Ambitions for Myanmar," IISS Strategic Comments, Vol. 16, No. 6 (July 2000).

56. Marvin Ott, "From Isolation to Relevance: Policy Considerations," in Rotberg, ed., op. cit., n. 44, p. 83.

57. David I. Steinberg, "Japanese Economic Assistance to Burma," in Koppel and Orr, eds., op. cit., n. 9, p. 149.

58. Ministry of Foreign Affairs of Japan, "Press Conference by the Press Secretary," September 10, 1999. (www.mofa.go.jp, December 20, 1999).

59. Ministry of Foreign Affairs of Japan, "Japan-Indonesia Relations," November 1999 (www.mofa.go.jp/region/asia-paci/indonesia, December 20, 1999).

60. "Japan Won't Cut Aid to Indonesia Because of Timor Killings, Vice Minister Says," *Japan Digest,* January 17, 1992; Jeff Kingston, "Bolstering the New Order: Japan's ODA Relationship with Indonesia," in Koppel and Orr, eds., op. cit., n. 9, pp. 46–47.

61. Marc Castellano, "Japan Contributes Funds, Not Troops, to East Timor Peacekeeping Force," *Japan Economic Institute Report,* No. 36B, September 24, 1999, p. 11.

62. "*Indonesia Saisei heno Michi*" (A Path for a Rebirth of Indonesia), *Mainichi Shimbun,* May 27, 1998.

63. "*Higashi Timōru Taiou "Nihon Seifu, Indonesia Yori," Bero ga Hihan,*" (Father Bello Criticizes Japanese Government for Being Too Pro-Indonesia), *Asahi Shimbun,* October 9, 1999.

64. "Blamed for Fattening Suharto & Friends, Tokyo Will Shift Aid Policy in Indonesia," *Japan Digest,* May 22, 1998.

65. "*Ajia no Chiiki Funsou to Nihon, Heiwa Kakuho he Yobou Gaikou wo*" (Asian Crises and Japan: Time for Preventive Diplomacy and Peace Making), *Nihon Keizai Shimbun,* October 18, 1999.

66. "*Shubi Han'i de Ugokenu Nihon, Keizaiseisai niha Futatsu no Ashi, Higashi Timōru Souran*" (East Timor Rioting: Japan Unable to Move within Its Own Fortress Walls), *Asahi Shimbun,* September 11, 1999.

67. "*Nishi Timor ni Kūjiki ga Chakuriku*" (JASDF Plane Arrives in West Timor), *Mainichi Shimbun,* November 28, 1999. Japan also prepared for JASDF evacuation when rioting spread in Jakarta in the spring of 1998; "Tokyo Keeps Its Planes & Ships in Place for an Indonesian 'Evacuation,'" *Japan Digest,* May 22, 1998.

68. Ministry of Foreign Affairs of Japan, "Japan's Contribution for Assistance to East Timor, December 16, 1999.

69. Jeannie Henderson, *Reassessing ASEAN, Adelphi Paper 328* (London: The International Institute for Strategic Studies, 1999), p. 62.

70. Kwangwen Kin, "Asian Governments not Keen on Joint Piracy Patrols," *The Straits Times,* May 4, 2000.

71. "*Nichi In, Anpo Taiwa Kaishi he*" (Japan and India Start Security Dialogue), *Yomiuri Shimbun,* August 15, 2000.

72. These were the words of Ogura, op. cit., n. 17, p. 136.

73. This view is argued in a paper by the former Japanese ambassador to Burma, Yamaguchi Yōichi, "Myanmar: The Present Situation and Future Prospects," discussion paper prepared January, 1999 for the Council on Foreign Relations roundtable discussion on Japanese foreign policy toward Cambodia and Burma.

Chapter 7

1. Japan Ministry of Foreign Affairs, *Waga Gaikou no Kinkyou* (Diplomatic Blue-book: Our Recent Diplomacy), September 1957, pp. 7–8.
2. See Akiko Fukushima, *Japanese Foreign Policy: The Emerging Logic of Multilateralism* (New York: St. Martins Press, 1999). Fukushima found the UN highlighted in domestic speeches by Kaifu Toshiki in 1991, Miyazawa Kiichi in 1993 and 1994, and Hata Tsutomu in 1994.
3. The Japan Ministry of Foreign Affairs, Challenge 21, January 4, 1999 (http://www.mofa.go.jp/policy/other/challenge21.html).
4. Robert Keohane, "Multilateralism: An Agenda for Research," *International Journal*, No. 45, No. 4 (Autumn 1990), p 731.
5. John Ruggie, "Multilateralism: The Anatomy of an Institution," in John Ruggie, ed, *Multilateralism Matters: The Theory and Praxis of an Institutional Form* (New York: Columbia University Press, 1993), p. 11. Emphasis added.
6. Peter J. Katzenstein and Takashi Shiraishi, *Network Power: Japan and Asia* (Ithaca, NY: Cornell University Press, 1997).
7. Article 53 of the UN Charter states: "1. The Security Council shall, where appropriate, utilize such regional arrangements or agencies for enforcement action under its authority. But no enforcement action shall be taken under regional arrangements or by regional agencies without the authorization of the Security Council, with the exception of measures against any enemy state, as defined in paragraph 2 of this Article, provided for pursuant to Article 107 or in regional arrangements directed against renewal of aggressive policy on the part of any such state, until such time as the Organization may, on request of the Governments concerned, be charged with the responsibility for preventing further aggression by such a state. 2. The term enemy state as used in paragraph 1 of this Article applies to any state which during the Second World War has been an enemy of any signatory of the present Charter." Article 77 states: "1. The trusteeship system shall apply to such territories in the following categories as may be placed thereunder by means of trusteeship agreements: a. territories now held under mandate; b. territories which may be detached from enemy states as a result of the Second World War . . . Article 107 states: "Nothing in the present Charter shall invalidate or preclude action, in relation to any state which during the Second World War has been an enemy of any signatory to the present Charter, taken or authorized as a result of that war by the Governments having responsibility for such action." (http://www.un.org/Overview/Charter).
8. The former enemies clause remains unchanged in the UN charter, even though the General Assembly approved the deletion, because of the bureaucratic complexities of completing the revision.

9. The Advisory Group on Defense Issues, *The Modality of the Security and Defense Capability of Japan: Outlook for the 21st Century* (August 12, 1994—official English translation), p. 3.

10. Asian Forum Japan, *A Call for a Multilateral Strategy for Japan,* May 1995, p. 42.

11. The principle limitations were that the JSDF soldiers could not be armed and would be withdrawn in the event of an outbreak of hostilities.

12. *Jiyū Minshu Tou* (LDP), *Kokusai Shakai ni okeru Nihon no Yakuwari: Anzen Hoshou Mondai ni Kansuru Teigen* (Japan's Role in International Society: Proposals on Security Issues), February 3, 1993.

13. The law set forth five principles for Japanese participation in UN peacekeeping: (1) agreement on a cease-fire shall have been reached among the parties to the conflict; (2) parties to the conflict, including the territorial states, shall have given their consent to the deployment of peacekeeping forces and Japan's participation in such forces; (3) the peacekeeping forces shall strictly maintain impartiality, not favoring any party to the conflict; (4) should any of the above guideline requirements cease to be satisfied, the Government of Japan may withdraw its contingent; (5) use of weapons shall be limited to the minimum necessary to protect lives of personnel.

14. Article 4 of the 1951 U.S.-Japan security treaty states: "This Treaty shall expire whenever in the opinion of the Governments of the United States of America and Japan there shall have come into force such United Nations arrangements or such alternative individual or collective security dispositions as will satisfactorily provide for the maintenance by the United Nations or otherwise of international peace and security in the Japan Area." Security Treaty Between the United States and Japan; September 8, 1951 (http://www.yale.edu/lawweb/avalon/diplomacy/japan001.htm#art4). Article 10 of the 1960 U.S.-Japan security treaty states: "This Treaty shall remain in force until in the opinion of the Governments of the United States of America and Japan there shall have come into force such United Nations arrangements as will satisfactorily provide for the maintenance of international peace and security in the Japan area." (Treaty of Mutual Cooperation and Security between the United States of America and Japan, 1960 (http://www.yokota.af.mil/usfj/Treaty1.htm).

15. *Asahi Shimbun* championed the ARF as the future of Asian security in a May 3, 1995, and in subsequent commentary on the 1996 Joint Security Declaration and the revision of the Defense Guidelines. For details on the liberal idealist versus realist views of multilateral security in Japan, see Kawasaki Tsuyoshi, "Between Realism and Idealism in Japanese Security Policy: The Case of the ASEAN Regional Forum," paper prepared for the annual meeting of the Association of Asian Studies, 16 March 1997, Chicago, Illinois.

16. *Purojekuto 2010, "Jouji Chūryū Naki Anpo," Bunkakai Katsudou no Kiroku* (Records of the Project 2010 "No Base Alliance Analysis Group") (Tokyo: Project 2010 Jimukyoku, February 1997-January 1998), p. 17.

17. Terashima Jitsurō, *Kokka no Ronri to Kigyo no Ronri* (The Logic of the State and the Logic of the Firm) (Tokyo: Chūou Kouron, 1998), pp. 94–98.

18. Suzuki Yoshikatsu, "*Takyokuka/Ikkyoku Yuui ka: Asia Taieheiyo de Hajimatta Aratana Pawaa Geimu*" (Multilaterlization or Unilateral Hegemony: The New

Power Game Beginning in Asia), *Sekai Shūhou,* Vol. 78, No. 46, December 16, 1997, p. 25.

19. Nishihara Masashi, "*Ajia Taiheiyou Chiiki to Takokukan Anzen Hoshou Kyouryoku no Wakugumi*" (The Framework of Multilateral Security Cooperation in the Asia Pacific Region), *Kokusai Mondai,* No. 415 (October 1994), pp. 60–74; and "*Takokukan Kyouchou Shugi no Zeijyakusei: Ikouki no Anzen Hoshou Taisei wo Kangaeru*" (The Vulnerability of Multilateralism: Thinking about Security Systems in Transitory Periods), *Bouei Daigaku Kiyou,* No. 69 (March 1994), pp. 19–29.

20. Okazaki Hisahiko, "*Nihon no Jonin Rijikoku Iri to Ajia*" (Japan's Permanent UN Security Council Seat and Asia), *Shokun!,* November 1994, pp. 26–33.

21. In the mid-1980s for example, Prime Minister Nakasone used the G-7 forum to protest the transfer of Soviet SS-20 missiles to the Russian Far East under the terms of the Intermediate Nuclear Forces (INF) negotiations.

22. Aoki Tamotsu, "*Ima Koso Takokukan Bunka Gaikou wo*" (Now Is the Time for Multilateral Cultural Diplomacy), *Chūou Kouron,* August 1998, pp. 52–64.

23. See Saya S. Shiraishi, "Japan's Soft Power: Doraemon Goes Overseas," in Peter Katzenstein and T. Shiraishi, Network Power, pp. 234–272.

24. See, for example, Michael Blaker, "Evaluating Japan's Diplomatic Performance," in Gerald L. Curtis, ed., *Japan's Foreign Policy After the Cold War: Coping with Change* (New York: M. E. Sharpe, 1993), pp. 1–42.

25. See Fukushima, op. cit., n. 2, pp. 54–65.

26. Ueki Yasuhiro, "Japan's UN Diplomacy: Sources of Passivism and Activism," in Curtis, ed., op. cit., n. 24, p. 352.

27. Ibid., p. 351.

28. Robert M. Immerman, "Japan in the United Nations," in Robert M. Immerman and Toby Trister Gati, eds., *Japan in a Multilateral Dimension* (New York: East Asian Institute, Columbia University, 1992).

29. Toshima Ryuichi, *1991nen Nihon no Haiboku* (Japan's Defeat in 1991) (Tokyo: Shinchou Bunko, 1996), p. 174.

30. Immerman, op. cit., n. 28, p. 189.

31. "*Gunjimen no Yakuwari Bimyou, Nihon, Anpori Jonin Riji Koku ni Rikkouho–Kaisetsu*" (Military Role Sensitive as Japan Bids for UNSC Permanent Membership—News Analysis), *Asahi Shimbun,* July 6, 1993.

32. "Bidding for UN Seat," *Japan Economic Journal,* June 13, 1994.

33. Ibid.

34. Barbara Wanner, "United Nations Reform Shines Spotlight on Japan's Leadership Potential," *JEI Report* No. 15-A, Japan Economic Institute, April 19, 1996, p. 12. MOFA put forward its arguments in a variety of forms and forums, including an October 1994 pamphlet called "*Kokuren Anzen Hoshou Rijikai no Kaikaku: Wagakuni no Jonin Riji Koku Iri*" (The Reform of the UN Security Council: Japan's Entry as a Permanent Member). See Asai Motofumi, "*Jonin riji koku iri no hitsuyo wa nai*" (There Is No Need to Become a Permanent UNSC Member), *Hougaku Seminā,* No. 482, February 1995, pp. 14–19. On the contemporary debate, see also Shinyo Takahiro, "*Kokuren Anpori Jounin Rijikoku iri Koredake Jouken*" (These Are the Only Conditions for Permanent Membership on the UN Security Council), *Chūou Kouron,* April 1994, pp. 136–149; and an

interview with then UN Ambassador Owada Hisahiko, "*Nihon ga Anpori Jounin Rijikoku ni Hairu noha Tozen toiu Kūki desu*" (The Atmosphere Is That It Is Natural for Japan to Become a Permanent Member of the UNSC), *Economisuto,* March 28, 1995, pp. 74–77.

35. Prime Minister's Office (http://www.sorifu.go.jp/survey/Gaikō/index.html).
36. This recommendation reflected the majority view. Fukushima, op. cit., n. 2, p. 174.
37. Yamazaki Shinji, *"Jounin Rijikoku Nihon wa Jitsugen Suru Ka?"* (Will a Japanese Permanent Security Council Seat Be Realized?), *Seikai Shūhou,* November 15, 1994, pp. 21–26.
38. Wanner, op. cit., n. 33, p. 14.
39. Asian Forum Japan, *A Call for a Multilateral Strategy for Japan,* 1995, p. 6.
40. Immerman, op. cit., n. 28, p. 190.
41. Fukushima, op. cit., n. 2, p. 182.
42. "Statement by Foreign Minister Keizo Obuchi at the 52nd Session of the General Assembly of the United Nations," September 23, 1997, Ministry of Foreign Affairs of Japan, p. 2.
43. See "Paying 20% of Regular UN Budget with No Council Seat Irks Japan," *Japan Digest,* September 23, 1999. See also H. E. Yukio Sato, "Japan's Security Perceptions in a Changing World," address to the National Committee on American Foreign Policy, April 18, 2000, in *American Foreign Policy Interests,* Vol. 22, No. 3 (June 2000), p. 33.
44. "Holbrooke Promises to Work Hard to Get Japan a Security Council Seat," *Japan Digest,* September 15, 1999.
45. In a 1998 special edition of *Gaikō Forum* on Japan and the UN, the chief UN policymaker from MOFA's Comprehensive Foreign Policy Bureau chose to focus on the need for more Japanese to apply to the UN as international civil servants. See Ueda Hideaki, *"Tanomu, Nihonjin Kokusai Komuin,"* (Help Wanted: Japanese to Work as International Civil Servants), *Gaikō Forum,* Special 10th Anniversary Issue, November 1998, pp. 100–103.
46. Yoshinobu Yamamoto and Tsutomu Kikuchi, "Japan's Approach to APEC and Regime Creation in the Asia-Pacific," in Vinod K. Aggarwal and Charles E. Morrison, eds., *Asia-Pacific Crossroads* (New York: St. Martin's Press, 1998), p. 192. See also Tsutomu Kikuchi, "Asia-Pacific Economic Regionalism," in Chihiro Hosoya and Tomohito Shinoda, eds., *Redefining the Partnership: The United States and Japan in East Asia* (Washington, DC: University Press of America, 1998), pp. 195–215.
47. Yōichi Funabashi, *Asia-Pacific Fusion: Japan's Role in APEC* (Washington, DC: Institute for International Economics, 1995), p. 53; Lawrence Woods, *Asia-Pacific Diplomacy: Non-governmental Organizations and International Relations* (Vancouver: University of British Columbia Press, 1993).
48. Funabashi, Ibid., p. 56.
49. Ibid., p. 194.
50. *Gaimushou* (MOFA), *Gaikou Seisho* 1993 (Japan Diplomatic Blue Book 1993) (Tokyo: Ministry of Foreign Affairs, 1994), p. 84.
51. Marc Castellano, "What Happened to APEC? A Decade of Taking Two Steps Forward, One Back," *JEI Report,* Japan Economic Institute, May 7, 1999.

52. Funabashi Yōichi,"*Nihon ga Kokutoku wo Shimesu*" (Time for Japan to Demonstrate National Virtue), *Chūou Kouron,* December 1995, p. 30.

53. Hiroshi Hashimoto, Japanese Government press spokesman, "Japan's Views on APEC," November 15, 1999 (http://www.mofa.go.jp/policy/economy/apec/1995).

54. Ministry of Foreign Affairs of Japan, "Highlights of Japan's Individual Action Plan," November 1999 (http:www.mofa.go.jp/policy/economy/apec/1996), p. 2; "Asia–Pacific Economic Cooperation Ministerial Meeting Joint Statement," Manila, November 22–23, 1996.

55. Castellano, op. cit., n. 51, p. 5

56. Interview with senior MITI official, June 18, 1999.

57. "*APEC Koukyū Jimu Reberu Kyougi: Bei no Ito ni Gishin*" (APEC Senior Working Level Meeting: Suspicion of U.S. Intentions), *Sankei Shimbun,* November 13, 1999.

58. "*Bunya Betsu Jiyūka de Saishū Chousei: APEC Kakuryou Kaigi ga Kaimaku*" (Final Adjustment on Sectoral Liberalization: Current Rises on the APEC Cabinet Meeting), *Nihon Keizai Shimbun,* November 14, 1999.

59. Interview with senior MITI official, June 19, 1999.

60. "*APEC Kakuryou Kaigi Nihon, Jiyūka no Nagare ni Gyakkou*" (Japan Does an About Face on Liberalization Move in APEC Cabinet Meeting), *Sankei Shimbun,* November 16, 1999.

61. "*APEC Kakuryou Kaigi Kaimaku: Rinsuisanbutsu no Jiyūka, Nichibei no Mizo Umarazu Saitougi he*" (As Curtain Rises on APEC Cabinet Meeting, U.S. and Japan Stalemated, Move to New Debate), *Yomiuri Shimbun,* November 15, 1999.

62. "*98 APEC Kuararumpūru Bunya Betsu Jiyūka, Nihon no Kyohi—Ajia Shokoku ni Shien*" (APEC 98, Kuala Lumpur: Japan Looks for Support from Asian Countries for Rejection of Sectoral Liberalization), *Mainichi Shimbun,* November 14, 1999.

63. "Tokyo Will Likely Refuse APEC Tariff Plan at Session Beginning This Weekend," *Japan Digest,* November 10, 1998; "Seoul Nixes Tokyo Plea to Block APEC Opening of Forest & Fish Market," *Japan Digest,* October 30, 1998.

64. "*Rin, Suisanbutsu no Kanzei Teppai: Nihon no Kyohi Younin: ASEAN, Bei wo Kensei*" (ASEAN Acknowledges Japan's Rejection of Total Tariff Reductions on Forestry and Fishery Products: Warns U.S.), *Nihon Keizai Shimbun,* November 14, 1998.

65. "*Tsūka Kiki ni Yureta APEC*" (APEC Shaken by Financial Crisis), *Sankei Shimbun,* November 19, 1998.

66. "*Soshiki no Yowasa Rotei: APEC Heimaku*" (As Current Closes on APEC, Its Organizational Weakness Is Revealed), *Asahi Shimbun,* November 19, 1998.

67. "Japan Wins APEC Backing for Broad WTO Talks; U.S. Also Claims Victory," *Japan Digest,* September 13, 1999; "*APEC Shunou Teigen*" (APEC Summit Statement), *Yomiuri Shimbun,* September 14, 1999; Marc Castellano, "APEC Summit Overshadowed by Conflict in East Timor," *JEI Report,* Japan Economic Institute, September 17, 1999, pp. 9–10; "Eleventh APEC Ministerial Meeting Joint Statement," Auckland, New Zealand, September 9–10, 1999.

68. Funabashi, op. cit., n. 47, p. 214.
69. "International Law, the WTO, and the Japanese State: Assessment and Implications of the New Legalized Trade Politics," *Journal of Japanese Studies,* Vol. 27, No. 1 (Winter 2001).
70. Daniel K. Tarullo, "Seattle Light," *International Economy,* November–December 1999, p. 40.
71. For details, see Tsuyoshi Kawasaki, "Between Realism and Idealism in Japanese Security Policy: The Case of the ASEAN Regional Forum," *Pacific Review,* Vol. 10, No. 4 (1997), pp. 480–503; see also Fukushima, op. cit., n. 2, p. 141.
72. Masaharu Kōno, "In Search for Proactive Diplomacy: Increasing Japan's Diplomatic Role in the 1990's: with Cambodia and the ASEAN Regional Forum (ARF) as Case Studies," Draft policy paper, Brookings Institution, June 10, 1999, pp. 39–40.
73. "*Haikei ni Chūgoku no Nyūnan Shisei; Kouno Gaishou no Sekkyoku Hatsugen; ASEAN Kakkoku ha Kouiteki*" (China's Flexible Posture and Foreign Minister's Assertive Speech Set the Background for Goodwill from ASEAN Countries), *Mainichi Shimbun,* August 2, 1998.
74. "*ASEAN Kakudai Gaishou Kaigi de Nihon Gaikou, Ajia Anpo no Wakudukuri Nerau*" (At the ASEAN Post-Ministerial Conference, Japanese Diplomacy Aims at Framework for Asian Security), *Yomiuri Shimbun,* August 4, 1995.
75. Nishihara Masashi, "*Chiiki Anzen Hoshou no Atarashii Chitsujo wo Mezashite: ARF no Genjou*" (Searching for a New Regional Order, the Current Status of ARF), *Gaikō Forum,* November 1997, pp. 38, 40.
76. "*Towareru Funsou Yokushi Kinou: Chūgoku wo Ishiki: ASEAN Chiiki Forum*" (ASEAN Regional Forum's Sensitivity to China Brings Conflict Prevention Capabilities into Question), *Asahi Shimbun,* July 27, 1999; "*Tenbou Mienu Yobou Gaikou: Chūgoku ga Shoukyoku Shisei: ASEAN Forum*" (Hopes for Preventive Diplomacy Unrealized with China's Reticent Posture at ASEAN Forum), *Yomiuri Shimbun,* July 27, 1999.
77. The chairman's statement from the Sixth Meeting of the ASEAN Regional Forum, Singapore, July 26, 1999, reinforced the glacial pace of forward movement by stating: "The Ministers agreed that ASEAN would remain the driving force of the ARF process and that the ARF would maintain its evolutionary approach as the process progresses from confidence building to preemptive diplomacy and, as the eventual goal, the elaboration of approaches to conflict resolution. The ARF process will continue to move at a pace comfortable to all ARF participants on the basis of consensus." The forum put off the second stage of preventive diplomacy, noting in the chairman's report that "The Ministers also requested the ISG on CBMs to further explore the overlap between CBMs and Preventive Diplomacy for the next inter-sessional year, focusing, inter alia, on the development of the concept and principles of preventive diplomacy."
78. "Komura, Albright & Hong Issue Their Own Warning to Pyongyang," *Japan Digest,* July 28, 1999.
79. Morimoto Satoshi, "The Political and Security of Asia's Economic Crisis," October 8, 1998, p. 4. (English translation of "*Ajia Tsūka Kiki to Anzen Hoshou*"), unpublished paper.

80. Shimada Kazuyuki, "*Ajiaryū ni Mieru Genkai: Kyūshinryoku Kaifuku ga Mondai ARF*" (The Limits of "Asian Way" Have Appeared: ARF's Inability to Restore Cohesion), *Gunshuku Mondai Shiryou,* October 1998, pp. 13–16.

81. In February 1994 in Tokyo, JIIA, together with CSIS in Washington and IMEMO in Moscow, held the first meeting of the Trilateral Forum on North Pacific Security. The second meeting of this forum was held in November 1994 in Moscow, and the third one in Washington, D.C., in June 1995 (http://www.iijnet.or.jp/JIIA/exchange.html).

82. Courtney Pourington, "U.S.-Japan Relations in International Arms Control after the Cold War," in Peter Gourevich, Takashi Inoguchi, and Courtney Purrington, eds., *United States-Japan Relations in International Institutions after the Cold War* (San Diego: Graduate School of International Relations and Pacific Studies, 1995), pp. 85–108.

83. Recognizing this suspicion but unrepentant about its own idealism is *Asahi Shimbun*. See for example, "*Hikaku Power: Haibokushugi Tsuranuki Ginen Harae*" (Nonnuclear Power: Sustain 'Defeatism' and Expel Skepticism of Other Countries), *Asahi Shimbun,* August 4, 1999.

84. "NPT Extension Issue Left Vague by G-7 to Accommodate Tokyo," *Japan Digest,* July 9, 1993.

85. "South Korean Ambassador Asks Japan to Explain Its NPT Stance," *Japan Digest,* July 15, 1993; see also Selig Harrison, "A Yen for the Bomb," *Washington Post,* October 31, 1993.

86. "Hashimoto Says Japan Will Work Hard for New Non-Proliferation Framework," *Japan Digest,* June 5, 1998.

87. Japan had committed U.S. $133 billion to India and $63 billion to Pakistan in yen loans. See Satu P. Limaye, "A Blast to Business: The Economic Costs of a Nuclear Test by India or Pakistan Could Be High," *Business South Asia* (Economist Intelligence Unit), May 1996.

88. Interview with State Department official, July 23, 1998.

89. Japan Ministry of Foreign Affairs, "Fourth Meeting of Tokyo Forum for Nuclear Non-proliferation and Disarmament," July 13, 1999 (http://www.mofa.go.jp/announce/announce/1999/7/713.html). The full report is available at the Hiroshima Peace Institute's web site. (http://serv.peace.hiroshima-cu.ac.jp/English/anew/tfhoukoku1-e.htm).

90. "Nuclearization Possible Technically," *Mainichi Shimbun,* July 12, 1968, cited in Selig S. Harrison, ed., Japan's Nuclear Future (Washington, DC: Carnegie Endowment for International Peace, 1996), pp. 8, 9.

91. "*Fukushima Daiichi Genpatsu 3-gouki, Tsūsan, MOX ni Goukakushou*" (MITI Gave an Approval Notice to the MOX for Fukushima Nuclear Reactor), *Yomiuri Shimbun,* August 11, 2000.

92. The Japan Atomic Industrial Forum sponsored an innovative study group on nonproliferation in 1999–2000, for example, but the group's recommendations for increased Japanese activism in nonproliferation policy were in striking contrast to the lack of attention to Japan's own plutonium program. Defenders of the Japanese plutonium program point out that the International Atomic Energy Agency spends more time and energy in Japan than any other country. The Study Group on Peaceful Uses of Nuclear Energy and Non-proliferation

Policy, "The Statement on the Peaceful Uses of Nuclear Energy and Non-proliferation: Action Plan towards 21st Century," Tokyo, March 27, 2000.

93. NPT/CONF.2000/WP.1 (NPT Conference Document), April 24, 2000; and interviews with U.S. and Japanese delegates to the NPT review conference. For further details see Michael J. Green and Katsuhisa Furukawa, "New Ambitions, Old Obstacles: Japan and Its Search for an Arms Control Strategy," *Arms Control Today*, Vol. 30, No. 6 (July/August 2000), pp. 17–24.

94. No-first-use (NFU) discussion was actively pursued, for example, in the Tokyo Foundation Study Group on U.S.-Japan Alliance and Nuclear Disarmament and a group organized by the National Institute for Research Advancement (NIRA) in 1999–2000. MOFA resisted the NFU proposal in its own policies, however. Hisao Yamaguchi, Japanese minister to the Geneva Conference on Disarmament, told NGO's in New York in May 1999 that "Considering the present global situations, circumstances are not yet ready for Japan to accept the proposal of no first use." See "*Saitenken Kakasenu Nihon*" (Japan Needs to Constantly Review Its Nuclear Policy), *Asahi Shimbun,* August 10, 1999.

Chapter 8

1. IMF Annual Reports summarized in Yoshiko Kōjō, "Burden-sharing under U.S. Leadership: The Case of Quota Increases of the IMF Since the 1970's," in Henry Beinen, ed., *Power, economics, and security: the United States and Japan in focus* (Boulder: Westview Press, 1992), p. 294.

2. Shiratori Masaki, *Sekai Ginkou Group:Tojoukoku Enjo to Nihon no Yakuwari* (The World Bank Group: Aid to Developing Countries and Japan's Role) (Tokyo: Kokusai Kaihatsu Jaanaru, 1993), pp. 225–254.

3. Gary Evans, "Japan Takes over the IMF," *Euromoney,* September 1988, p. 98.

4. Ibid., p. 107.

5. Sadako Ogata, "Shifting Power Relations in Multilateral Development Banks," *Journal of International Studies* (Institute of International Relations, Sophia University, Tokyo), No. 22 (January 1989), pp. 9, 18.

6. Kōjō, op. cit., n. 1, p. 292.

7. Meredith Woo Cummings, "The Asian Development Bank and the Politics of Development in East Asia," in Peter Gourevitch, Takashi Inoguchi, and Courtney Pourington, eds., *United States-Japan Relations and International Institutions after the Cold War* (La Jolla, CA: Graduate School of International Relations and Pacific Studies, 1995), p. 241; Edward J. Lincoln, *Japan's New Global Role* (Washington, DC: Brookings Institution, 1992), p 136.

8. Kōjō, op. cit., n. 1, p. 300.

9. Ogata, op. cit., n. 5, p. 16.

10. *The Report of the Advisory Group on Economic Structural Adjustment for International Harmony Submitted to the Prime Minister Yasuhiro Nakasone,* April 7, 1986. This Advisory Group is an ad hoc panel headed by the former chairman of the Bank of Japan Maekawa Haruo. It issued a set of recommendations commonly called "*The Maekawa Report.*" On April 23, 1987, the Special Committee on Economic Restructuring of the Economic Council, which is an official organ of the government and also headed by Maekawa, and an advisory body to the

prime minister, issued a report entitled "Action for Economic Restructuring," the so-called "New Maekawa Report."

11. The Japan Export-Import Bank (JEXIM) was given $9 billion of this amount to disperse. JEXIM's own institutional history was a microcosm of the rapid changes in Japan's overall international profile. Established during the Occupation to finance exports, the bank added foreign investment lending capability in 1953, foreign aid tied to exports in 1958, and a small number of untied loans beginning in 1972. In order to give the bank the flexibility to handle the massive amounts of capital it would be recycling (and to compensate for the erosion of its traditional mission of supporting Japanese industry, which now had adequate capital resources), the Japanese government dramatically increased the amount of untied loans after 1987. JEXIM also began focusing its financing on bilateral projects and cofinancing with the World Bank and other multilateral banks, including $2 billion in parallel financing to the IMF for Mexico. This pattern of cofinancing and cooperation with the international financial institutions allowed Japan to maintain an independent profile for its loans, backed by the credibility that the IMF and World Bank brought to the policy at home and abroad. Based on interviews with senior JEXIM officials, April 28, 1999. See also Anne L. Emig, "Activating the Export Import Bank of Japan as A Development Lending Agency," draft chapter in *Rising to the Challenge: Development Finance and Japanese Burden Sharing*, Ph.D. diss., Columbia University, February 24, 1998 draft.

12. This is a disbursed total amount of external debt outstanding of Latin American countries. See Inter-American Development Bank, *Economic and Social Progress in Latin America (IPES) 1998/99*, p. 241. (http://www.iadb.org/int/sta/ENGLISH/staweb/statship.htm).

13. Evans, op. cit., n. 5, p. 100.

14. "Japanese Bearing Gifts," *Wall Street Journal*, October 14, 1988.

15. "Assistant U.S. Treasury Secretary David Mulford Said He Is Somewhat Concerned by Recent Data Suggesting that Progress in Reducing Japan's Trade Surplus Is Stalling," Reuters, December 5, 1988.

16. "The Brady Plan Explained: What Has Happened," *International Economy*, Vol. 3, No. 3 (May/June 1989), p. 40.

17. Remarks by the Secretary of the Treasury Nicholas F. Brady to the Brookings Institute and the Bretton Woods Committee Conference on Third World Debt, March 10, 1989.

18. Yanagihara Tōru, "*Miyazawa Kousou wo Torikonda Bureidhi Teian*" (The Miyazawa Plan Turned into the Brady Plan), *Economisuto*, April 11, 1989, pp. 37–41. See also Douglas Oustrom, "Japan Slated for Big Role in New Debt Plan," *Japan Economic Institute Report*, No. 11B, March 17, 1989.

19. Walter S. Mossberg and Marcus W. Brauchli, "Japan's Support for Brady Plan May Lead to a Bigger Role in IMF," *Wall Street Journal*, March 27, 1989; NHK Shuzaihan, *Nichibei no Shoutotsu* (U.S.-Japan Collision) (Tokyo: NHK Shuppan Kyoukai, 1990), p. 58.

20. For details, see Edith Terry, "How Asia Got Rich: World Bank vs. Japanese Industrial Policy," *JPRI Working Paper*, No. 10 (June 1995); and Anne L. Emig, "Japan's Challenge to the World Bank: An Attempt at Intellectual Leadership," draft dissertation chapter in op. cit., n. 11, May 15, 1998, draft.

21. Susumu Awanohara, "The U.S. and Japan at the World Bank," in Gourevitch, Inoguchi, and Pourington, eds., op. cit., n. 7, p. 167.

22. Emig, op. cit., n. 20, p. 29.

23. See World Bank, *The East Asian Miracle: Economic Growth and Public Policy* (New York: Oxford University Press, 1993).

24. Yōichi Funabashi, "Japan and America: Global Partners," *Foreign Policy,* No. 86 (Spring 1992), p. 29.

25. Quoted in Awanohara, op. cit., n. 21, p. 167.

26. Richard P. Cronin, "Asian Financial Crisis: An Analysis of U.S. Foreign Policy Interests and Options," *Congressional Research Service Report* 98–75F, April 23, 1998, p. 3.

27. Morris Goldstein, "The Asian Financial Crisis," *International Economics Policy Brief,* Institute for International Economics, March 1998, p. 2.

28. C. Fred Bergsten, "The Asian Monetary Crisis: Proposed Remedies," Statement before the Committee on Banking and Financial Services, U.S. House of Representatives, November 13, 1997.

29. Ibid.

30. Japan Ministry of Finance, Subcommittee on Asian Financial and Capital Markets, Committee on Foreign Exchange and Other Transactions, "Lessons from the Asian Currency Crises: Risks Related to Short-Term Capital Movement and the 21st Century-Type Currency Crisis," May 19, 1998.

31. Ibid., pp. 2, 5.

32. Gyōten Toyoo, Kusukawa Toru, Taida Hideya, Honda Keikichi, and Kondō Seiichi, "*Zadankai: Nihon ga Kawareba, Amerika ga Kawaru, Sekai ga Kawaru*" (Roundtable Discussion: If Japan Changes, America Will Change and the World Will Change," *Gaikō Forum,* February 1999, pp. 35–36.

33. Martin N. Baily, Diana Farrell, and Susan Lund, "The Color of Hot Money," *Foreign Affairs,* Vol. 79, No. 2 (March/April 2000), pp. 100–101.

34. Ibid., p. 105.

35. MOF, Subcommittee on Asian Financial and Capital Markets, op. cit., n. 31, p. 49.

36. Ron Chernow, "Grim Reckoning in Japan—and Beyond," *New York Times,* November 17, 1997, quoted in Cronin, op. cit., n. 26, p. 4.

37. Japan Ministry of International Trade and Industry, *Heisei 8-nendo Tsūshou Hakusho* (*White Paper on Trade and Industry 1994*) Part 2, p. 7; and *Heisei 8-nendo Tsūshou Hakusho* (*White Paper on Trade and Industry 1998*), Part 2, p. 6.

38. Martin Feldstein, "Japan's Folly Drags Asia Down," *Wall Street Journal,* November 26, 1997.

39. Nishida Makoto, "Japan and the Asian Economic Crisis: False Villain?" *The Oriental Economist,* September 1988, p. 14 (reprinted from the original Japanese version in *Touyou Keizai*).

40. "*Ajia Keizai 'Gensoku,' Nikkei Kigyou ni Dageki*" (Asian Economies' "Slowdown" a Blow to Japanese Subsidiaries), *Mainichi Shimbun,* July 4, 1997. Also Paul M. Sherer, "Asia-Pacific Politics and Policy: Aid Plan Seen as Crucial for Economic Recovery," *Asian Wall Street Journal,* July 18, 1997.

41. Subcommittee on Asian Financial and Capital Markets, op. cit., n. 31, p. 19.

42. "*Kokusai KinYū Fuan wo Yobou, Takokukan no Jouhoumou Seibi: Sammitto Goui he Denbâ Sammitto*" (Towards a Summit Agreement at Denver on Multilateral

Network to Prevent International Financial Instability), *Nihon Keizai Shimbun,* June 16, 1997.

43. Interview with MOF official, October 6, 1999.

44. "*Tai Zoushou ga Kinkyū Yūshi Yousei*" (Thai Finance Minister Requests Emergency Funds), *Yomiuri Shimbun,* July 11, 1997.

45. "*Ajia heno Kinkyū Kinyū Shien: Ōkurashou ga Kentou Kaishi*" (MOF Opens Consideration of Emergency Financial Assistance to Asia), *Mainichi Shimbun,* July 12, 1997.

46. Jacob Schlezinger and Jathon Sapsford, "Japan to Provide Biggest Portion of Thai Aid Plan: But It's Less Willing to Assert Full Clout, Shifting Role to IMF," *Asian Wall Street Journal,* August 11, 1998.

47. International Monetary Fund, "IMF Approves Stand-by Credit for Thailand," Press Release No. 97/37, August 20, 1997 (http://www.imf.org/external/np/sec/pr/1997/PR9737.htm).

48. Ibid.

49. Interview with MOF official, April 20, 1999. MOF and ASEAN officials had discussed the idea in Bangkok in July.

50. David Wessel and Bob Davis, "Limits of Power: Global Crisis Is a Match for Crack U.S. Economists," *Asian Wall Street Journal,* September 25, 1998.

51. Interview with JEXIM Bank senior official, April 28, 1999.

52. "*Tai Shien wa Enkokusaika no Kouki*" (Aid to Thailand a Good Chance for Internationalization of the Yen), *Sankei Shimbun* editorial, August 13, 1997.

53. Former MOF Vice Minister for International Affairs Gyōten Toyoo argued that the AMF would never have caused the internationalization of the yen. See Gyōten, et al., op. cit., n. 32, p. 42.

54. Interview with MOF officials in Washington and Tokyo, October 6, 1998, and April 20, 1999.

55. Itō Takeshi, "*Ajia Keizai Kiki to Wagakonu no Yakuwari*" (The Asian Economic Crisis and Our Nation's Role), *Gaiko Forum,* February 1999, p. 2.

56. Interview with MOF official, op. cit., n. 49.

57. Sakakibara Eisuke, *Shihonshugi wo Koeta Nippon* (Japan Beyond Capitalism) (Tokyo: Toyo Keizai Shinposha, 1990).

58. Jathon Sapsford, "Japan's Sakakibara Set for Promotion, Adding to His Clout in Currency Market," *Wall Street Journal,* July 3, 1997.

59. Interview with Vice Minister of Finance Sakakibara Eisuke, April 1999.

60. Interview with senior IMF official, April 30, 1999.

61. Interview with MOF officials, op. cit., n. 43 and 49.

62. Interview with JEXIM official, op. cit., n. 51.

63. Sakakibara Eisuke, "Thai Crisis Played a Part in IMF Idea," Special to *Yomiuri Shimbun,* November 29, 1999.

64. "*Ajiaban IMF Kousou, Nihon ni Kyouryoku Yousei, ASEAN Zoushou to Hikoushiki Kaidan*" (Japanese Cooperation on Asian IMF Requested at Informal ASEAN Meeting with Finance Minister), *Asahi Shimbun,* September 22, 1997.

65. Anthony Rowley, "The Battle of Hong Kong: Tokyo's Proposal to Establish a Regional Emergency Fund Upsets the IMF, Western Governments," *Nikkō Capital Trends,* Vol. 2, No. 13 (November 1997), p. 1.

66. Sakakibara, op. cit., n. 63.

67. "*Ajia Tsūka Kikin, Nihon, Chū-Kan Sanka Teian he, IMF Kyouchou Gensoku ni*" (Japan to Propose Asian Monetary Fund with Chinese and Korean Participation; In Principle Compatible with IMF*), Nihon Keizai Shimbun,* September 22, 1997; and "*Ajia Keizai, Tanki Shikin Izon wa Kiken, Segin/IMF Soukai, Mitsuzuka Zoushou ga Enzetsu*" (Finance Minister Mitsuzuka in Speech at World Bank/ IMF Annual Meeting: Dependence on Short-term Capital Is Dangers for Asian Economies), *Nihon Keizai Shimbun,* September 24, 1997.

68. Ibid. See also "Japan is Pressing Ahead with Its Plan for a Regional Emergency Fund to Deal with Currency Crises in Asia," *Financial Times,* September 23, 1997.

69. Rowley, op. cit., n. 65, p. 1.

70. "*Insaido Ajia Tsūka Kikin*" (Inside the AMF), *Mainichi Shimbun,* September 28, 1997; and interview with Sakakibara Eisuke, November 1998.

71. "*Jimin Chousakai de Icchi, Ajia Tsuuka Kikin, IMF to Kyouchou de*" (LDP Policy Research Committee Agreed Thar AMF Initiative Should be Proceeded in Accordance with Japan's Consultation with IMF), *Nihon Keizai Shimbun,* October 4, 1997.

72. Rowley, op. cit., n. 65, p. 2.

73. "*Sakakibarashi no 'Kyakuhon' ni Dannen: Ajia Tsūka Kikin*" (Mr. Sakakibara Changes His Script on the Asian Monetary Fund), *Asahi Shimbun,* October 5, 1997.

74. Interview with MOF official, op. cit., n. 49.

75. Interview with MOF official, December 14, 1999.

76. Ibid.; see also Jonathon Sapsford and David Wessel, "Japan Pushes Asian Monetary Fund Despite U.S., IMF Concerns," *The Wall Street Journal,* November 6, 1997.

77. MOF, Subcommittee on Asian Financial and Capital Markets, op. cit., n. 30, p.20.

78. "IMF Moves to Center State in Asia Crisis," *Financial Times,* November 20, 1997; "Clinton Team Wins Most of APEC Tricks," *Financial Times,* November 27, 1997.

79. Itō, op. cit., n. 55, p. 26.

80. "*AMF, Seikyū Sugita Nihon*" (Japan Too Impatient on AMF), *Sankei Shimbun,* December 7, 1997.

81. See Gyōten, et al., op. cit., n. 32, p. 34.

82. Eric Altbach, "Japan, United States Press Suharto to Speed IMF Reforms, Shelve Currency Board," *Japan Economic Institute Report* No. 9B, March 6, 1998, pp. 6–9; MOF, Subcommittee on Asian Financial and Capital Markets, op. cit., n. 30, pp.8–9.

83. Altbach, Ibid., p. 7.

84. International Monetary Fund, "IMF Approves Stand-By Credit for Indonesia," Press Release No. 97/50, November 5, 1997 (http://www.imf.org/external/np/sec/pr/1997/PR9750.htm).

85. Cronin, op. cit., n. 26, p. 9.

86. *Keizai Kikakuchou* (the Economic Planning Agency), *Getsurei Keizai Houkoku (Monthly Report of Japanese Economy),* February 6, 1998 (Japanese version is available at: http://www.epa.go.jp/98/f/19980206getsurei.html).

87. David E. Sanger, "U.S. Sees New Villain in Asia Crisis: Tokyo's Leadership," *New York Times,* February 22, 1998.

88. Saitō Takahiro, "*Nihon no Zaisei Shutsudou wo Kakukoku ga Yousei—London G7*" (Each Nation Requests Fiscal Stimulus of Japan at London G-7 Meeting), *Sekai Shūhou,* Vol. 79, No. 9, March 17, 1998.

89. Douglas Oustrom, "American Worries Mount about Japan's Economy," *Japan Economic Institute Report,* No. 9B, March 6, 1998, p. 1.

90. Toshikawa Toshio, "*Amerika ga Kimeta 'KinYū Saisei' Saku*" (America Decided the Financial Revitalization Policy), *Shukan Touyou Keizai,* July 25, 1998.

91. "Regional Fund Plan Is Well Received: Developing World Wants the Same," *Japan Digest,* October 5, 1998.

92. Japan Export-Import Bank, *JEXIM's Role in Japanese Assistance for the Asian Economy: Status Report,* Revised as of March 1999, pp. 1–6.

93. Interview with MOF official, op. cit., n. 49.

94. Henny Sender, "Japan Is Likely to Pledge Aid to Support Asia," *Asian Wall Street Journal,* September 29, 1998.

95. Interview with senior JEXIM officials, op. cit., n. 51.

96. "Outline of Emergency Economic Package" (Provisional Translation), Economic Planning Agency, November 16, 1998.

97. Japan Export-Import Bank, op. cit., n. 92, p. 6.

98. Marc Castellano, "Japanese Foreign Aid: A Lifesaver for East Asia?" *Japan Economic Institute Report* No. 6A, February 12, 1999, p. 6.

99. Japan Ministry of Finance, "Japanese Financial Support to Malaysia under the Framework of the New Miyazawa Initiative," March 31, 1999; Marc Castellano, "Japan Continues Crisis Aid for East Asia," *Japan Economic Institute Report,* No. 11B, March 19, 1999, p. 10.

100. "The Asian Growth and Recovery Program," MOF International Finance Bureau, Development Policy Division, November 17, 1999; see also Castellano, ibid.

101. Castellano, op. cit., n. 99., p. 8.

102. Mark Castellano, "Japanese Bank Lending to Asia Continues to Decline," *Japan Economic Report,* No. 44B, November 19, 1999, p. 8.; Akiko Nakazawa, "East Asian Corporate Debt Problems," *Fuji Research Paper 17,* Fuji Research Institute, January 2000, p. 28.

103. "ADB Approves New US$3.06 Billion Facility to Aid Asia's Currency Crisis-Hit Countries," *ADB News Release,* No. 14/99, March 23, 1999.

104. Japan Ministry of Finance, "Resource Mobilization Plan for Asia: The Second Stage of the New Miyazawa Initiative," May 15, 1999, p. 1. (http://www.mof.go.jp/english/if/e1b068.htm); see also Japan Ministry of Finance, "Beyond the Asian Crisis: Speech by Mr. Kiichi Miyazawa on the Occasion of the APEC Finance Ministers Meeting in Langkawi, Malaysia on May 15, 1999" (http://www.mof.go.jp/english/if/e1b067.htm).

105. Interview with MOF official, March 8, 2000.

106. "*ASEAN, Ajia Kiki Boushi No 'Miyazawa Kousou' Kakudai, Seidoka wo Youbou*" (ASEAN Requests Expansion and Institutionalization of 'Miyazawa Initiative' to Prevent Asian Crisis), *Sankei Shimbun,* November 27, 1999; "*Ajia Kakukoku, Nihon Manē ni Atsui Shisen*" (Asian Nations Show Strong Desire for Japan Money), *Nihon Keizai Shimbun,* November 29, 1999.

107. Japan Ministry of Finance, The Joint Ministerial Statement of the ASEAN + 3 Finance Ministers Meeting, 6 May 2000, Chiang Mai, Thailand (http://www.mof.go.jp/english/if/if014.htm).

108. *"Ajia Tsūka Kikin Kousou Sainen"* (AMF Concept Heats Up Again), *Asahi Shimbun,* February 19, 2000.

109. E-mail interview, Japan Bank for International Cooperation official, March 1, 2000.

110. *Asahi Shimbun,* op. cit., n. 108.

111. William Jefferson Clinton, "Remarks on the Global Economy," presentation to the Council on Foreign Relations, September 14, 1998, New York, NY.

112. Interview with JEXIM official, op. cit., n. 51; and with senior IMF official, op. cit., n. 60.

113. "Statement by the Honorable Kiichi Miyazawa, Minister of Finance of Japan at the Fifty-Third Joint Annual Discussion, October 6. 1998; see also Japan Ministry of Finance, *"Kokusai KinYū Sisutemu Kaikaku no Jūyou Mondai"* (Major Issues in the Reform of the International Financial System) (http://www.mof.go.jp, May 18, 1999).

114. MOF, Subcommittee on Asian Financial and Capital Markets, op. cit., n. 30, p. 34. The same advisory council first recommended the internationalization of the yen in a report in 1984. See Japan Ministry of Finance, Commission on Foreign Exchange and Other Transactions, Sub-commission on the Internationalization of the Yen, *Internationalization of the Yen* (Interim Report) (Provisional Translation), November 12, 1998, p. 1.

115. MOF, Subcommittee on Asian Financial and Capital Markets, (*Internationalization of the Yen*), op. cit., n. 114, p. 10.

116. Gyōten, et al., op. cit., n. 32, p. 37.

117. Ibid., p. 38.

118. See for example, Eisuke Sakakibara, "Reform of the International Financial System," Speech at the Manila Framework Meeting, Melbourne, Australia, March 26, 1999; C. H. Kwan, "Sayonara Dollar Peg: Asia in Search of a New Exchange Rate Regime," Nomura Research Institute, December 1999; Kan Shiyū, *Enken no Keizaigaku* (Economics of Yen Zone) (Tokyo: Nikkei Shimbunsha, 1995).

119. Interview with MOF official, op. cit., n. 49.

120. MOF, Subcommittee on Asian Financial and Capital Markets, op. cit., n. 30, p. 35.

121. *Jiyū Minshutou, Seimu Chousakai* (LDP Policy Research Committee), *Tounan Ajia KinYū, Tsūka Kiki heno Kinkyū Taisaku nitsuite* (On Emergency Measures for Financial and Currency Crisis in Southeast Asia), *Gaikou Chousakai* (Foreign Policy Committee), February 19, 1998, p. 6.

122. "Miyazawa Proposes 'Flexible' Currency System, 'Basket' for Asian Exchanges," *Japan Digest,* January 19, 1999.

123. MOF, Commission on Foreign Exchange and Other Transactions, op. cit., n. 114, p. 2.

124. Noted in interview with MOF official, op. cit., n. 49; and by former Vice Minister for International Affairs Gyōten Toyo in Gyōten, et al., op. cit., n. 32, p. 41.

125. Interview with Sakakibara Eisuke, op. cit., n. 70.

126. MOF, Council on Foreign Exchange and Other Transactions, *Internationalization of the Yen for the 21st Century–Japan's Response to Changes in Global Economic and Financial Environments -,* April 20, 1999 (http://www.mof.go.jp/english/if/e1b064a.htm).

127. Douglas Ostrom, "Tokyo's Changing Role in Financial Markets: Taking a Step Backward?" *Japan Economic Institute Report,* No. 43A, November 12, 1999.

128. Makoto Ebina and Atsushi Niigata, "The Impact of the Euro's Launch on the Japanese Yen," *Fuji Research Paper,* 15 (Tokyo: Fuji Research Institute, July 1999), p. 1.

129. Other steps, such as denominating more trade and loans in yen, might help, although this is limited because most commodity trade is traditionally done in dollars. See Robert Brusca, "A Yen Bloc: Allure of Yen Invoicing," *Nikkō Capital Trends,* Vol. 3, No. 4 (March 1998), p. 6.

130. The more significant was the contingent credit line. "Global Financial Reform: The Evolving Agenda," remarks by Michel Camdessus, Managing Director of the International Monetary Fund at the Council on Foreign Relations, New York, June 4, 1999, p. 5.

131. Interview with MOF officials December 14, 1999, and U.S. Treasury official, June 4, 1999.

132. Marc Castellano, "Tokyo, Washington Clash over Reshaping IMF's Role," *Japan Economic Institute Report,* No. 1B, January 7, 2000, p. 10.

133. Interview with MOF official, op. cit., n. 75.

134. *Strengthening the International Financial Architecture: Report from G-7 Finance Minister to the Heads of State and Governments,* Fukuoka, Japan, July 18, 2000.

135. Bergsten, op. cit., n. 28. He stated: "There is a clear need to launch new regional arrangements to reinforce the efforts of the International Monetary Fund to help prevent and respond to future monetary crises in the region. The Asia Pacific Economic Cooperation (APEC) forum is the logical institutional home for the 'Asian monetary fund' that has been discussed so widely since the onset of the current financial problems in Southeast Asia and should initiate such arrangements at its summit meeting in Vancouver on November 25 . . . Widespread support has therefore developed for an 'Asian monetary fund' to supplement the IMF. But Japan's proposal for an Asia-only facility was rejected by all concerned, including its intended beneficiaries, and has now been withdrawn. ASEAN is obviously too small. The 'Six Markets Group' (or G-6) that met last spring included the United States but excluded many key Asian countries. The IMF itself has reportedly proposed that a regional grouping be created and staffed by its own new office in Tokyo. APEC is the logical institutional venue for such arrangements" (http://www.iie.com/TESTIMONY/crisis.htm).

136. Christopher B. Johnstone, "Strained Alliance: US-Japan Diplomacy in the Asian Financial Crisis," *Survival,* Vol. 41, No. 2 (Summer 1999), pp. 121–137.

137. *"APEC Miyazawa Kousou Haijakku Mondai"* (The Problem of the Miyazawa Initiative Hijacking at APEC), *Sankei Shimbun,* November 17, 1998.

138. Esuke Sakakibara, "Thai Crisis Played Part in IMF Idea," *Yomiuri Shimbun,* November 19, 1999.

139. Itō, op. cit., n. 55, p. 31.

140. Japan Ministry of Foreign Affairs, "Council on ODA Reforms for the 21st Century, Final Report," 1998 (http://www.mofa.go.jp).

141. Nancy Dunne and Mark Suzman, "The Global Standard," *The Financial Times,* April 18, 1998.

Chapter 9

1. Interview with a JDA official, Washington, D.C., May 17, 2000.

Index